On Retaliation

Integration and Conflict Studies

Published in Association with the Max Planck Institute for Social Anthropology, Halle/Saale

The objective of the Max Planck Institute for Social Anthropology is to advance anthropological fieldwork and enhance theory building. 'Integration' and 'conflict', the central themes of this series, are major concerns of the contemporary social sciences and of significant interest to the general public. They have also been among the main research areas of the institute since its foundation. Bringing together international experts, Integration and Conflict Studies includes both monographs and edited volumes, and offers a forum for studies that contribute to a better understanding of processes of identification and intergroup relations.

For a full volume listing, please see back matter

On Retaliation

Towards an Interdisciplinary Understanding of a Basic Human Condition

Edited by

Bertram Turner and Günther Schlee

berghahn
NEW YORK • OXFORD
www.berghahnbooks.com

Published in 2017 by
Berghahn Books
www.berghahnbooks.com

First paperback edition published in 2019

Library of Congress Cataloging-in-Publication Data

Names: Turner, Bertram, editor. | Schlee, Günther, editor.
Title: On retaliation : toward an interdisciplinary understanding of a basic human condition / edited by Bertram Turner and Günther Schlee.
Description: New York : Berghahn Books, 2017. | Series: Integration and conflict studies ; Volume 15 | Includes bibliographical references and index.
Identifiers: LCCN 2016054918 (print) | LCCN 2017008870 (ebook) | ISBN 9781785334184 (hardback : alk. paper) | ISBN 9781785334191 (ebook)
Subjects: LCSH: Punishment--Social aspects. | Revenge--Social aspects. | Ethnological jurisprudence. | Law and anthropology. | Lex talionis.
Classification: LCC GT6710 .O6 2017 (print) | LCC GT6710 (ebook) | DDC 303.3/6--dc23
LC record available at hlps://lccn.loc.gov/2016054918

British Library Cataloguing in Publication Data

A catalogue record for this book is available from the British Library

ISBN 978-1-78533-418-4 (hardback)
ISBN 978-1-78920-077-5 (paperback)
ISBN 978-1-78533-419-1 (ebook)

Contents

Figures and Tables

Figures

Tables

Acknowledgements

This volume reflects on and unpacks basic assumptions about the concept of retaliation, which is one of the three constitutive concepts comprising the research agenda of the International Max Planck Research School 'Retaliation – Mediation – Punishment' (IMPRS–REMEP). It was in the course of the many stimulating intellectual exchanges with colleagues and students provided within the framework of the IMPRS–REMEP that this new, transdisciplinary approach to retaliation was conceived and realized.

The editors are grateful to the members of the IMPRS–REMEP network for their support, especially Carolin Hillemanns and Karl Härter. For assistance in preparing the manuscript for publication, we are indebted to Gesine Koch, Anne Vatter and especially Conny Schnepel, who managed the preparation of the manuscript from start to finish. Brian Donahoe's careful language editing has tremendously improved the volume. We also acknowledge the encouragement and advice of the members of the editorial board of the 'Integration and Conflict Studies' series. We are indebted to the Max Planck Institute for Social Anthropology and the Max Planck Institute for Foreign and International Criminal Law for their continued financial and logistical support of the IMPRS–REMEP. Most of all, we wish to express our thanks to all those who have contributed to the passionate discussions on the topic of retaliation across disciplinary boundaries. We have benefited greatly from these discussions in the process of preparing this manuscript for publication, particularly in writing the Introduction and the Conclusion.

Bertram Turner and Günther Schlee
Halle, Germany, 11 April 2016

Introduction

On Retaliation

Conceptual Plurality, Transdisciplinary Research, Rifts, Blurrings and Translations

Bertram Turner

The study of retaliation as a concept addressing the regulation of imbalances in social relations is pursued in a variety of disciplines and has attained the status of an established field of research; in fact, attention to retaliation has even increased in recent years. The spectrum of disciplines in which retaliation is considered an object of research ranges from economics (fields such as organization management and macroeconomics – see, e.g., Mesmer-Magnus and Viswesvaran 2005; Feinberg and Reynolds 2006; Kudisch, Fortunato and Smith 2006) to various subdisciplines of psychology (Eisenberger et al. 2004; Paul 2005; Denson, Pederson and Miller 2006; Orth, Montada and Maercker 2006; Barash and Lipton 2011) to law, criminology, sociology, history, religious studies, sociobiology and so on. Yet recent developments in the various disciplines have not significantly raised awareness of one another's scientific agendas. The increase in interest seems to be less attributable to the identification of a common project than to different trends in the various disciplines and to different conceptual and empirical challenges. We also observe, however, a countertendency to this disciplinary isolation in the general reasoning about basic concepts. To give an example, the analyses of concepts of retaliation and their political and social frameworks (Waldmann 2001; Aase 2002; Grutzpalk 2002) have recently been substantially influenced by the current interdisciplinary discourse in conflict and human security studies. From that perspective, retaliation has been identified as pertaining to a range of thematic fields such as terrorism and causes of war, which are examined by scholars from a variety of disciplines (see, e.g., Gehring 2003; Rees 2003; Sue and Rodin 2007; Diamond 2008).

With this volume we intend to invest in and advance the emerging insight that various approaches and directions of research must be pooled, an insight that replaces the conventional claims of individual disciplines to supremacy regarding conceptual design. With this in mind, it is worthwhile, I suggest, to continue elaborating on the concept of retaliation and to broaden our perspective in a transdisciplinary effort. As regards the use of the terms 'transdisciplinary' and 'interdisciplinary', it is the objective of this volume to show how a specific topic is addressed *throughout* and *across* a number of disciplines, and not *between* them. It also implies a methodological approach and a certain degree of interaction among and across the contributing disciplines. I have therefore made a conscious decision to frame this discussion in terms of *trans*disciplinarity, which more accurately represents my approach and the overall intention of the volume, rather than the more common concept of *inter*disciplinarity. Thus, this introduction is designed to take the first step towards an *integrative* approach without pretending to have already resolved all concomitant problems.[1]

In analysing recent developments without neglecting the historical context within which they unfold, our aim is to make a contribution to an upgraded, theoretically informed, empirical understanding of the concept of retaliation as such and the ways in which actors refer to it in various circumstances. In light of the recent interest in the principle of retaliation in the human sciences, this book presents an inventory of approaches to retaliation in selected disciplines and an overview of the most recent theoretical innovations and research perspectives on this subject.

Addressing transdisciplinary convergence as a common challenge, we are particularly sensitive to scalar arrangements and to the interface between, on the one hand, local variability in the ways in which retaliation informs processes of conflict settlement and, on the other hand, references to retaliation as a universal normative template at a transnational scale. Recent developments in law and politics, such as the scalar rearrangements of the relationship between the global and the multitude of diverse local spheres and the role nation-states play as the interface between these spheres, prompt us to reconsider incoherent combinations or co-occurrences of causal explanations that conflate retaliation with issues that are related to human security.

Recent interventions in trans-scalar arenas of conflict have assigned the discourse on retaliation a prominent position on the transnational agenda. Many cases in which retaliation was a major component have attracted international attention in recent years and have raised awareness of various facets of the concept among the broader public. Thus, the variety in scientific approaches to retaliation goes along with a renewed and diversified public awareness.

An example concerning the involvement of NATO troops in local affairs in Afghanistan can serve to highlight the impact of retaliatory logics in scalar entanglements – and its misinterpretation. In related newspaper articles in the German newspaper *Süddeutsche Zeitung*,[2] retaliation is addressed as an important component of local normative culture, which therefore must be taken into consideration. The articles also convey the message that the foreign forces are culturally sensitive and well-integrated into local Afghan communities. This official statement about normative principles of local disputing was triggered by an incident that became known as the 'Kundus bombing', in which German army officers were responsible for bombing fuel tanker trucks that had been stolen by Taliban forces and were considered a threat to German troops near Kundus. According to *Süddeutsche Zeitung*, the German government was negotiating – in line with the government's understanding of the logic of retaliation – 'compensation payments' for the injured Afghan civilians and the surviving dependants of Afghan civilians killed in the bombing. The problem was that the German government wanted to provide compensation locally while denying its responsibility at the international scale for the very act it was ready to compensate for. Therefore, what should locally be understood as compensation was officially declared voluntary *ex gratia* payments.

Here two notions, a local normative one and a formal legal one, become conflated. In many retaliatory constellations, as in the local Afghan context, the perpetrator's acknowledgement of responsibility is considered a prerequisite for any negotiations about compensation between the parties. However, responsibility in this sense does not amount to an acknowledgement of culpability in formal legal terms. Thus, from an Afghan perspective, the German government's offer of compensation is not only incomprehensible without the accompanying acknowledgement of responsibility, but is even offensive to local sensibilities.

The scenario would have been a real opportunity to demonstrate that the foreign allies were willing to take local actors seriously and to show their ability to negotiate an honourable arrangement. In the end they would not only have enhanced their reputation locally, they would even have had to pay a much-reduced compensation, as the victims' side clearly also had some responsibility for the events, facts that usually would have to be brought forward in real local negotiations between the parties. The crucial point addressed in the newspaper articles in this context was the interface between local legal orders, German jurisdiction and the incongruent *ex gratia* payment standards of NATO allies in Afghanistan. The articles do not mention the locally established procedures for managing conflict and determining 'blood money tariffs' nor the option of referring to *diya* (compensation) arrangements on the basis of Islamic law.[3] In August 2010 the German government acknowledged reimbursing the civilian victims' families in the form of equal lump sums labelled 'voluntary support'. In so doing, the government insisted that the payments could not be interpreted as an admission of guilt for the deaths, as acknowledgement that the decision to bomb the fuel tankers was misguided or as compensation in the spirit of the law of retaliation. As noted above, the latter point reveals a blatant misunderstanding of the concept of retaliation. The chance to honour local normative standards was missed because the German government was overly concerned with avoiding the appearance of admitting guilt.[4]

The social reality of retaliation has always contained a great deal of dramatic potential, and has found ample and widely varied representation not only in the media, but also in the fine arts, visual arts, music and literature. The manifold adaptations of the concept reveal the effects of differing social circumstances and the influence of religious, cultural and other kinds of role models.[5] Themes such as the avenging hero, the tragic protagonist fulfilling his duty to retaliate at the expense of his own life, and the executor of equalizing justice are to be found in all of the world's literatures and continue to influence existing values and ideals. The hero may well be described in ambivalent terms; he or she does not necessarily embody positive character traits. Nevertheless, the stock character of the intelligent protagonist who anticipates the consequences of his or her actions and who always defends the underprivileged, the exploited and the oppressed – like Robin Hood and comparable heroes around the world – contributes to the positive image of the retaliator as the embodiment of equalizing and retaliatory justice.

Violent rhetoric and retaliation also play a prominent role in contemporary musical genres such as hip-hop, rap and heavy metal (see, e.g., Gollwitzer and Sjöström, this volume). Some of this music glorifies honour codes and other lifestyle elements that involve social transgression and delinquency or are critical of mainstream culture and those who conform to it.[6] We could just as well refer to the lyrics of some national anthems or pieces of European military music to exemplify musical adaptations of retaliation. It seems that these conventional and modern artistic adaptations of the topic also inform recent media representations of retaliatory events and allow one to make inferences about perceptions and social practices.

Such references to retaliation in modern times throughout the world provide useful data to ongoing discussions of the apparent disciplinary differences and logics that contribute to the various conceptual frameworks, and thus help establish a process of mutual sensitization. In fact, different explanatory models (religious, ethical/moral, normative/legal, psychological, etc.) are often set against one another, as if in competition, when spectacular retaliatory events are analysed in science and in public discourse. The point is that not much attention has been paid to these differences. Media representations operate with selective reference to certain meanings and connotations, evoke 'archaic survivals' or emphasize the entrapment of humans in predefined patterns of behaviour or emotional entanglements (Isak 2003). Such representations, in turn, summon and combine templates from various intellectual backgrounds, and in so doing pave the way for finding a common ground. Hence, recent cases and their representation in the media help to identify basic framework conditions that influence the social effectiveness of the concept. For instance, the religious reference to retaliation used by former U.S. president George W. Bush to justify the 'War on Terror' and the

Iraq war is not an isolated case (see, e.g., Austin, Kranock and Oommen 2003). A legitimizing rhetoric of retaliation is frequently used in the media if violence is characterized as reactive or defensive. In this vein, for instance, Jewish settlers label and present their actions against Palestinians in Israel as 'price-tag' attacks in an effort to justify them as retributive.[7] To highlight another illustration, the Internet hacker attacks of transnationally active movements such as Anonymous are imbued with the symbolic paraphernalia of revenge culture (Coleman 2012).

Framework Conditions: Scientification, Securitization, Religiosification and Juridification

This introduction and the volume's concluding chapter comprise two halves of a single overview bookending the intervening chapters. In this overview, I intend to delineate such references to retaliation that involve translation processes across scales (Herod and Wright 2002) from a perspective that emerges from a transdisciplinary approach to conflict studies. This effort to revisit a concept that deals with one of the most fundamental drivers of human action is motivated by the observation that retaliation has resurfaced in various discourses and scientific debates, and has gained momentum in contexts that, at first glance, appear to have little in common.

Taking these tendencies as a point of departure, in this volume we pose the question of the circumstances and framework conditions that may have contributed to this resurgence of the concept of retaliation in diverse disciplines and in public discourses. This renewed attention to retaliation in the areas of research that are dealt with in this volume – human nature, crime, deviance and punishment, religion, social and political organization, and postwar scenarios – resonates with four corresponding trends or framework conditions: *scientification*, *securitization*, *religiosification* and *juridification*. These conditions constitute subsequent normative specifications of the project of globalization and the establishment of a neoliberal world order (Benda-Beckmann and Benda-Beckmann 2007). They are selected from the multitude of ongoing global trends that have amplified retaliation to the point where it is presented – by researchers and commentators of various stripes – as the most efficacious or foundational issue in a number of contexts.[8]

Scientification

There are, first, processes that may be labelled *scientification* – the search for objectified epistemologies. The production of knowledge in the natural sciences regarding basic human conditions increasingly entails far-reaching consequences in 'real lifeworlds' and is poised to have an impact on the realms of the judiciary and conflict management. The question is: to what extent does this also apply to the growing body of research looking at retaliation as a basic condition of human cognition? This search for the basic conditions of human existence has been associated with a wide range of topics, from retaliation in everyday interpersonal dealings such as situations in the workplace to its impact on individual economic and social decision making (see, e.g., Gollwitzer 2005; Tripp and Bies 2009; Barash and Lipton 2011). Disciplines in which the individual human being is at the centre of research, such as psychology, provide provocative data on predispositions that are, at their most fundamental level, presumed to be shared by all human beings.

Such data, generally generated in formal experimental settings focusing on individual study participants, have increasingly been taken into account in other social sciences; they have even found their way into the analysis of the manifestations of universal human characteristics (such as retaliation) as drivers of human societal organization and in the dynamics of social relations. Thus, two questions emerge: first, whether the application of data generated in the analysis of *individuals* to studies on human collectivities may lead to misrepresentation; second, where the epistemological limits are set. Here various strands come together, ranging from psychology and economy to history and social anthropology. In the process, the data produced in the so-called hard sciences, which were formerly presumed to be neutral and unchallengeable, are reframed and assessed in relation to the social and political conditions of their production or discovery. Without going into detail here, new developments in neuroscience have led to a vibrant renewal of the debate about the free will of the individual, his or her position as an autonomous legal person, and the concept of individual and collective responsibility (e.g., McCullough 2008; Goodenough and Tucker 2010; Rilling and Sanfey 2011; see also Bies and Tripp, this volume).[9] Both scientific research on retaliation (especially in psychology) and the public debate on retaliation have been affected by these new developments.[10]

Securitization

The second framework condition is the global discourse on human security, which takes into account the insight to link the enforcement of human rights to the question of individual and collective responsibility (Martin and Owen 2014). The process of globalization has given global governance institutions ever-increasing influence, especially in the politics of securitization. In this field, the issue of human security is often conflated, via causal explanations, with retaliation, particularly with respect to the concept of social and political order. The maintenance and restoration of order as a prerequisite for human security entails a shift in perspective away from retaliation's preventive capacity towards its capacity to give rise to violence. Retaliation from this perspective constitutes a threat to security, and the moment in which the actor must choose either violence or compensation needs to be normatively regulated. Here the concept of retaliation is apparently a promising instrument that allows for the anticipation of potential reactive consequences. At the same time, however, if the preventive power fails, it would seem to legitimize the offended party's right to react violently. Such a right, in turn, is challenged by those institutions that claim that security can only result from the state's exclusive monopoly on the use of force and, increasingly, the legitimacy claimed by institutionalized global governance organs.[11] In sum, the relationship between human security and retaliation addresses the temporalities of law at the interface of precaution, avoidance and prohibition. Subsequently, if all deterrence has failed, retaliation entails the reactive power, which is also inherent in the same logic of normative temporality (Holbraad and Pedersen 2013).

Religiosification

The third phenomenon of global significance that finds expression in recent treatments of the concept of retaliation is the re-enchantment of the modern world and the increasing impact of faith-based convictions in the realm of the political, the economic, the legal and the social (Turner and Kirsch 2009). The amalgamation of spiritual capital, spiritual motivations, eschatological reflections and quests for salvation seems to inform the decision making of individuals in all spheres of life and to take effect even without being explicitly referred to as religious guidance (Benda-Beckmann et al. 2013). The notion of freedom of religious expression as a right laid down in national constitutions may be stretched to include claims to legal retaliation on the basis of religious conviction. Religion may stipulate forbearance towards those who have wronged someone or, on the contrary, emphasize the exercise of retaliation as a religious duty, thereby fostering an intertwining of the religious and the secular in various domains. Tenets of faith may thus appear inextricably linked with notions of retaliation and reflect religious ideas about justice, repentance and remorse, punishment and salvation. In any case, one must acknowledge that a religious interpretation of retaliation has gained momentum in many parts of the world (see, e.g., Greer et al. 2005), both within the mundane realm of conflictive human interaction and for the relationship between the individual and the divine.

The emphasis on a fundamentally religious logic of retaliation has consequences for the political realm and political concepts of action. The United States' legitimizations of the 'War on Terror' and the Iraq war exemplify this. Political actors portray themselves as executors of God's will and as instruments of a higher justice, all in the name of religion.[12] These examples illustrate that the increasing importance of religion in this age of globalization also confers additional weight upon a religiously informed logic of retaliation, with dogmatic and confrontational religious trends apparently gaining in influence.

Juridification

The fourth factor of globalization to be mentioned here is the ongoing process of juridification or judicialization – in other words, the increasing pervasiveness of normative models in all spheres of human existence (Comaroff and Comaroff 2006; Blichner and Molander 2008). The observation of this process has triggered a debate that revolves around all sorts of rights-based approaches, issues of individual and collective responsibility, the criteria for the assessment of culpability of human action and the consequences thereof. It is about the power of the legal argument and the displacement of political and moral principles to the realm of law.

This process finds expression in the proliferation of formal legal institutions such as international tribunals and special courts; in the global boom of law-oriented non-governmental organizations (NGOs) and rights-claiming movements; in the proliferation of new constitutions and constitutional reform the world over; and in the production of transnational legal templates within the framework of global governance (Turner and Kirsch 2009). As a basic principle of justice and a technique of normative ordering, retaliation becomes, once again, absorbed into norm-setting processes while simultaneously gaining legitimacy because it is incorporated into legal systems in a hybridized form and expressed in terms of 'rights'. As will be shown, for the concept of retaliation, this translates into fragmented integration into formal law systems, whereby components excluded from this integration may resurface as possible threats to the state monopoly on violence.

Taking these framework conditions, superimposed upon one another, into account allows us to explore the concept of retaliation in its multifarious manifestations and to unpack disciplinary approaches in order to arrive at transdisciplinary insights.

We learn from each other to identify both common strands and specific markers of distinction that can be associated with the specific epistemologies of the different disciplines. In sum, the spectrum of research presented in this volume addresses retaliation as a concept that informs the scope of human agency – in all its variation involving both interpersonal and intergroup relations – in the maintenance of order and in the settlement of disputes, conflicts and imbalances of interest.

The ways in which these framework conditions are reflected in the six thematic sections of this volume and in the specific contributions are outlined in the volume's concluding chapter. For the purposes of this introduction, however, I prefer to sketch out in greater detail the *antecedents* of the epistemological project pursued here, that is, to revisit retaliation by adjusting the analysis to the fields outlined in the sections. I think it is reasonable and legitimate to begin a transdisciplinary enterprise like this one with a disclosure of my own theoretical and conceptual framework. Against this background, I hope I can make it clear that the choice and composition of sections and chapters in this book follows a comprehensible logic, and that the chapters, while coming from disparate disciplinary perspectives, are fully complementary with one another.

I begin with a brief outline in which I derive the concept of retaliation from the broader notion of reciprocity and ultimately define retaliation as the human disposition to strive for a reactive balancing of conflicts and other situations perceived as unjust. Next, I address the plurality of theoretical portfolios and inventories of knowledge on retaliation, delineate the basic components of a theory of retaliation, and show their affinities to the realms of conflict and violence as the point of departure for the combination of topics in the present volume. Then I look at the manifestations of the concept of retaliation in situations of conflict and the consequences it may entail, highlighting its transformative power. A subsequent section is devoted to the process of analysing and contextualizing the tension between retaliation as a code of instruction for human agency, on the one hand, and its representation and stereotyping, on the other. I conclude by briefly introducing the chapters of the volume and outlining the six thematic fields in which they are embedded.

The scientific discourse on the universality, timelessness and complexity of the concept of retaliation has a long history in Western scholarship. However, while disciplinary interaction has always played a role, a dialogue only developed after the classic fields of study had diversified into the modern range of disciplines, and especially after the emergence of new, empirically informed epistemologies and the paradigmatic shifts at the end of nineteenth century and into the twentieth century. At that time, theology, history and jurisprudence were the disciplines in which the benchmarks for all further reflection on retaliation had already been established. In the concluding chapter, the six thematic sections of this volume are revisited in greater detail. Therein I briefly touch upon this development in the Western history of science, as it helps to understand recent steps towards transdisciplinary comparative analysis. Towards the end of the concluding chapter, I briefly summarize the main topics and come back to the ostensible scientific demarcations and apparent incommensurability between disciplines, and the common ground that a synopsis of the various chapters in the volume allows us to discern.

The Transdisciplinary Career of a Basic Concept

Retaliation and Reciprocity

As a point of departure for the study of retaliation in modern social sciences, I suggest starting with the superordinate axiom of reciprocity. This principle of the balancing of service and return service or of action and reaction manifests its formative power in all spheres of human existence. It takes on different shapes in different social environments and frameworks of action. The balanced and symmetrical exchange of goods and services in the shape of highly formalized systems and forms of economic cooperation is but one example of the above principle in human interaction. As an ethical rule, reciprocity calls on people to treat others as they themselves would want to be treated. This is often called the 'golden rule', which, as the expression of an unconditional mutual respect, provides one foundation of modern human rights.

As formalized, anticipatory decisions to act, reciprocity-based action–reaction schemes logically contribute to the occurrence of a wide range of operational and institutional arrangements, be it in the economy, social life, religion or other interconnectivities examined in the contributions to this volume. Thus, reciprocal action is further differentiated according to relational and reactional patterns as generalized, direct, indirect, delayed, serial, 'negative' or immediate reaction to an action in either formalized or nonspecified progressions. Reciprocity may therefore be understood, on the one hand, as the desired and positive result of an investment in social relationships. On the other hand, it may entail a restriction of human agency, as behaviour that is classified as deviant or as a social transgression will trigger a (reciprocal) counteraction. This hints at the moral implications of reciprocal action. Whether in the case of a formalized gift exchange or of a reaction to perceived injustice, what distinguishes reciprocity in social life from other action–reaction schemes is the moment of commitment (Gouldner 1960; Narotzky and Moreno 2002).

Retaliation is one concretization of this principle. With the coining of the term 'regulated reciprocity' by Richard Thurnwald (1921) and its later use by Bronislaw Malinowski (1984 [1922]; 1926),[13] a new avenue to the complex of retaliation, usually described in terms such as revenge, vengeance, feud, self-help and so on, was opened in empirical social sciences. As the specific form of reciprocity that manifests itself in constellations of conflict, retaliation is, in turn, embedded in a wider framework of mutually constitutive and intertwined basic principles of human interaction. Such principles can at times take the form of institutional arrangements that formalize mutual dependencies and entanglements, and that can therefore prove to be particularly efficacious. In choosing their strategies of action in situations of conflict, actors operate with these interdependencies. Institutional arrangements of retaliatory claims between parties may thus be connected to an institutionalized grant of protection, asylum or exile, which, in turn, may carry over to established forms of negotiations (Turner 2005). This framework may add, after a fashion, a moment of calculability to the assessment of conflictive dynamics, despite the apparent unpredictability and vast range of optional or hypothetical courses of a conflict. At this point, it seems necessary to emphasize that the principle of retaliation may materialize in accordance with differing cultural and social logics and be integrated in very different conceptual frameworks that are themselves subject to constant renegotiation.

The spectrum of courses of action (reactions) associated with retaliation ranges from refusal to communicate (ignoring or avoiding someone) to affronts (which also include bullying), claims to compensation and the use of violence, even in its most excessive forms. The moments of transition – when avoidance turns into confrontational reaction that, again, may turn into compensation-oriented negotiations and vice versa – seem to be the vital juncture in this field of action where the social conditions in which the principle of retaliation comes into play and its consequences can be empirically observed.

Disciplinary Diversification

As a basic pattern of human behaviour, retaliation exerts a pull far beyond disciplinary boundaries and also beyond the realms of the interdisciplinary framework presented here. It serves in a variety of scientific disciplines as an explanatory model for the most diverse of human actions. A few examples will suffice to illustrate this point. In addition to the abovementioned use of the concept of retaliation in organizational economic models of negotiation and accommodation, entire economic and political theories of rational action can be traced back to this basic directive (Fehr and Gächter 2003; Axelrod 2006). In this context, retaliation is considered to be the application of the principle of reciprocity in situations of competitive relations. The best-known example is the description of the *tit-for-tat* strategy in game theory as 'equivalent retaliation'. Following this strategy, one actor responds to his or her opponent's actions with identical reactions. If the opponent cooperates, the actor does as well; if the opponent defects (ceases to cooperate), the actor retaliates by ceasing to cooperate. This strategy has proven to be the most successful in market and competitive constellations, but it also risks leading to perpetual retaliation. Thus, two actors engaging with each other on the basis of this strategy will reach the point of perpetual conflict as soon as one of them defects, unless one of them has learned through experience (i.e., multiple iterations of the game) that it sometimes pays to give the other the benefit of the doubt and assumes that the first act of retaliation was either accidental or the result of a mistaken understanding of the previous action.[14]

Sociobiology, evolutionary behavioural sciences and evolutionary economics also invoke retaliation as an explanatory model in their analysis of human development (in part drawing on concepts from game theory). Reciprocal altruism, selection processes and explanations for cooperative behaviour are put in a context with retaliation as instantiations of reciprocity (Bowles and Gintis 2011). In return, disciplines such as sociobiology pursue their specific approaches to explaining retaliation. In my view, however, such explanations remain speculative because they are usually not empirically grounded. Sociobiological and evolutionary explanations become questionable (at the latest) when they address degrees of violence and homicide rates in different eras of human history (Boehm 2011; Pinker 2011). Some representatives of these disciplines suggest that retaliatory logic has claimed more victims throughout human history than jealousy, greed and war put together (Voland 2000), a statement that already proceeds from dubious categorical distinctions. In contrast, it is one concern of this introduction to show that retaliation discourses, even regarding the gravest offences such as homicide, do not mechanically instruct people to kill in response. Rather, they are an integral part of complex institutional configurations that include avoidance and compensation and aim to regulate and channel violence.

Towards a Theory of Retaliation: Basic Components and Terminological Framings

The concept of retaliation refers broadly to the full range of reactions to circumstances that are perceived to be deviant or socially transgressive. Such a constellation presupposes two opposed, but nominally equal parties. Understood in this sense, retaliation occurs at all levels of sociopolitical organization, from individual face-to-face interaction to nuclear families to nation-states and transnational organizations.

Retaliatory logics may inform the entire gamut of conflict resolution procedures, from consensual settlement through various forms of compensation to violent reprisal and escalation. Taking the principle of reciprocity as a point of departure, the question of how to explain the variety within the scheme of retaliatory reactions arises. The most fundamental common property seems to be the equalizing and balancing quality that is inherent in the principle of reciprocity. Thus, retaliatory reaction may in the first place exhibit two properties. First, it guarantees that a perpetrator is prevented from gaining an advantage from a deviant or socially transgressive act. The concept of punishment only seems subordinately associated with retaliation and reflects a logic of power stratification and of the judiciary of the state. This will be addressed below in the section on crime and deviance.

Second, retaliation implies the notion of appropriateness; it presumes proportionality. However, both appropriateness and proportionality connote a variety of criteria, a comparative examination of which shows that the requirement of proportionality can lead to highly differentiated consequences. The quality of the initial act is of critical importance here, but the assessment of this quality also depends on the particularities of the social relationship between the opposed parties, an issue that will be discussed in the context of the formation and identification of conflictive parties. Further criteria come into play. Should retaliation be proportional to the damages suffered or to the unjustly acquired advantage? Does a responsible party pay damages according to fixed rates corresponding to a classification of the offence or according to his or her wealth? Should a reaction take into account the social status or the asset situation of the victim or of the perpetrator? There are many different interpretations and sometimes they compete against one another.

Whether perceived as legitimate or not, retaliation thus appears on the one hand as a preventive principle: the fear of retaliation can prevent somebody from committing an inappropriate act against another. On the other hand, it is viewed as a right to react in a way that allows for the restoration of balance following a perceived injustice.

Relations between parties that are based on retaliatory logics, in turn, also exhibit a number of necessary determinants. A certain threshold must be transcended to warrant a reaction, not only in the view of the offended party, but also in the view of a concerned public. Such a threshold may depend on the seriousness of the offence, as well as on the individual accounts of actors involved and the history of offensive acts. Moreover, some effects of retaliation only manifest themselves if the initiator is a first offender. For example, the option to claim compensation for an offence may not materialize if the perpetrator is a repeat offender or notorious wrongdoer. Thus, retaliation is about the choice between violent and compensatory approaches towards a disruptive act, always taking into consideration the quality of the social relations between the parties involved.

The multifariousness of phenomena that are classified as retaliation has led to terminological plurality. Some terms refer to a set of specific properties and neglect others. Most frequently we observe implicit reference to the concept under the notions of revenge, vengeance, retribution, self-help (in the sense of taking the law into one's own hands), private revenge, vigilantism, payback, getting even, feud and vendetta. Some authors attempt to make a strict distinction between retaliation and revenge. They assert that the concept of retaliation only aims at and is motivated by equalizing justice, whereas revenge springs from vengefulness and thus has to be condemned (e.g., Sarat 2002a, 2002b; Murphy 2003). This fundamental distinction aims at a moral evaluation of the motivation for actions and may be useful for analytical purposes, but the available empirical data do not actually support it (Miller 2006). Furthermore, this distinction becomes thoroughly problematic when it is associated with different stages in the progress of societies, as will be emphasized below in the section on retaliation as a litmus test for social theories of cultural evolution. Other terms emphasize long-standing conflicts, such as vendetta and feud, while others imply reference to illegality, such as the 'private' in 'private revenge', which implies 'without the intervention of legitimate authorities' (or even against such intervention).

Manifestations of the Principle of Retaliation in Situations of Conflict: Violence and Compensation

Violence is necessarily an inherent part of the concept of retaliation, although both concepts connote more than can be derived from their specific co-conditionality. For example, when the emergence of planned and organized exchanges of violence is examined, retaliation can only explain the reactive moment. Some argue that in the evolution of humankind, the violent component of the concept of retaliation must have been primordial, while the idea of compensation as an alternative to it only emerged much later and appears to be of subordinate importance. I have no independent opinion on this subject; I can only say that, according to the empirical data available, neither of the two aspects of the principle ever seems to appear with such dominant exclusivity that it would be impossible to envision the other. This is not to deny that in some cases actors seem to expect greater benefits from a violent reaction. In this context, the reference to retaliation sometimes appears to be a legitimizing strategy to hide the desire for benefits of a violent intervention, whether with regard to material gains or reproductive success. In any case, the data suggest that the prevalence of the violent option in retaliatory relations, as asserted in many analyses, is neither self-evident nor the only possible interpretation (Turner and Schlee 2008).

Thus, an overemphasis on retaliatory violence does not take us very far. Moreover, a wide variety of considerations inform the decision to engage in violent retaliation, including the quality and intensity of the initial infraction, and the rules of and limitations on the use of violence. Factual constraints come into play: social proximity and even seasons and phases in the economic cycle may influence a decision. In some agrarian societies, for example, during the rainy season or harvest, the propensity for violent retaliation decreases as people are more concerned with essential activities sustaining their livelihood and have no interest in being distracted by a conflict during this time. Such circumstances can promote compensation-oriented conflict regulation. This does not, however, mean that a wrong will not be brought up again at a later time, for example, if someone needs justification in the future to move against the person who caused the wrong.

An epistemologically more promising approach aims at a synthesis of the violence-generating and violence-avoiding potentials of retaliation. In my view, it is not expedient to separate the violence-legitimizing power of retaliation, which refers to the repertoire of accepted violent reactions to an initial violent act, on the one hand, from its capacity to regulate the potential for violence or to avoid escalation on the other hand. The latter capacity basically enables the transformation of legitimate claims to the use of violence into compensation.

It is this interconnection that accounts for the concept of retaliation. There is indeed a categorical difference between its preventive dimension as regards initial violence and its justifying dimension as regards the use of reactive violence, but both aspects may arise out of the same logic. In cases where the violence prevention fails and an initial violent act takes place, reactive violence appears legitimized; otherwise, the preventive aspect of retaliation would lose its deterrent capacity. However, the legitimate right to violent retaliation does not presume its immediate execution. This proves to be true even in situations where there is not only a *right* to a violent reaction, but also an actual *duty*. Even then, there are usually a number of exit options available. These allow for the involved parties to avoid sustained violence without waiving their claims. All this is subject to negotiation.

Several contributions to this volume discuss various ways in which the concept of retaliation informs complex processes of conflict regulation. However, when we look at the public discourse, we see that the violence-legitimizing capacity of retaliation is singled out and overemphasized. In media debates on the legitimacy of reactive violence, for instance, another vital component of the concept of retaliation recedes into the background. This is the requirement of *proportionality* in retaliatory exchanges – the assessment of whether the reactive violence is proportionate to the initial act or surpasses it in intensity. It is exactly this aspect of balancing out between action and reaction that gives a retaliatory act its legitimacy. However, the assessment of proportionality is challenged when the boundaries between different staging areas of tensions – ranging from intrafamilial disputes to international crises – become blurred. This point is quite controversial and is sometimes dominated by insistence on codified ideologies of violent retaliation. On the one hand, the media represent spectacular performances of violence – identified as retaliation – as 'typical' of places such as Palestine, Iraq, Afghanistan, Albania and the Horn of Africa.[15] Incidents at the local or family scale are presented as characteristic of entire countries or 'cultures'. Yet, at the same time, the call for legitimate retaliation is increasingly detached from these concrete social contexts and becomes politicized and scaled up to the transnational level.[16] Claims to retaliation may have a unifying effect that transcends spatial boundaries for the sake of commonly shared markers of identity such as religion or language. In a similar manner, incidents of violence in the global North that have recently received considerable attention (such as honour crimes) are represented as the execution of the violent aspect of retaliation. This is all the more so when these acts can be distanced from the host culture by, for instance, explaining them in terms of a history of migration. In fact, there is much to suggest that this interpretation does not accurately reflect traditional repertoires. However, it is not only the majority population of the host country that misinterprets these acts. When members of the migrant communities themselves engage in these practices, they seem to be taken in by their own misconceptions about this component of their traditional repertoires of conflict settlement practices. They single out a presumed obligation to violent reaction, and fail to take into consideration both proportionality and the fact that intrafamilial retaliation is a contradiction in terms.

Our attempt at a transdisciplinary dialogue on retaliation has made it evident that the option of legitimate retaliation is as much a social fact as it is a juridical institution ensuring reciprocity. In the realm of everyday disputes arising in time and space, retaliation has not generated more violence, but rather contributes to its containment. This is even true for social settings in which retaliation is thought to be tantamount to violence. Its embeddedness in institutional arrangements of conflict regulation provides an analytical point of departure and the key to understanding how it affects human relations. When

I emphasize that retaliation is not *necessarily* sanction-oriented, perpetrator-oriented or based on central authorities, this does not mean that these qualifications must be excluded from those modes of conflict settlement in which actors operate with retaliatory claims. Thus, I consider retaliation to be an efficient means of balancing conflict management *irrespective* of any connection to sanctions and central authorities and *because* it does not deny the violent counterpart to compensation.

Again, the social relevance may rather be seen in the potential of retaliation to prevent one party from acquiring advantages from acts of social transgression and deviant behaviour. This is especially true when the conflicting parties, or the perpetrator and the victim, are separated from each other by a certain social and political distance. Now I come back to the interaction of the two criteria – appropriateness and the quality of the social relations between the parties involved – and bring them together with the option of reactive violence or compensation. I argue that a 'middle-range social distance' is most favourable for a negotiated settlement of retaliatory claims. While I am fully aware of the imprecision of the term 'middle-range' with regard to social proximity, I am nevertheless convinced of its usefulness as a relational concept. If the social distance is smaller, then the victim's and perpetrator's statuses converge too much for retaliation claims to be reasonably offset.[17] If the distance is greater, then the option of compensatory retaliation is often pushed to the background in favour of gaining the greatest possible advantage through retaliation claims beyond all proportionality. In all given conflict constellations of 'medium social distance' (Turner 2008), the actors effectively use institutional repertoires that show compliance with a retaliatory logic, irrespective of a political framework. When we look, in turn, solely at the violent component, the following question immediately arises: to what extent do organizational principles reflect specific reference to retaliatory violence in connecting actors with types of violent behaviour, whether it be vigilantism, gang violence, 'tribal conflict' or some other form of organized violent intervention? Reference to retaliation as an argument to justify such use of violence helps us to understand violent events in terms of the perceived legitimacy of war, civil unrest or acts of terrorism.

The Problem of Method and Empirical Data: Comparability and Interpretive Biases

In the study of basic principles of the human condition such as retaliation, it is not surprising that we are confronted with methodological and theoretical plurality, and with the problem of variation within and between disciplinary approaches, schemes of reference, sets of data and their terminological framing. In some disciplines, particularly in the psychological sciences, data are generated through experimentation. While data collected under 'unnatural conditions', for instance, in laboratory settings, may be doubted by some, such findings on individual decision making are taken up, compared and acknowledged by others. In the social sciences, quantitative data originating from surveys and questionnaires and qualitative data generated by means of interviews and participant observation are quite often analysed using different epistemological approaches and through different theoretical prisms, and therefore produce quite divergent results. To highlight just one discrepancy with regard to data on retaliation: there is a remarkable difference between individual decisions elicited in controlled laboratory settings and the narratives and representations of such decisions when actors explain the motivations behind their decisions. This leads analysts to assume that the same difference pertains to real-life situations. In short, everything comes down to the difference between representation and empirical facts; between people's conscious reference to an established rule and their actual behaviour. However, the discovery of this difference, of the gap between the rule and the practice, turns out to be epistemologically much less illuminating than the ways in which these different categories actually interconnect and interact. There is, for instance, the hypothesis that long-standing conflictive relationships between social groups can be explained as a typical result of retaliatory behaviour (e.g., Black-Michaud 1975; Verdier 1980–84). When asserted, however, this hypothesis generally appears to have been extrapolated from fragmented data. Such data may become entrenched, both in popular representation and in the literature, as the stereotype of the eternal feud between kin groups. Yet, in reality, such 'eternal feuding' may turn out to be nothing more than a way of referring to long-standing relations of peace, whereby all kinds of conflict are addressed in terms of a hypothetical balancing of accounts between the parties. These accounts are never expected to be settled, but they nevertheless do not lead to an incessant exchange of violence. Rather, the accounting is about unsettled retaliatory relationships that are referred to as 'periods' or 'cycles' of retaliation, which may include long-lasting phases of peaceful and nonviolent interaction between the parties punctuated by brief incidents of violence. These peaceful phases may resemble periods of truce that remain under the threat of an unresolved feud, but during which trade relations and even rather intimate social practices to remain in good standing with one another, such as bride exchange, are maintained. The very same time span may be addressed in oral or written tradition as a phase of deterrent retaliation in which only the few exchanges of violence are recounted and emphasized, while the prevailing periods of peaceful coexistence go unremarked. The focus on single events does not automatically allow for the observation of social routines, which only become evident over a long period of time, maybe even generations.

Another epistemological problem lies in the recognition of presumably known and familiar phenomena in the historical and ethnographic record. This may lead to misinterpretation and to the assignment of one's own values to circumstances that are unknown or misunderstood. Crucial here is the role of rhetorical representation that, if always taken literally, tricks us into believing in a worldview according to which retaliatory violence is predominant and ubiquitous.

We notice, for instance, that the media often appropriate the notion of retaliation as an interpretive framework that represents violent events in ways that may range from the exercise of archaic blood vengeance to military retaliation executed with the highest precision, but without acknowledging the fragmentary and incomplete nature of the data set they are working with. Thus, retaliation is associated with concepts ranging from backwardness and primitiveness to notions of a legitimate right or even a religious duty. In fact, the diverse sources and types of data have to be combined in a careful historical analysis to unpack such entanglements of fact, fiction, stereotypes and interpretations. Put briefly, the rhetoric and language of retaliation not only inform discourses on conflict settlement and dispute management, but also predetermine the representation of the very potential for conflict.

I recognize, of course, that automatic violent responses resulting from an ideology of retaliation have also been empirically documented, although relatively infrequently, and certainly less frequently than media and other representations would have us believe. The transformation of legitimate claims to violence into compensation appears to be by far the preferred option when compared to the actual execution of violence. This can be empirically demonstrated. But it is empirically much more difficult to show how many acts of violence have been prevented by the mere threat of retaliation, and how many more acts of retaliatory violence have been prevented by the payment of compensation when the threat of retaliation did not prevent an initial act, than it is to document empirically overt acts of retaliatory violence.

Conclusion: Structure and Composition of the Volume

After these reflections on the more contextual, epistemological and theoretical dimensions of the concept of retaliation, I turn now to the structure of the volume, which is organized thematically rather than along disciplinary lines. The book is divided into six sections, with each section comprising two chapters. The topics of the respective sections also feature as thematic axes running throughout the entire book. The topics – specified above as human universals, crime, deviance and punishment, faith-driven models, conflict management in social and political ordering, and transnational interventionism and postwar scenarios – shall be briefly introduced here. They are addressed in greater detail in the volume's concluding chapter, where I trace out how the framework conditions and major tendencies outlined here take effect in contexts in which references to retaliation imbue situations of everyday life and public discourse. The aim is to show how disciplinary expertise can be addressed in the light of global developments that have brought the issue of retaliation to the forefront of the scientific and public agenda, namely, as I have introduced, scientification, securitization, religiosification and juridification. I suggest that taking such references into consideration is all the more important because they convey connotations of retaliation that far exceed the scope of the accepted conceptual plurality of the concept in academic discourse.

To avoid pushing the anthropological perspective of the editors too much to the foreground, the first section of the volume offers two more general presentations in order to accentuate the plurality of approaches and perspectives that I have tried to outline in this introduction. These two chapters deal with retaliation as an expression of human nature and outline how retaliation is addressed in research on the human psyche, mind and emotions. First, Mario Gollwitzer and Arne Sjöström offer a psychological analysis of the individual and social functions of revenge. Robert J. Bies and Thomas M. Tripp, with a background in business management, follow by highlighting the influence of visceral factors on retaliation. In doing so, they open up the vast area relating the world of emotions to the human reactions elicited by the experience of perceived injustice.

The thematic conjunction continues with the sections on crime, deviance and punishment, drawing on contributions from legal history, psychology, econometrics and criminology. In the first chapter of this section, Horst Entorf, from the perspective of econometrics, explores 'the role of angry retaliation within economic reasoning' in the victim–offender overlap, noting that 'offenders are more likely than non-offenders to be victims, and victims are more likely than non-victims to be offenders'. Margit E. Oswald, from a psychological point of view, states that ordinary citizens adopt a generally retributive attitude towards punishable acts and explores what criteria further specify such an attitude.

The third section – on crime – looks at encounters between formal and informal normativities. Karl Härter investigates the historical process during which the nascent criminal justice system in early modern Europe positioned itself between the public and private spheres with regard to retaliation. Richard Wright, Volkan Topalli and Scott Jacques argue that 'the contagion of urban violence arises from dynamic, recursive cycles of victimization and retaliation that occur between criminally involved individuals, embedded within facilitative sociocultural settings and circumstances' and draw challenging conclusions on the basis of this assertion.

In the fourth and fifth sections (on religion and sociopolitical ordering, respectively), a social anthropological perspective is predominant. With reference to Islam, Yazid Ben Hounet's chapter shows that religion and social ordering can be so tightly intertwined that efforts to separate out their respective connections to retaliation are rendered highly problematic. Severin Lenart highlights the connection between retaliation and witchcraft in local disputing in Swaziland and the adjacent parts of South Africa. In the section on the organization of social and political order, Albert K. Drent examines the conscientious and intentional avoidance of retaliation in dispute configurations that involve state and nonstate actors at different scales in northern Cameroon. Günther Schlee focuses on the interconnectedness of Islamic perceptions, customary law and clan-based order in a failed state environment, which comes close to the anthropological *locus classicus* of a stateless society.

In section VI, the two contributions address how scenarios of transnational postconflict interventionism are affected by resurfacing notions of retaliation. From an anthropological perspective, Friederike Stahlmann analyses the complex fabric of retaliatory concepts in the postwar society of Bamyan, Afghanistan. In the same section, Pietro Sullo addresses retaliatory and punitive aspects of reparations in international law.

The structure of the book thus reflects areas of research in which the concept of retaliation is currently being revisited and new insights are generated. The contributions to this volume address different aspects of the topic that are usually not brought together. We do not claim to present all possible facets of the topic and to provide the complete, definitive overview of the treatment of retaliation in all of these disciplines, but want rather to take up significant questions in order to reveal interdisciplinary interfaces and to facilitate an exchange of ideas.

Trajectories of scientific knowledge production, which are most often seen in isolation from one another, are thus brought together. Ways of addressing social grievances, disputes and conflicts – ranging from the propensity to exercise violence to negotiations and mediation, and from individual strategies in decision making to the involvement of the state and global governance institutions in conflict management at various scales – are thus put into one context. Needless to say, the representatives of the various disciplines who have contributed to this transdisciplinary discourse on retaliation were bound to commence such an enterprise in a discipline-specific way. It is the nature of the beast. And I do fully concede that such an approach may produce some inconsistencies, rifts, distortions and overlaps. Nevertheless, I think that this has advantages and that it does not make sense to impose stringency and rigour where it cannot be given as a matter of fact. Thus, without privileging one approach or perspective over another, I believe that we can come closer to an empirically informed theory if we accept this plurality of overlaps, interfaces, similarities and contradictions that are lurking behind disciplinary boundaries, and learn to discover the common ground underlying them.

Acknowledgements

I am grateful to Brian Donahoe for his careful review and language editing, and the two anonymous reviewers for their very useful comments on the original version of this text.

Bertram Turner is Senior Researcher in the 'Law and Anthropology' department at the Max Planck Institute for Social Anthropology in Halle, Germany. He has conducted extended field research in the Middle East and North Africa, Germany and Canada, has held university teaching positions in Munich, Leipzig and Halle, and has published widely on the anthropology of law, religion, conflict, morality, development and resource extraction. Among his more recent publications is a special issue co-edited with Maarten Bavinck and Marc Simon Thomas in the *Journal of Legal Pluralism* 47(3): 375–410: 'Franz von Benda-Beckmann: Legal Pluralism in the Past and Future' (with a single-authored introduction by Turner).

Notes

1. *Transdisiplinarity* is not meant in the sense of a universal theoretical unity (see Nowotny et al. 2001; Nicolescu 2002; Mittelstrass 2011; Bernstein 2015). For further literature on transdisciplinarity, see the bibliography at http://ciret-transdisciplinarity.org (retrieved 25 February 2016).
2. 'Wieviel kostet ein toter Afghane?' ('How Much Does a Dead Afghan Cost?') and 'Tarife des Schreckens' ('Tariffs of Horror'), *Süddeutsche Zeitung*, 10 December 2009: 2.
3. One of the first cases of blood money payment and *diya* negotiations in the context of a foreign assignment of the German *Bundeswehr* (armed forces) took place in Somalia in the early 1990s. For an analysis of these events, the crucial importance of negotiations between the perpetrator party and the offended party, the necessity to establish social relations between them, the assessment of the appropriateness of compensatory payments and the concomitant misunderstandings, see Schlee and Turner (2008).
4. Individual claims for compensation were rejected by the district court in Bonn, Germany, at the end of 2013 with the argument that a culpable breach of duty of the German army officer in charge could not be proved and therefore the state was not liable (see www.tagesschau.de/inland/kundus-urteil100.html, accessed 14 March 2016).
5. Countless literary works feature the word 'retaliation' in their titles. Two works may suffice as examples of the ample variety: Oliver Goldsmith's 'Retaliation: A Poem' (1774), and *The Retaliation: A Novel* by Yasmin Shiraz (2008). See also Maynard, Kearney and Guimond (2010) for examples of literary and cinematic representation of 'illegal revenge'.
6. The rap album *Retaliation, Revenge & Get Back* by Daz Dillinger and the single 'Retaliation' by the hip-hop group Jedi Mind Tricks may serve as examples here.
7. See, e.g., http://www.btselem.org/settler_violence,_retrieved 1 August 2016.
8. There are, of course, other trends, such as neoliberalism, with all its consequences for the topics addressed in this volume. Likewise, there may well be research areas concerned with retaliation other than those selected for this book.
9. See also the respective chapters in Clausen and Levy (2014) on concepts such as 'justice', 'free will' and 'normality'.
10. See, e.g., the debate in the U.S. media about the 'evolutionary inevitability' of revenge following the killing of Osama bin Laden in 2011 (Harmon 2011).
11. In this sense, the monopoly on the legitimate use of force includes the right of the state to partially delegate it to commercial security providers while state control is sustained.

12. See, e.g., Austin, Kranock and Oommen (2003) and Scheer (2004) on U.S. president George Bush's Christian rhetoric and reference to religion in his justification of retaliatory war.
13. With reference to the literature quoted, I work within the broader field that is not limited to the economic aspects of reciprocity. Other early literature such as Mauss (1990 [1925]) also analyses reciprocity in the context of power relations – an understanding that is taken up below when reciprocity/retaliation among nominally equal, but politically and economically unequal parties is addressed. Regarding the normative–legal aspects, recent literature in legal studies addresses reciprocity, especially in the context of international law (see, e.g., Nasrolahi Fard 2016).
14. It is not the place here to refer in more detail to the *tit-for-tat* strategy as a specification of the principle of reciprocity. Building on its importance in game theory, it has become one of the most influential approaches in the social sciences and fields of application such as politics, and has generated an abundant literature (see Axelrod 2006).
15. See Prunier (1997); Schwandner-Sievers (2001); Schlee (2003); Schlee and Turner (2008). See also the conventional wisdom and stereotypes on retaliation and violence, e.g., on the basis of Google hits for terms like 'blood feud' in combination with country names such as Afghanistan, Iraq, Palestine or Albania.
16. Muslims all over the world are called upon to exercise retaliation for their brothers in faith in situations of crisis such as in Lebanon, Iraq and Pakistan. The U.S. media reacted with a sophisticated tale of retaliation to the threat of terrorism after the attacks of 11 September (see, e.g., Deveau and Fouts 2005; Al-Asaadi 2006; see also Rees 2003).
17. In this regard, there is, to an extent, correspondence between data in anthropology (see, e.g., Otterbein 1997) and criminology (e.g., Dugan and Apel 2005).

References

Aase, T. (ed.). 2002. *Tournaments of Power: Honour and Revenge in the Contemporary World.* Aldershot: Ashgate.

Al-Asaadi, M. 2006. 'Mosque Preacher Sacked for Inciting Hatred', *Yemen Observer*, 15 August.

Austin, G., T. Kranock and T. Oommen. 2003. *God and War. An Audit and an Explanation.* Bradford: Department of Peace Studies. Retrieved 1 August 2016 from http://news.bbc.co.uk/2/shared/spl/hi/world/04/war_audit_pdf/pdf/war_audit.pdf.

Axelrod, R. 2006. *The Evolution of Cooperation*, revised edn. New York: Basic Books.

Barash, D.P., and J.E. Lipton. 2011. *Payback: Why We Retaliate, Redirect Aggression, and Take Revenge.* Oxford: Oxford University Press.

Benda-Beckmann, F. v., and K.v. Benda-Beckmann. 2007. 'Transnationalisation of Law, Globalisation and Legal Pluralism: A Legal Anthropological Perspective', in C. Antons and V. Gessner (eds), *Globalisation and Resistance: Law Reform in Asia since the Crisis.* Oxford: Hart, pp. 53–80.

Benda-Beckmann, F. v., K.v. Benda-Beckmann, M. Ramstedt and B. Turner. 2013. 'Introduction: On the Pervasiveness of Religious Normativity in Disputing Processes', in F.v. Benda-Beckmann, K.v. Benda-Beckmann, M. Ramstedt and B. Turner (eds), *Religion in Dispute: Pervasiveness of Religious Normativity in Disputing Processes.* Basingstoke, Hampshire: Palgrave Macmillan, pp. VII–XX.

Bernstein, J.H. 2015. 'Transdisciplinarity: A Review of its Origins, Development, and Current Issues', *Journal of Research Practice* 11(1). Retrieved 1 August 2016 from http://jrp.icaap.org/index.php/jrp/article/view/510/412.

Black-Michaud, J. 1975. *Cohesive Force: Feud in the Mediterranean and the Middle East*. Oxford: Blackwell.

Blichner, L.C., and A. Molander. 2008. 'Mapping Juridification', *European Law Journal* 14(1): 36–54.

Boehm, C. 2011. 'Retaliatory Violence in Human Prehistory', *British Journal of Criminology* 51(3): 518–34.

Bowles, S., and H. Gintis. 2011. *A Cooperative Species: Human Reciprocity and its Evolution*. Princeton: Princeton University Press.

Clausen, J., and N. Levy (eds). 2014. *Handbook of Neuroethics*. Dordrecht: Springer.

Coleman, G. 2012. 'Our Weirdness is Free: The Logic of Anonymous – Online Army, Agent of Chaos, and Seeker of Justice', *Triple Canopy*. Retrieved 1 August 2016 from http://canopycanopycanopy.com/15/our_weirdness_is_free.

Comaroff, J., and J.L. Comaroff (eds). 2006. *Law and Disorder in the Postcolony*. Chicago: University of Chicago Press.

Denson, T. F., W.C. Pedersen and N. Miller. 2006. 'The Displaced Aggression Questionnaire', *Journal of Personality and Social Psychology* 60(6): 1032–51.

Deveau, V., and G. Fouts. 2005. 'Revenge in U.S. and Canadian News Magazines Post-9/11', *Canadian Journal of Communication* 20: 99–109.

Diamond, J. 2008. 'Vengeance is Ours: What Can Tribal Societies Tell Us about Our Need to Get Even?', *The New Yorker. Annals of Anthropology* 21(4): 74–82.

Dugan, L., and R. Apel. 2005. 'The Differential Risk of Retaliation by Relational Distance: A More General Model of Violent Victimization', *Criminology* 43(3): 697–729.

Eisenberger, R., P. Lynch, J. Aselage and S. Rohdieck. 2004. 'Who Takes the Most Revenge? Individual Differences in Negative Reciprocity Norm Endorsement', *Personality and Social Psychology Bulletin* 30(6): 787–99.

Fehr, E., and S. Gächter. 2003. 'Fairness and Retaliation: The Economics of Reciprocity', in E.L. Khalil and G.M. Hodgson (eds), *Trust*. Cheltenham: Edward Elgar, pp. 285–307.

Feinberg, R.M., and K.M. Reynolds. 2006. 'The Spread of Antidumping Regimes and the Role of Retaliation in Filings', *Southern Economic Journal* 72(4): 877–90.

Gehring, V.V. (ed.). 2003. *War after September 11*. Lanham, MD: Rowman & Littlefield.

Goldsmith, O. 1774. *Retaliation: A Poem*. London: G. Kearsly.

Gollwitzer, M. 2005. *Ist 'gerächt' gleich 'gerecht'?* Berlin: Wissenschaftlicher Verlag Berlin.

Goodenough, O.R., and M. Tucker. 2010. 'Law and Cognitive Neuroscience', *Annual Review of Law and Social Sciences* 6: 61–92.

Gouldner, A.W. 1960. 'The Norm of Reciprocity: A Preliminary Statement', *American Sociological Review* 25(2): 161–78.

Greer, T., M. Berman, V. Varan and S. Watson. 2005. 'We are a Religious People. We are a Vengeful People', *Journal for the Scientific Study of Religion* 44(1): 45–57.

Grutzpalk, J. 2002. 'Blood Feud and Modernity', *Journal of Classical Sociology* 2(2): 115–34.

Harmon, K. 2011. 'Does Revenge Serve an Evolutionary Purpose?', *Scientific American*. Retrieved 1 August 2016 from http://www.scientificamerican.com/article.cfm?id=revenge-evolution.

Herod, A., and M. Wright (eds). 2002. *Geographies of Power: Placing Scale*. Malden, MA: Blackwell.

Holbraad, M., and A. Pedersen (eds). 2013. *Times of Security: Ethnographies of Fear, Protest and the Future*. London: Routledge.

Isak, K. 2003. *Die Rachegesellschaft: Der Rachediskurs in den Printmedien; ein Beitrag zur Logistik der Medien*. Maria Saal: Vision+Mission-Verlag.

Kudisch, J.D., V.J. Fortunato and A.F. Smith. 2006. 'Contextual and Individual Difference Factors Predicting Individuals' Desire to Provide Upward Feedback', *Group and Organization Management* 31(4): 503–29.

Malinowski, B. 1984 [1922]. *Argonauts of the Western Pacific*. Prospect Heights, NY: Waveland Press.

———. 1926. *Crime and Custom in Savage Society*. London: Kegan Paul.

Martin, M., and T. Owen (eds). 2014. *Routledge Handbook of Human Security*. London: Routledge.

Mauss, M. 1990 [1925]. *The Gift: The Form and Reason for Exchange in Archaic Societies*. New York: Norton.

Maynard, K., J. Kearney and J. Guimond. 2010. *Revenge versus Legality: Wild Justice from Balzac to Clint Eastwood and Abu Ghraib*. Oxford: Birkbeck Law Press.

McCullough, M.E. 2008. *Beyond Revenge: The Evolution of the Forgiveness Instinct*. San Francisco: Jossey-Bass.

Mesmer-Magnus, J.R., and C. Viswesvaran. 2005. 'Whistleblowing in Organizations: An Examination of Correlates of Whistleblowing Intentions, Actions, and Retaliation', *Journal of Business Ethics* 62(3): 277–97.

Miller, W.I. 2006. *Eye for an Eye*. Cambridge: Cambridge University Press.

Mittelstrass, J. 2011. 'On Transdisciplinarity', *Trames* 15(4): 329–38.

Murphy, J.G. 2003. *Getting Even – Forgiveness and its Limits*. Oxford: Oxford University Press.

Narotzky, S., and P. Moreno Feliu. 2002. 'Reciprocity's Dark Side: Negative Reciprocity, Morality and Social Reproduction', *Anthropological Theory* 2(3): 281–305.

Nasrolahi Fard, Shahrad 2016. *Reciprocity in International Law: Its Impact and Function*. Abingdon: Routledge.

Nicolescu, B. 2002. *Manifesto of Transdisciplinarity*. New York: State University of New York Press.

Nowotny, H., P. Scott and M. Gibbons. 2001. *Re-thinking Science: Knowledge and the Public in an Age of Uncertainty*. Cambridge: Polity Press.

Orth, U., L. Montada and A. Maercker. 2006. 'Feelings of Revenge, Retaliation Motive, and Posttraumatic Stress Reactions in Crime Victims', *Journal of Interpersonal Violence* 21(2): 229–43.

Otterbein, K.F. 1997. *Feuding and Warfare*. Amsterdam: Gordon & Breach.

Paul, R.A. 2005. 'Reconciliation and the Craving for Revenge in Psychotherapy', in A.B. Brown and K.M. Poremski (eds), *Roads to Reconciliation: Conflict and Dialogue in the Twenty-First Century*. Armonk, NY: M.E. Sharpe, pp. 107–19.

Pinker, S. 2011. *The Better Angels of Our Nature: Why Violence Has Declined*. New York: Viking Adult.

Prunier, G. 1997. 'Segmentarité et violence dans l'espace somali, 1840–1992', *Cahiers d'Études Africaines* 37: 379–401.

Rees, B. 2003. *Terrorism, Retaliation, and Victory: Awaken the Soul of America to Defeat Terrorism without Casualties*. Philadelphia: Xlibries.

Rilling, J.K., and A.G. Sanfey. 2011. 'The Neuroscience of Social Decision-Making', *Annual Review of Psychology* 62: 23–48.

Sarat, A. 2002a. 'Vengeance, Victims and the Identities of Law', in M. Mundy (ed.), *Law and Anthropology*. Aldershot: Ashgate, pp. 347–73.

———. 2002b. 'When Memory Speaks: Remembrance and Revenge in *Unforgiven*', in M. Minow (ed.), *Breaking the Cycles of Hatred: Memory, Law and Repair*. Princeton: Princeton University Press, pp. 236–59.

Scheer, R. 2004. 'With God on His Side… By Invoking a Higher Power, Bush Sidesteps Pesky Constitutional Issues', *Los Angeles Times*. Retrieved 7 March 2016 from http://articles.latimes.com/2004/apr/20/opinion/oe-scheer20.

Schlee, G. 2003. 'Introduction: Identification in Violent Settings and Situations of Rapid Change', *Africa* 73(3): 333–42.

Schlee, G., and B. Turner. 2008. 'Rache, Wiedergutmachung und Strafe: Ein Überblick', in G. Schlee and B. Turner (eds), *Vergeltung. Eine interdisziplinäre Betrachtung der Rechtfertigung und Regulation von Gewalt*. Frankfurt: Campus, pp. 49–67.

———. (eds). 2008. *Vergeltung. Eine interdisziplinäre Betrachtung der Rechtfertigung und Regulation von Gewalt*. Frankfurt: Campus.

Schwandner-Sievers, S. 2001. 'The Enactment of "Tradition": Albanian Constructions of Identity, Violence and Power in Times of Conflict', in B.E. Schmidt and I.W. Schröder (eds), *Anthropology of Violence and Conflict*. London: Routledge, pp. 97–120.

Shiraz, Y. 2008. *Retaliation: A Novel*. Alexandria, VA: Rolling Hills Press.

Sue, H., and D. Rodin. 2007. *Preemption: Military Action and Moral Justification*. Oxford: Oxford University Press.

Thurnwald, R. 1921. *Die Gemeinde der Bánaro. Ehe, Verwandtschaft und Gesellschaftsbau eines Stammes im Inneren von Neuguinea*. Stuttgart: Enke.

Tripp, T.M., and R.J. Bies. 2009. *Getting Even: The Truth about Workplace Revenge and How to Stop it*. San Francisco: Jossey-Bass.

Turner, B. 2005. *Asyl und Konflikt: von der Antike bis heute*. Berlin: Reimer.

———. 2008. 'Recht auf Vergeltung? Soziale Konfigurationen und die prägende Macht der Gewaltoption', in G. Schlee and B. Turner (eds), *Vergeltung. Eine interdisziplinäre Betrachtung der Rechtfertigung und Regulation von Gewalt*. Frankfurt: Campus, pp. 69–103.

Turner, B., and G. Schlee. 2008. 'Wirkungskontexte des Vergeltungsprinzips in der Konfliktregulierung', in G. Schlee and B. Turner (eds), *Vergeltung. Eine interdisziplinäre Betrachtung der Rechtfertigung und Regulation von Gewalt*. Frankfurt: Campus, pp. 7–47.

Turner, B., and T. Kirsch. 2009. 'Law and Religion in Permutation of Order: An Introduction', in T. Kirsch and B. Turner (eds), *Permutations of Order: Religion and Law as Contested Sovereignties*. Farnham: Ashgate, pp. 1–24.

Verdier, R. et al. (eds). 1980–84. *La Vengeance*. 4 vols. Paris: Éditions Cujas.

Voland, E. 2000. *Grundriß der Soziobiologie*. Stuttgart: Spektrum.

Waldmann, P. 2001. 'Revenge Without Rules: On the Renaissance of an Archaic Motif of Violence', *Studies in Conflict & Terrorism* 24: 435–50.

Section I

Retaliation and the Human Nature

The Search for Universalities?

Chapter 1

Revenge and Retaliation

A Social-Functionalist Approach

Mario Gollwitzer and Arne Sjöström

Introduction and Overview

'When you put me down / Revenge is the first thing on my mind', sings Tom Barman of dEUS, a Belgian alternative rock band, in their song 'Pocket Revolution' from the 2005 album of the same title. This quote is quite informative because it nicely summarizes some of the main psychological features of revenge: it is a reaction to being put down (and other equivalent provocations); it does not take long for the desire for revenge to arise; it is a personal experience; and, finally, it may not be the last thing that is on one's mind (the potential avenger might contemplate other reactions).

This chapter analyses this quote from the dEUS song in more detail from a social-psychological perspective. More precisely, we will look at some questions that psychologists usually ask about revenge and retaliation, such as: what kinds of events or situations trigger vengeful reactions? How can we understand why revenge is perhaps the most immediate and frequent reaction to being put down? What exactly is on people's minds when they think about revenge?

We will try to provide some more or less conclusive answers to these questions by drawing upon social-psychological research on revenge and retribution. We thereby argue that a 'social-functionalist' perspective is probably the most fruitful scientific approach to investigating revenge. This perspective is based on the following premises: (a) revenge is a reaction to perceived injustice and its ultimate goal is to re-establish a subjective state of justice; (b) revenge is not a mindless, irrational impulse that belongs to our animal heritage and that needs to be tamed and overridden by legal law, but is rather a comprehensible and functional reaction to injustice that we may be able to shape, but not to tame; (c) revenge can – under certain circumstances – actually be capable of establishing a desired end-state (that is, subjective justice), although there are other mechanisms that might be more effective (and more socially desirable) for solving social conflicts in the long run; (d) while the particular functions that revenge seems to fulfil can be achieved by other (again, more socially desirable) forms of reaction, such as accepting an apology and forgiving the harmdoer, such alternative reactions can nevertheless be better understood (and tailored) if we know what goals people hope to achieve when they take revenge.

The chapter is organized around these four central arguments. In the next section, we will briefly discuss the relationship between revenge and (in)justice. We will argue that revenge is often sparked by the perception that one's entitlement to be treated respectfully by others has been violated and that revenge aims at re-establishing a sense of justice by making it clear that one is indeed entitled to be treated respectfully. The third section will elaborate on the notion of revenge as a functional and goal-driven type of behaviour. In this section, we will also introduce and briefly review some empirical studies that have investigated the circumstances under which revenge can be satisfying for the avenger. Moreover, we will develop testable hypotheses regarding the questions *whether* revenge can lead to satisfaction when the vengeful action is targeted at a different person than the original source of the injustice ('displaced revenge') and, if so, *when* it can do so. The fourth section, 'Alternative Responses to Perceived Injustices', will discuss other forms of reaction to injustice, such as seeking legal help, engaging in restorative procedures, demanding and accepting an apology, and forgiving the offender. In the fifth and final section, we will speculate a little about the extent to which our arguments are universal or, conversely, specific to Western cultures.

Revenge as a Reaction to Perceived Injustice

In line with other authors (e.g., Skarlicki and Folger 1997), we argue that revenge is a reaction to perceived injustice. The term 'perceived' hereby qualifies *and* dilutes our argument at the same time. Perceived injustice means that notions of what is fair and what is not lie, to a large degree, in the eyes of the beholder. There might be a shared social consensus on what fairness means and what kinds of behaviour count as fair or unfair. And, of course, this shared consensus on notions of fairness is, in many instances, explicitly codified in statutes, bills and laws, or in more or less implicit rules of social conduct. Nevertheless, the feeling of what it means to be harmed or wronged is a personal and subjective experience, and so is the feeling of what it means to establish a sense of justice and deservingness.

Such subjective experiences give legal scholars a headache, and legal practitioners can only approximate these experiences in the application of penal law. For instance, how much harm does it cause when my best friend calls me a liar? How much harm does it cause when a reckless speeder on the highway scratches my beloved automobile? How much harm does it cause when a thief steals my wallet with the single remaining photo of my grandmother in it? The injustice implied in harm cannot be objectively measured because it is contingent on the actor's degree of responsibility and blameworthiness (Fincham and Jaspars 1980; Alicke 2000), and on the amount of disrespect that the actor shows. Many psychological studies suggest that it is not the harm itself that evokes retaliatory reactions, but the interpersonal message that is conveyed in the harmful act. It is a message of disrespect and disregard for norms of respectful treatment (Bies and Shapiro 1987; Greenberg 1994; Bies and Tripp 1996; Miller 2001). In line with that reasoning, it has been repeatedly shown that when people are asked about typical events that sparked their desire to take revenge, they usually report cases in which norms of interactional fairness were wilfully violated by another person, such as betrayal, abuse of confidence, abuse of power and authority, and dishonesty (see Bies and Tripp 1996; Mikula, Scherer and Athenstaedt 1998; Crombag, Rassin and Horselenberg 2003).

Just as the harmful act (for example, being put down by a significant other) is measured on a subjective fairness scale, so is the appropriateness of one's reaction. What is deserved and appropriate also lies in the eye of the beholder. An act of retribution that may be considered 'just' in the eyes of the victim may be vastly exaggerated and intolerable in the eyes of the targeted offender or a neutral observer (Stillwell, Baumeister and Del Priori 2008). In addition, perceptions of what is just, appropriate and desirable are socially shared, and these perceptions are transmitted via cultural, societal or group-specific normative systems. Some systems may deem it appropriate to take a life for a life (capital punishment in response to first-degree murder – see Ellsworth and Ross 1983); some may deem it appropriate (or even normative) to kill the son of a man who insulted one's family (see Schwandner-Sievers 1999); some may deem it appropriate to exchange money for blood (see Hounet, this volume); some may deem it appropriate to shame thieves by making them wear signs announcing their crimes in busy public areas (Schwarcz 2003); and some may engage in mystical practices to retaliate against actual sufferings or malevolent intentions (see Lenart, this volume). Yet, despite the fact that responses to criminal offences are often codified or subject to a socially shared normative system, what feels right in terms of giving the offender his or her 'just deserts' (see, e.g., Carlsmith, Darley and Robinson 2002; Carlsmith and Darley 2008) varies considerably from situation to situation, context to context, and individual to individual.

Many definitions of revenge emphasize that it is a response to perceived injustice, which, in turn, is in many cases rooted in the perception that one has been disrespectfully treated by the harmdoer (see Stuckless and Goranson 1992; Frijda 1994). The notion that revenge aims at getting even and giving the offender what he or she deserves is likewise central to most definitions of revenge and retaliation (see Tripp and Bies 1997; Feather 1999). The question then becomes: what exactly does 'getting even' mean? One might argue that this is a trivial question, since the only reasonable meaning of 'getting even' can be to make the offender suffer just as the victim has suffered himself or herself. This is 'payback' in its ultimate sense. But things are not so simple, as we shall see in the next section.

Revenge as a Functional and Goal-Driven Response

Revenge can take multiple forms (see, e.g., Bies and Tripp 2005; Bies and Tripp, this volume) and, despite its one ultimate ('higher-order') goal (that is, to achieve subjective justice), it can be directed towards achieving a number of 'lower-order' goals, such as making the offender experience guilt, shame or remorse; teaching him or her a lesson; deterring future harm; re-equilibrating power differentials; rebalancing gains and losses; restoring one's self-esteem; or expunging the pain, anger and humiliation that the provocation had evoked (Frijda 1994). The crucial aspect of our argument is that revenge *is* actually a goal-driven response, just as other justice-related phenomena are (Skitka and Wisneski 2012).

The Rationality of Revenge

Although revenge may be the first thing on one's mind after being put down, this by no means signifies that revenge is an irrational, mindless, animalistic impulse, as legal scholars and some philosophers sometimes tend to see it (see Gollwitzer 2009). The wish to retaliate may be more universal, more fundamental and less complex than other justice-related behavioural systems (Hogan and Emler 1981), but this only substantiates, rather than undermines, its psychological significance. Some scholars have argued that revenge is the opposite of a rational and enlightened response to provocations and that, unlike law-based retribution, it is inherently irrational, savage, unlimited, unprincipled and disproportionate (see, e.g., Nozick 1981). This view has been challenged by psychologists (e.g., Vidmar 2001; Gollwitzer 2009). We shall not reprise these arguments here; for our present purposes, it will suffice to stress that it makes no sense to label either revenge or the emotions that usually accompany it (such as anger, moral outrage and disappointment) as 'irrational'. On the contrary, these emotions are functional, adaptive and *ecologically rational* in that they direct the organism's attention to important aspects of a situation (Solomon 1990) and prepare the organism to respond to problems that arise in social interactions (Keltner and Haidt 1999). For example, empirical studies show that anger involves a shift of blood away from the internal organs towards the hands and arms (Levenson, Ekman and Friesen 1990), and it increases one's sensitivity to potential injustices and the moral implications of other people's actions (Keltner, Ellsworth and Edwards 1993). Of course, anger can also trigger disproportionate retaliatory behaviours (Tripp and Bies 2009; Bies and Tripp, this volume), but this does not mean it is inherently 'irrational'. Most behavioural systems with which the human organism is equipped are 'irrational' in that they may be incompatible with logical, deductive reasoning and a stringent cost-benefit analysis of gains, risks and losses, but they are nevertheless functional in that they enable us to deal with complex (social or nonsocial) problems and to make appropriate decisions in an even more complex and unpredictable environment (Gigerenzer 2000; Gigerenzer and Gaissmeier 2011).

Revenge belongs to the human behavioural system just as communication, competition and cooperation do. And like these systems, it has important societal and individual functions. Revenge is not something that humans should try to overcome and it is definitely not a psychological dysfunction (as some authors argue – see Horney 1948; Summerfield 2002; Murphy 2003). On the contrary, revenge can be functional when it teaches the offender a lesson or makes it clear that one is worthy of respectful treatment (see also McCullough, Kurzban and Tabak 2010). To put it differently, revenge tells the offender (and possibly other people as well) that 'I am not the kind of person you can do this to' – or simply 'Don't mess with me!'. In this vein, taking revenge is directly related to one's social status and feelings of self-worth (Shnabel and Nadler 2008; Zdaniuk and Bobocel 2012).

Evolutionary biologists and anthropologists have argued that revenge (or having the reputation of being vindictive) improves an organism's (or a group's) reproductive fitness by deterring others from disregarding one's entitlement to respectful treatment in the future (McCullough, Kurzban and Tabak 2010). Observational studies have shown that by swiftly retaliating, a group can demonstrate its power, which in turn helps to deter attackers from committing the same or similar offences in the future (Chagnon 1988). In the same vein, conflict researchers (e.g., Schelling 1960) argue that nations may signal their willingness to take revenge in order to deter conflict in the first place. In other words, retaliation produces fitness gains for an avenger by reducing the likelihood of being attacked, provoked, injured or treated disrespectfully (for an extensive discussion of the deterrent functions of revenge and on game-theoretical approaches to vengeful behaviours, see McCullough, Kurzban and Tabak 2013, as well as the many thought-provoking commentaries on their target article).

How Sweet is Revenge?

Coming back from the evolutionary or biological functions of a potentially evolved 'revenge system' to a social-psychological perspective on revenge, we may ask whether taking revenge can be a rewarding and pleasurable experience, as the popular saying 'revenge is sweet' suggests. If we argue that revenge is functional, then it should also be rewarding if it fulfils its function. Interestingly, the empirical evidence regarding the 'sweetness' of revenge is mixed. Carlsmith, Wilson and Gilbert (2008) have shown that people who were given the opportunity to punish a free-rider for behaving uncooperatively in a social dilemma game expected themselves to feel better after punishing the target, but in fact felt worse than those people who had no opportunity to punish. The authors argue that engaging in retaliatory actions makes people ruminate more about the harmdoer and his or her deed, whereas those who have no opportunity to punish are more likely to move on and think about something else. These findings suggest that taking revenge is not necessarily satisfying per se. Under what circumstances, then, might revenge lead to the experience of satisfaction? Can it be satisfying when it teaches the offender a lesson by effectively signalling 'Don't mess with me!'?

Empirical evidence from some of our own studies suggests that this is indeed the case. In one study (Study 3 in Gollwitzer, Meder and Schmitt 2011), participants were confronted with an ostensible partner who behaved extremely selfishly when given the opportunity to divide lottery tickets between himself or herself and the real participant. Half of the participants were given an opportunity to punish their respective partners by taking lottery tickets away from them. Two-thirds of these participants did so (that is, they took revenge). More importantly, all participants were also told that they could communicate with their partner via an online messenger tool after the distribution of lottery tickets. The messages participants received from their ostensible partners were manipulated beforehand. Half of the participants received a message from their partner saying: 'When I learned that you could take tickets from me, I thought, "Hmm, you'll probably do that because I divided the tickets unfairly"' (understanding message). The other half received a message saying: 'When I learned that you could take tickets from me, I thought, "Hmm, why would you do that?"' Thus, the design consisted of four experimental conditions: revenge and understanding message; revenge and no understanding message; no revenge and understanding message; no revenge and no understanding message. After messages were exchanged, we asked participants to what extent they felt satisfied and had the impression that justice had been re-established and everybody got what they deserved. These 'satisfaction/deservingness' scores were significantly higher among avengers who received the understanding message from their partner than among participants in the other three conditions. In other words, when partners supposedly understand *why* revenge has been taken on them, revenge can indeed be satisfying for the avenger. We were able to replicate this pattern of results in different contexts and with different measures (see, e.g., Gollwitzer and Denzler 2009; Funk, McGeer and Gollwitzer 2014), and we interpret it as evidence for the notion that revenge can be satisfying when it effectively delivers a message such as: 'Don't mess with me!'

The idea that revenge can be a pleasurable experience when it restores the victim's self-worth and social status is also in line with other theoretical arguments put forth in the literature (see, e.g., Shnabel and Nadler 2008; Zdaniuk and Bobocel 2012), and also with anecdotal and empirical evidence that witnessing acts of revenge can evoke perceptions of satisfaction and deservingness among observers (for instance, audiences watching a Western) when the villain eventually knows why he or she is being punished (Miller 1998; French 2001). Nonetheless, the degree to which such explicit acknowledgements of 'understanding' by the villain actually occur in the real world is an open question – besides experimentally controlled settings and fictitious (or imagined) acts of revenge, people seem to have a hard time remembering an episode in which revenge actually did taste 'sweet' (Crombag, Rassin and Horselenberg 2003; Boon, Deveau and Alibhai 2009).

Revenge as 'Comparative Suffering'?

Besides putting the – as we refer to it – 'understanding hypothesis' to an empirical test, our research also tested another notion of what could make revenge satisfying. This notion is commonly referred to as the 'comparative suffering' hypothesis (Frijda 1994). The comparative suffering hypothesis states that revenge simply aims at balancing the suffering score between the victim and the offender: the offender has made the victim suffer, and now the offender must suffer to an equal degree (at least). This notion of payback would also be in line with a very rough and basic idea of re-establishing justice (Doob and Wood 1972). But is mere payback (seeing the offender suffer) also satisfying for the avenger? We reasoned that if it is only the amount of suffering that needs to be balanced in order to make revenge satisfying, then it should make no difference whether the offender's suffering has been caused by the harmed victim or by fate. In other words, if the comparative suffering hypothesis were true, then fateful accidents that make the offender suffer should be just as satisfying as making the offender suffer by taking revenge against him or her (see Frijda 1994; Vidmar 2001). In turn, an accident befalling the offender might be construed as 'just deserts' from the victim's point of view.

The empirical evidence, however, tends to speak against the comparative suffering hypothesis (Gollwitzer and Denzler 2009; Gollwitzer, Meder and Schmitt 2011). Seeing the offender suffer from fate is, by and large, not as satisfying for the victim as taking revenge and learning that the offender has actually understood the message. In one study (Gollwitzer 2005), participants completed an online survey in which they were asked to imagine that some other person had behaved disrespectfully or unfairly towards them. For instance, they should imagine themselves working in a team in which one of the other members repeatedly behaved selfishly, missed important deadlines and delegated unpleasant work tasks to other team members. One group of participants was then asked to imagine that, one day, the chance for revenge had come: when the obnoxious team member left the office, they could give his keys, which he had left on his desk, a little shove and let them fall into the dustbin, where he would most probably have a hard time finding them. Participants who decided to engage in this vengeful reaction were further assigned to a 'revenge accomplished' condition (in which the colleague actually did spend quite some time looking for his keys, which made him furious and nervous) or to a 'revenge failed' condition (in which he instantly found his keys after looking for them in the dustbin). A third group of participants learned that one day during an important meeting with the CEO, the colleague's presentation went awry because his computer did not work properly ('fate condition'). And, finally, a fourth group of participants learned that the obnoxious team member had been promoted and the chances that they would ever meet again were small ('control condition').

After these stories were finally told, we asked participants to what extent they felt satisfied, perceived that justice had been re-established and believed that everyone had got what he or she deserved. These 'satisfaction/deservingness' scores significantly differed between the four conditions (see Figure 1.1): they were highest when revenge had been accomplished, but they were much lower when revenge failed, when nothing happened ('control condition') or when the offender suffered from fate.

This pattern of results, which we also replicated in more experimentally controlled settings (Gollwitzer and Denzler 2009; Gollwitzer, Meder and Schmitt 2011), suggests that seeing the offender suffer from fate does not seem to be the ultimate goal of revenge and that revenge is therefore about more than merely establishing a balance in suffering. It should be noted, however, that all of our studies have been conducted in Germany; thus, our argument may only be valid within the Western cultural sphere. In the conclusion we will speculate about cultural differences with regard to the role of fate and other mystical agents in the context of vengeful episodes.

Taken together, the 'understanding hypothesis' has received stronger empirical support in our studies than the 'comparative suffering' hypothesis. One should note, however, that most of the vengeful contexts we investigated in our research involved noncriminal and therefore somewhat trivial offences (such as dividing tickets unfairly, giving disrespectful feedback on an essay, and imagining

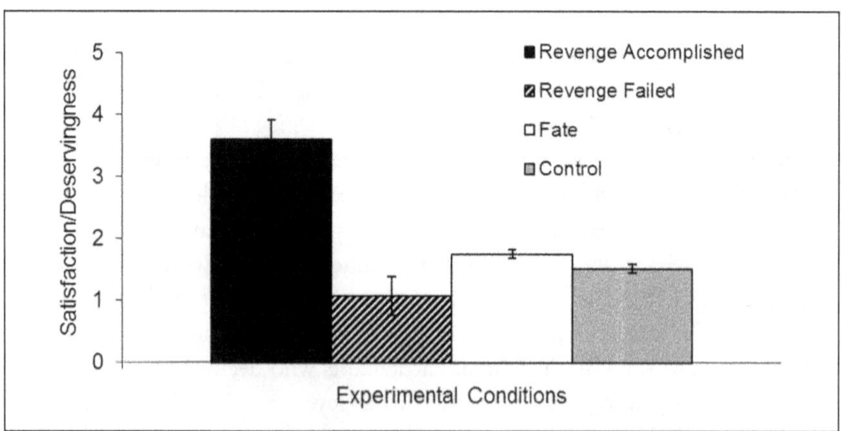

Figure 1.1 Mean scores on satisfaction/deservingness across the four experimental conditions (n = 881; 64% female), aggregated across 7 different revenge vignettes (for more information, see Gollwitzer 2005: Chapter 6.2). Response scales ranged from 0 to 5. Capped vertical lines denote standard errors of means in each condition

a selfish and uncooperative coworker). For example, we cannot be sure whether kinsmen of a murdered victim do indeed experience more satisfaction and deservingness when the murderer who faces capital punishment (which fortunately happens only in some parts of the world) expresses understanding for his or her punishment than when the defendant pleads not guilty. But we do have empirical evidence for the notion that – even in real-life instances – people experience more satisfaction and deservingness when they believe that punishment has effectively sent a message to the perpetrator. For example, we were able to show that, after the assassination of Osama bin Laden in May 2011, U.S. citizens felt a stronger sense of 'justice achieved' when they believed that the killing of bin Laden sent a strong message to al-Qaeda and other terrorist groups not to mess with the United States (Gollwitzer et al. 2014).

Displaced Revenge

Considering the numerous ongoing conflicts in the world, such as terrorist attacks and retributive reactions to such attacks, it becomes obvious that acts of revenge and retribution often spread beyond the initial agents (victim and perpetrator). Thus, an intriguing question that follows from our research is whether revenge can also be satisfying when the target of one's revenge is not the original harmdoer, but rather a third person who was not directly involved in the original harmdoing. Such acts of 'displaced revenge' or 'vicarious retribution' (Lickel et al. 2006; Lickel 2012) interestingly have not received a lot of attention in the social-psychological literature thus far. Although research on '(triggered) displaced aggression' (which describes the phenomenon that provoked parties tend to aggress against uninvolved third parties when the original source of the provocation is no longer available - see Dollard 1938) exists and has been thoroughly investigated (see, e.g., Marcus-Newhall et al. 2000; Bushman et al. 2005), we do not know yet whether acts of displaced revenge can actually be as satisfying as direct revenge.

If the target of one's revenge and the original harmdoer are entirely unconnected, then revenge should not be satisfying and not accompanied by feelings of deservingness in any way for the avenger. However, if the target of one's revenge and the original harmdoer belong to the same group or share certain social features, then the situation becomes a bit more complex. Given our notion of 'understanding' as described above, we propose that if, for example, social circumstances prevent direct retaliation, displaced revenge can indeed be satisfying if the message ('Don't mess with me!') is effectively delivered and understood (French 2001). When the fact that the harmdoer belongs to a group is salient in a given vengeful context (for instance, if the harmdoer belongs to another street gang, another religious group or another university), the message is addressed not only to the individual harmdoer; it is likely to be important that the message be effectively delivered to and understood by the entire group. Thus, displaced revenge is expected to be all the more satisfying the greater the chances are that the word is spread.

This reasoning leads us to hypothesize that displaced revenge can be more satisfying when the offender and the target of revenge belong to what social psychologists refer to as a highly *entitative* group. Group entitativity describes the extent to which a group of individuals is perceived as a unified and coherent whole (Campbell 1958). However, the meaning of entitativity can be twofold (Ip, Chiu and Wan 2006). First, it could mean that group members share certain similarities merely on a perceptual or superficial level: 'they' all look alike. For example, surveys of U.S. citizens found that: (a) the desire to avenge the terrorist attacks from 11 September 2001 predicted support for the invasion of U.S. troops into Iraq in 2003 simply for vengeance, and (b) that hate crimes in the United States against Arab-Americans, Muslims and similar targets increased dramatically after the 9/11 incident (Skitka et al. 2009). It is conceivable that the mere superficial similarity with a stereotypical al-Qaeda terrorist makes innocent Muslims an 'appropriate' target for U.S. avengers. Anger, fear, conspiracy beliefs or a strong identification with one's own group might even increase perceptions of outgroup entitativity among victims (Stenstrom, Denson and Miller 2008).

Second, entitativity can mean that group members share common goals and engage in concerted behaviour (Ip, Chiu and Wan 2006). Within entitative groups, members act as a collective unit, frequently interact with one another and are mutually interdependent regarding their respective actions (see, e.g., Lickel et al. 2000; Igarashi and Kashima 2011). Given the high level of interaction and interdependence among entitative groups, displaced revenge may be more effective in delivering the message (see above) to the group and all of its members.

Distinguishing between these two conceptions of group entitativity is important for deriving the following empirically testable hypothesis. There is ample evidence that phenomena such as '(triggered) displaced aggression' or 'displaced revenge' exist: victims sometimes lash out at those who are entirely unconnected to the original harm. And such acts of displaced revenge are more likely to occur if the target of revenge shares some similarities with the original offender – even if these similarities are merely superficial (see, e.g., Marcus-Newhall et al. 2000). However, we propose that superficial similarity alone does not make displaced revenge satisfying for the avenger. Superficially similar groups may spark a retributive intention, but such retribution would be ineffective in 'spreading the word' as long as the group does not *act* or *interact* as a collective entity. To put it the other way round, we hypothesize that displaced revenge can be satisfying, but only if the target of one's revenge and the original harmdoer belong to a group that shares collective goals and normative beliefs, and whose members frequently interact and communicate with each other. Only such 'structurally entitative' groups present the necessary conditions whereby retaliating against any one of them increases the chances that the message embedded in revenge ('Don't mess with me!') is spread within the perpetrator group and leads to genuine satisfaction.

Alternative Responses to Perceived Injustices

Despite the observation that revenge can have evolutionary, biological, psychological and social functions, the functionalistic perspective on revenge by no means implies that revenge is necessarily the most effective or the most socially desirable way of trying to re-establish a sense of justice. Criminal justice systems in the seventeenth and eighteenth centuries gradually started to criminalize private retaliation in order to implement a system of social control over crime, and a side-effect of these – more visible – public punishment trials might have been a decline in homicide rates (see Härter, this volume). Thus, one might argue that installing a criminal justice system is more effective in a larger sense. In many societies around the world, the state now has a monopoly on punishing those who violate its normative standards. Revenge has become taboo, and victims who seek to re-establish justice are required to address the police and the criminal justice system in order to get what they want.

Interestingly, the criminal justice system has always justified its existence by claiming that its central function is to eradicate the savageness and unfairness inherent in private revenge. The criminal justice system is often considered to be more rational, less emotional and therefore more 'just' than private revenge (Nozick 1981). But in fact, it would be a gross oversimplification to say that private revenge is always and necessarily irrational and emotional, and that the criminal justice system is not. For example, capital punishment lacks every criterion of rationality (see Ellsworth and Ross 1983), and emotions do come into play even in highly standardized court procedures (see Solomon 1999). However, criminal justice systems are usually more 'procedurally just' in defining how court trials have to be set up, who is given voice, who decides upon the verdict and the punishment, and how society comes up with developing a system of contingency between features of a crime and 'just' punishment.

Then there is restorative justice as a viable alternative to revenge. Restorative procedures aim to bring the affected parties – that is, the victim(s), the offender(s) and the community – back to where they were before the transgression occurred (Bazemore 1998; Braithwaite 2002; Strang 2002). On this view, punishment functions to compensate, benefit and heal rather than to punish and reciprocate (Braithwaite and Strang 2001). Typically, suitable sanctioning forms are restorative justice conferences, formal apologies, monetary compensation or community service. By engaging in a restorative justice conference, the affected parties can gain a shared understanding of the offence, the harm caused and ways to repair this harm.

A number of empirical studies have shown that victims are more satisfied with restorative justice conferences than with traditional court-based procedures (see Gromet 2009 for a review), but research has also shown that restorative justice procedures are not more likely than traditional court-based processes to reduce recidivism, and that restorative justice procedures do not necessarily result in perceptions of fairness and re-established justice among the afflicted parties. Particularly for more severe criminal offences, it appears that victims (and neutral third-party observers) more strongly prefer a combination of restorative and retributive sanctioning forms. Making the victim 'whole' again and allowing him or her to 'save face' is important, but not at the cost of letting the offenders go unpunished and sparing them their 'just deserts' (Gromet and Darley 2006).

A central element of restorative procedures entails an explicit apology from the offender and a request for forgiveness (Braithwaite 2002). Forgiveness has been considered the opposite of revenge (McCullough 2008), and there now exists a large body of research on the positive aspects, functions and effects of forgiveness on both the offending and the victimized party (Karremans et al. 2003; Baskin and Enright 2004; Lundahl et al. 2008). Despite these many positive features of seeking apologies and granting forgiveness in terms of resolving social conflicts, the pitfalls associated with forgiveness should, in our opinion, not be overlooked. We believe that, under certain circumstances, forgiving somebody may not always be rooted in a desire to heal and improve the relationship. There may be instances in which forgiving an offender signals to others that one is morally superior to the offender, or that the offender does not even deserve to be punished. Thus, forgiving may sometimes feel like taking revenge, both for the offender and for the victim/forgiver (Wenzel and Okimoto 2012). Such cases have been referred to as 'hollow forgiveness' (Baumeister, Exline and Sommer 1998).

Our brief discussion here rather suggests that the relationship between revenge and forgiveness is more complex. First, forgiveness and retaliation are not mutually exclusive; they may sometimes complement each other (Strelan and van Prooijen 2013). In the context of forgiveness in close relationships, Fitness and Peterson (2008) have noted that acts of forgiveness are often accompanied by punishing the partners and reminding them of their offences. Second, as described above, what looks like forgiveness on the surface might just be revenge in disguise. In line with the latter argument, it seems that the U.S. humourist Josh Billings was right when he once said: 'There is no revenge so complete as forgiveness.'

Conclusion and Outlook

In this chapter we have talked about revenge, what sparks revenge, what revenge aims at, whether revenge can be 'functional' and satisfying, and whether revenge can be replaced by more socially desirable and – possibly – more effective strategies to re-establish a state of justice. We are well aware that we have spoken of revenge as if we were advocates of it. We have done so in order to contribute a different (and notably provocative) flavour to the discussion, which typically demonizes revenge (and, on the other hand, glorifies either the criminal justice system or the willingness to forgive). By sketching how social psychology has addressed questions of revenge and retribution, we hope to have put forward convincingly that revenge can be fruitfully looked at from a social-functionalist perspective, and that exploring these functions and the conditions under which revenge can be satisfying can possibly tell us something about what people hope to achieve when they take revenge. We also hope to have suggested what kind of alternative responses to injustice might be able to achieve the same goals. Nevertheless, we are fully aware of the fact that revenge is not the optimal strategy in interpersonal or intergroup conflicts, and that alternative routes to conflict resolution (such as sincere forgiveness) are – in most cases – clearly preferable.

Most of the empirical research that we have reviewed in the present chapter has been conducted in Western societies, as we have already noted. This possibly limits the generalizability of these results. For example, our argument that revenge aims at delivering to the offender the message 'Don't mess with me!' might be specific to Western cultures. Although the need for positive self-regard and a sensitivity to being treated respectfully are universal human motives, different cultures may have a different understanding of what 'respectful treatment' precisely means. Some cultures are particularly sensitive to violations of *autonomy* norms (individual rights and freedom), others are sensitive to violations of *community* norms (communal codes and hierarchies), and some (sub)cultures may be particularly sensitive to violations of *divinity* norms (purity and sanctity - see Shweder et al. 1997). Depending on which norm a culture is most sensitive to, transgressions may be construed differently and, consequently, the exact message that the revenge-taker intends to send may also differ.

Cultures also differ with regard to how much they honour victims who take matters into their own hands. In more individualistic cultures, the norm of paying back the injustice may more likely be placed on single individuals, whereas in more collectivistic cultures, this norm (and the notion of who has been victimized and who is responsible for taking revenge) may be distributed across the group of close kin (see Drent, this volume). In the latter cultures, seeking help from one's family members after being victimized may not be considered cowardice or weakness. On the other hand, cultures (or subcultures) that value the concept of honour and are highly sensitive to being dishonoured by others (such as in some Mediterranean countries, but also the southern part of the United States - see Nisbett and Cohen 1996) would not approve of victims who cannot defend themselves properly, particularly if they are male. The same might be true among adolescent street gangs, for whom violent retaliation may be a means to regulate their social status and self-esteem (see Wright, Topalli and Jacques, this volume).

And finally, cultures – but also individuals within a culture – may differ with regard to the role they assign to mystical or divine agents in re-establishing justice. In the Bible, the Lord says 'It is mine to avenge, I will repay' (Deuteronomy 32:35), and so it comes as no surprise that the more victims believe in ultimate justice (that is, that all harmdoers will eventually pay for their sins and all victims will eventually be compensated – see Maes 1998), the more they refrain from taking revenge (Gollwitzer 2005). Likewise, beliefs regarding the effectiveness with which other mystical agents can bring about 'just deserts' may alleviate the desire to take revenge oneself (see Lenart, this volume). It is still an open – and interesting – question whether such fate-based acts of revenge can also be satisfying for victims. If we are right in assuming that revenge aims at delivering a message and that this is true universally, then victims might only experience satisfaction when they believe that the offenders on whom a curse is cast understand that they are being punished for a wrong they committed. However, this is highly speculative and requires empirical research within respective cultures.

To sum up, revenge may be the first thing on Tom Barman's mind after being put down, but then he goes on to say: 'But that's just stupid, man / I need a better plan / Delicate and refined.' Revenge may be stupid, and it can make things worse than they already are, but it can also be delicate and refined, and it can even be satisfying if it effectively delivers a message to the offender in which one of the core human motives – the need to be treated respectfully – is justifiably reinforced.

Mario Gollwitzer is Professor of Methodology and Social Psychology at the Department of Psychology at Philipps-University Marburg, Germany. He received his doctoral degree from the University of Trier in 2004. His research focuses on: (a) social psychological research on retributive justice; (b) individual differences in 'justice sensitivity' and their relation to moral reasoning and moral behaviour; (c) the effects of violent video games on cognition, emotion, and behaviour; and (d) public understanding of and engagement with (social) scientific research programmes and findings.

Arne Sjöström studied psychology at Georg-August University Göttingen and Philipps-University Marburg, Germany. In 2009 he was a visiting research scholar at the University of Southern California, Los Angeles. From 2011 to 2015, he worked as a research associate in psychological methods. He received his doctoral degree in Psychology from Philipps-University Marburg in 2015.

References

Alicke, M.D. 2000. 'Culpable Control and the Psychology of Blame', *Psychological Bulletin* 126: 556–74.

Baskin, T.W., and R.D. Enright. 2004. 'Intervention Studies on Forgiveness: A Meta-analysis', *Journal of Counseling and Development* 82: 79–90.

Baumeister, R.F., J.J. Exline and K.L. Sommer. 1998. 'The Victim Role, Grudge Theory, and Two Dimensions of Forgiveness', in E.L. Worthington (ed.), *Dimensions of Forgiveness: Psychological Research and Theological Forgiveness*. Philadelphia, PA: Templeton Foundation Press, pp. 79–104.

Bazemore, G. 1998. 'Restorative Justice and Earned Redemption', *American Behavioral Scientist* 41(6): 768–813.

Bies, R.J., and D.L. Shapiro. 1987. 'Interactional Fairness Judgments: The Influence of Causal Accounts', *Social Justice Research* 1: 199–218.

Bies, R.J., and T.M. Tripp. 1996. 'Beyond Distrust: "Getting Even" and the Need for Revenge', in R.M. Kramer and T.R. Tyler (eds), *Trust in Organizations: Frontiers of Theory and Research*. Thousand Oaks, CA: Sage, pp. 246–60.

———. 2005. 'The Study of Revenge in the Workplace: Conceptual, Ideological, and Empirical Issues', in S. Fox and P.E. Spector (eds), *Counterproductive Work Behavior: Investigations of Actors and Targets*. Washington DC: American Psychological Association, pp. 65–81.

Boon, S.D., V.L. Deveau and A.M. Alibhai. 2009. 'Payback: The Parameters of Revenge in Romantic Relationships', *Journal of Social and Personal Relationships* 26: 747–68.

Braithwaite, J. 2002. *Restorative Justice and Responsive Regulation*. New York: Oxford University Press.

Braithwaite, J., and H. Strang. 2001. 'Introduction: Restorative Justice and Civil Society', in H. Strang and J. Braithwaite (eds), *Restorative Justice and Civil Society*. Cambridge: Cambridge University Press, pp. 1–13.

Bushman, B.J., A.M. Bonacci, W.C. Pedersen, E.A. Vasquez and N. Miller. 2005. 'Chewing on it Can Chew You Up: Effects of Rumination on Triggered Displaced Aggression', *Journal of Personality and Social Psychology* 88: 969–83.

Campbell, D.T. 1958. 'Common Fate, Similarity, and Other Indices of Status of Aggregates of Persons as Social Entities', *Behavioral Science* 3: 14–25.

Carlsmith, K.M., and J.M. Darley. 2008. 'Psychological Aspects of Retributive Justice', *Annual Review of Psychology* 40: 193–236.

Carlsmith, K.M., J.M. Darley and P.H. Robinson. 2002. 'Why Do We Punish? Deterrence and Just Deserts as Motives for Punishment', *Journal of Personality and Social Psychology* 83: 284–99.

Carlsmith, K.M., T.D. Wilson and D.T. Gilbert. 2008. 'The Paradoxical Consequences of Revenge', *Journal of Personality and Social Psychology* 95: 1316–24.

Chagnon, N. 1988. 'Life Histories, Blood Revenge, and Warfare in a Tribal Population', *Science* 239: 985–92.

Crombag, H., E. Rassin and R. Horselenberg. 2003. 'On Vengeance', *Psychology, Crime & Law* 9: 333–44.

Dollard, J. 1938. 'Hostility and Fear in Social Life', *Social Forces* 17: 15–25.

Doob, A.N., and L.E. Wood. 1972. 'Catharsis and Aggression: Effects of Annoyance and Retaliation of Aggressive Behavior', *Journal of Personality and Social Psychology* 22: 156–62.

Ellsworth, P.C., and L. Ross. 1983. 'Public Opinion and Capital Punishment: A Close Examination of the Views of Abolitionists and Retentionists', *Crime and Delinquency* 29: 116–69.

Feather, N.T. 1999. *Values, Achievement and Justice: Studies in the Psychology of Deservingness.* New York: Kluwer Academic/Plenum Publishers.

Fincham, F.D., and J.M. Jaspars. 1980. 'Attribution of Responsibility: From Man the Scientist to Man as Lawyer', in L. Berkowitz (ed.), *Advances in Experimental Social Psychology* 13. New York: Academic Press, pp. 81–138.

Fitness, J., and J. Peterson. 2008. 'Punishment and Forgiveness in Close Relationships: An Evolutionary, Social Psychological Perspective', in J. Forgas and J. Fitness (eds), *Social Relationships: Cognitive, Affective, and Motivational Processes.* New York: Psychology Press, pp. 255–69.

Funk, F., V. McGeer and M. Gollwitzer. 2014. 'Get the Message: Punishment is Satisfying if the Transgressor Responds to its Communicative Intent', *Personality and Social Psychology Bulletin* 40: 986–97.

French, P.A. 2001. *The Virtues of Vengeance.* Lawrence: University Press of Kansas.

Frijda, N.H. 1994. 'The Lex Talionis: On Vengeance', in S.H.M. van Goozen, N.E. van der Poll and J.A. Sergeant (eds), *Emotions: Essays on Emotion Theory.* Hillsdale, NJ: Erlbaum, pp. 263–89.

Gigerenzer, G. 2000. *Adaptive Thinking: Rationality in the Real World.* New York: Oxford University Press.

Gigerenzer, G., and W. Gaissmaier. 2011. 'Heuristic Decision Making', *Annual Review of Psychology* 62: 451–82.

Gollwitzer, M. 2005. *Ist Gerächt 'Gleich' Gerecht? Eine Analyse von Racheaktionen und Rachebezogenen Reaktionen unter Gerechtigkeitspsychologischen Aspekten* [*Does 'Avenged' Equal 'Just'? An Analysis of Vengeful Reactions and Revenge-Related Reaction from a Psychology of Justice Perspective*]. Berlin: wvb.

———. 2009. 'Justice and Revenge', in M.E. Oswald, S. Bieneck and J. Hupfeld-Heinemann (eds), *Social Psychology of Punishment of Crime.* Hoboken, NJ: Wiley, pp. 137–56.

Gollwitzer, M., and M. Denzler. 2009. 'What Makes Revenge So Sweet: Seeing the Offender Suffer or Delivering a Message?' *Journal of Experimental Social Psychology* 45(4): 840–44.

Gollwitzer, M., M. Meder and M. Schmitt. 2011. 'What Gives Victims Satisfaction When They Seek Revenge?', *European Journal of Social Psychology* 41: 364–74.

Gollwitzer, M., L.J. Skitka, D. Wisneski, A. Sjöström, P. Liberman, S.J. Nazir and B.J. Bushman. 2014. 'Vicarious Revenge and the Death of Osama bin Laden'. *Personality and Social Psychology Bulletin* 40: 604–16.

Greenberg, J. 1994. 'Using Socially Fair Treatment to Promote Acceptance of a Worksite Smoking Ban', *Journal of Applied Psychology* 79: 288–97.

Gromet, D.M. 2009. 'Psychological Perspectives on the Place of Restorative Justice in Criminal Justice Systems', in M.E. Oswald, S. Bieneck and J. Hupfeld-Heinemann (eds), *Social Psychology of Punishment of Crime.* Hoboken, NJ: Wiley, pp. 39–54.

Gromet, D.M., and J.M. Darley. 2006. 'Restoration and Retribution: How Including Retributive Components Affects the Acceptability of Restorative Justice Procedures', *Social Justice Research* 19: 395–432.

Hogan, R., and N.P. Emler. 1981. 'Retributive Justice', in M.J. Lerner and S.C. Lerner (eds), *The Justice Motive in Social Behavior.* New York: Plenum Press, pp. 125–43.

Horney, K. 1948. 'The Value of Vindictiveness', *American Journal of Psychoanalysis* 8: 3–12.

Igarashi, T., and Y. Kashima. 2011. 'Perceived Entitativity of Social Networks', *Journal of Experimental Social Psychology* 47: 1048–58.

Ip, G.W.M., C.Y. Chiu and C. Wan. 2006. 'Birds of a Feather and Birds Flocking Together: Physical versus Behavioral Cues May Lead to Trait- versus Goal-Based Group Perception', *Journal of Personality and Social Psychology* 90: 368–81.

Karremans, J.C., P.A.M. van Lange, J.W. Ouwerkerk and E.S. Kluwer. 2003. 'When Forgiving Enhances Psychological Well-Being: The Role of Interpersonal Commitment', *Journal of Personality and Social Psychology* 84(5): 1011–26.

Keltner, D., P.C. Ellsworth and K. Edwards. 1993. 'Beyond Simple Pessimism: Effects of Sadness and Anger on Social Perception', *Journal of Personality and Social Psychology* 64: 740–52.

Keltner, D., and J. Haidt. 1999. 'Social Functions of Emotions at Four Levels of Analysis', *Cognition & Emotion* 13: 505–21.

Levenson, R.W., P. Ekman and W.V. Friesen. 1990. 'Voluntary Facial Action Generates Emotion-Specific Autonomic Nervous System Activity', *Psychophysiology* 27: 363–84.

Lickel, B. 2012. 'Retribution and Revenge', in L. Tropp (ed.), *Oxford Handbook of Intergroup Conflict.* New York: Oxford University Press, pp. 89–105.

Lickel, B., D.L. Hamilton, G. Wieczorkowska, A. Lewis, S.J. Sherman and A.N. Uhles. 2000. 'Varieties of Groups and the Perception of Group Entitativity', *Journal of Personality and Social Psychology* 78(2): 223–46.

Lickel, B., N. Miller, D.M. Stenstrom, T.F. Denson and T. Schmader. 2006. 'Vicarious Retribution: The Role of Collective Blame in Intergroup Aggression', *Personality and Social Psychology Review* 10: 372–90.

Lundahl, B.W., M.J. Taylor, R. Stevenson and K.D. Roberts. 2008. 'Process-Based Forgiveness Interventions: A Meta-analytic Review', *Research on Social Work Practice* 18(5): 465–78.

Maes, J. 1998. 'Immanent Justice and Ultimate Justice: Two Ways of Believing in Justice', in L. Montada and M.J. Lerner (eds), *Responses to Victimizations and Belief in a Just World.* New York: Plenum Press, pp. 9–40.

Marcus-Newhall, A., W.C. Pedersen, M. Carlson and N. Miller. 2000. 'Displaced Aggression is Alive and Well: A Meta-analytic Review', *Journal of Personality and Social Psychology* 78: 670–89.

McCullough, M.E. 2008. *Beyond Revenge: The Evolution of the Forgiveness Instinct.* New York: Jossey-Bass.

McCullough, M.E., R. Kurzban and B.A. Tabak. 2010. 'Evolved Mechanisms for Revenge and Forgiveness', in P.R. Shaver and M. Mikulincer (eds), *Understanding and Reducing Aggression, Violence, and their Consequences.* Washington DC: American Psychological Association, pp. 221–39.

———. 2013. 'Cognitive Systems for Revenge and Forgiveness', *Behavioral and Brain Sciences* 36: 1–58.

Mikula, G., K.R. Scherer and U. Athenstaedt. 1998. 'The Role of Injustice in the Elicitation of Differential Emotional Reactions', *Personality and Social Psychology Bulletin* 24: 769–83.

Miller, D.T. 2001. 'Disrespect and the Experience of Injustice', *Annual Review of Psychology* 52: 527–53.

Miller, W.I. 1998. 'Clint Eastwood and Equity: Popular Culture's Theory of Revenge', in A. Sarat and T.R. Kearns (eds), *Law in the Domains of Culture.* Ann Arbor: University of Michigan Press, pp. 161–202.

Murphy, J.G. 2003. *Getting Even: Forgiveness and its Limits.* New York: Oxford University Press.

Nisbett, R.E., and D. Cohen. (1996). *Culture of Honor: The Psychology of Violence in the South.* Boulder, CO: Westview Press.

Nozick, R. 1981. *Philosophical Explanations.* Cambridge, MA: Harvard University Press.

Schelling, T. 1960. *The Strategy of Conflict.* Cambridge, MA: Harvard University Press.

Schwandner-Sievers, S. 1999. 'Humiliation and Reconciliation in Northern Albania: The Logic of Feuding in Symbolic and Diachronic Perspectives', in G. Elwert, S. Feuchtwang and

D. Neubert (eds), *Dynamics of Violence: Processes of Escalation and De-escalation in Violent Group Conflicts*. Berlin: Duncker & Humblot, pp. 127–45.

Schwarcz, D. 2003. 'Shame, Stigma, and Crime: Evaluating the Efficacy of Shaming Sanctions in Criminal Law', *Harvard Law Review* 116(7): 2186–207.

Shnabel, N., and A. Nadler. 2008. 'A Needs-Based Model of Reconciliation: Satisfying the Differential Emotional Needs of Victims and Perpetrators as a Key to Promoting Reconciliation', *Journal of Personality and Social Psychology* 94: 116–32.

Shweder, R.A., N.C. Much, M. Mahapatra and L. Park. 1997. 'The "Big Three" of Morality (Autonomy, Community, Divinity) and the "Big Three" Explanations of Suffering', in A. Brandt and P. Rozin (eds), *Morality and Health*. New York: Routledge, pp. 119–69.

Skarlicki, D.P., and R. Folger. 1997. 'Retaliation in the Workplace: The Roles of Distributive, Procedural, and Interactional Justice', *Journal of Applied Psychology* 82: 434–43.

Skitka, L.J., and D.C. Wisneski (2012). 'Justice Theory and Research: A Social Functionalist Perspective', in H. Tennen and J. Suls (eds), *Handbook of Psychology*, vol. 5: *Personality and Social Psychology*, 2nd edn. Hoboken, NJ: Wiley, pp. 407–28.

Skitka, L.J., B. Saunders, G.S. Morgan and D. Wisneski. 2009. 'Dark Clouds and Silver Linings: Socio-psychological Responses to September 11, 2001', in M.J. Morgan (ed.), *The Day that Changed Everything? Looking at the Impact of 9-11*. New York: Palgrave Macmillan, pp. 63–79.

Solomon, R.C. 1990. *A Passion for Justice: Emotions and the Origins of the Social Contract*. Reading, MA: Addison-Wesley.

———. 1999. 'Justice v. Vengeance: On Law and the Satisfaction of Emotion', in S.A. Bandes (ed.), *The Passions of Law*. New York: New York University Press, pp. 123–48.

Stenstrom, D.M., T.F. Denson and N. Miller. 2008. 'The Roles of Ingroup Identification and Outgroup Entitativity in Intergroup Retribution', *Personality and Social Psychology Bulletin* 34: 1570–82.

Stillwell, A.M., R.F. Baumeister and R.E. Del Priori. 2008. 'We're All Victims Here: Toward a Psychology of Revenge', *Basic and Applied Social Psychology* 30: 253–63.

Strang, H. 2002. *Repair or Revenge: Victims and Restorative Justice*. Oxford: Oxford University Press.

Strelan, P., and J.-W. van Prooijen. 2013. 'Retribution and Forgiveness: The Healing Effects of Punishing for Just Deserts', *European Journal of Social Psychology* 43: 544–53.

Stuckless, N., and R. Goranson. 1992. 'The Vengeance Scale: Development of a Measure of Attitudes Toward Revenge', *Journal of Social Behavior and Personality* 7: 25–42.

Summerfield, D. 2002. 'Effects of War: Moral Knowledge, Revenge, Reconciliation, and Medicalised Concepts of "Recovery"', *British Medical Journal* 325: 105–107.

Tripp, T.M., and R.J. Bies. 1997. 'What's Good about Revenge? The Avenger's Perspective', in R.J. Lewicki, R.J. Bies and B.H. Sheppard (eds), *Research on Negotiation in Organizations* 6. Greenwich, CT: JAI Press, pp. 145–60.

———. 2009. *Getting Even: The Truth about Workplace Revenge – and How to Stop it*. San Francisco, CA: Jossey-Bass.

Wenzel, M., and T.G. Okimoto. 2012. 'The Varying Meaning of Forgiveness: Relationship Closeness Moderates How Forgiveness Affects Feelings of Justice', *European Journal of Social Psychology* 42: 420–31.

Vidmar, N. 2001. 'Retribution and Revenge', in J. Sanders and V.L. Hamilton (eds), *Handbook of Justice Research in Law*. New York: Kluwer Academic/Plenum Publishers, pp. 31–63.

Zdaniuk, A. and D.R. Bobocel. 2012. 'Vertical Individualism and Injustice: The Self-Restorative Function of Revenge', *European Journal of Social Psychology* 42: 640–51.

Chapter 2

In the Heat of the Moment

The Influence of Visceral Factors on Retaliation

Robert J. Bies and Thomas M. Tripp

Understanding why people engage in acts of retaliation has been the focus of research from a variety of disciplines, including psychology (Adams 1965; Deutsch 1973), sociology (Homans 1961; Morrill 1995), economics (Axelrod 1984), international relations (Zartman 1995) and management (Bies and Tripp 1996; Skarlicki and Folger 1997; Tripp and Bies 2009). For the most part, this multidisciplinary body of theory and research has taken a *cognitive control* perspective on explaining when and why people engage in acts of retaliation (Tripp and Bies 2009). Specifically, a key trigger of retaliation is a causal judgement to blame another person for the harm, which is primarily a cognitive process. Assigning blame focuses one's motivation and volitional behaviour on retaliation.

We propose an alternative framework for analysing retaliation: a *visceral factors* perspective, which highlights the importance of drive states such as moods and emotions, and physical pain (Loewenstein 1996). Emotions such as anger and environmental conditions such as intense heat or aggressive cues are experienced visceral factors. These visceral factors have direct hedonic consequences and a disproportionate effect on behaviour, 'crowding out' virtually all goals other than that of mitigating the visceral factor (Loewenstein 1996).

In this chapter, we analyse the role of visceral factors on retaliation. Drawing on recent research from the social sciences and neurosciences, we shall demonstrate how visceral factors: (a) preclude decision making by focusing a person's attention and motivation on the external behaviour that elicited the visceral response; and (b) collapse one's time perspective to the present and direct one's focus inward to facilitate the retaliation response. We conclude our analysis with a discussion of the practical implications of a visceral factors perspective on retaliation.

Note that our approach, while rooted in psychology, is largely informed by the workplace (organizational) context in which we have conducted our research for the past twenty years. Also, the vast majority of this research stream on the psychological roots of workplace revenge has been conducted in North America and Europe. These two facts differentiate our chapter from most of the other chapters in this volume. First, while our conceptualization overlaps with Gollwitzer's psychological approach, our approach does not overlap much with the studies from the other social sciences represented here, such as anthropology and criminal justice. Second, because so much of the research stream on the psychological roots of workplace revenge has been studied in so few countries, and Western countries at that, crosscultural variation and qualifiers are not well understood, and thus we will not discuss them in this chapter. Nonetheless, the variety of disciplines and nations represented in this volume illustrate just how varied is the conceptualization of revenge and retaliation by scholars and by 'practitioners' of revenge and retaliation.

The Emotion of Anger: Visceral Influences on Retaliation

Our research has shown that anger, particularly *righteous* anger, is the key emotional state triggering retaliation (Tripp and Bies 2009). The righteousness of the anger provides a moral foundation to this visceral state. While the anger fuels the retaliation, it is the righteousness of the anger that accelerates the response, often without thinking.

What we have discovered in our research is that righteous anger is a complex emotion with different dimensions (Tripp and Bies 2009), and each dimension provides clues to the desire and motivation for retaliation. One of these dimensions focuses on a sense of violation – *violation of expectations* and *violation of a sacred trust.* The second dimension focuses on the pain of the emotion and how it is experienced, which we describe with reference to *intensity* and *tyrannical quality*. A third dimension is the *social labelling* of the visceral state of anger.

Sense of Violation: Expectations and Sacred Trust

One sense of violation that people experience is a *violation of expectations.* The victim simply did not see it coming, and thus victims often report feeling 'confused' or 'stunned' by the harm caused. Indeed, in most of the incidents of revenge we have examined in the course of our research programme, the victims were 'surprised' by the harm (Tripp and Bies 2009). However, victims are usually more than just stunned and mad, as the feeling of a *violation of a sacred trust* comes into play. They were not just hurt – they were *wronged.* And that wrong is viewed as a violation of trust.

This sense of violation can accelerate the negative generalizations that people make about the harmdoer. For example, Porath, MacInnis and Folkes (2010) conducted four different experiments in which participants witnessed an act of incivility in a consumer context. Across these studies, they find consistent and converging evidence that the participants in the studies: (a) became angry when that act was between an employee and another employee (and also between an employee and a consumer); and (b) made negative generalizations about the firm, its other employees and future interactions with the company. Further, the participants' response time to making these generalizations was much faster the angrier they were, suggesting the influence of visceral factors on individual judgements.

Other social psychological research underscores the influence of visceral factors on social cognitive processes and behaviour. For example, Weiner (1985) found that spontaneous attributional activity was greater for negative than for positive events. Leith and Baumeister (1996) found that highly aroused, unhappy people engaged more in patterns of high-risk and self-defeating behaviour than neutral-mood or good-mood people.

Pain: Intensity and Tyrannical Quality

Victims often describe the *intensity* of the emotions they experience (Bies and Tripp 2002). The intensity reveals a strong visceral response of physiological and psychological pain. In fact, the initial emotions are often described as 'white hot', 'furious' or 'bitter', words that are clear expressions of pain, anger and rage.

The intensity of the pain is not just psychological; it is also physiological. Many people in our studies report a variety of physiological symptoms, including uncontrollable crying, 'knots in the stomach' and physical exhaustion (Bies and Tripp 2002). Based on these findings, it is clear that the righteous anger is an intensely *felt* experience.

But the emotional pain of anger also can have a *tyrannical quality*, creating a psychological and physiological stranglehold over the individual. Consider the words used by a manager at a consumer products company to describe his anger: 'Despite my efforts to control my feelings, they just overtake me.' What often sustains the tyrannical quality of anger is *obsession*. Victims often obsess about their situation. Obviously, these are not happy thoughts; they are negative thoughts about the offence that they replay repeatedly in their heads, which sustains the visceral response of anger and can crowd out other thoughts and goals.

The tyranny of righteous anger can endure over time, sometimes for days, weeks and even months, if not longer (Tripp and Bies 2009). Indeed, the emotion of anger can be like a 'social toxin' for some people, 'poisoning' their professional and personal lives over time. And, as we have found in our research, often the emotions endure due to the social support of coworkers who continually participate in conversations about the injustice.

These findings are consistent with a review of how people respond to bad events and good events of the everyday or major-life kind, which found that bad events wear off more slowly than good events (Baumeister et al. 2001). The authors also found that undesirable (bad) events had more pervasive effects on subsequent mood than desirable (good) ones. Further, in what has been termed *affective forecasting* (Gilbert et al. 1998), people estimate that negative events will affect them longer than positive events.

The Naming of Anger: The Social Labelling of Arousal

As we described above, the harm a person experiences creates a state of arousal. Whether or not that visceral state is labelled as anger may depend on the social labelling of the arousal state. As Schachter and Singer (1962) demonstrated, the social cues provided to people when they are in an aroused state can label the emotion in different ways. In a laboratory experiment, Schachter and Singer injected subjects with the drug epinephrine, which causes physiological arousal. The aroused subjects were then placed in a waiting room with a confederate of the experimenters. In one condition, the confederate acted angry, complaining about the experiment; in the other condition, the confederate acted happy as he shot wadded-up paper balls into the wastebasket. Even though in both conditions the subjects experienced the same physiological arousal, how they thought about and labelled the emotional arousal differed significantly across conditions: in the first condition, they reported feeling angry; and in the second condition, they reported feeling happy. Crucially, the only difference between the conditions was the social context. Thus, how an emotion gets labelled after the fact can be dramatically influenced by social context and salient social cues (Taylor and Fiske 1978). This is a key tenet of both Social Comparison Theory (Festinger 1954) and Social Information Processing Theory (Salancik and Pfeffer 1978): in ambiguous circumstances, people will look to other people for interpretive information.

Perhaps one of the most remarkable demonstrations of the power of social context to label, if not 'mislabel', emotions is an experiment performed by Dutton and Aron (1974). In their experiment they had an attractive woman (or man in the control condition) interview men who crossed either a 'scary' bridge (the Capilano Canyon Suspension Bridge in Vancouver, Canada, which crosses a deep canyon, wobbling and tilting, with only low wire handrails to hold on to) or a nonscary bridge (a lower, solid wood bridge). The interview contained a survey that included a psychological projection test known as the Thematic Apperception Test (TAT). The men who crossed the scary bridge and were interviewed by the woman showed significantly higher sexual content in their TAT items and were also significantly more likely to contact the interviewer later (he or she gave a phone number to the men 'in case you have any questions about the survey') than the men in the other conditions. These results demonstrate that the scary bridge generated strong emotions of fear in the men, which the men then labelled as sexual arousal when in the presence of the attractive female interviewer.

Regarding the impact of social context on injustice and retaliation, we first turn to a study by Folger et al. (1979). In a laboratory experiment, these researchers found that peer opinions on inequity – where peers either confirmed or disconfirmed to an individual that he or she had suffered an inequity – influenced the individual's perception of whether the process was fair. Moreover, the social context influences not only the perception of injustice, but also retaliation. For instance, Morrill (1995) found that executives who engage in revenge first discuss their feelings and attributions in social 'bitch sessions' after work with other executives. Goldman (2001) studied recently terminated employees who visited various unemployment offices. Whether terminated employees filed discrimination claims against their former employers depended on the advice of their families and legal counsels. Such advice influenced whether terminated employees believed they were terminated illegally, a belief that was usually necessary for them to file suits, and influenced how angry they got (Goldman 2003).

Our research suggests that social information is often provided to those who are harmed and that social information can shape the naming of anger (Tripp and Bies 2009). When a victim is aroused but unsure as to what emotion is appropriate, he or she may adopt the group's opinion – more so when there is consensus within the group. Simply put, when individuals are unsure about something, they more likely think what everyone else claims to think, wrong or right.

Of course, anger is not the only emotion that may influence retaliation. For example, in their review of the approach–avoidance literature (which includes the study of 'fight-or-flight' responses), Carver and Harmon-Jones (2009) focused on anger and fear, noting that both can activate approach mechanisms. Thus, fear represents another visceral factor that can motivate retaliation (Shorris 1981).

But not all such emotions are excitatory. In fact, fear may *inhibit* revenge. If an act of revenge would require taking risks (for example, when retaliating against one's boss, who can powerfully counter-retaliate), fear may inhibit risk taking. While we know of no studies that have investigated which emotions inhibit revenge, there is evidence that revenge against powerful others is less likely than revenge against weak others. For instance, Aquino, Tripp and Bies (2001, 2006) have shown that victims are more likely to get even with their peers and subordinates than they are with their bosses. Alternatively, fear may inhibit some forms of revenge while encouraging other forms. Common wisdom suggests that fear of powerful offenders/targets may not exactly eliminate revenge, but rather force it 'underground'. That is, when would-be avengers fear counter-retaliation from offenders, they may choose covert rather than overt acts of revenge, and may enlist the involvement of others (for example, badmouthing the offenders 'behind their backs' to others instead of insulting the offenders 'to their faces'). In our own interviews with avengers and victims, many described their fear of counter-retaliation and how it influenced the type of revenge they took (Tripp and Bies 1997).

Which Comes First? The Interplay of Cognition and Emotion

Our analysis thus far illustrates that while emotions and judgements are separate psychological constructs, they do not occur independently. Indeed, in the 1980s, a famous debate occurred between Richard Lazarus and Robert Zajonc about such interdependence – specifically, over which came first: cognitions or emotions. In response to the claim by Lazarus (1984) that cognition precedes emotion, Zajonc (1984) argued that emotion often precedes cognition, that individuals may feel an emotion before knowing what caused it. Evidence exists for both views. Sometimes people experience arousal and then look to label that arousal with social cues available in the situation. This is what the Schachter and Singer (1962) and Dutton and Aron (1974) studies demonstrate. Moreover, Keltner, Ellsworth and Edwards (1993) demonstrate that anger also increases one's judgement that the other is responsible for negative events. However, other scholars have shown that emotions follow judgements. In summarizing many of these studies, Lerner and Keltner (2000: 476) describe how such 'cognitive-appraisal' mechanisms work regarding anger: 'Anger arises from appraisals of: (a) other-responsibility for negative events, (b) individual control, and (c) a sense of certainty about what happened.'

Regarding injustice and emotions such as anger, Cohen-Charash and Byrne (2008; see also De Cremer 2007) review this literature and find ample evidence that emotion both precedes and follows judgements of injustice. For example, in a study of customers who blog online after a service failure with a firm, Gregoire, Laufer and Tripp (2010) found that anger mediated the relationship between the judgement of the perceived greed of the firm and the customer's desire for revenge or retaliation.

Neuroscience research may be able to help explain the apparently reciprocal influence of emotion and judgement. Feelings of anger, and even a sense of injustice and desire for revenge, must also occur in the 'deeper', more 'animal' parts of the brain; after all, evidence exists that animals feel anger and injustice and seek revenge. For example, a recent study by Range et al. (2009) showed that even dogs experience inequity aversion. In their study, dogs performed tricks and then were offered food rewards. However, in one condition, dogs saw other dogs receive food rewards, but received no reward themselves. The dogs that received no rewards 'got even' by refusing to perform the tricks. Note that in the control conditions (other dogs getting no rewards either, or when the dog performed alone unable to see what other dogs received), the dogs continued to perform tricks. Cats, too, may get even. Consider the story of the Siberian tiger that was shot by poacher Vladimir Markov (Valiant 2011). Markov shot and wounded the tiger, and then left it alone to die. But the tiger did not die, and in fact tracked Markov's scent to his home miles away. When the tiger did not find Markov home, he destroyed everything that had Markov's scent, and waited forty-eight hours for Markov to return. When Markov returned, the tiger killed him and then ate him. This story suggests that tigers are capable of seeking revenge.

So, where in our 'animal brain' do feelings of anger, judgements of injustice and thoughts of revenge reside? Much research in the last decade using brain imaging equipment (for example, functional Magnetic Resonance Imaging (fMRI) and positron emission tomography (PET) scanners) has explored the locations in the human brain where various processes occur, including emotional responses such as anger, perceived injustice and revenge. For instance, Sanfey et al. (2003) had subjects play the 'ultimatum game' while lying in an fMRI scanner. In the ultimatum game two people are given a fixed sum of money to divide. One person, the proposer, gets to propose a split of the money, and the other person, the decider, decides to accept or reject the split. If the decider rejects the proposed split, neither person gets any money. Typically, offers that allocate 80 per cent or more for the proposer (and thus 20 per cent or less for the decider) are usually rejected. That is, the deciders get even when proposers make such 'greedy' offers. In Sanfey et al.'s experiment, each subject saw thirty offers believed to be from either another subject or from a computer. Some offers were even ($5 each), and some were uneven (for example, $9 to the proposer, $1 to the decider). When subjects received even offers from persons or any kind of offer from the computer, the dorsolateral prefrontal cortex (DLPFC) – where thought, but not feeling, occurs – was involved. However, when subjects saw uneven offers from people, then not only was the DLPFC involved, but so too was the anterior insula region of the brain, which is associated with negative emotion.

Other studies, such as those conducted by Rebecca Saxe and colleagues (e.g., Young and Saxe 2009) show that a specific brain area (the right temporo-parietal junction) is involved when people make moral judgements about other people's intentions. As other research has shown (e.g., Weiner 1995; Crossley 2009), a victim's judgement of an offender's motivation as intentional is nearly a prerequisite for revenge. Moreover, recent research (Quervain et al. 2004; Singer et al. 2006) shows that witnessing the punishment of others who have acted unfairly activates the 'reward circuits' of the brain (that is, the left ventral striatum, specifically, the nucleus accumbens).

Taken together, the neuroscience research provides evidence that many different areas and circuits of the brain – both in the more rational neo-frontal cortex and in the more emotion-driven anterior insula region – interact to produce emotions and judgements reciprocally. Furthermore, it is also clear that the anterior insula region, which is associated with negative emotions, is activated when a person engages in revenge or retaliation. Clearly, then, much of revenge is visceral, not merely cognitive. As such, this neuroscience research provides direct evidence for the layperson's common-sense observation that revenge and retaliation are acts that occur 'in the heat of the moment', albeit shaped by social context, as argued above.

Visceral Factors and Retaliation: Psychosocial and Environmental Influences

Drawing on research from neuroscience and the social sciences, we identify two categories of factors that can trigger visceral anger, which often leads to retaliation: psychosocial factors and environmental factors.

Psychosocial Factors

Psychosocial factors that create a visceral response are different types of harm that create the emotion of anger. These harms are *goal obstruction, breaking of rules or norms* and *attacks on one's reputation.*

Goal Obstruction

Perhaps the most basic or primal motivation for revenge is when one person frustrates another person in attaining some goal or reward. Psychologists call it the 'frustration-aggression' hypothesis. When one is frustrated by interference in goal-directed activity, one is more likely to aggress. So we aggress against the person who frustrates us, and sometimes immediately and reflexively, without much contemplation. When a person stops others from getting what they want, people get angry and want to get even. It's as simple as that, much like the sibling rivalry that many of us grew up with.

Being a roadblock to others can motivate revenge, but often a simple sense of injustice or being unfairly treated can be the motivating force. And it is those 'injustice' triggers to which we now turn our attention: breaking rules or social norms and damaging another's reputation.

Breaking Rules and Norms

In our research in the workplace, we have been struck by just how sensitive people can be when those around them 'break' the rules or violate social norms. Let's begin with a look at why people seek revenge when they perceive that rules have been broken. In every organization, there are rules that govern how decisions are made. Whether it is decisions about hiring and promotion or about salary increases and budget allocations, there are rules that govern these decision-making processes. When the rules are broken, people get angry. First, a *violation of the formal rules* is a frequent trigger of revenge. *Changing the rules 'after the fact'* is a second common form of rule breaking.

Of course, not all the rules are written down or even declared as 'rules'. Often, people come to understand that there are just some ways people do and should behave. Sociologists refer to such commonly understood expectations as social norms. Acting in accordance with the prevailing social norms of conduct is important to people, and a violation can create the visceral response of righteous anger. More specifically, when someone violates the standard of honour, people distrust the violator. In our studies (Tripp and Bies 2009) of the workplace, we have found six such social norm violations.

First, *shirking job responsibilities* is viewed as a norm violation. This is a common trigger of revenge among teams, particularly when one team member does not fulfil his or her job responsibilities, thus leaving the other team members to 'carry the load'. Such shirking violates an implicit, if not explicit, trust among team members to work 'together', as one person put it, and 'share the load' equally.

Broken promises represent a second norm violation and an action that can trigger a visceral response. For example, a coworker promises that she will 'help you out' at a difficult client meeting, but then she backs out at the last minute with no explanation. Or consider the boss who made explicit promises to support a subordinate's candidacy for a promotion, but in the end did not follow through.

Lying is a third violation that creates feelings of distrust and outrage – for example, the boss who promises an employee a raise when, in fact, no raise was even considered. In the face of being lied to, then, the typical reaction is to feel that one has been 'duped' and 'manipulated' – reactions similar to those of victims of broken promises. In such cases, people are unable to trust the liar again.

Stealing ideas or credit from others is a fourth violation that triggers revenge. Whether it be a boss who puts his name on a subordinate's report and claims public credit for it or a team member who claims primary responsibility for an innovation to which she contributed very little, stealing credit creates a visceral response among victims – and observers.

The *disclosure of private confidences and secrets* is an action that violates a fundamental trust between people and often triggers a vengeful response. Whether it be disclosing a subordinate's private matter that was supposed to be held in confidence by the boss, or a coworker who receives secret information disclosed by another and then uses it to his own advantage, such actions are viewed as a fundamental betrayal and 'a knife in the back', resulting in what one person described as 'not just a splintering, but a shattering of trust'.

Finally, the *abuse of authority* represents a violation of a special kind of social norms or codes of conduct – those to which we hold our leaders accountable. The *intolerable boss* and the *corrupt boss* represent two such types of leaders. The *intolerable boss* is a classic example of abuse in action. Specifically, such bosses are hypercritical, overdemanding, overly harsh and even, in the words of one person, 'cruel' in their dealings with subordinates *over time*. The *corrupt boss* is another classic example of abuse in action. The word *corrupt* was used to describe bosses who 'padded expense reports' or made sure they 'flew in first class *at company expense*, while the rest of the team flew in coach class on the airplane', as well as those who would hire their children for a prime job or overlook theft of company resources by their 'friends'.

Attacks on Reputation

When people believe that they are the targets of interpersonal attacks that have the effect of impugning or undermining their reputation, it creates an immediate visceral response, which is often very intense and lasting (Tripp and Bies 2009). Such attacks include *public criticism*, *wrong or unfair accusations* and *insults to the self or collective.*

Public criticism is viewed as a direct and focused attack on one's social reputation. The criticism is not only negative, but also usually personal and berating.

Being *accused wrongly or unfairly* represents a second kind of attack on one's identity. A wrongful accusation involves a person being blamed for a mistake or failure when, in fact, that person was not at fault. An unfair accusation is similar to a wrongful accusation in that in both cases, the accusations are not true.

Finally, an *insult to one's self or collective* represents a third kind of attack on one's social identity that we have observed. We found that insults on a personal level typically involve 'name-calling', as in questioning an employee's intellectual capacities by referring to him or her as a 'moron', or in disparaging a male employee's lack of assertiveness by calling him a 'wimp' or saying that he 'has no balls'. Insults to the collective involve any attack not on a specific individual, but on some characteristic of the demographic group to which the individual belongs, such as one's gender, ethnicity, age or religion. This category also extends to attacks on one's professional background characteristics, such as the school or university from which one graduated or what one studied.

Environmental Factors

As we discussed earlier, revenge is not only prompted by the more cognitive factors listed above; it is also prompted by visceral internal states, some of which may have very little rational basis at all. That is, sometimes people can experience negative emotions not due to an act of another person, but simply due to their environment. Yet, as the Schachter and Singer (1962) and Dutton and Aron (1974) studies showed, people can misinterpret the cause of those negative emotions and then make the wrong choices. Indeed, based on the literature, we list two ways in which environmentally induced emotions can cause retaliation: (a) negative emotions cause more hostile attributions and intense blame of an offender, in part by focusing a person's attention and motivation on the behaviour that gave rise to the visceral response; and (b) negative emotions 'crowd out' all other goals besides revenge by collapsing one's time perspective to the present and narrowly directing one's focus inward, which in turn facilitates the retaliation response. To demonstrate this, we focus on two environmental conditions known to cause negative emotions and increase the likelihood of revenge: (a) external stimuli that negatively affect a person's senses, such as heat, noise and odour; and (b) aggressive cues.

Heat, Noise and Odour

Criminologists have known for some time that more violent crimes are committed when temperatures rise (though only up to a point – when it becomes too hot, people remain indoors instead of going out to commit crimes; see Rotton and Cohn 2004). In his review of the aggression literature, Anderson (2001) proposes that heat makes people 'cranky', which then distorts the social interaction process. Such distortion increases anger:

> which in turn primes aggressive thoughts, attitudes, preparatory behaviors (e.g., fist clenching), and behavioral scripts (such as 'retaliation' scripts). A minor provocation can quickly escalate, especially if both participants are affectively and cognitively primed for hostility by their heightened level of discomfort. A mild insult is more likely to provoke a severe insult in response when people are hot than when they are more comfortable. This may lead to further increases in the aggressiveness of responses and counterresponses. An accidental bump in a hot and crowded bar can lead to the trading of insults, punches, and (eventually) bullets. (Anderson 2001: 36)

As an example of heat-induced retaliation, Larrick et al. (2011) analysed nearly 60,000 Major League Baseball games to see if high temperatures increased the prevalence of batters being hit by a pitch. They found that when one of a pitcher's teammates had been hit by the opposing team's pitcher earlier in the game, the probability of that pitcher hitting a batter in retaliation increased abruptly at higher temperatures.

Heat is but one of the nonsocial aversive conditions that can increase aggressive responses. Other such conditions include loud noises and unpleasant odours (Berkowitz 1993). Indeed, any general discomfort or pain can increase aggression, an effect that is mediated primarily by negative affect, a visceral state (Anderson et al. 2000).

But how do such aversive conditions increase aggressive responses such as retaliation? Anderson (2001) suggests two ways: (a) by increasing misattribution of one's emotions, perhaps to an aggressive cue (for example, misattributing heat-induced stress as due not to the heat, but to a minor social provocation such as another's complaining); or (b) by suppressing normal mechanisms that inhibit aggression. Thus, in the chain of events that lead to retaliation – offence → blame → desire for revenge → revenge (Tripp, Bies and Aquino 2007) – aversive conditions may increase the likelihood of retaliation by: (1) amplifying the 'offence→blame' link by attributing more intentionality to the offender's motives (Crossley 2009); and (2) by amplifying the 'desire for revenge→revenge' link by reducing the self-control that victims are able to exercise. Evidence exists for both explanations.

First, evidence suggests that aversive conditions can cause arousal, which is then misattributed to some offence. According to 'excitation transfer' theory (Zillman 1983; Anderson 2001), excitation caused by one stimulus lingers and is then attributed to another, subsequent stimulus. Anderson, Deuser and DeNeve (1995) found in two experiments that heat does indeed cause physiological arousal that transferred to hostile cognition, and that subjects did not perceive their hostile cognitions as being due to the heat.

Second, evidence suggests that heat and other aversive stimuli can affect self-control. In particular, the arousal created by aversive stimuli may crowd out other emotions that may otherwise attenuate or offset hostile affect. Zillman makes several observations on this point. To begin with, he notes that strong arousal leads to a loss of cognitive control: 'At very high levels of excitation, then, hostile and aggressive behaviors are expected to become impulsive – that is, to become behaviors composed of learned reactions associated with great habit strength' (1983: 94). He also notes that excitation can lead to rumination, which thereby maintains excitation, leading to a sustained feedback cycle of angry obsession that crowds out other thoughts and that may continue until some other 'absorbing stimulus disrupts the rehearsal of grievances' (1983: 92).

In our own research (Tripp and Bies 2009), we have found similar reports of those who retaliate after having first obsessed about the mistreatment they experienced. This obsession not only sustained the anger, but also in many cases deepened the anger of the person who was harmed. Those whose obsession led to a deeper, and more intense, anger were the ones who acted out that anger through retaliation. Moreover, they often regretted their actions later because, as they recounted, they were too shortsighted to think through the obvious negative implications of their revenge actions (Tripp and Bies 1997).

More recent research suggests that when individuals are depleted of their self-regulatory resources, they are more likely to behave unethically, in part because they lose their ability to identify their own potentially morally questionable behaviour (Gino et al. 2011). To the extent that revenge is a morally questionable behaviour, those whose cognitive resources are diminished would lose one important source of inhibition of the revenge impulse. Although Gino et al. examined the depletion of cognitive resources through decision fatigue (making many moral decisions exhausts one's ability to make yet another moral decision), emotions, and not just cognitions, may also deplete cognitive resources. Colloquially speaking, anger may 'hijack' one's mind. That is, anger leads to a loss of self-control, which otherwise would help resist the temptation to engage in morally questionable behaviour such as retaliation. Exercising self-control over aggressive feelings may follow a similar pattern. Muraven and Baumeister (2000) propose that exercising self-control is like exercising a muscle: the more one flexes it, the more tired and the less able to flex it one becomes. Muraven and Baumeister furthermore propose that negative affect prompts the exercise of self-control, and that stress, such as noise (Glass, Singer and Friedman 1969), weakens self-control. Therefore, building upon their rationale and our earlier arguments, we suggest that sustained anger (from the vicious feedback cycle of anger – rumination – anger that is angry obsession) depletes the self-control necessary for victims to resist acting on their desire for revenge. Eventually, after enough self-control attempts, they will give into this temptation.

Although the previous studies did not examine organizational life per se, we would expect to observe the same effects in organizations. Many organizations contain aversive and stressful stimuli such as unrealistic workloads and deadlines that may build up negative affect and sap cognitive resources. Many manufacturing, warehousing and construction settings are characterized by loud noise and stifling heat. Perhaps this partially explains why such 'blue-collar' workers are more combative with coworkers than are 'white-collar' office workers, a difference that cannot be explained by the testosterone factor alone (the fact that such workplaces generally have a large proportion of male employees) (Dabbs Jr. 1992; Dabbs Jr., Alford and Fielden 1998).

Aggressive Cues

One of the consistent findings in aggression research is that people who are angry act more aggressively (see, e.g., Baron 1971). Furthermore, when individuals are angry, their aggression can be even greater if social cues associated with violence, like a weapon, are present. For example, in a classic experiment, Berkowitz and Le Page (1967) found that angered subjects administered a greater number of retaliatory shocks against the person who harmed them when a shotgun or a revolver (rather than a badminton racquet or no object at all) was lying on a table in front of them. This so-called 'weapons effect' was a controversial finding, and attempts to replicate it have met with mixed results. However, using meta-analytic procedures, Carlson, Marcus-Newhall and Miller (1990) found confirmation of the weapons effect, although the effect was restricted to cases where subjects' sophistication and evaluation apprehension were low.

Other studies have focused on different aggressive cues. In particular, there is a body of research that has focused on name-mediated negative associations such as language associated with violence (e.g., Berkowitz and Geen 1966), aggressive verbalizations and hostile attitudes (e.g., Loew 1967), and unpleasant physical characteristics (e.g., looks, speech) of the target of the aggression (e.g., Berkowitz and Frodi 1979). These studies provide converging evidence that aggressive cues increase aggression. Indeed, using meta-analytic procedures, Carlson, Marcus-Newhall and Miller (1990) found confirmation that these name-mediated aggression cues augment aggressive responses, particularly in those who are negatively aroused.

Aggressive cues are prevalent in many organizations and may, in part, explain acts of revenge or retaliation. For example, we found that insults to coworkers or hypercritical comments and demeaning public statements by a boss to a subordinate were viewed as acts of aggression, frequently eliciting a quick retaliatory response of some kind from the target of such aggressive language (Tripp and Bies 2009). In a richly textured analysis of conflict at the executive level, Morrill (1995) describes many examples of executives who engage in confrontational behaviour in public meetings with other executives, including name-calling and making pejorative comments about the character or competence of others, often leading to heightened emotions and conflict. Moreover, this type of aggressive behaviour was acceptable in the culture of the organizations that Morrill studied!

Practical Implications

The above arguments suggest two types of recommendations: (a) encouraging and enhancing *self-control strategies* for when one is feeling angry and about to retaliate; and (b) developing *social control strategies* for organizations that wish to avoid provoking, enabling or facilitating their workers' retaliation impulses.

Self-Control Strategies

Anger management strategies developed for those high in trait anger (see Howells and Day 2003) should enhance self-control. For instance, being aware of one's own arousal and agitation, and how environmental factors unrelated to social provocation may stimulate it may help one reduce mislabelling such arousal to aggression cues. Also, one could avoid engaging in conflict 'resolution' when one is aroused. We are reminded of Ambrose Bierce's warning: 'Speak when you are angry, and you will make the best speech you will ever regret.' Similarly, one should delay conflict resolution when one is tired or when one has been involved in other conflicts recently in order to avoid the temptations that result from decision fatigue. As Thomas Jefferson once said: 'If angry, count to ten. If really angry, count to one hundred.'

Social Control Strategies

Organizations that wish to reduce conflict and chaos among their employees should implement the following strategies to contain aggression. First, organizations can increase social norms that reduce aggressive cues and inhibit aggressive expression (for example, by supporting norms against name-calling and destructive public criticism of ideas). Second, organizations in which employees work long shifts could reduce shifts to ten hours or less so that employees do not become so overtired as to have decision fatigue. Third, organizations can control the physical climate. By controlling heat levels, maintaining fresh air and lowering the noise level (or enforcing the wearing of hearing protection), workers should become less aroused with negative emotions that they may misattribute to other, social causes.

Conclusion

The current paradigm governing research on revenge and retaliation in the workplace is a cognitive perspective, one that focuses on the importance of attributions and blame assignment. By contrast, we have proposed a visceral factors perspective as an alternative framework for analysing revenge and retaliation. Our review of the research on the role of visceral factors highlights the importance of emotions (such as anger and fear) and environmental conditions (such as heat and the salience of aggressive cues) as key drivers of revenge and retaliation.

We cannot escape acts of revenge and retaliation in the workplace, as they are woven into the fabric of organizational life. We can, however, develop a more complete understanding of what triggers acts of revenge and retaliation. Our focus on the importance and role of visceral factors in shaping acts of revenge and retaliation increases our understanding of such acts and our ability to manage them. Indeed, it should keep us vigilant to conditions that can cause one to act 'in the heat of the moment'.

Robert J. Bies is Professor of Management and Founder of the Executive Master's in Leadership Program at the McDonough School of Business at Georgetown University, United States. He is a Faculty Fellow of the Center for Social Justice Research, Teaching, and Service at Georgetown University. His current research focuses on leadership, the delivery of bad news, organizational justice, trust and distrust dynamics, and revenge, forgiveness and mercy in the workplace. His research has been published in leading journals (e.g., the *Academy of Management Annals*, *Academy of Management Journal*, *Academy of Management Review*, *Journal of Applied Psychology*, *Journal of Management* and *Organizational Behavior and Human Decision Processes*). He is also coauthor of the book *Getting Even: The Truth about Workplace Revenge – and How to Stop it* (Jossey-Bass, 2009).

Thomas M. Tripp is Professor of Management and Associate Dean of Academic Programs, Carson College of Business, at Washington State University, United States. He has specialized in the area of workplace conflict, publishing on workplace conflict in journals including the *Journal of Applied Psychology*, *Academy of Management Annals*, *Organizational Behavior and Human Decision Processes* and the *Journal of Marketing*. He is coauthor with Robert Bies of the 2009 book *Getting Even: The Truth about Workplace Revenge – and How to Stop it* (Jossey-Bass). He earned a Ph.D. in organizational behaviour from the Kellogg School of Management at Northwestern University and a BS in Psychology from the University of Washington.

References

Adams, J.S. 1965. 'Inequity in Social Exchange', in L. Berkowitz (ed.), *Advances in Experimental Social Psychology*, vol. 2. New York: Academic Press, pp. 267–99.

Anderson, C.A. 2001. 'Heat and Violence', *Current Directions in Psychological Science* 10: 33–38.

Anderson C.A., K.B. Anderson, N. Dorr, K.M. DeNeve and M. Flanagan. 2000. 'Temperature and Aggression', in M. Zanna (ed.), *Advances in Experimental Social Psychology*. New York: Academic Press, pp. 63–133.

Anderson, C.A., W.E. Desuser and K.M. DeNeve. 1995. *Personality and Social Psychology Bulletin* 21: 434–48.

Aquino, K., T.M. Tripp and R.J. Bies. 2001. 'How Employees Respond to Personal Offense: The Effects of Blame Attribution, Victim Status, and Offender Status on Revenge and Reconciliation in the Workplace', *Journal of Applied Psychology* 86: 52–59.

———. 2006. 'Getting Even or Moving on? Power, Procedural Justice, and Types of Offense as Predictors of Revenge, Forgiveness, Reconciliation, and Avoidance in Organizations', *Journal of Applied Psychology* 91: 653–58.

Axelrod, R. 1984. *The Evolution of Cooperation.* New York: Basic Books.

Baron, R.A. 1971. 'Magnitude of Victim's Pain Cues and Level of Prior Anger Arousal as Determinants of Adult Aggressive Behavior', *Journal of Personality and Social Psychology* 17: 236–43.

Baumeister, R.F., E. Bratslavsky, C. Finkenauer and K.D. Vohs. 2001. 'Bad is Stronger than Good', *Review of General Psychology* 5: 323–70.

Berkowitz, L. 1993. *Aggression: Its Causes, Consequences, and Control.* New York: McGraw-Hill.

Berkowitz, L., and A. Frodi. 1979. 'Reactions to a Child's Mistakes as Affected by Her/His Looks and Speech', *Social Psychology Quarterly* 42: 420–25.

Berkowitz, L., and R.G. Geen. 1966. 'Film Violence and the Cue Properties of Available Targets', *Journal of Personality and Social Psychology* 3: 525–30.

Berkowitz, L., and A. LePage. 1967. 'Weapons as Aggression-Eliciting Stimuli', *Journal of Personality and Social Psychology* 7: 202–7.

Bies, R.J., and T.M. Tripp. 1996. 'Beyond Distrust: Getting Even and the Need for Revenge', in R. Kramer and T.R. Tyler (eds), *Trust in Organizations.* Newbury Park, CA: Sage Publications, pp. 246–60.

———. 2002. 'Hot Flashes, Open Wounds: Injustice and the Tyranny of Its Emotions', in S. Gilliland, D. Steiner and D. Skarlicki (eds), *Emerging Perspectives on Managing Organizational Justice.* Greenwich, CT: IAP Press, pp. 203–23.

Carlson M., A. Marcus-Newhall and N. Miller. 1990. 'Effects of Situational Aggression Cues: A Quantitative Review', *Journal of Personality and Social Psychology* 58: 622–33.

Carver, C.S., and E. Harmon-Jones. 2009. 'Anger is an Approach-Related Affect: Evidence and Implications', *Psychological Bulletin* 135: 183–204.

Cohen-Charash, Y., and Z.S. Byrne. 2008. 'Affect and Justice: Current Knowledge and Future Directions', in N.M. Ashkanasy and C.L. Cooper (eds), *Research Companion to Emotion in Organizations.* Cheltenham: Edward Elgar, pp. 360–91.

Crossley, C.D. 2009. 'Emotional and Behavioral Reactions to Social Undermining: A Closer Look at Perceived Offender Motives', *Organizational Behavior and Human Decision Processes* 108: 14–24.

Dabbs, J.M. Jr. 1992. 'Testosterone and Occupational Achievement', *Social Forces* 70: 813–24.

Dabbs, J.M. Jr., E.C. Alford and J.A. Fielden. 1998. 'Trial Lawyers and Testosterone: Blue-Collar Talent in a White-Collar World', *Journal of Applied Social Psychology* 28: 84–94.

DeCremer, D. 2007. *Advances in the Psychology of Justice and Affect.* Greenwich, CT: Information Age Publishing.

Deutsch, M. 1973. *Conflict Resolution: Constructive and Destructive Processes.* New Haven, CT: Yale University Press.

Dutton, D.G., and A.P. Aron. 1974. 'Some Evidence for Heightened Sexual Attraction under Conditions of High Anxiety', *Journal of Personality and Social Psychology* 30(1): 510–17.

Festinger, L. 1954. 'A Theory of Social Comparison Processes', *Human Relations* 7: 117–40.

Folger, R., D. Rosenfield, J. Grove and L. Corkran. 1979. 'Effects of "Voice" and Peer Opinions on Responses to Inequity', *Journal of Personality and Social Psychology* 37: 2243–61.

Gilbert, D.T., E.C. Pinel, T.D. Wilson, S.J. Blumberg and T.P. Wheatley. 1998. 'Immune Neglect: A Source of Durability Bias in Affective Forecasting', *Journal of Personality and Social Psychology* 75: 617–38.

Gino, F., M.E. Schweitzer, N.L. Mead and D. Ariely. 2011. 'Unable to Resist Temptation: How Self-Control Depletion Promotes Unethical Behavior', *Organizational Behavior and Human Decision Processes* 115: 191–203.

Glass, D.C., J.E. Singer and L.N. Friedman. 1969. 'Psychic Cost of Adaptation to an Environmental Stressor', *Journal of Personality and Social Psychology* 12: 200–10.

Goldman, B.M. 2001. 'Toward an Understanding of Employment Discrimination Claiming: An Integration of Organizational Justice and Social Information Processing Theories', *Personnel Psychology* 54: 361–86.

———. 2003. 'The Application of Referent Cognitions Theory to Legal-Claiming by Terminated Workers: The Role of Organizational Justice and Anger', *Journal of Management* 29: 705–28.

Gregoire, Y., D. Laufer and T.M. Tripp. 2010. 'A Comprehensive Model of Customer Direct and Indirect Revenge: Understanding the Effects of Perceived Greed and Customer Power', *Journal of the Academy of Marketing Sciences* 38: 738–58.

Homans, G.C. 1961. *Social Behavior.* New York: Harcourt, Brace & World.

Howells, K., and A. Day. 2003. 'Readiness for Anger Management: Clinical and Theoretical Issues', *Clinical Psychology Review* 23(2): 319–37.

Keltner, D., P.C. Ellsworth and K. Edwards. 1993. 'Beyond Simple Pessimism: Effects of Sadness and Anger on Social Perception', *Journal of Personality and Social Psychology* 64: 740–52.

Larrick, R.P., T.A. Timmerman, A.M. Carton and J. Abrevaya. 2011. 'Temper, Temperature, and Temptation: Heat-Related Retaliation in Baseball', *Psychological Science* 22: 423–28.

Lazarus, R.S. 1984. 'On the Primacy of Cognition', *American Psychologist* 39: 124–29.

Leith, K.P., and R.F. Baumeister. 1996. 'Why Do Bad Moods Increase Self-Defeating Behavior? Emotion, Risk-Taking, and Self-Regulation', *Journal of Personality and Social Psychology* 71: 1250–67.

Lerner, J.S., and D. Keltner. 2000. 'Beyond Valence: Toward a Model of Emotion-specific Influences on Judgment and Choice', *Cognition and Emotion* 14(4): 473–93.

Loew, C.A. 1967. 'Acquisition of a Hostile Attitude and its Relationship to Aggressive Behavior', *Journal of Personality and Social Psychology* 5: 335–41.

Loewenstein, G. 1996. 'Out of Control: Visceral Influences on Behavior', *Organizational Behavior and Human Decision Processes* 65: 272–92.

Morrill, C. 1995. *The Executive Way: Conflict Management in Corporations.* Chicago: University of Chicago Press.

Muraven, M., and R.F. Baumeister. 2000. 'Self-Regulation and Depletion of Limited Resources: Does Self-Control Resemble a Muscle?', *Psychological Bulletin* 126: 247–59.

Porath, C.L., D.J. MacInnis and V.S. Folkes. 2010. 'Witnessing Incivility among Employees: Effects on Consumer Anger and Negative Inferences about Companies', *Journal of Consumer Research* 37: 292–303.

Quervain, de D.J.F., U. Fischbacher, V. Treyer, M.Schellhammer, U. Schnyder, A. Buck and E. Fehr. 2004. 'The Neural Basis of Altruistic Punishment', *Science* 305: 1254–58.

Range, F., L. Horn, Z. Viranyi and L. Huber. 2009. 'The Absence of Reward Induces Inequity Aversion in Dogs', *Proceedings of the National Academy of Sciences* 106: 340–45.

Rotton, J., and E.G. Cohn. 2004. 'Outdoor Temperature, Climate Control, and Criminal Assault: The Spatial and Temporal Ecology of Violence', *Environment and Behavior* 36: 276–306.

Salancik, G.R., and J. Pfeffer. 1978. 'A Social Information Processing Approach to Job Attitudes and Task Design', *Administrative Science Quarterly* 23: 224–53.

Sanfey, A.G., J.K. Rilling, J.A. Aronson, L.E. Nystrom and J.D. Cohen. 2003. 'The Neural Basis of Economic Decision-Making in the Ultimatum Game', *Science* 300: 1755–58.

Schachter, S., and J. Singer. 1962. 'Cognitive, Social, and Physiological Determinants of Emotional State', *Psychological Review* 69: 379–99.

Shorris, E. 1981. *The Oppressed Middle: The Politics of Middle Management: Scenes from Corporate Life.* New York: Anchor/Doubleday.

Singer, T., B. Seymour, J.P. O'Doherty, K.E. Sephan, R.J. Dolan and C.D. Frith. 2006. 'Empathic Neural Responses are Modulated by the Perceived Fairness of Others', *Nature* 439: 466–69.

Skarlicki, D.P., and R. Folger. 1997. 'Retaliation in the Workplace: The Roles of Distributive, Procedural, and Interactional Justice', *Journal of Applied Psychology* 82: 434–43.

Taylor, S.E., and S.T. Fiske. 1978. 'Salience, Attention, and Attribution: Top of the Head Phenomena', *Advances in Experimental Social Psychology* 11: 249–88.

Tripp, T.M., and R.J. Bies. 1997. 'What's Good about Revenge? The Avenger's Perspective', in R.J. Lewicki, R.J. Bies and B.H. Sheppard (eds), *Research on Negotiation in Organizations*, vol. 6. Greenwich, CT: JAI Press, pp. 145–60.

———. 2009. *Getting Even: The Truth about Workplace Revenge – and How to Stop it.* San Francisco: Jossey-Bass.

Tripp, T.M., R.J. Bies and K. Aquino. 2007. 'A Vigilante Model of Justice: Revenge, Reconciliation, Forgiveness, and Avoidance', *Social Justice Research* 20: 10–34.

Valiant, J. 2011. *The Tiger: A True Tale of Vengeance.* New York: Knopf.

Weiner, B. 1985. '"Spontaneous" Causal Thinking', *Psychological Bulletin* 97: 74–84.

———. 1995. *Judgments of Responsibility: A Foundation for a Theory of Social Conduct.* New York: Guilford Press.

Young, L., and R. Saxe. 2009. 'Innocent Intentions: A Correlation between Forgiveness for Accidental Harm and Neural Activity', *Neuropsychologia* 47: 2065–72.

Zajonc, R.B. 1984. 'On the Primacy of Affect', *American Psychologist* 39: 117–23.

Zartman, I.W. (ed.). 1995. *Elusive Peace: Negotiating an End to Civil Wars*. Washington DC: Brookings Institution Press.

Zillman, D. 1983. 'Arousal and Aggression', in R.G. Geen and E. Donnerstein (eds), *Aggression: Theoretical and Empirical Reviews*, vol. 1. New York: Academic Press, pp. 75–102.

Section II

Retaliation in Psychological and Economic Analyses of Crime and Deviance

Chapter 3

A Criminal is a Victim is a Criminal?

An Economist's View on the Victim–Offender Overlap

Horst Entorf

Introduction

In economics, the concept of *retaliation* is allocated to the 'economics of reciprocity', made popular in a series of articles by the Austrian economist Ernst Fehr (Zurich University, Switzerland) and co-authors. In a seminal article published in the *Journal of Economic Perspectives* (Fehr and Gächter 2000), the authors term cooperative reciprocal tendencies 'positive reciprocity', while the retaliatory aspects (at the centre of this book) are called 'negative reciprocity': people gain utility by acting altruistically towards those who treat them fairly and by acting spiteful towards those who treat them unfairly. The views published in Fehr and Gächter (2000) have become common knowledge in modern economics. The basic contribution of this and related work (see, e.g., Fehr and Gächter 2002) is that they have provided evidence on important conditions in which the traditional self-interest theory of the *homo oeconomicus* is unambiguously refuted. *Reciprocity* (negative and positive) has become part of *behavioural economics*, which has changed mainstream economics in the last ten years or so. In the field of the 'economics of crime', traditional (rational choice) models are likewise often criticized because they ignore the fact that cognitive restrictions or emotional factors such as time pressure, peer-group influence or anger restrict the long-run 'optimality' of individual decisions (see Garoupa 2003; McAdams and Ulen 2009; Mehlkop and Graeff 2010; Van Winden and Ash 2012; Entorf 2014).

Although many crimes would fit well into the category of retaliatory behaviour, even the more recent literature on the behavioural economics of crime is rather silent on negative reciprocity or retaliation as a motivation for crime. This is somewhat surprising because emotional factors such as anger provide an important theoretical link between behavioural economics and crime. A remarkable exception to the rule is the recent article by Van Winden and Ash (2012), which emphasizes the role of angry retaliation not only as a factor in crime, but also as a crime deterrent. McAdams and Ulen (2009) also point to the preference for fairness that may underlie certain crimes of 'self-help' retaliation by victims against their perpetrators (see also Fehr and Gächter 2002; Garoupa 2003). This observation is in line with one of the *stylized facts* in the crime literature, that is, the victim–offender overlap, whereby offenders are more likely than non-offenders to be victims, and victims are more likely than nonvictims to be offenders.[1] In the criminological literature, the overlap between offenders and victims has been well documented since the early contributions by Hentig (1941) and Wolfgang (1958), and it has been analysed in a considerable number of articles, in particular in recent years (see, for instance, Ousey, Wilcox and Fisher 2011; Silver et al. 2011). Lauritsen, Sampson and Laub (1991) represent an early seminal work. In the field of economics, empirical studies are scarce – Deadman and MacDonald (2004), Foreman-Peck and Moore (2010) and Entorf (2012) are rare exceptions.

This chapter is grounded on the empirical observation that being a victim of crime is strongly correlated with having a criminal record. The chapter gives a survey of theoretical explanations leading to the phenomenon of victim–offender overlaps, with a focus on the role of angry retaliation within economic reasoning. It highlights insights based on behavioural economics, with findings relying on rationality, bounded rationality and ecological rationality. A second focus will be on the statistical and empirical approach to the victim–offender overlap, including the significance of important underlying criminological and economic factors.

Considerations of the Victim–Offender Overlap: A Survey

Explanations Based on Individual Behaviour: Bounded Rationality and Behavioural Economics

Rational choice models are often criticized because they ignore the cognitive restrictions and emotional factors – such as time pressure, peer group influence or anger – that restrict the long-run 'optimality' of individual decisions. Traditional models clearly lack explicit consideration of the human cognitive decision process. As was first pointed out by Simon (1957; see also Simon 1982 for an overview of his models), the complexity of situations and limitations of both available information and cognitive capacity lead to decisions being taken under the condition of 'bounded rationality'. Such decisions are often suboptimal. Simon also demonstrated that, rather than being utility 'maximizers', humans are 'satisficers', seeking satisfactory solutions that make them happy enough. Bounded rationality is at the heart of modern behavioural economics. Of crucial importance for 'behavioural' explanations of crime are anger, 'uncertainty' (dealing with small probabilities and loss aversion), hyperbolic discounting (discounting future events), time pressure and shame/guilt (norms) (see Englerth 2010; Entorf 2014 for recent surveys of these findings; Garoupa 2003; McAdams and Ulen 2009; Van Winden and Ash 2012).

As regards the overlap of victimization and offending, anger seems to be a major motivation of retaliatory behaviour, as stressed by many criminological and psychological research papers (see, e.g., Agnew 1992; Kubrin and Weitzer 2003; Jacobs and Wright 2010; Simons and Burt 2011). Anger in response to perpetrated injury, frustration and unfair treatment is a triggering event that motivates 'striking back', not necessarily against the perpetrator himself or herself but also against non-involved bystanders and other available victims, and not necessarily right away, but at some later point in time (see Haidt 2003; Van Winden and Ash 2012). Such behaviour is often the consequence and origin of norms of honour and respect (or fear of dishonour and shame, respectively), prevailing and potentially escalating in subcultural societies (Anderson 1999; Kubrin and Weitzer 2003). However, punishing the 'unkind' behaviour of others ('negative reciprocity') is not limited to deprived subgroups, but seems to be a social norm rooted in general human behaviour, as suggested by the findings in Fehr and Gächter (2002). Participants in their experiments revealed some 'altruistic punishment' behaviour, that is, they punished defectors even when the retaliation was costly to them. This so-called prosocial behaviour has its origin in the notion of fairness, as can be seen from the outcome of many ultimatum-game experiments. In such games, responders often forgo their own (guaranteed) gains in order to prevent the proposer from receiving any gains when they perceive that the proposal was unfairly low. As is known from experiments with public-good games (Fehr and Gächter 2002), punishing defectors is even more effective than rewarding cooperators. Thus, the individual motivation behind anger might be impulsive and 'irrational' (in the sense of traditional rational-choice models), but its social effect can be deterrence (Van Winden and Ash 2012), at least in pre-legal or subcultural spaces. Moreover, although individual behaviour based on cognitive and emotional factors significantly diverges from decisions of the *homo oeconomicus*, human behaviour can be characterized as 'ecologically rational' (Frank 1988; Gigerenzer 2005), as human decision making is evolutionarily adapted and designed to survive natural selection and to solve fitness-related problems (Van Winden and Ash 2012). Here economics meets evolutionary psychology and neuroscience, which leads to the new field of 'neuroeconomics'. The future will show whether studying the human brain will have a sustainable impact on economic thinking (see Camerer, Loewenstein and Prelec 2005 for a survey).

Criminological and Economic Approaches in the Literature

The human behaviour of angry retaliation (or 'negative reciprocity' as economists would put it) is presumably one of the major explanations of the victim–offender overlap, although not all publications address this 'deep' factor of crime. The most prominent 'explanations'[2] found in the literature focus on the sociodemographic similarities between victims and offenders (male, young, black, urban) as laid out in routine activity/lifestyles theories (Hindelang, Gottfredson and Garofalo 1978; Cohen and Felson 1979): daily risky activity brings attractive and poorly guarded targets for crime into close proximity and interaction with potential offenders. A similar explanation for the victim–offender overlap is the subculture-of-violence approach (Singer 1981), according to which individuals who attack others risk retaliation from former victims, something often reinforced by subcultural norms such as the 'code of the street' of gang behaviour (see Anderson 1999; Levitt and Venkatesh 2000). This has been confirmed by in-depth interviews with street criminals (Jacobs and Wright 2010), which have shown that retaliation is not necessarily addressed against the perpetrator, and that random redirection might lead to a climate of urban violence. This adverse effect of social interaction is not limited to violence. Falk and Fischbacher (2002) report that, on average, the more individuals steal, the more others steal. Agnew's (1992) general strain theory and Akers' (1985) social learning theory also emphasize the role of former victimization within subcultural societies that provide motivation and specific training to commit crimes.

A different prominent theory providing a foundation for the correlation between victimization and offending is low self-control (Gottfredson and Hirschi 1990). These authors argue that crime evolves from sensation-seeking behaviour that ignores long-term consequences. Individuals who find themselves in places and situations of low self-control are equally likely to become victims or to commit crimes. Heavy drinking and illicit drug use are prime examples.

Some criminological theories of criminal behaviour might be considered observationally equivalent to economic theories of crime. The same applies to explanations of the victim–offender overlap. Merton's strain theory (1938), for instance, proposes that crime is an illegal attempt to be economically and socially successful. 'Offenders are essentially strivers for the American dream' (Schreck, Stewart and Osgood 2008: 878) who became frustrated by their relatively weak position within the social structure, which interferes with the achievement of their expectations (see also Agnew 1992). Schreck, Stewart and Osgood (2008) argue that, according to strain theory, victimizing people who are lower in the social hierarchy would produce little gain. The same prediction would follow from rational choice theory in the tradition of Becker (1968): given utility-maximizing behaviour and the potential (expected) risks of being detected and punished, would-be offenders choose *attractive* targets in order to maximize net awards. Thus, potential victims of rational offenders are typically economically and socially successful people who are less guarded, those in the proximity of offenders, and those who are visible and available ('exposed'). Papadopoulos (2011) points out that this description also fits the basic elements of routine activity/lifestyle theory. As basic economic theory seems to be closely related to criminological views, Papadopoulos presents ideas of a two-stage theory of offending and victimization that borrows from the early economic models by Becker (1968) and Ehrlich (1973). In the same vein, Foreman-Peck and Moore (2010) examine the behaviour of rational potential victims of violence who minimize the probability of injury under the given budgetary constraints and the need to achieve other objectives. However, a clear weakness of this reasoning – and of classical rational choice theory in general – is that it ignores the possibility of the same person being both a victim and an offender.

The approach of modern economics to retaliation is based on the concept of reciprocity. Traditional rational choice theory seems to be generally called into question by the 'irrational' retaliatory behaviour of victims and criminals. However, as highlighted above, 'altruistic punishment' and 'prosocial behaviour' can be seen as a rational deterrence strategy in a 'pre-legal' or 'pre-societal' community. In such areas, without access to or trust in the criminal law systems in modern societies, victims might be tempted to take the law into their own hands. Particularly in disadvantaged neighbourhoods and subcultural societies where the retaliatory ethic of the 'code of the street' (Anderson 1999) is used in lieu of criminal codes, the credible threat of punishment by strong retaliation might deter potential future perpetrators. For would-be victims, the potential threat of future retaliation by any other member of subcultural groups might be an incentive to join the group and can prevent violent crimes that would otherwise have taken place. This reasoning has been confirmed in the literature: Sobel and Osoba (2009) argue that youth gangs form in response to governments' failure to protect youths against violence. Jacobs and Wright (2010) point to the increased specific deterrence effect when retaliation is addressed within a close microstructural or relational space: violators may be deterred even though they have suffered no direct punishment.

Empirical Studies on the Victim–Offender Overlap

The best way to study interacting cycles of offending and victimization and the emergence of retaliatory situations would be to observe actions, reactions and counter-reactions of the same people over time. Unfortunately, this is almost impossible in empirical practice unless one observes people in unrealistic laboratory situations. In order to capture risky environments and microstructural conflicts, empirical studies are often based on in-depth interviews with criminals (see, in particular, Jacques and Wright 2008; Jacobs and Wright 2010). While this technique has the advantage of allowing experienced interviewers to delve more deeply into relevant questions asked to relevant players, the disadvantage is that the rather small number of observations[3] limits the external validity and statistical inference of the interview data. The alternative is to use relatively large samples from relevant subpopulations (see, e.g., Deadman and MacDonald 2004;

Silver et al. 2011; Entorf 2012). However, the disadvantage of this approach is that it fails to identify disastrous individual conflicts between offenders and their victims. Instead, the milieu of victims and offenders has to be approximated by data on age, education, parents, alcohol and drug abuse, peers, health conditions, labour market status and so forth. Thus, there is no silver-bullet approach for empirical studies analysing the interaction of criminals and victims in general and of retaliation in particular. Both narrative interviews and the use of standardized survey data have their merits and drawbacks; as such, they should be considered complements rather than substitutes.

Historically, the empirical evidence of most published studies on the victim–offender overlap focuses on how offending influences victimization. This can be seen from the example of Lauritsen, Sampson and Laub (1991), one of the most frequently cited articles in the literature on the victim–offender overlap. The main conclusions of this seminal study are based on least squares regressions, with victimization as the dependent variable and current and lagged delinquent lifestyles as regressors (controlling for lagged victimization and socioeconomic factors). A second strand of empirical literature, following Singer (1981), Akers (1985) and Agnew (1992), employs the statistical explanatory power of former victimization on offending. Here angry retaliation may be an important factor, although it cannot be observed in most empirical applications. In a survey of existing results on 'victimization causes subsequent offending', Ousey, Wilcox and Fisher (2011) report mixed results regarding this direction of influence. Hay and Evans (2006), Cullen et al. (2008) and studies characterized as 'intergenerational transmission of violence'[4] find that former victimization is positively related to future offending, whereas other authors conclude that victimization *decreases* future offending. Ousey, Wilcox and Brummel (2008) and Jacques and Wright (2008), for instance, propose a 'victimization termination' rationale, according to which victimization represents a seminal traumatic turning point causing individuals to reassess their involvement in risky activities (frequenting bars, alcohol and drug abuse and so on), and ultimately curtails the committing of property and violent crimes. It should be noted, however, that the majority of studies lack external validity because results are based on the views and experiences of small samples of subcultural groups.

As regards the causal structure of offending and victimization and the role of retaliation therein, the more realistic view is to consider the relationship as simultaneous or at least reciprocal (think, for instance, of repeated angry retaliation where the role of victim and offender might change over time). It is only recently that researchers have widened their perspective to study both the influence of victimization on offending and the reverse causation. In their review of the 'reciprocal' literature, Ousey, Wilcox and Fisher (2011) mainly refer to two studies, Schreck, Stewart and Osgood (2006) and Wilcox, May and Roberts (2006), both of which use repeated panel waves to study the dynamics of the victimization–offending–victimization feedback. Both studies confirm what Ousey, Wilcox and Fisher (2011) call the 'reciprocal escalation hypothesis': victimization increases offending, which in turn provokes higher victimization. By contrast, results by Ousey, Wilcox and Fisher (2011) based on dynamic panel data from four follow-up surveys among 12- to 15-year-old students are in line with the conclusion that offending is reduced by one's own previous victimization.

Silver et al. (2011), Foreman-Peck and Moore (2010) and Shaffer (2004), independently of one another, follow a different approach. They consider victimization and offending to be a joint process, that is, both variables are treated as dependent variables that are determined by exogenous factors. A crucial element of these so-called seemingly unrelated regression models (SUR) or, if dependent variables are dichotomous (or binary), the bivariate probit model is the consideration of correlated residuals – latent factors that obscure unobserved heterogeneity influencing the joint victimization–offending process. Silver et al. (2011) consider violent offending and victimization within a sample of psychiatric patients. The authors confirm previous results indicating that most significant factors of victimization also hold for offending. Their important finding is that both offending and victimization are affected by some positively correlated unobserved factors not accounted for in the data. The authors presume that violence and victimization may be linked through interactional processes such as provocation and retaliation, or chronic relationship conflicts. The same positive interrelationship between unobserved drivers of victimization and offending has been documented by Shaffer (2004) and Foreman-Peck and Moore (2010). Their empirical models only differ with respect to included explanatory variables: Shaffer (2004) has a strong focus on the significant role of peer effects, whereas Foreman-Peck and Moore (2010) highlight the importance of risk aversion (low risk aversion increases the likelihood of becoming a victim) and time preference (more impatient people are more likely to be violent). The strong positive effect of a joint latent factor found in all three articles is highly significant after controlling for numerous socioeconomic, parental, lifestyle/routine activity, peer-group and clinical variables, as well as time preferences and risk aversion. The robustness of these results suggests that, despite the long list of well-known factors, both victimization and offending are still subject to positively associated latent factors, of which the tendency to retaliate is probably a very important one.

A further example of bivariate probit not covered above is Deadman and MacDonald (2004). Their approach is atypical in that they estimate a recursive bivariate probit system (without naming it as such). They view victimization as the equation of interest and treat offending as one of its explanatory factors. Offending is explained in a second equation using variables that the authors consider truly exogenous (that is, causal) to the system of victimization and offending (such as truancy and expulsion from school, excessive drinking and drug use); in other words, these variables are significantly associated with the offending variable, but not the victimization variables. Entorf (2012) follows a similar recursive bivariate probit approach, but he also tests the 'victimization causes offending' direction of influence. His paper employs German survey data and uses retrospective information on individual offending and victimization, as well as a rich list of social, demographic, economic and further criminological factors. Exogeneity tests do not contradict exogeneity of criminal activities and endogeneity of victimization. Among the most important factors in crime, broken homes (a term that covers any previous conviction of parents or siblings, as well as the divorce of parents) and alcohol or drug abuse are the most important factors in crimes. Problems with excessive debt also play a significant role. Besides prior criminal involvement, very large peer groups and high levels of education are factors that increase the risk of victimization, while married and healthy people have a significantly lower risk of becoming victims of crime. Results also confirm previous findings by Silver et al. (2011), Deadman and MacDonald (2004), Shaffer (2004) and Foreman-Peck and Moore (2010), according to which offending and victimization are significantly driven by common unobserved factors. Retaliatory conflicts and motivations certainly belong to the most influential factors that were neglected in previous empirical work. In the future, better data should cover longitudinal information on retaliatory interactions.

Summary and Conclusions

Theoretical explanations based on individual decision-making processes of the empirically well-documented individual victim–offender overlaps are rare. Retaliatory behaviour is one of the most prominent explanations. This chapter focuses on the view of modern behavioural economics and highlights the role of cognitive restrictions and emotional factors that restrict the long-run 'optimality' of individual decisions. As becomes obvious, anger in particular is of crucial importance for 'behavioural' explanations of the victim–offender overlap and retaliatory behaviour. Anger in response to perpetrated injury, frustration and unfair treatment is a triggering event that motivates 'striking back'. This chapter argues that such behaviour is not necessarily irrational. Whereas the retaliatory behaviour of victims and criminals would seem to call traditional rational choice theory into question, recent findings by Fehr and Gächter (2002) suggest that punishing the 'unkind' behaviour of others ('negative reciprocity') is a social norm rooted in general human behaviour. As detailed in this chapter, angry retaliatory behaviour can also be seen as a rational crime deterrent, at least in 'pre-legal' or 'pre-societal' communities. The deterrent effect is reinforced by the fact that prosocial behaviour is not only addressed to the perpetrator himself or herself, but also to non-involved bystanders.

Empirical evidence is in line with these predictions. Retaliatory behaviour is often the consequence and origin of norms of honour and respect prevailing and potentially escalating in subcultural societies (Anderson 1999; Kubrin and Weitzer 2003). In general, however, empirical studies often suffer from the small number of observations (in the case of narrative interviews) or from not being able fully to capture risky environments and microstructural conflicts (in the case of survey data). If large data sets are to be used, the milieu of victims and offenders needs to be approximated by rich information on age, education, parents, alcohol and drug abuse, peers, health conditions, labour market status and so on. The given empirical evidence suggests that a large portion of the victim–offender overlap is driven by joint factors such as risky daily activities, drinking habits and relational conflicts, mainly arising in subcultural and microstructural spaces. However, unobserved heterogeneity is an important issue when studying crime and victimization. Again, here microstructural retaliatory conflicts are supposed to be of crucial importance, but have been omitted from statistical models because they escape the observation of empirical researchers.

The best way to study dynamic 'cycles' of offending and victimization would be through the analysis of panel data, in particular using network information. This would allow the researcher to observe actions, reactions and counter-reactions as cause and response affecting the same individuals over time. It is hoped that future research will have such data at hand so that the true forces of the victim–offender overlap can be studied in greater detail.

Horst Entorf is Professor of Econometrics at the Goethe University of Frankfurt, Germany. He was previously Professor at Darmstadt University of Technology and at the University of Würzburg. He held previous research and teaching positions at Université Catholique de Louvain-la-Neuve, CREST-INSEE (Paris) and CERGE (Prague). He received his Ph.D. in economics from the University of Mannheim. His main research interests include empirical econometrics applied to labour economics, education, migration and the economics of crime. He has published in the *Journal of Econometrics*, *Journal of Labor Economics*, *European Economic Review*, *Scandinavian Journal of Economics*, and *European Journal of Political Economy*.

Notes

This chapter is based on the paper presented for the Conference on Retaliation (Max Planck Institute for Foreign and International Criminal Law in Freiburg, Germany, 26–29 October 2011), as well as on the more detailed paper 'Criminal Victims, Victimized Criminals, or Both? An Econometric Analysis of the Victim–Offender Overlap' (Entorf 2012). According to a survey provided by Shaffer (2004), results in the literature indicate that offenders are 1.5–7 times more likely than non-offenders to be victims, and victims are 2–7 times more likely than nonvictims to be offenders.

1. According to a survey provided by Shaffer (2004), results in the literature indicate that offenders are 1.5–7 times more likely than non-offenders to be victims, and victims are 2–7 times more likely than nonvictims to be offenders.

2. Note, however, that these theories do not deal explicitly with victimization, but rather focus on criminal behaviour.
3. Jacobs and Wright (2010), for instance, interviewed fifty-two active street criminals.
4. The psychometric literature on 'intergenerational transmission' is subsumed under 'cycle of violence' (Widom 1989a, 1989b) and goes rather undetected in the criminological literature (as, for instance, in the survey by Schreck, Stewart and Osgood 2008). Recent contributions to this strand of literature include Kim (2008), Maas, Herrenkohl and Sousa (2008) and Yun, Ball and Lim (2011).

References

Agnew, R. 1992. 'Foundation for a General Strain Theory', *Criminology* 30(1): 47–87.

Akers, R.L. 1985. *Deviant Behavior: A Social Learning Approach.* Belmont, CA: Wadsworth.

Anderson, E. 1999. *Code of the Street.* New York: Norton.

Becker, G.S. 1968. 'Crime and Punishment: An Economic Approach', *Journal of Political Economy* 76(2): 169–217.

Camerer, C.F., G. Loewenstein and D. Prelec. 2005. 'Neuroeconomics: How Neuroscience Can Inform Economics', *Journal of Economic Literature* 43(1): 9–64.

Cohen, L.E., and M. Felson 1979. 'Social Change and Crime Rate Trends: A Routine Activities Approach', *American Sociological Review* 44: 588–608.

Cullen, F.T., J.D. Unnever, J.L. Hartman, M.G. Turner and R. Agnew. 2008. 'Gender, Bullying Victimization, and Juvenile Delinquency: A Test of General Strain Theory', *Victims and Offenders* 3(4): 346–64.

Deadman, D., and Z. MacDonald. 2004. 'Offenders as Victims of Crime? An Investigation into the Relationship between Criminal Behaviour and Victimization', *Journal of the Royal Statistical Society Series A* 167(1): 53–67.

Ehrlich, I. 1973. 'Participation in Illegitimate Activities: A Theoretical and Empirical Investigation', *Journal of Political Economy* 81(3): 521–65.

Englerth, M. 2010. *Der beschränkt rationale Verbrecher: Behavioral Economics in der Kriminologie.* Berlin: Lit Verlag.

Entorf, H. 2012. 'Criminal Victims, Victimized Criminals, or Both? An Econometric Analysis of the Victim–Offender Overlap'. Mimeo. Manuscript prepared for the IZA Conference on the Economics of Risky Behaviour, Istanbul, April.

———. 2014. 'Certainty and Severity and their Deterrent Effects', in G. Bruinsma and D. Weisburd (eds), *Encyclopedia of Crime and Criminal Justice.* Heidelberg: Springer, 319–28. Extended version: IZA DP 6516 (2012).

Falk, A., and U. Fischbacher. 2002. Social Norms: '"Crime" in the Lab – Detecting Social Interactions', *European Economic Review* 46: 859–69.

Fehr, E., and S. Gächter. 2000. 'Fairness and Retaliation: The Economics of Reciprocity', *Journal of Economic Perspectives* 14(3): 159–81.

———. 2002. 'Altruistic Punishment in Humans', *Nature* 45: 137–40.

Foreman-Peck, J., and S.C. Moore. 2010. 'Gratuitous Violence and the Rational Offender Model', *International Review of Law and Economics* 30(2): 160–72.

Frank, R.H. 1988. *Passions within Reason.* New York: Norton.

Garoupa, N. 2003. 'Behavioral Economic Analysis of Crime: A Critical Review', *European Journal of Law and Economics* 15(1): 5–15.

Gigerenzer, G. 2005. 'Is the Mind Irrational or Ecologically Rational?', in F. Parisi and V.L. Smith (eds), *The Law and Economics of Irrational Behavior.* Stanford, CA: Stanford University Press.

Gottfredson, M.R., and T. Hirschi. 1990. *A General Theory of Crime.* Stanford, CA: Stanford University Press.

Haidt, J. 2003. 'The Moral Emotions', in R.J. Davidson, K.R. Scherer and H.H. Goldsmith (eds), *Handbook of Affective Sciences.* Oxford: Oxford University Press, pp. 853–54.

Hay, C., and M.M. Evans. 2006. 'Violent Victimization and Involvement in Delinquency: Examining Predictions from General Strain Theory', *Journal of Criminal Justice* 34(3): 261–74.

Hentig, H. van. 1941. 'Remarks on the Interaction of Perpetrator and Victim', *Journal of Criminal Law, Criminology, and Police Science* 31: 303–9.

Hindelang, M.J., M.R. Gottfredson and J. Garofalo. 1978. *Victims of Personal Crime: An Empirical Foundation for a Theory of Personal Victimization.* Cambridge: Ballinger.

Jacobs, B.A., and R. Wright 2010. 'Bounded Rationality, Retaliation, and the Spread of Urban Violence', *Journal of Interpersonal Violence* 25(10): 1739–66.

Jacques, S., and R. Wright. 2008. 'The Victimization–Termination Link', *Criminology* 46(4): 1009–38.

Kim, J. 2008. 'The Protective Effects of Religiosity on Maladjustment among Maltreated and Nonmaltreated Children', *Child Abuse and Neglect* 32: 711–20.

Kubrin, C.E., and R. Weitzer. 2003. 'Retaliatory Homicide: Concentrated Disadvantage and Neighborhood Culture', *Social Problems* 50(2): 157–80.

Lauritsen, J.L., R.J. Sampson and J.H. Laub. 1991. 'The Link between Offending and Victimization among Adolescents', *Criminology* 29: 265–91.

Levitt, S.D., and S.A. Venkatesh. 2000. 'An Economic Analysis of a Drug-Selling Gang's Finances', *Quarterly Journal of Economics* 115(3): 755–89.

Maas, C., T. Herrenkohl and C. Sousa. 2008. 'Review of Research on Child Maltreatment and Violence in Youth', *Trauma, Violence, and Abuse* 9(1): 56–67.

McAdams, R.H. and T.S. Ulen. 2009. 'Behavioral Criminal Law and Economics', in N. Garoupa (ed.), *Criminal Law and Economics.* Cheltenham: Edward Elgar, pp. 403–25.

Mehlkop, G., and P. Graeff. 2010. 'Modelling a Rational Choice Theory of Criminal Action: Subjective Utilities, Norms, and Interactions', *Rationality and Society* 22: 189–222.

Merton, R. 1938. 'Social Structure and Anomie', *American Sociological Review* 3: 672–82.

Ousey, G.C., P. Wilcox and S. Brummel 2008. '*Déjà Vu* All over Again: Investigating Temporal Continuity of Adolescent Victimization', *Journal of Quantitative Criminology* 24: 307–35.

Ousey, G.C., P. Wilcox and B.S. Fisher 2011. 'Something Old, Something New: Revisiting Competing Hypotheses of the Victimization–Offending Relationship among Adolescents', *Journal of Quantitative Criminology* 27: 53–84.

Papadopoulos, G. 2011. 'The Relationship between Immigration Status and Victimization. Evidence from the British Crime Survey'. Mimeo. University of Essex. Paper presented to the European Economic Association meeting in Oslo.

Schreck, C.J., E.A. Stewart and B.S. Fisher 2006. 'Self-Control, Victimization, and their Influence on Risky Lifestyles: A Longitudinal Analysis Using Panel Data', *Journal of Quantitative Criminology* 22: 319–40.

Schreck, C.J., E.A. Stewart and D.W. Osgood 2008. 'A Reappraisal of the Overlap of Violent Offenders and Victims', *Criminology* 46(4): 871–904.

Shaffer, J.N. 2004. 'The Victim–Offender Overlap: Specifying the Role of Peer Groups', *U.S. Department of Justice Report Document No 205126.* (Thesis at the Pennsylvania State University, December 2003.)

Simon, H.A. 1957. *Models of Man, Social and Rational: Mathematical Essays on Rational Human Behavior in a Social Setting.* New York: Wiley.

———. 1982. *Models of Bounded Rationality*, vol. 2. Cambridge, MA: MIT Press.

Silver, E., A.R. Piquero, A.R. Jennings, G. Wesley, N.L. Piquero and M. Leiber. 2011. 'Assessing the Violent Offending and Violent Victimization Overlap among Discharged Psychiatric Patients', *Law and Human Behavior* 35(1): 49–59.

Simons, R.L., and C. H. Burt 2011. 'Learning to Be Bad: Adverse Social Conditions, Social Schemas and Crime', *Criminology* 49(2): 553–98.

Singer, S. 1981. 'Homogeneous Victim–Offender Populations: A Review and Some Research Implications', *Journal of Criminal Law and Criminology* 72: 779–88.

Sobel, R.S., and B.J. Osoba. 2009. 'Youth Gangs as Pseudo-governments: Implications for Violent Crime', *Southern Economic Journal* 75(4): 996–1018.

Van Winden, F., and E. Ash. 2012. 'On the Behavioral Economics of Crime', *Review of Law & Economics* 8: 181–213.

Widom, C.S. 1989a. 'The Cycle of Violence', *Science* 244: 160–66.

———. 1989b. 'Child Abuse, Neglect, and Violent Criminal Behavior', *Criminology* 27: 251–71.

Wilcox, P., D.C. May and S.D. Roberts. 2006. 'Student Weapon Possession and the "Fear and Victimization Hypothesis": Unraveling the Temporal Order', *Justice Quarterly* 23: 502–29.

Wolfgang, M.E. 1958. *Patterns in Criminal Homicide.* New York: Wiley.

Yun, I., J.D. Ball and H. Lim. 2011. 'Disentangling the Relationship between Child Maltreatment and Violent Delinquency: Using a Nationally Representative Sample', *Journal of Interpersonal Violence* 26(1): 88–110.

Chapter 4

Laypeople's Reactions to Deviancy as Determined by Retributive Motives

Margit E. Oswald

Introduction

This chapter examines three different empirical studies that highlight important psychological insights into the problem of whether laypeople (that is, people who are not professionally involved in sentencing or otherwise determining the punishment for crimes) rely more on retributive or utilitarian motives when determining appropriate punishment. It appears to be necessary to apply *indirect methods* to measure punishment motives because self-reports tend to reflect people's beliefs about their motives rather than what actually drives their decisions. If indirect measures like the Behavioural Process Tracing (BPT) tasks are used, it can reliably be shown that retributive motives play the major role (Study I: Keller et al. 2010). However, *cultural differences* may exist with regard to the general importance of retributive motives. Thus, while findings from studies in the United States suggest that judgements about punishment are broadly consistent with the principles of retributive justice, retributive justice seems to be less important in Switzerland unless the suspect is one of the ingroup (Study II: Fischer, Oswald and Seiler 2013). Punishment decisions are biased by several extra-legal variables, such as the victim's reputation and the offender's ethnicity, gender or attractiveness. Under certain conditions, people are eager to *correct for the extra-legal biases* that may influence their punishment decisions. However, their corrections are quite often either limited or excessive, and are sometimes even inappropriate (Study III: Oswald and Stucki 2010).

Laypersons are very seldom in the position where they have to decide if and how severely an offender should be punished. They are in general not very well informed about crime-specific sentences of the court (Robinson and Darley 2004) and have inaccurate perceptions of crime and crime rates. In general, they strongly overestimate the severity and the rate of crimes (Stalans 1993, 2009;

Windzio and Kleimann 2009). However, if they are asked about punishment and punishment goals, they usually do not hesitate to give an answer via self-report.

Interestingly, self-reports differ tremendously from results that researchers obtain if they use indirect measurements where people are unaware of the fact that their goal preferences have been measured. According to results of those indirect measurements, punishment seems mainly to be driven by *retribution* (just deserts), whereas self-reports show clear preferences for the *utilitarian goal* that punishment should prevent recidivism. If people prefer the goal of retribution, they want the offender to pay for the harm she or he has done or, to put it another way, they want to *retaliate* for the culpable damage caused by the offender. Strictly speaking, retribution does not rest on utility considerations, but on the moral that justice has to be re-established after it was challenged by a crime. Conversely, the utilitarian goal strives explicitly for future benefits to society, and justifies punishment only if it reduces the likelihood of crime. Indirect measures of people's goal preferences may be more valid because they are less influenced by self-presentation strategies than self-reports are. However, there may be circumstances in which self-reports also deliver a valid picture of goal preferences; this possibility requires further investigation.

Utilitarian motives may play a bigger role when people are less emotional and less concerned about the norms and values of their group or society. Thus, it can be shown that the severity of the treatment of a suspect is more influenced by utilitarian than retributive considerations if the offender belongs to an outgroup rather than to the ingroup. Whether this dynamic is peculiar to countries with a continental European legal system (as opposed to those with an Anglo-American one) remains an open question.

The overwhelming predominance of retributive motives may hold for quick and intuitive judgements, but less so for carefully deliberated ones. More deliberate judgements may take into account not only utilitarian goals, but also the biasing influences of such extra-legal variables as outrage, accidental damage and social threat. This assertion will be stressed in the last section of this chapter. It will be shown that people may very well be motivated to correct for biasing influences, but that it is no simple matter to do so; correcting a judgement appropriately presupposes at least some specific knowledge about when, where and how far the decision should be corrected.

Is 'Retribution' the Main Motive for Punishment?

Punishment goals can be differentiated beyond the dichotomy of retribution (just deserts) and utilitarianism. Oswald et al. (2002) demonstrated empirically that all punishment goals can be classified with reference to two dimensions: first, to which social entity the goal is mainly targeted, that is, towards a specific person (perpetrator or victim) or towards the general public; and, second, whether the sanction has negative or positive objectives, that is, whether it aims at deterrence or rehabilitation. Thus, special positive prevention, one of the utilitarian goals, refers to a specific person (perpetrator) and to a positive objective (rehabilitation), while general negative prevention, another utilitarian goal, refers to the general public (all prospective offenders) and to a negative objective (deterrence).

Empirical studies have generally shown that all goals are regarded as important (Darley 2002; Doble 2002) and that 'special prevention' seems to be in general the most important goal (Oswald et al. 2002). However, goal preferences have almost exclusively been measured explicitly via self-report. Some authors argue that self-reports reflect people's beliefs about their motives rather than what actually drives their decisions (Carlsmith 2008), and that indirect approaches that avoid asking people directly are better suited to infer underlying punishment motives. One of those indirect approaches is the Behavioural Process Tracing (BPT) task, which was originally described by Jacoby et al. (1987) and was applied to research on punishment motives by Carlsmith (2006).

What is the rationale behind this method? People read that a crime has been committed and they are asked how severely they would punish the offender. To help them in completing this task, they can then select from and get answers to a list of questions such as 'Is the offender a repeat offender?' and 'Are the crime and the trial attracting a lot of media attention?' If these questions about the crime can be mapped *uniquely* in advance onto specific 'sentencing goals', one can then trace back the preferred sentencing goals by using the kind of information the person asked for. Researchers can study which pieces of information people selected, how many and in what order. In contrast to earlier studies that used explicit measures, Carlsmith (2006) showed that when participants engaged in a BPT task, they strongly focused on the retributive perspective. This result is also in line with studies using other indirect measurement approaches (e.g., Carlsmith, Darley and Robinson 2002; Darley and Gromet 2010).

Keller et al. (2010) (Study I) tried to replicate Carlsmith's findings in their first experiment (Experiment 1), but in two further experiments (Experiments 2 and 3) also adjusted for some shortcomings in Carlsmith's research that may have artificially strengthened the expected outcome. First, the participants in Carlsmith's research were not informed about what type of crime the offender had committed; rather, they had the option of selecting this information in the BPT task as an item related to retribution. It can be argued, however, that selecting 'type of crime' does not indicate a desire for retribution, but rather a desire for basic information. In Experiments 2 and 3 carried out by Keller et al., the participants were informed from the beginning of the type of crime that had been committed. Second, Carlsmith's study only included three punishment goals: retribution, general prevention and incapacitation. Including more than these three motives might affect the pattern of results. Hence, Experiment 3 carried out by Keller et al. (2010) included special prevention as a fourth motive, and controlled additionally for the length and concreteness of questions that participants were selecting.

In what follows, I will focus on Experiment 3 because it can be considered the strongest test of Carlsmith's finding that people punish out of retributive motives. Fifty-four participants (67 per cent female), mostly students from various disciplines, were told that a person was convicted of residential burglary and that their task was to select an appropriate punishment. In order to complete this task, participants could gather out of a list of fourteen items *five pieces* of information that they deemed most important for making their decision. These items had been separately pretested, and each one can be uniquely and exclusively associated with a specific sentencing goal (see Table 4.1).

As the main dependent variable, a rank preference score was computed for each participant to assess the relative importance of the four punishment goals. The first selected item received a weight of 5, the second item a weight of 4, the third a weight of 3 and so on. Adding weights for each punishment motive resulted in a motive-specific rank preference score. If, for example, a participant selected first two retribution items, then two general prevention items, and then one special prevention item, then retribution received a score of 9 (= 5 + 4), general prevention a score of 5 (= 3 + 2) and special prevention a score of 1. In addition, a self-report measure of goal preference was applied after short descriptions of the four goals of punishment in order to estimate the degree of convergence between the indirect and the self-report method.

As in Experiments 1 and 2, mean rank preference scores differed between the four punishment motives (Friedman's ANOVA: *Chi-square* (3.54) = 73.17,

Table 4.1 Classification of items to punishment justifications (Pretest)
Note: N = 36. Chi-square tests indicate whether an item was significantly more often classified as belonging to a respective punishment goal than to any other punishment goal. All $p < .001$. (Table adapted from Table 2 in Keller et al. 2010: 109)

Sentencing goal	**Example of item associated with goal (14 items in all)**	**Correct classification (%)**	**df**	**Chi-square**
Retribution	How big is the financial, physical and psychological harm the offender has caused?	86	2	55.17
General prevention	Will this type of crime become more frequent if the punishment is too lenient?	86	3	71.78
Incapacitation	What is the probability of the perpetrator being a repeat offender?	94	2	60.50
Special prevention	How can the offender be supported to live without committing crimes?	100		
Filler items	Where did the crime take place?	67	4	50.94

p<.001). The mean score for retribution (M = 6.89) was significantly higher than the mean score for incapacitation (M = 4.38), special prevention (M = 3.64) and general prevention (M = 1.92). Incapacitation did not differ significantly from special prevention, but yielded higher scores than general prevention. Also, the mean score of special prevention was significantly higher than the mean score of general prevention. However, in spite of the modifications in Experiment 3, the mean rank preferences for retribution items still yielded higher scores than for any other punishment goal (Figure 4.1). Thus, the experiments provide additional support for Carlsmith's (2006) conclusion that people's subjective punishment motives are largely shaped by a desire to see the offender punished and to have the punishment fit the crime.

However, a completely different pattern of results emerged when punishment goals were measured via self-reports. In line with earlier research, participants rated each goal as relatively important. Except for general prevention (M = 3.77), all mean values were above the theoretical midpoint of the scale (4). Moreover, special prevention was preferred over incapacitation, while retribution and general prevention received the lowest support.

How can we explain the discrepancy between the results of explicit and implicit measures? Explicit measures of punishment motives are much more vulnerable to self-deception and self-presentational strategies than implicit measures. Thus, the findings of the implicit measurement of punishment motives seem to be in accordance with Hogan and Emler's (1981: 131) assertion that the 'the process of retribution is [evolutionarily] older, more primitive, more universal, and socially more significant' than other justice-related goals. Still, explicit measures may not only be the result of self-deception and thus an invalid predictor of

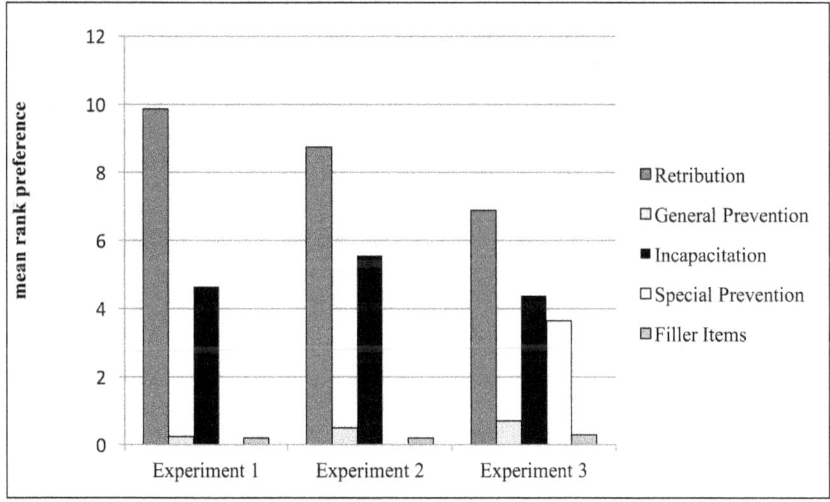

Figure 4.1 Comparison of implicit measures (mean rank preference scores) between Experiments 1–3 of Study I (Keller et al. 2010)

behaviour, but rather the result of a profound deliberate reasoning. For example, when people have enough cognitive capacity at their disposal and feel accountable for their punishment decisions, their intuitive judgements will be influenced by reasoning about mitigating circumstances and foreseeability, as we will see later (e.g., Oswald and Stucki 2010).

Cultural Variation in the Influence of 'Just Deserts' Reasoning

It is well known that the penal system in the United States is extremely harsh, and many American social scientists refer to America as a 'punitive society' (Tyler et al. 1997: 106; Whitman 2003). A recent study (Study II) by Fischer, Oswald and Seiler (2013) has shown that in Switzerland, 'retribution' seems to especially play a role if suspects belong to the ingroup rather than to an outgroup, whereas Carlsmith and Sood (2009) demonstrated in a similar study that in the United States, retribution seems to play a more general role.

Carlsmith and Sood (2009) examined ordinary US citizens' motives to support harsh interrogation techniques in a fictitious scenario of a suspected Afghan terrorist detained by U.S. and coalition forces. Their findings suggest that supporters of harsh interrogation techniques were motivated by utilitarian considerations, but even more by a desire to punish suspects out of a retributive or 'just deserts' motive. Fischer et al. (2013) wanted to investigate further the motives for supporting harsh interrogation techniques in another country with a continental European legal system. They asked participants in Switzerland (N = 219, 34 per cent female) to recommend different legal and illegal interrogation techniques of varying severity for a terrorism suspect in an experimental vignette study. The main dependent variable was the *number of accepted interrogation techniques of increasing severity* (NumberTechniques). Retributive motivation was manipulated by varying the terrorist past of the suspect (yes vs. no) and utilitarian motivation by varying the probability (5 per cent vs. 95 per cent) that the suspect could provide valuable information that might prevent a terrorist attack and save lives of innocent civilians (Knowledge).

In addition, Fischer et al. (2013) wanted to examine the influence of group membership of terrorism suspects and, in particular, the effect of the relationship between their group membership and participants' retributive goals upon the acceptance of severe interrogation techniques. The suspect in their study was a student at the University of Zurich, and either an Afghani with the name Farid Bakthiri or a Swiss with the name Urs Bachmann. Recent research suggested that group membership often interacts with offenders' personal characteristics such as criminal history by establishing the frame within which people perceive a certain transgression as a threat to the norms and values of their own group (Boeckmann and Tyler 1997; Vidmar 2002; Okimoto and Wenzel 2008; Wenzel et al. 2008). For example, Gollwitzer and Keller (2010) found that personal factors such as a criminal history had a stronger effect on punitive responses if the offender belonged to the ingroup than if she or he belonged to an outgroup. Repeat offenders from the ingroup evoked more anger and outrage and more societal concerns, and were therefore deemed deserving of harsher punishment than first-time ingroup offenders, whereas criminal history was a less important factor in judging outgroup offenders.

Additional variables such as the political attitude of participants, the attributed moral status of the suspect and perceived interrogation effectiveness were measured in order to investigate mediation processes between independent and dependent variables. As in Carlsmith and Sood's study (2009), retributive motives should be activated if the effects of a suspect's terrorist past on the interrogation severity measures are mediated by the perceived moral status of the suspect. The suspect's moral status was closely related to the NumberTechniques variable ($r = -.35, p < .01$). Likewise, Fischer et al. (2013) expected that utilitarian considerations would play a crucial role only if the manipulation of the likelihood that the suspect had useful information was mediated by the participant's belief in the effectiveness of harsh interrogation. The Knowledge variable was closely related to NumberTechniques ($r = .34, p < .01$).

To test these mediation hypotheses, Fischer et al. (2013) analysed the indirect effects of each of the independent variables (Terrorist Past, Knowledge, Group Membership) through the two proposed mediators (moral status of the suspect and interrogation effectiveness) upon the dependent measure (NumberTechniques), controlling for the covariate political attitude in a multiple mediator model (for details on the method, see Preacher and Hayes 2008). Figure 4.2 contains all the significant results of the multiple mediation analyses for NumberTechniques.[1] The direct effects of Terrorist Past ($b = .82, p < .05$) and Knowledge ($b = .74, p < .05$) on NumberTechniques were substantially reduced after controlling for the mediators (Terrorist Past: $b = .42$ (not statistically significant); Knowledge: $b = .24$ (not statistically significant)).

As expected, only moral status substantially contributes to the mediation between the manipulation of suspect's terrorist past and NumberTechniques, while interrogation effectiveness was the only significant contributor to the mediation between Knowledge and NumberTechniques.

The findings for the main effects of the independent variables were only partly consistent with the findings reported by Carlsmith and Sood (2009). As in their study, Fischer et al. (2013) found a main effect of Knowledge on NumberTechniques, $F(1, 210) = 4.29, p < .05, \eta^2 = .02$. Thus, a high probability that the suspect was withholding useful information went along with a greater willingness of participants to recommend more interrogation techniques of increasing severity ($M = 8.03, SD = 3.37$) than a low probability ($M = 7.07, SD = 2.82$). A significant main effect of Terrorist Past was also found for NumberTechniques, $F(1, 210) = 5.22, p < .05, \eta^2 = .02$, although this main

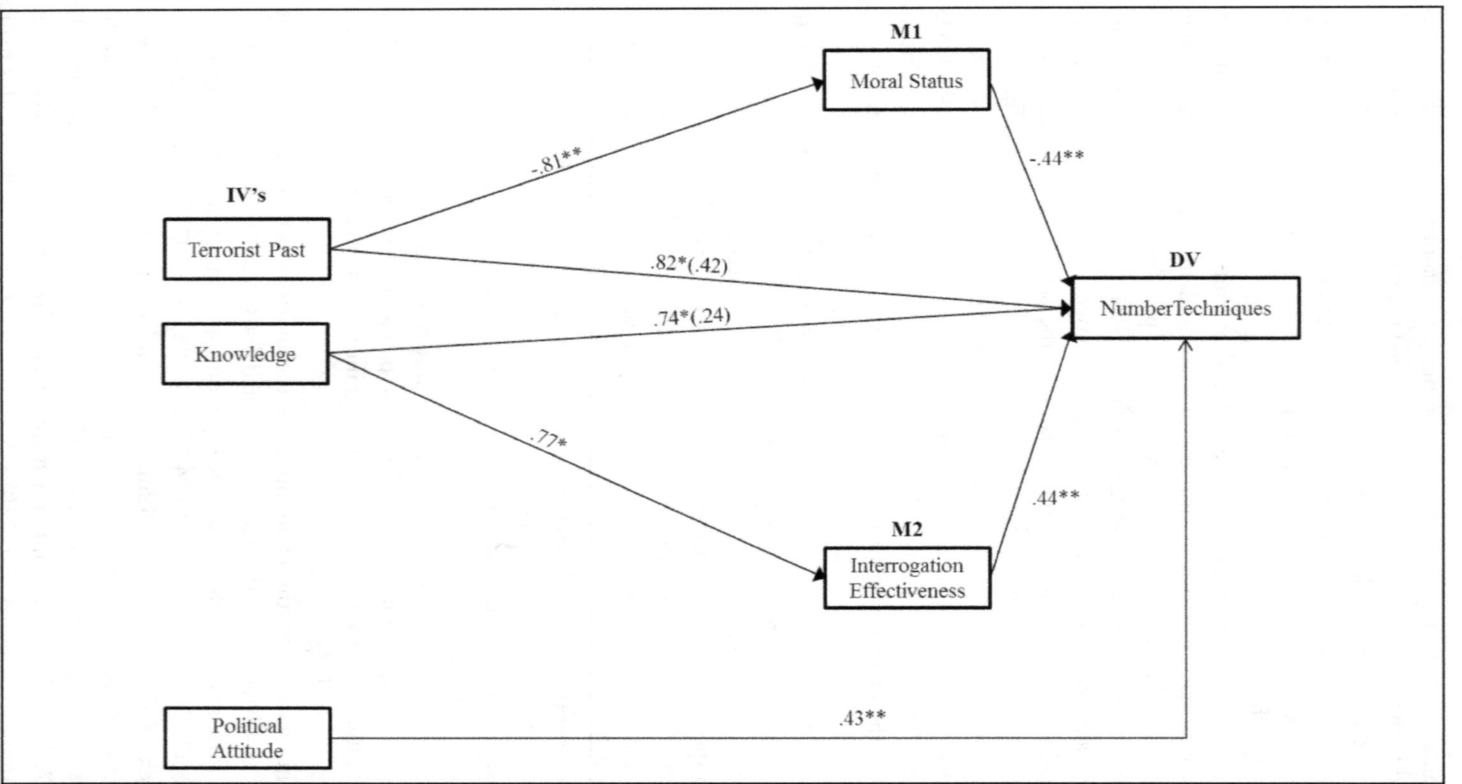

Figure 4.2 An aggregation of the effects of multiple mediation analyses for Terrorist Past and Knowledge on NumberTechniques (= number of accepted interrogation techniques of increasing severity) through Moral Status and Interrogation Effectiveness (with standardized path coefficients). * $p < .05$; ** $p < .001$

effect was qualified by an interaction effect between Group Membership and Terrorist Past for NumberTechniques, $F(1, 210) = 6.27, p < .05, \eta^2 = .03$. A post hoc analysis revealed that, in the case of an ingroup suspect, information about a terrorist past (as opposed to no such information) tends to lead participants to assume more readily that a suspect is in fact guilty, of lower moral status and a threat to the group's normative cohesion. As a result, participants try to protect the status of the ingroup by recommending a greater number of physically and psychologically stressful interrogation techniques with a higher average interrogation severity. If the suspect belongs to an outgroup, however, transgressions are more likely to be perceived as threats to the power and status of the group as a whole and not to the validity of ingroup norms or to the normative cohesion of the ingroup (Okimoto and Wenzel 2008; Wenzel et al. 2008). Thus, the suspect's terrorist past seems to be a less important factor in deciding on appropriate interrogation techniques.

In general, Fischer et al. (2013) confirmed the findings by Carlsmith and Sood (2009) insofar as they showed that utilitarian as well as retributive motives are at work when people decide how severely someone who is suspected of terrorism should be treated. Nevertheless, the Swiss sample seemed to be influenced mainly by utilitarian considerations, and retributive motives were less important *unless* the suspect was one of their own group. These findings differ from other research (Carlsmith and Darley 2008; Carlsmith and Sood 2009), which suggests that judgements about justice are broadly consistent with the principles of retributive justice. We may speculate that the varying degrees of importance of retributive motives in Switzerland and the United States are due to different legal systems (van Koppen 2009; Whitman 2003) and social attitudes towards punishment.

Retribution and the Problem of Extra-Legal Variables

Whenever we talk about the question of whether people want to punish norm-deviant behaviour out of utilitarian motives or retributive motives, we have to admit that there is nothing wrong with retributive or 'just deserts' considerations. This is at least true as long as 'just deserts' considerations clearly refer to the blameworthiness or culpability of the offender, like the severity of the intended harm or the number of previous convictions. However, retributive reactions in particular are quite often influenced by emotional outrage (Tetlock et al. 2007; Ask and Pina 2011) caused by, for example, very severe injury or damage, even if the injury or damage occurred entirely accidentally (Robbennolt 2006) or by the race, gender, reputation and socioeconomic status (SES) of the defendant or victim (Mazzocco, Alicke and Davis 2004). Vidmar (2002) provides a taxonomy of these influences, and calls them 'extra-legal' because they rest on prejudices that violate legal rules or ethical principles. His taxonomy differentiates between:

(a) interest prejudice (the judge or juror has a personal stake in the outcome of the trial); (b) case-specific prejudice, such as improperly obtained confessions or erroneous facts disseminated, for example, via mass media; (c) generic prejudice due, for example, to offender type (for example, child molesters), or the attractiveness, race or gender of the defendant or victim; and (d) conformity prejudice, such as pressure from the community, a prosecutor or the mass media. According to Two-Process Models (e.g., Tetlock et al. 2007), the first intuitive intention to punish will be influenced especially by social threat and variables of the offence, like the severity of injury to the victim or damage or the victim's reputation, even if the offender cannot be blamed for it (Figure 4.3). Such variables can also trigger a so-called 'prosecutorial mindset', which is a combination of anger, character attribution and the goal of retribution. However, this first intuitive judgement may be corrected in a second, revised judgement.

There is a vivid debate about the conditions concerning both the inhibition of automatic, intuitive processes and the post hoc correction of automatically triggered biases (Bodenhausen, Todd and Richeson 2009). Interestingly, empirical findings on the correction of judgement biases are not uniformly encouraging, even if people are motivated to do so. First, the conscious suppression of biasing thoughts may, somewhat incongruously, lead to undesired results, for example, the intensification of the thought that one wanted to suppress (Wegener et al. 2000). Second, individuals may not have a clear idea of what has caused their judgement (Bargh 1999) and may thus correct for the wrong bias on the wrong dimension, or undercorrect or even overcorrect their intuitive judgement (Wegener and Petty 1997).

Oswald and Stucki (2010) ran two experiments to test whether and how well individuals are able to correct for the influence of extra-legal variables – in the sense of false assumptions and prejudices – under rather optimal conditions (Study III). They manipulated the victim's reputation alone (Experiment 1), as well as the victim's reputation combined with the severity of outcomes that occurred accidentally and without the intention of the offender (Experiment 2). For the sake of simplicity, only Experiment 1 will be described in more detail here. Seventy-seven students (78 per cent female) were presented a crime vignette in which a victim had been assaulted. The victim's reputation (good vs. bad) was manipulated by varying the description. In one condition, the victim was a physician and was described as a nice person. In the other case, the victim was a small-time criminal. The processing depth (low vs. high) was manipulated along the dimensions of cognitive capacity, awareness and perceived accountability. Participants in the low processing depth condition had to solve a dual task (pressing the left key on the keyboard every time the letter K or a red letter appeared on the screen, and pressing the right key if any other letter appeared) while they were listening to the case with headphones. Those in the deep processing condition had no dual task to solve while listening to the case, and they were also informed that they would have to justify their final decision on punishment, and that their final statement would be videotaped. The main dependent variable was the punishment decision. Punishment was measured with five items, using a seven-point Likert rating scale (Cronbach's alpha: .80).[2]

The results showed a main effect of processing depth on punishment $F(1, 73) = 4.07$, $p <.05$, $\eta^2 = .05$. Recommended punishment was more severe if participants were in the low processing depth condition than in the high processing

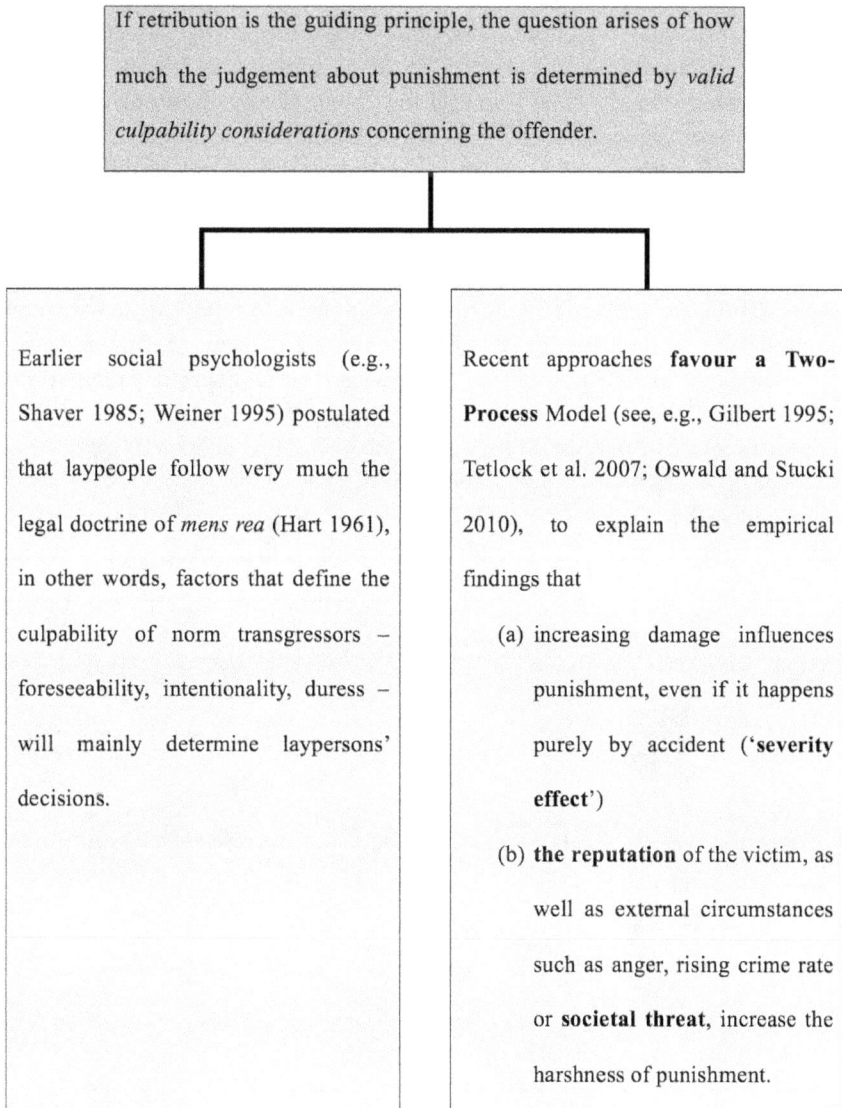

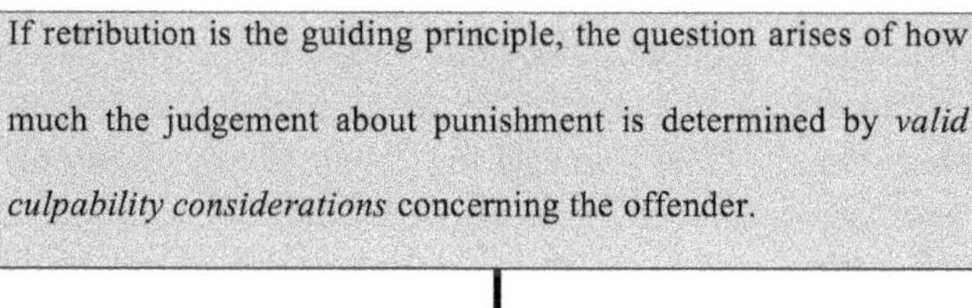

Earlier social psychologists (e.g., Shaver 1985; Weiner 1995) postulated that laypeople follow very much the legal doctrine of *mens rea* (Hart 1961), in other words, factors that define the culpability of norm transgressors – foreseeability, intentionality, duress – will mainly determine laypersons' decisions.

Recent approaches **favour a Two-Process** Model (see, e.g., Gilbert 1995; Tetlock et al. 2007; Oswald and Stucki 2010), to explain the empirical findings that

(a) increasing damage influences punishment, even if it happens purely by accident (**'severity effect'**)

(b) **the reputation** of the victim, as well as external circumstances such as anger, rising crime rate or **societal threat,** increase the harshness of punishment.

Figure 4.3 Overview of earlier and more recent culpability conceptions in social psychology

depth condition. However, more important was a significant interaction between the victim's reputation and processing depth $F(1, 73) = 8.30, p < .01, \eta^2 = .10$. Under conditions of low processing depth, a harsher punishment was recommended in the case of the 'good' victim than in the case of the 'bad' victim, whereas under conditions of high processing depth, a harsher punishment was recommended in the case of the 'bad' victim than in the case of the 'good' victim (Figure 4.4).

Thus, we can conclude that people are intuitively biased because they prefer a harsher punishment for an offender if the victim has a good rather than a bad reputation. However, this biasing preference can be changed if an opportunity to deliberate on the judgement is provided. In that case, however, it is not easy to explain why the condition enabling the higher depth of processing did not really have a de-biasing effect. What we actually found was a *reverse influence* rather than the *disappearance* of any influence of the extra-legal factor 'victim's reputation'. Interestingly, the punishment was not harsher for an offender who had attacked a small-time criminal, but was more lenient for an offender who had attacked a physician. Thus, participants in the high depth of processing condition seemed to be more concerned about punishing too harshly than about punishing too leniently. But why then do participants recommend even more lenient punishment if the victim had a good rather than a bad reputation? According to Wegener and Petty (1995, 1997), participants probably noticed the nature of the likely bias in their judgement, but had difficulties calibrating its magnitude, leading them to overcorrect their initial decision.

Results of both studies clearly confirm that the motivation to correct for the influence of extra-legal variables increases in general with the processing

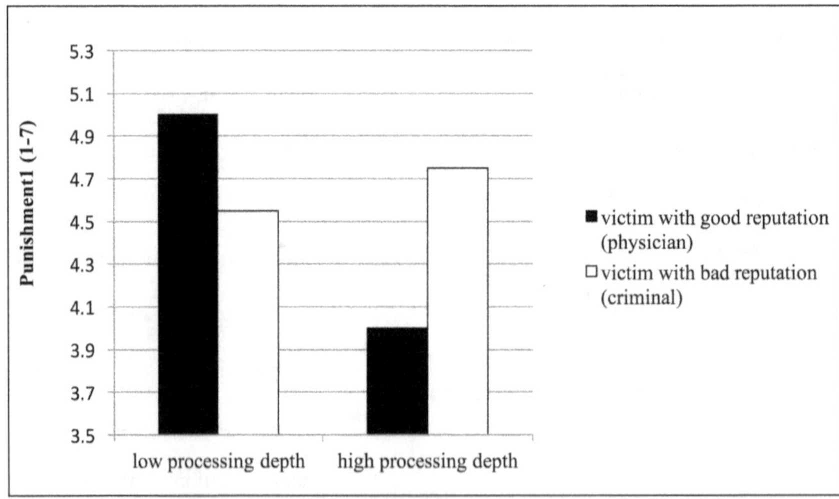

Figure 4.4 Mean punishment for an offender as a function of the victim's reputation and depth of information processing (Oswald and Stucki 2010)

depth. However, the corrections do not entirely comply with normative standards: they can either go too far, as in Experiment 1, or not far enough and even be partly erroneous, as in Experiment 2. Thus, instead of punishing offenders *equally severely* and independent of the victim's status in conditions of high processing depth, participants now punished the offender even more severely if she or he attacked a victim with a good rather than a bad reputation (see Experiment 2). Overcorrection or correction in the wrong direction may occur whenever participants lack a frame of reference for the appropriate amount of punishment to be meted out. Insufficient corrections may occur in cases where more than one extra-legal variable is apparent. Participants may then focus only on the most salient influence and may conclude their critical reasoning as soon as one correction is accomplished.

Let us finally ask whether some people are more motivated than others to correct their first, intuitive judgement according to their own moral standards. Several authors assume that it is mainly political attitudes such as conservatism or liberalism (see Carroll et al. 1987; Skitka and Bauman 2008) or right-wing authoritarianism (Feather 1996; Altemeyer 1998; Sibley, Wilson and Duckitt 2007) that influences the harshness of punishment. To date, Skitka et al. (2002) seem to be the only ones who have tested the question of whether the willingness of liberal people to be more prosocial than conservatives is an automatic/intuitive reaction or an effortful process of correcting for biases. However, they actually asked whether liberal people 'help more' and not whether they punish less. If we transform their results into our context of punishment, we would predict that under restricted cognitive capacity (for example, the presence of cognitive load), conservatives and liberals will have the same intuitive tendency to act as a prosecutor and that only if full cognitive capacity is at their disposal will liberals be more willing than conservatives to take into account external circumstances like excuses and justifications. This extrapolation has to be corroborated in future research.

Conclusion: Putting the Puzzle Together

The retributive motive seems to be the guiding principle of laypeople's punishment decisions, especially if the judgements have to be made under conditions of restricted cognitive capacity such as time pressure or multiple tasking. Utilitarian considerations such as deterrence or special prevention do play an additional role if people feel obliged to deliberate on and explain their judgements and if the offender is a member of the outgroup rather than the ingroup. The latter effect might possibly be more pronounced in countries with a continental European legal system than in those with an Anglo-American system. However, cultural differences in punishment decisions and their justification have to be investigated further.

Considerations of deservingness (retribution) are only problematic if they do not rely on valid proof of the culpability of the offender and if punishment is consequently not strictly guided by the degree of blameworthiness. Otherwise, retribution can hardly be separated from revenge or transgression. Unfortunately, deservingness considerations are error-prone, especially if there is neither the time nor the motivation to deliberate on the initial intuitive judgement. Many studies show a strong influence of such extra-legal variables on punishment as the victim's reputation, anger caused by independent sources, the severity of the damage (even if it was unintended and purely accidental) and several aspects of social threat. Self-correction for those extra-legal influences is possible, but depends on situational circumstances as well as political attitudes (for example, conservatism or liberalism). Situational circumstances not only include the motivation to elaborate on one's decision (for example, when one is held accountable for the decision), but also the availability of specific knowledge about when, where and how far the decision should be corrected. Otherwise the corrections could go astray.

Nevertheless, it seems worthwhile to think about whether an intuitive goal of retribution that is likely driven by emotions should be differentiated from a more reasoned goal of retribution that is reached via a process of deliberation. Such a differentiation could possibly disentangle existing confusion in the literature over what retribution really means.

Margit E. Oswald is Professor Emeritus of Social Psychology and Psychology and Law at the University of Bern, Switzerland. Her main research interests are rationality and biases of human information processing, treatment and punishment of deviancy by laypeople and professionals, aggression, social justice and conflict resolutions, and development of social stereotypes and prejudices. One of her main publications on punishment include (with S. Bieneck and J. Hupfeld-Heinemann) *The Social Psychology of Punishment of Crime* (Wiley-Blackwell, 2009).

Notes

1. Mediation analyses are employed to understand a known relationship by exploring the underlying mechanism or process by which one variable (X) influences another variable (Y). Thus, if the suspect's terrorist past (X) is thought to be the cause of interrogation severity (Y), we assume the presence of another psychological mechanism, the participant's perception of the moral status of the suspect (Z), that can explain how participants' different interrogation severities associated with suspect's terrorist past arise. Such a mechanism (Z) is called a mediator, the explicit inclusion of which should reduce the direct correlation between X and Y significantly.
2. The scale is named after its inventor, psychologist Rensis Likert, and is a psychometric scale commonly used in research that employs questionnaires. When responding to a

Likert questionnaire item, respondents specify their level of agreement or disagreement on a symmetric agree–disagree scale for a series of statements. Thus, the range captures the intensity of their feelings for a given item.

References

Altemeyer, B. 1998. 'The Other "Authoritarian Personality"', in M. Zanna (ed.), *Advances in Experimental Social Psychology*, vol. 30. San Diego: Academic Press, pp. 47–92.

Ask, K., and A. Pina. 2011. 'On Being Angry and Punitive: How Anger Alters Perception of Criminal Intent', *Social Psychology and Personality Science* 2(5): 494–99.

Bargh, J.A. 1999. 'The Cognitive Monster: The Case against the Controllability of Automatic Stereotype Effects', in S. Chaiken and Y. Trope (eds), *Dual-Process Theories in Social Psychology*. New York: Guilford Press, pp. 361–82.

Bodenhausen, G.V., A.R. Todd and J.A. Richeson. 2009. 'Controlling Prejudice and Stereotyping: Antecedents, Mechanisms, and Contexts', in T. Nelson (ed.), *Handbook of Prejudice, Stereotyping, and Discrimination*. New York: Psychology Press, pp. 111–35.

Boeckmann, R.J., and T.R. Tyler. 1997. 'Commonsense Justice and Inclusion within the Moral Community: When Do People Receive Procedural Protections from Others?', *Psychology, Public Policy and Law* 3: 362–80.

Carlsmith, K.M. 2006. 'The Roles of Retribution and Utility in Determining Punishment', *Journal of Experimental Social Psychology* 42: 437–51.

———. 2008. 'On Justifying Punishment: The Discrepancy between Words and Action', *Social Justice Research* 21: 119–37.

Carlsmith, K.M., and J.M. Darley. 2008. 'Psychological Aspects of Retributive Justice', *Advances in Experimental Social Psychology* 40: 193–236.

Carlsmith, K.M., J.M. Darley and P.H. Robinson. 2002. 'Why Do We Punish? Deterrence and Just Deserts as Motives for Punishment', *Journal of Personality and Social Psychology* 83: 284–99.

Carlsmith, K.M., and A.M. Sood. 2009. 'The Fine Line between Interrogation and Retribution', *Journal of Experimental Social Psychology* 45: 191–96.

Carroll, J., W. Perkowitz, A. Lurigio and K. Weaver. 1987. 'Sentencing Goals, Causal Attributions, and Personality', *Journal of Personality and Social Psychology* 52: 107–18.

Darley, J. 2002. 'Just Punishment: Research on Retributional Justice', in M. Ross and D.T. Miller (eds), *The Justice Motive in Everyday Life*. Cambridge: Cambridge University Press, pp. 314–33.

Darley, J.M., and D.M. Gromet. 2010. 'The Psychology of Punishment: Intuition and Reason, Retribution and Restoration', in D.R. Bobocel, A.C. Kay, M.P. Zanna and J.M. Olson (eds), *The Psychology of Justice and Legitimacy*. New York: Psychology Press, pp. 229–49.

Doble, J. 2002. 'Attitudes to Punishment in the US – Punitive and Liberal Opinions', in J.V. Roberts and M. Hough (eds), *Changing Attitudes to Punishment*. Cullompton: Willan, pp. 128–47.

Feather, N.T. 1996. 'Reactions to Penalties for an Offense in Relation to Authoritarianism, Values, Perceived Responsibility, Perceived Seriousness, and Deservingness', *Journal of Personality and Social Psychology* 71(3): 571–87.

Fischer, A., M.E. Oswald and S. Seiler. 2013. 'Terrorists among Us: Effects of a Suspect's Group Membership, Terrorist Past and Knowledge on Lay Persons' Interrogation Severity Recommendations', *Swiss Journal of Psychology* 72(1): 13–23.

Gilbert, D.T. 1995. 'Attribution and Interpersonal Perception', in A. Tesser (ed.), *Advanced Social Psychology*. New York: McGraw-Hill, pp. 99–147.

Gollwitzer, M., and L. Keller. 2010. 'What You Did Only Matters if You are One of Us: Offender's Group Membership Moderates the Effect of Criminal History on Punishment Severity', *Social Psychology* 41(1): 20–26.

Hart, H.L.A. 1961. 'Negligence, Mens Rea and Criminal Responsibility', in A.G. Guest (ed.), *Oxford Essay in Jurisprudence: A Collaborative Work*. New York: Oxford University Press, pp. 29–49.

Hogan, R., and N.P. Emler. 1981. 'Retributive Justice', in M.J. Lerner and S.C. Lerner (eds), *The Justice Motive in Social Behavior*. New York: Plenum Press, pp. 125–43.

Jacoby, J., J. Jaccard, A. Kuss, T. Troutman and D. Mazursky. 1987. 'New Directions in Behavioral Process Research: Implications for Social Psychology', *Journal of Experimental Social Psychology* 23: 146–75.

Keller, L.B., M.E. Oswald, I. Stucki and M. Gollwitzer. 2010. 'A Closer Look at an Eye for an Eye: Laypersons' Punishment Decisions are Primarily Driven by Retributive Motives', *Social Justice Research* 23(2–3): 99–116.

Mazzocco, P.J., M.D. Alicke and T.L. Davis. 2004. 'On the Robustness of Outcome Bias: No Constraint by Prior Culpability', *Basic and Applied Social Psychology* 26: 131–46.

Okimoto, T.G., and M. Wenzel. 2008. 'The Symbolic Meaning of Transgressions: Toward a Unifying Framework of Justice Restoration', in K.A. Hegtvedt and J. Clay-Warner (eds), *Advances in Group Processes: Justice* vol. 25. Oxford: Elsevier, pp. 291–326.

Oswald, M.E., J. Hupfeld, S.C. Klug and U. Gabriel. 2002. 'Lay-Perspectives on Criminal Deviance, Goals of Punishment, and Punitivity', *Social Justice Research* 15: 85–98.

Oswald, M.E., and I. Stucki. 2010. 'Automatic Judgment and Reasoning about Punishment', *Social Justice Research* 23(4): 290–307.

Preacher, K.J., and A.F. Hayes. 2008. 'Contemporary Approaches to Assessing Mediation in Communication Research', in A.F. Hayes, M.D. Slater and L.B. Snyder (eds), *The Sage Sourcebook of Advanced Data Analysis Methods for Communication Research*. Thousand Oaks, CA: Sage, pp. 13–54.

Robbennolt, J.K. 2006. 'Outcome Severity and Judgments of "Responsibility": A Meta-analytic Review', *Journal of Applied Social Psychology* 30: 2575–609.

Robinson, P.H., and J.M. Darley. 2004. 'Does Criminal Law Deter? A Behavioural Science Investigation', *Oxford Journal of Legal Studies* 24: 173–205.

Shaver, K.G. 1985. *The Attribution of Blame*. New York: Springer.

Sibley, C.G., M.S. Wilson and J. Duckitt. 2007. 'Effects of Dangerous and Competitive Worldviews on Right-Wing Authoritarianism and Social Dominance Orientation over a Five-Month Period', *Political Psychology* 28(3): 357–71.

Skitka, L., and C.W. Bauman. 2008. 'Moral Conviction and Political Engagement', *Political Psychology* 29(1): 29–54.

Skitka, L.J., E. Mullen, T. Griffin, S. Hutchinson and B. Chamberlin. 2002. 'Dispositions, Scripts, or Motivated Correction? Understanding Ideological Differences in Explanations for Social Problems', *Journal of Personality and Social Psychology* 83(2): 470–97.

Stalans, L.J. 1993. 'Citizens' Crime Stereotypes, Biased Recall, and Punishment Preferences in Abstract Cases: The Educative Role of Interpersonal Sources', *Law and Human Behavior* 17(4): 451–70.

———. 2009. 'Measuring Attitudes Towards Sentencing and Sentencing Goals', in M.E. Oswald, S. Bieneck and J. Hupfeld-Heinemann (eds), *Social Psychology of Punishment of Crime*. Chichester: Wiley, pp. 231–54.

Tetlock, P.E., P.S. Visser, R. Singh, M. Polifroni, A. Scott, B. Elson and P. Mazzocco. 2007. 'Alleged Biases and Errors in Attribution of Responsibility: Defensive Intuitive Scientists or Prudent Intuitive Prosecutors?', *Journal of Experimental Social Psychology* 43: 195–209.

Tyler, T.R., R.J. Boeckmann, H.J. Smith and Y.J. Huo. 1997. *Social Justice in a Diverse Society*. Boulder, CO: Westview Press.

Van Koppen, P.J. 2009. 'The Diversity of Nations and Legal Systems – Contrasting the Dutch and the Americans', in M.E. Oswald, S. Bieneck and J. Hupfeld-Heinemann (eds), *Social Psychology of Punishment of Crime*. Chichester: Wiley, pp. 3–19.

Vidmar, N. 2002. 'Retributive Justice: Its Social Context', in D.T. Miller and M. Ross (eds), *The Justice Motive in Everyday Life*. New York: Cambridge University Press, pp. 291–313.

Wegener, D.T., and R.E. Petty. 1995. 'Flexible Correction Processes in Social Judgment: The Role of Naive Theories in Corrections for Perceived Bias', *Journal of Personality and Social Psychology* 68: 36–51.

———. 1997. 'The Flexible Correction Model: The Role of Naive Theories of Bias in Bias Correction', *Advances in Experimental Social Psychology* 29: 141–208.

Wegener, D.T., N.L. Kerr, M.A. Fleming and R.E. Petty. 2000. 'Flexible Corrections of Juror Judgments: Implications for Jury Instructions', *Psychology, Public Policy, and Law* 6(3): 629–54.

Weiner, B. 1995. *Judgments of Responsibility: A Foundation for a Theory of Social Conduct.* New York, London: Guilford Press.

Wenzel, M., T.G. Okimoto, N.T. Feather and M.J. Platow. 2008. 'Retributive and Restorative Justice', *Law and Human Behavior* 32: 375–89.

Whitman, James Q. 2003. *Harsh Justice: Criminal Punishment and the Widening Divide between America and Europe*. New York: Oxford University Press.

Windzio, M., and M. Kleimann. 2009. 'Criminal Society and Criminal Immigrants: A Social Construction of Reality by Mass Media?', in M.E. Oswald, S. Bieneck and J. Hupfeld-Heinemann (eds), *Social Psychology of Punishment of Crime*. Chichester: Wiley, pp. 93–112.

Section III

Retaliation and Punishment

Encounter of Formal and Informal Normativities

Chapter 5

Violent Crimes and Retaliation in the European Criminal Justice System between the Seventeenth and Nineteenth Centuries

Karl Härter

Introduction

Early modern courts dealing with violent crimes constitute an exemplary field to study historical changes in the function and significance of retaliation as a measured reaction to criminal behaviour. The burgeoning research on the history of violence and criminal justice has produced a range of case studies covering many European countries, namely the Holy Roman Empire of the German Nation (mostly specific territorial states and imperial cities), the Netherlands, the Swiss Confederation, France, England, Italy and Spain.[1] Drawing on these recent studies on violence in early modern Europe and exemplary court records – in particular from the criminal high court of the German territorial state of Kurmainz[2] – this chapter analyses the significance and the different functions of retaliation in the legal practice of European criminal justice systems that were mainly based on European common law: the *ius commune*.[3] The survey focuses on the eighteenth and nineteenth centuries – the so-called *Sattelzeit* (c. 1750–1850) – to analyse changes in the concept and function of retaliation as a pivotal purpose of criminal justice and punishment in response to violent behaviour that was regarded (or conceptualized) as a crime.

In pre-modern times, it was socially acceptable for individuals to respond to violations of honour, body and property with appropriate violence; violent assaults could also be compensated for with material recompense. Penal justice also partially pursued the purpose of retaliation in the sense of retribution, as is evidenced by the fact that criminal courts punished manslaughter or murder with the death penalty. The ambivalent nature of retaliation with regard to violence became even more pronounced with the emergence of a public[4] criminal justice system in most countries of continental Europe from the sixteenth century onwards. It was based on comprehensive criminal codes, inquisitorial criminal procedure (the *Offizial- und Instruktionsmaxime* – the principles of public prosecution of crimes, the investigation of substantive facts and the establishment of objective truth), new penalties (such as the prison workhouse and forced labour) and the central concepts of security and 'good order' (*gute Policey*). As a consequence, a new system of state-based formal punitive control emerged, and criminal justice pursued more and more utilitarian purposes, and punished violent crimes in order to maintain social control or to 'discipline' and 'civilize' perpetrators.[5]

Many studies in the history of crime and violence agree that public criminal justice, based on a monopoly on power and legitimate force, ultimately achieved a decline in violent crimes – notably homicide. This was accompanied by a reduction in violent retributive corporal and capital punishment starting in the eighteenth century, thereby resulting in the elimination of retaliation as an element of the criminal justice system.[6] However, the overview presented here does not take that assumption at face value: retaliation as a measured reaction to violence[7] did not totally vanish; private compensation and conflict settlement persisted to a certain degree and influenced court decisions as well as legal practice. It will be argued that the function of retaliation and the relations between the different actors shifted from private compensation (between perpetrators and victims) to material public recompense ('public compensation') and punitive damages ('private punishment' – *Privatstrafe*) as an amalgamation of private and public retaliation that served the interests of the state: fiscal recompense, the juridification (*Verrechtlichung*) of vindicatory violence and private retaliation, and the extension of social control through the criminal justice system. Hence, the main objective of this chapter is to demonstrate that private and legal retaliation to violence significantly changed from legitimate vindicatory violence, private compensation and retributive public punishment to a system of formal social control and public retaliation that prevented violence, but preferred public compensation at the expense of the interests of victims. In the final analysis, the criminal history of violence and retaliation may demonstrate that the concept of retaliation was and still is a pivotal element of the justice system, closely related to and intermingled with mediation and punishment.

Violence and Violent Crimes: Long-Term Developments and Models

Historical research has stressed the dominant role of interpersonal male violence within in the pre-modern European society of orders (*vormoderne Ständegesellschaft*), resulting in violent crimes such as assault, battery, manslaughter and murder. Physical injury was often coupled with verbal insults, intimidation and the violation of honour. In the pre-modern period, many manifestations of violence can be characterized as affective and irrational (notably domestic and sexual violence), but also implied more or less rational elements: material benefits, defending or elevating someone's honour, or vindication. Thus, violence can be characterized as a ubiquitous resource used frequently in private conflicts, as well as a legal means used by the state and nonstate actors. Even the parties involved in private conflicts could exercise legitimate or legal violent actions such as feuding or retorsion (legitimate retribution)[8] to deal with conflicts and to assert claims and interests.[9]

All in all, the social ubiquity and importance of violence resulted in a considerable amount of violent crime (or the behaviour that was defined and labelled as such), and homicide in particular, with an annual average of 35 homicides per 100,000 inhabitants in Europe in the late Middle Ages.[10] Recent studies discern a significant decline in the rate of homicide calculated in relation to the population as well as to other crimes (notably property crimes) in Europe from the sixteenth century onwards, especially between the eighteenth and nineteenth centuries (Spierenburg 2008). The digression of violence was interpreted as the civilizing of violent crime, the disciplining of affective, irrational violent behaviour and a shift from 'violence to theft', related to historical changes such as the shift from a feudal to a bourgeois society, the emergence of a state-based criminal justice and penal system, and the implementation of the public monopoly on the legitimate use of violence and state-based penal power (*staatliches Gewaltmonopol*) (Johnson and Monkkonen 1996; Mantecón 2007; Spierenburg 2011). However, a direct correlation between property crimes and violent crimes was largely rejected due to insufficient empirical evidence, and some authors have also questioned the overemphasis on homicide as the principal (and only) indicator of the level of interpersonal violence. They have argued that the decline in homicide could result, for instance, from improved medical care that reduced the lethality of assaults or from a shift from interpersonal to collective or state violence, and, as such, indicates a change in the expression or form of violence more than it does a civilizing of violence (Lindenberger and Lüdtke 1995; Dinges 1998; Schwerhoff 2002, 2004).

Moreover, violent crimes below the threshold of homicide are not thoroughly researched and remain within a grey area. Only recently has research produced some evidence that in the eighteenth and nineteenth centuries, interpersonal violence manifested in crimes such as battery and assault remained frequent and intense, but was prosecuted and punished differently (King 1996; Lacour 2000). It is remarkable that the developments are quite inverse to the homicide rate: violent crimes such as assault and battery were prosecuted and punished more frequently in the nineteenth century than in the eighteenth century, as a study of England shows. Peter King observes an increase in the number of indictments and verdicts, as well as an aggravation of punishment from fines to imprisonment (King 2000, 2003). In addition, some studies indicate that homicide was punished more harshly starting in the sixteenth century and that the practice of pardoning declined in the eighteenth century as well.[11]

Though the effectiveness and even the existence of the 'civilizing of violence' is still questioned, many studies recognize the importance of the criminal justice system and legal responses to violent crime to the analysis of the changes in patterns of violence between the early modern period and the nineteenth century. However, neither the legal history of penal law (*Strafrechtsgeschichte*) nor the history of crime (*Historische Kriminalitätsforschung*) paid much attention to the complex interdependencies between retaliation and violence within the framework of the criminal justice system, which – in my opinion – are crucial to understanding the ambivalent historical developments of violence and the legal responses to violent crimes in early modern Europe (Schlee and Turner 2008). I will argue that the changing and ambivalent legal responses to violence cannot only be attributed to the 'process of civilization' or the 'humanization of punishment', but are also related to the legal practice of 'retaliation': on the one hand, the early modern authorities and states criminalized vindicatory violence and private means of legitimate violence such as feuding, duelling and retorsion; on the other hand, they integrated patterns of social or private retaliation and compensation into the criminal justice system.

Functions of Retaliation in the Early Modern Criminal Justice System

In the following, I use a broader historical concept of retaliation, which can be defined as a measured reaction – a repayment in kind – based on religious, social or legal rules and principles such as reciprocity, equality, adequacy and the principle of talion or the *lex talionis*. 'Retaliation' was used by a variety of actors (including the state) to react to different kinds of conflicts – notably violent ones – to achieve various purposes such as 'getting even', restoring or achieving a balance, gaining satisfaction or securing restitution via compensation or punishment (Miller 2006; see also Günther 1889–95). With regard to the patterns of violence and the legal responses to violent crime, we can categorize the different functions of retaliation in early modern Europe in the following way:[12]

- as a violent practice that can be characterized as vengeance and revenge, often lethal, but somewhat measured in accordance with the initial conflict and damage (Nassiet 2007, 2008; Boehm 2011);[13]
- as a legitimate (and sometimes 'legal') practice such as feuding, duelling or retorsion, which followed rules and rituals, but included vindicatory violence to assert legitimate claims or titles;[14]

- as a social and legal practice of engaging in conflict and conflict resolution that aimed at the compensation of material damage and injury, redress, restitution (financial as well as honour-related) and the re-establishment of peace by means of money (*Wergeld*), compromise agreements and treaties (*Sühne- und Vergleichsverträge, transactio*), punitive damages (*Strafschadenersatz*) or public religious rituals (requiem, penance, pilgrimage);[15]
- as a religious concept that provided penance that could substitute for retaliatory punishment, but on the other hand emphasized the wrath of God as retaliatory punishment for deviant behaviour;
- as public retributive punishment, notably manifested in capital and corporal penalties mirroring the crime;
- as public retaliation that could include private compensation between perpetrators and victims as well as social sanctions.

Altogether retaliation constituted a pivotal purpose of early modern European criminal law as part of the *ius commune*, which entailed ambiguous norms, functions and means, ranging from retributive public punishment and public compensation to private sanctions and compensation.[16] In short, retaliation indicates measured legal, social and/or economic relations to different actors and elements of the early modern criminal justice system, including the crime, the culprit/perpetrator (and his or her family and kin), the victim (and his or her family and kin), the legally protected interests (*Rechtsgüter*) comprising rights, goods, bodies, honour, order or security, and the interests of other third-party actors such as authorities, rulers, mediators, jurists, lawyers, communities and so on. As a result, the early modern criminal justice systems in Europe used different means of measured reciprocal action to implement or achieve retaliation, ranging from harsh capital punishment and a variety of public penalties to pardoning, compensation and private sanctions.

These different functions and means of retaliation most notably shaped the ambiguous responses of the European criminal justice systems to violence and influenced criminal legislation, court practice and punishment. Concerning early modern criminal law, we can observe the criminalization of violent behaviour and the differentiation of violent crimes, in the long run resulting in a (by no means coherent) normative system of violent crimes (as defined and conceptualized by the European *ius commune*), notably:

- homicide, comprising premeditated murder, manslaughter and accidental homicide (*homicidium qualificatum* and *homicidium simplex*), as well as atrocities such as familicide, regicide and suicide;[17]
- property-related violent crimes, especially robbery, murder with robbery (*Raubmord*) and church robbery (*Kirchenraub*), often committed by (or ascribed to) so-called robber bands and gangs (Ortalli 1986; Rousseaux 1989; Härter 2005: Chapter 9);
- furtive crimes such as arson, poisoning and witchcraft;

- collective, popular and political violence such as riots and breach of peace (*Landfriedensbruch*), as well as feuding and duelling;[18]
- infanticide, abortion, rape and other sex-related violent crimes, including husband–wife homicide;[19]
- interpersonal physical violence such as assault, battery and brawls (*Schlägerei, Raufhändel*), further classified as physically severe and less serious injuries (bleeding and non-bleeding wounds).[20]

From the late sixteenth century onwards, we can observe an increasing criminalization and penalization of deviant violent behaviour, particularly concerning manslaughter, which was criminalized as a serious crime that should be punished, like murder, with the death penalty (Pohl 1999; Spierenburg 2008). Likewise, penal laws and *ius commune* defined physical injuries, assault and battery as public crimes, established the obligation of the authorities/states to prosecute and punish such crimes via inquisitorial procedure, and threatened serious punishment. Thus, retaliation in such cases was no longer a private matter of civil litigation only.[21] Moreover, penal law criminalized different modes of previously legitimate violent retaliation such as the feud and the duel. However, the enforcement of such laws remained deficient (notably as regards duelling), and different forms of more or less legitimate violent retaliation continued into the eighteenth and even the nineteenth centuries.[22]

On the whole, early modern penal law prioritized capital and corporal punishment as the retributive answer to violent crimes. While laws and legal discourses stressed harsh bloody retaliation via penalties that mirrored the crime, they also developed concepts such as simple or accidental homicide, diminished responsibility, vindication (against an assault) and self-defence, all of which allowed greater flexibility in sentencing and meting out punishment.

In most early modern European countries, such violent crimes were dealt with by higher and lower/local criminal courts and judicial authorities. Cases of verbal abuse and less serious physical injury and interpersonal physical violence were often dealt with by lower courts and local authorities, for which public punishment formed only one option and whose decisions mostly aimed at private compensation and maintenance of the peace (Rummel 1993; Frank 1995; Thauer 2001). Nevertheless, the state-based higher criminal courts staffed with professional jurists seized jurisdiction over serious violent crimes and over the course of the early modern period increasingly expanded their judicial powers to include all kinds of violent crimes. However, lower courts operated by intermediary powers to a certain degree maintained jurisdiction or participation in cases of less serious violent crimes. Moreover, in their judicial practice, higher criminal courts adopted certain modes and purposes of social or private retaliation and compensation.

Violent Crimes, Punishment and Retaliation in Judicial Practice

The decision making and punishment of early modern criminal justice concerning violent crimes and retaliation exhibited a certain ambivalence.[23] First of all, premeditated murder and atrocities, as well as the death penalty, remained an exception. Only in the case of infanticide do some studies discern an increase in capital punishment, which, however, was followed by a more or less rapid decrease in the second half of the eighteenth century induced by the debates and reforms of 'enlightened absolutism' (Jackson 2002). Although courts could also impose capital punishment for homicide (manslaughter), the majority of convicts were able to negotiate a mitigation of punishment or obtain a pardon. Concerning assaults, battery and brawls, courts can be characterized as hesitant or reluctant to mete out (severe) public punishment. The high courts – and more so the lower or local courts – of many countries preferred conflict settlement, maintenance of the peace and compensation as the model (or means) of retaliation and achieving the purposes of criminal justice.[24]

Only in response to violent property crimes – notably robbery – committed by marginal groups and 'dangerous classes' (vagabonds and vagrants, strangers, Gypsies, Jews, bandits, gangs) did most criminal courts mete out exemplary harsh and 'socially two-tracked' capital punishment, which mirrored the deed and aimed at both general deterrence and bloody retribution as one pattern of public retaliation.[25] For example, in most cases of violent property crimes between 1650 and 1800, the Criminal High Court of the Electorate of Mainz convicted members of marginal groups and meted out harsh punishment to them – more than 80 per cent of the death penalties concerned violent property crimes and delinquents who belonged to marginal groups (or were labelled as such) (Härter 2005: 1080–1122).

In contrast, homicide, manslaughter and assault were punished more leniently. Planned premeditated murder was very hard to prove, and many judicial authorities in Europe tended to leniently punish common homicide or manslaughter committed by regular male subjects[26] who were defending their honour or who acted unintentionally, or permitted them the option of supplication and pardon. Serious or lethal violent crimes were often adjudicated as simple or accidental homicide and were therefore punished with extraordinary penalties (the so-called *poena extraordinaria*, a penalty that was not explicitly prescribed in penal law) ranging from banishment to imprisonment to fines. In addition, the courts sometimes included a private settlement or compensation in the decision. Although up to the eighteenth century homicide and other serious violent crimes formed the majority of criminal cases, 'the authorities did not see the punishment of interpersonal violence as one of their central tasks', concludes Smith (2008: 209) with regard to the English example. Many case studies on the judicial practice of criminal courts in other European countries and Central

European territories and cities have produced corresponding results and often observe that criminal courts adjudicating violent crimes in the eighteenth and even in the nineteenth century still referred to traditional patterns of private retaliation. Courts accepted supplications and other modes of negotiating compensation and punishment, and often mitigated penalties or even abandoned the trial or pardoned perpetrators of violence if they compensated victims or if an infrajudicial settlement was achieved.[27]

With regard to eighteenth-century England, Shoemaker mentions the following example: 'When complaints of assault were brought to Justice Henry Norris of Hackney … his main concern was to settle them informally, typically with apologies or the payment of damages.' Shoemaker concludes that 'the main purpose of going to law was to facilitate informal agreements between the parties concerned' (2004: 218).[28] Using the example of Central European cities, Eibach has shown that even in the eighteenth century, conflicting parties went to the courts to get compensation and ask for 'satisfaction'. The city courts not only accepted extrajudicial settlements, but aimed to settle violent conflicts by imposing monetary compensation and rarely punished violence in neighbourhoods or the domestic sphere with harsh penalties (Eibach 2008: 65–67). Similar patterns can be found in France. In 1790, a French court formally recognized the infrajudicial settlement of a violent interpersonal conflict through a mediator, and in the long run 'infrajudicial resolution of disputes not only survived but became institutionalised' in the French justice system (Ruff 2008: 45–46).[29] Still during the nineteenth century, the court of the Canton of Zurich negotiated and imposed compensatory damages in cases of violent sexual crimes such as rape, and mitigated punishment if a sufficient material compensation was achieved and the honour of victims and families was restored, even accepting the offer of a rapist to marry his victim (Loetz 2012: 138–40, 176–78).

In cases of interpersonal violence ranging from manslaughter to assault and battery, the Criminal High Court of Mainz, for example, often mitigated or even waived harsh penalties – and therefore public retaliation – and included into its decisions a so-called private compensation (*Privatsatisfaktion*), which was also considered a part of public punishment. To adjudicate punishment and appropriate retaliation in such cases, the court (that is, the jurists who conceived the legal opinion or legal counsel and the elector, who could approve and modify the proposed verdict) evaluated, calculated and measured the violent actions, the circumstances and the damages, as well as the motives and the social status of perpetrators and victims. Based on the variety of legal arguments that the *ius commune* provided, and taking into consideration social arguments and utilitarian purposes, the court considered in detail many aspects of retaliation and violence, such as who started the brawl, whether both the aggressor and the victim used violence or caused a violent reaction through verbal injuries that infringed the honour of a person, and whether the violent action could be 'measured' and 'reckoned up' (regarding the damage, the wounds, the intent and so on). This included the consideration of whether a violent action could be legally classified as appropriate, reciprocal or retaliatory, and therefore could be subsumed under the so-called right of retorsion (Beling 1894), or as self-defence concerning life and limb or the honour of a person or family. Of crucial importance was the evaluation of the intentions and motives of a perpetrator to harm or kill, and whether he or she had committed the violent crime intentionally or involuntarily. Moreover, social factors and 'special prevention' played a role; courts and authorities particularly considered whether it was appropriate to classify a perpetrator as a 'useful' and 'regular' subject (*nützlicher Untertan*) who consequently could be disciplined via arbitrary noncapital penalties such as prison workhouse (*Zuchthaus*), forced labour, imprisonment or fines.

Though the Criminal High Court of Mainz adjudicated according to the infringement of penal law and the public order, the actual decision also took into account the damage caused by perpetrators or suffered by victims (concerning body and/or honour), the nature and amount of satisfaction and compensation, the medical costs, the consequential costs of an inability to work and the costs of the procedure, as well as the potential disciplining of a perpetrator (Härter 2003, 2005).

To achieve public as well as private retaliation in violent crimes (with the exception of robbery and infanticide), many criminal courts in Europe used a variety of legal options and means of compensation and control, and included them in public punishment. For example, the sentence could compel a delinquent to swear an oath that intentional damage had not been the intrinsic purpose of violent action (*juramentum de non offendo; Eid, daß nichts Schädliches beabsichtigt war*). This oath should also prevent future retaliatory violence (vengeance). In cases of less serious injury, perpetrators had to formally apologize to the victim in public (*öffentliche Abbitte*), sometimes coupled with the ritual of handshaking and public amends to make a statement of honour (*Ehrenerklärung*). Criminal courts also determined the amount of money for private compensation; in such cases, the verdict preceded the civil decision. From this perspective, (inquisitorial) criminal procedure could be more favourable for conflicting parties than litigation in civil courts, to which perpetrators and victims sometimes resorted. If the court adjudicated violent actions and damages as reciprocal and equivalent or based on the right of retorsion, the crimes could annul or compensate each other and the court would waive the legally stated punishment, impose a lenient *poena extradordinaria* (often a fine) or consider material compensation as the punishment. Fines and material compensation formed the base for a hybrid concept of retaliation and punishment: the so-called private punishment (*peine privée* or *Privatstrafe*) or punitive damages (*Strafschadenersatz*).[30] This approach not only built upon traditional concepts of 'private satisfaction' (*Kompensation/Komposition*) such as the *Wergeld* and incorporated private redress and compensation for victims, but also took public fiscal interests into account. To enforce such decisions, some courts threatened an aggravation of punishment if the convict did not comply or did not behave in a peaceful manner from that time forward. Early modern English courts frequently used so-called recognizances as a means to keep the peace and to secure the future disciplined behaviour of perpetrators (Smith 2008: 205). Moreover, during the procedure and after the verdict, both convicts and victims had the opportunity to supplicate and to negotiate punishment, retaliation, pardon or letters of remission. The courts also used this to urge opponents to conclude private settlements and offered the mitigation or even the waiving of punishment, especially if it was presumable that future vindicatory violence could be prevented and public order could be restored.[31]

Contemporary jurists of the *ius commune* discussed these ambiguous legal practices of private and public retaliation within the criminal justice system under the title of public composition (*herrschaftliche oder fiskalische Composition oder Vergleichung*) and private punishment/punitive damages (*Privatstrafe/Strafschadenersatz*), which admittedly did not fully conform to the *ius commune*, but nevertheless were frequently used in court practice.[32] In this regard, the state-based criminal justice system offered an opportunity for private retaliation within the framework of inquisitorial procedure and public punishment. The early modern state, on the other hand, transferred the concept of private compensation to the public sphere, claiming that violent crimes were also an infringement on the public order or the public weal (*Wohlfahrt*), which could be compensated through a regress in (charitable) payment or community service instead of regular public punishment. This flexible system of private and public retaliation suited the utilitarian purposes and fiscal interests of the state, which could at last extend the functions of the criminal justice system to the social control of violence (Schwerhoff 2004; Smith 2008).

In the eighteenth century, the option of retaliation and compensation via criminal justice was used more frequently in cases of assault, battery, brawls and less serious injuries because the criminal justice system provided private compensation and a more advantageous conflict regulation. This allowed the state to extend the penalization of violent crimes below the threshold of homicide. Moreover, with the Enlightenment and the emerging civil society (*bürgerliche Gesellschaft*), the perception of violence started to change slowly, especially among the elites. The elites used less interpersonal violence to solve conflicts and developed a sort of disgust towards affective, irrational and uncontrolled violence, especially of the lower classes. The changing attitudes influenced legal discourse, legislation (we can observe an increase in ordinances dealing with assault, brawling, weapons and prevention) and penal practice as well.[33]

Many studies observe an intensification of the prosecution and public punishment of violent crimes such as assault and battery, and a concomitant decrease in pardoning and mitigation concerning homicide, starting in the last decades of the eighteenth century. Notably, the courts meted out harsher public punishment if the opponents did not resort to compensation or if the perpetrators were perceived as savage, disorderly or habitual offenders who used violence not to defend themselves, but for base motives and with an antisocial effect, or violated the 'good order' and the public weal. In addition, the shape of public retaliation and punishment changed. In cases of assault and even manslaughter, 'modern' penalties such as imprisonment and forced labour were used more frequently, and the courts no longer accepted vindicatory violence, passion, anger, rage or inebriety as mitigating circumstances. In this regard, the criminal justice system augmented the purposes of punishment, aiming at the disciplining and policing of interpersonal violence, especially of the lower classes, and also intending the deterrence of crime among the middle classes and the elite. On the one hand, this resulted in a more or less stable low homicide rate, often interpreted as the 'civilization of violence'; on the other hand, it led to an increase in the rate of less serious violent crimes such as assault and battery (Johnson and Monkkonen 1996; Eisner 2001a; Spierenburg 2008, 2011).

Conclusion: Changes and Continuities in Violence and Retaliation

All in all, since the end of the eighteenth century we can observe contradictory changes in the adjudication of violent crimes and the intertwined concepts of retaliation and punishment. Many states reduced public retaliation through exemplary retributive capital punishment for violent property crimes (robbery with murder), especially if committed by vagrants and bandits, and for violent political crimes such as assassination. In this regard, the criminal justice system reduced retributive violence – notably torture, corporal punishment and the death penalty. However, in the nineteenth (and even the twentieth) century, the death penalty remained an option of the criminal justice system to retaliate against violent crimes, justified on the concept of exemplary mirroring punishment and prosecution, while criminal procedure and imprisonment still used forms of violence to control and discipline perpetrators and delinquents (Evans 1996; Martschukat 2006; Härter 2011). Nevertheless, since the second half of the eighteenth century and more so in the nineteenth century, homicide and more serious interpersonal violence were increasingly punished with imprisonment, prison workhouse, forced labour and other non-bloody penalties that aimed at disciplining and 'betterment', especially of violent men who belonged to the lower classes. These, in fact, can be seen as more lenient punishments when compared to the harsh penalties of the early modern penal codes, and they concur with the decline in the homicide rate and the decrease in vindicatory violence and vengeance.[34]

However, these changes were based on an intensification of the prosecution and punishment of violent crimes below the threshold of homicide, and they indicate the expansion of the disciplining and policing of violence via the criminal justice system. These developments still may fit well into the model of the civilizing of violence, the humanization of retributive punishment and the establishment of a state-based monopoly on violence (or power), but they were nonetheless accompanied by the persistence of early modern patterns of retaliation (Härter 2008). Though former legitimate practices of violent retaliation such as feuding and duelling had been criminalized, in the nineteenth century elites and other social groups still resorted to vindicatory violence – notably the duel.[35] Moreover, the criminal justice system still provided options for dealing with vindicatory violence and violent conflicts among elites and citizens that were not only based on public punishment, but also utilized lenient non-public penalties such as fines as well as private compensation, private punishment and punitive damages, particularly in cases of less serious violent crimes.[36]

In this regard, traditional pre-modern modes of retaliation for violent crimes did not entirely cease in the nineteenth century, but were partially transformed and integrated into the 'modern' criminal justice system. The Prussian penal code of 1851, for instance, allowed compensation for simple assault and the option to waive public punishment (*Strafgesetzbuch* 1851: §§ 188, 189). Beyond the normative level, criminal courts still considered compensation for material damage and injury, and redress and restitution between perpetrator and victim in deciding cases of violent crimes and meting out (and often waiving) public punishment, and therefore offered even better options for private retaliation, compensation and conflict settlement. However, the motives of the early modern and emerging modern state for integrating patterns of social or private retaliation went beyond safeguarding the interests of victims or settling conflicts without retributive punishment. The integration and juridification (*Verrechtlichung*) of retaliation also permitted functional gains for the criminal justice system: the monopolization of punitive powers and the intensification of prosecution and social control with regard to such violent crimes as assault and battery and the violent behaviour of the lower classes.

These objectives influenced the function of private compensation between perpetrators and victims, which developed into the legal institution of the *Privatstrafe*: punitive damages that, on the one hand, should ensure the compensation of victims, but, on the other hand, should also deter and prevent perpetrators of violence (Montazel 2001; Sonntag 2005). From the nineteenth century onwards, the relationship between perpetrator and victim became an increasingly less important element of retaliation as far as the state was concerned. Private compensation should not only serve as punitive damages; the state also claimed recompense for legal expenses and the infringement of the (legal) order and offered the mitigation of public punishment, which in the long run emerged as the modern concept of *Wiedergutmachung des Schadens durch eine bestimmte Leistung*: redress by paying a charitable contribution (sometimes directly to the state) (Albrecht 2008).

As a consequence, the function of retaliation and the relations between the different actors shifted from private compensation (perpetrators and victims) and public punishment (state and perpetrators) to public compensation and private punishment, ultimately becoming an amalgamation of private and public retaliation that served the interests of the state: fiscal recompense, the juridification (*Verrechtlichung*) of vindicatory violence and private retaliation, and the extension of social control through the criminal justice system. Commencing with the legal practice of the early modern criminal justice systems in Europe, private and legal retaliation to violence had significantly changed from legitimate vindicatory violence, private compensation and retributive public punishment to a system of formal social control and public retaliation that prevents violence, but neglects the interests of victims in favour of public compensation. However, it is doubtful whether violence – especially vindicatory violence – and private retaliation are nowadays really prevented or even controlled by the state and formal social control, and it is still a question whether the modern criminal justice system really does justice to the complex purposes and functions of retaliation.

Karl Härter is Professor, Research Group Leader and Senior Research Scientist at the Max Planck Institute for European Legal History in Frankfurt/Main, Germany. He is a member of the International Max Planck Research School on Retaliation, Mediation and Punishment, the Association for Constitutional History, the Commission for Hessian History and other academic and historical institutions. His recent publications include 'Images of Dishonoured Rebels and Infamous Revolts: Political Crime, Shaming Punishments and Defamation in the Early Modern Pictorial Media', in C. Behrmann (ed.), *Images of Shame* (De Gruyter, 2016); 'Political Crime in Early Modern Europe: Assassination, Legal Responses and Popular Print Media', *European Journal of Criminology* 11 (2014); 'Early Modern Revolts as Political Crimes in the Popular Media of Illustrated Broadsheets', in M. Griesse (ed.), *From Mutual Observation to Propaganda War: Premodern Revolts in Their Transnational Representations* (Transcript Verlag, 2014); 'Security and Cross-border Political Crime: The Formation of Transnational Security Regimes in 18th and 19th Century Europe', *Historical Social Research* 38 (2013); 'The Early Modern Holy Roman Empire of German Nation (1495–1806): A Multi-layered Legal System', in J. Duindam et al. (eds), *Law and Empire: Ideas, Practices, Actors* (Brill, 2013).

Notes

1. See Muchembled 1989; Conley 1991; Frank 1995; Johnson and Monkkonen 1996; Eibach 1998, 2005, 2008; Sieferle and Breuninger 1998; Spierenburg 1998, 2008; Kurgan-van Hentenryk 1999; Rousseaux 1999; King 2000; Lacour 2000; Blok 2001; Ruff 2001; Wittke 2002; Eriksson and Krug-Richter 2003; Shoemaker 2004; Wiener 2004; Wood 2004; Emsley 2005; Ulbrich, Jarzebowski and Hohkamp 2005; Ambroise-Rendu 2006; Carroll 2006, 2007; Mantecón 2007; Musin, Rousseaux and Vesentini 2008; Follain et al. 2008; Body-Gendrot and Spierenburg 2009; Mucchielli and Spierenburg 2009; Nassiet 2011; Loetz 2012.
2. In Härter (2005), I have analysed more than 3,500 trials and criminal records; the results of my research are largely comparable to the other case studies cited in note 1 above.
3. See in general Bellomo 1995; Grossi 2010.
4. In this chapter I use the term 'public' in the sense of state-based (*staatlich*), whereas 'private' indicates the sphere of social actors.
5. See Weisser 1979; Spierenburg 1991; Rousseaux and Lévy 1997; Härter 1999; Tedoldi 2008.
6. See Spierenburg 1996, 2011; Weinberger 1996; Eisner 2001a, 2001b, 2003; Thome 2001; Kaspersson 2003; Nassiet 2008. On the decline of capital punishment, see Evans 1996; Martschukat 2006.
7. Regarding the concept of retaliation within a legal/judicial framework, I refer in general to Miller (2006).
8. The pre-modern *ius commune* recognized the *ius retorsionis*, the legal capacity of private persons (and later on also states) to retaliate with injuries in kind if formal justice was not available.
9. See Eisner 2001a; Ruff 2001; Wood 2003; Ulbrich, Jarzebowski and Hohkamp 2005; Carroll 2007; Body-Gendrot and Spierenburg 2009; Eibach 2009; Schwerhoff 2011; McMahon, Eibach and Roth 2013.
10. See Spierenburg 1996; Thome 2001; Eisner 2003; Kaspersson 2003.
11. See Roth 2001; Wittke 2002; Carroll 2006; Mucchielli and Spierenburg 2009; Härter 2011.
12. This is based on the case studies cited in the introduction and note 1, and also refers to the European *ius commune*.
13. Frauenstädt (1980 [1881]) is also still of relevance.
14. See Billacois 1990; Chauchadis 1997; Spierenburg 1998; Netterstrøm and Poulsen 2007; Israel and Ortalli 2009; Ludwig, Krug-Richter and Schwerhoff 2012; Schwerhoff 2013.
15. See Lange 1955; Schaffstein 1987; Montazel 2001; Sonntag 2005.
16. See Günther 1889–95; Beling 1894; Hoffmann 1995; Evans 1996; Maihold 2005; Hilgendorf and Weitzel 2007; Schulze et al. 2008.
17. See Kröner 1958; Eibach 1998; Bulst 1999a; Pohl 1999; Härter 2005: 565–75; David 2009; Mucchielli and Spierenburg 2009.
18. On violent political crimes and revolts, see Caron et al. 2008; Härter and de Graaf 2012; De Benedictis and Härter 2013. On feuding and duelling, see Kiernan 1988; Billacois 1990; Frevert 1991; Chauchadis 1997; Netterstrøm and Poulsen 2007; Israel and Ortalli 2009; Ludwig, Krug-Richter and Schwerhoff 2012; Schwerhoff 2013.
19. For example, see Nolde 2003; Jackson 2002; Loetz 2012.
20. See Rummel 1993; Rousseaux 1999; Lacour 2001; Wittke 2002; Shoemaker 2004; Eibach 2008; Ruff 2008; Spierenburg 2008.
21. See King 1996, 2000; Härter 2000; Lacour 2000.

22. See Kiernan 1988; Billacois 1990; Frevert 1991; Chauchadis 1997; Spierenburg 1998; Netterstrøm and Poulsen 2007; Israel and Ortalli 2009.
23. Based on the case studies of Muchembled 1989; King 2000; Lacour 2000; Härter 2005; Carroll 2006; Mantecón 2007; Chaulet 2008; Eibach 2008; Ruff 2008; Spierenburg 2008; Mucchielli and Spierenburg 2009; Loetz 2012.
24. See Muchembled 1989; Frank 1995; Eibach 1998; Bulst 1999a, 1999b; Eriksson and Krug-Richter 2003; Eibach 2005, 2008; Mantecón 2007; Follain et al. 2008.
25. See Ortalli 1986; Rousseaux 1989; Blok 2001; Härter 2003, 2005. Many other studies on early modern violence somewhat neglect the issue of violent property crimes and marginal groups.
26. For the role of women, see van der Heijden 2013.
27. See Kurgan-van Hentenryk et al. 1999; King 2000; Lacour 2000; Wiener 2004; Wood 2004; Härter 2005; Ambroise-Rendu 2006; Carroll 2006; Mantecón 2007; Caron et al. 2008; Chaulet 2008; Eibach 2008; Piant 2008; Ruff 2008; Spierenburg 2008; Loetz 2012. On the negotiation of compensation, punishment and pardon via the procedure of supplicating, see Härter 2000; Nubola and Würgler 2002; Härter and Nubola 2011.
28. For more examples from nineteenth-century England, see Conley 1991: 49–67.
29. For more examples from nineteenth-century France, in particular on the adjudication of everyday violence in Blois (1815–48), see Vautier (2008: 137–45) and the contributions in Caron et al. (2008). On the concept of infrajustice, see Härter 2012.
30. See Lange 1955; Großfeld 1961; Holzhauer 1984; Schaffstein 1987; Montazel 2001; Sonntag 2005.
31. See Muchembled 1989; King 1996; Nubola and Würgler 2002; Carroll 2006; Ruff 2008; Härter and Nubola 2011.
32. See Beling 1894; Schaffstein 1987; Montazel 2001; Sonntag 2005.
33. See King 1996, 2000, 2003; Lacour 2000; Shoemaker 2004; Wood 2004; Emsley 2005; Härter 2005; Eibach 2008; Piant 2008.
34. See Kurgan-van Hentenryk 1999; King 2000; Shoemaker 2004; Wiener 2004; Wood 2004; Ambroise-Rendu 2006.
35. See Frevert 1991; Spierenburg 1998; Ludwig, Krug-Richter and Schwerhoff 2012; Schwerhoff 2013.
36. See Kurgan-van Hentenryk 1999; Wiener 2004; Ambroise-Rendu 2006; Bernaudeau 2008; Caron et al. 2008; Smith 2008; Spierenburg 2008; David 2009.

References

Albrecht, H.-J. 2008. 'Strafrecht und Strafe. Belastung oder Entlastung', in G. Schlee and B. Turner (eds), *Vergeltung. Eine interdisziplinäre Betrachtung der Rechtfertigung und Regulation von Gewalt*. Frankfurt: Campus, pp. 127–48.

Ambroise-Rendu, A.-C. 2006. *Crimes et délits. Une histoire de la violence de la Belle Époque à nos jours*. Paris: Nouveau Monde Édition.

Beling, E. 1894. *Die geschichtliche Entwicklung der Retorsion und Kompensation von Beleidigungen und Körperverletzung*. Breslau: Schletter.

Bellomo, M. 1995. *The Common Legal Past of Europe, 1000–1800*. Washington DC: Catholic University of America Press.

Bernaudeau, V. 2008. 'Invectives, injures et diffamations: les violences verbales et leur réparation devant les justices de paix au XIXe siècle', in A. Follain, B. Lemesle, M. Nassiet, É.

Pierre and P. Quincy-Lefebvre (eds), *La violence et le judiciaire du Moyen Age à nos jours. Discours, perception, pratiques.* Rennes: Presses Universitaires de Rennes, pp. 161–72.

Billacois, F. 1990. *The Duel: Its Rise and Fall in Early Modern France.* New Haven, CT: Yale University Press.

Blok, A. 2001. *Honour and Violence.* Cambridge: Polity Press.

Body-Gendrot, S., and P. Spierenburg (eds). 2009. *Violence in Europe: Historical and Contemporary Perspectives.* New York: Springer.

Boehm, C. 2011. 'Retaliatory Violence in Human Prehistory', *British Journal of Criminology* 51: 518–34.

Bulst, N. 1999a. 'Kriterien der Rechtsprechung zur Gewalt. Zum Problem strafrechtlicher Normen im Übergang vom Mittelalter zur Neuzeit', *ZIF Mitteilungen* 1: 9–18.

———. 1999b. 'Wirkungen von Normen zur Regulierung von Gewaltverhalten im Übergang vom Mittelalter zur Frühen Neuzeit', in H. Hof and G. Lübbe-Wolff (eds), *Wirkungsforschung zum Recht I. Wirkungen und Erfolgsbedingungen von Gesetzen.* Baden-Baden: Nomos, pp. 279–88.

Caron, J.-C., F. Chauvaud, E. Fureix and J.-N. Luc (eds). 2008. *Entre violence et conciliation. La résolution des conflits sociopolitiques en Europe au XIXe siècle.* Rennes: Presses Universitaires de Rennes.

Carroll, S. 2006. *Blood and Violence in Early Modern France.* Oxford: Oxford University Press.

———. (ed.). 2007. *Cultures of Violence. Interpersonal Violence in Historical Perspective.* Basingstoke: Palgrave Macmillan.

Chauchadis, C. 1997. *La loi du duel. Le code du point d'honneur dans l'Espagne des XVIe–XVIIe siècles.* Toulouse: Presses Universitaires du Mirail.

Chaulet, R. 2008. 'Royal Justice, Popular Culture and Violence: Homicide in Sixteenth- and Seventeenth-Century Castile', in R. McMahon (ed.), *Crime, Law and Popular Culture in Europe, 1500–1900.* Cullompton: Willan, pp. 74–95.

Conley, C.A. 1991. *The Unwritten Law: Criminal Justice in Victorian Kent.* New York: Oxford University Press.

David, A. 2009. *Die Entwicklung des Mordtatbestandes im 19. Jahrhundert.* Frankfurt: Lang.

De Benedictis, A., and K. Härter (eds). 2013. *Revolts and Political Crime from the 12th to the 19th Century: Legal Responses and Juridical-Political Discourses.* Frankfurt: Klostermann.

Dinges, M. 1998. 'Formenwandel der Gewalt in der Neuzeit. Zur Kritik der Zivilisationstheorie von Nobert Elias', in R.P. Sieferle and H. Breuninger (eds), *Kulturen der Gewalt. Ritualisierung und Symbolisierung von Gewalt in der Geschichte.* Frankfurt: Campus, pp. 171–94.

Eibach, J. 1998. 'Städtische Gewaltkriminalität im Ancien Régime', *Zeitschrift für Historische Forschung* 25: 359–82.

———. 2005. 'Institutionalisierte Gewalt im urbanen Raum: "Stadtfrieden" in Deutschland und der Schweiz zwischen bürgerlicher und obrigkeitlicher Regelung (15.–18. Jahrhundert)', in C. Ulbrich, C. Jarzebowski and M. Hohkamp (eds), *Gewalt in der Frühen Neuzeit. Beiträge zur 5. Tagung der Arbeitsgemeinschaft Frühe Neuzeit im VHD.* Berlin: Duncker & Humblot, pp. 189–205.

———. 2008. 'The Containment of Violence in Central European Cities, 1500–1800', in R. McMahon (ed.), *Crime, Law and Popular Culture in Europe, 1500-1900.* Cullompton: Willan, pp. 52–73.

———. 2009. 'Gibt es eine Geschichte der Gewalt? Zur Praxis des Konflikts heute, in der Vormoderne und im 19. Jahrhundert', in R. Habermas and G. Schwerhoff (eds), *Verbrechen im Blick Perspektiven der neuzeitlichen Kriminalitätsgeschichte.* Frankfurt: Campus, pp. 182–216.

Eisner, M. 2001a. 'Modernization, Self-Control and Lethal Violence: The Long-Term Dynamics of European Homicide Rates in Theoretical Perspective', *British Journal of Criminology* 41: 618–38.

———. 2001b. 'Individuelle Gewalt und Modernisierung in Europa, 1200–2000', in G. Albrecht, O. Backes and W. Kühnel (eds), *Gewaltkriminalität zwischen Mythos und Realität*. Frankfurt: Suhrkamp, pp. 71–100.

———. 2003. 'Long-Term Historical Trends in Violent Crime', *Crime and Justice* 30: 83–142.

Emsley, C. 2005. *Hard Men: The English and Violence since 1750*. London: Bloomsbury Academic.

Eriksson, M., and B. Krug-Richter (eds). 2003. *Streitkulturen. Gewalt, Konflikt und Kommunikation in der ländlichen Gesellschaft der frühen Neuzeit*. Cologne: Böhlau.

Evans, R.J. 1996. *Rituals of Retribution. Capital Punishment in Germany 1600–1987*. Oxford: Oxford University Press.

Follain, A., B. Lemesle, M. Nassiet, É. Pierre and P. Quincy-Lefebvre (eds). 2008. *La violence et le judiciaire du Moyen Age à nos jours. Discours, perception, pratiques*. Rennes: Presses Universitaires de Rennes.

Frank, M. 1995. *Dörfliche Gesellschaft und Kriminalität. Das Fallbeispiel Lippe 1650–1800*. Paderborn: F. Schöningh.

Frauenstädt, P. 1980 [1881]. *Blutrache und Todtschlagsühne im deutschen Mittelalter. Studien zur deutschen Kultur- und Rechtsgeschichte*. Leipzig: Duncker & Humblot.

Frevert, U. 1991. *Ehrenmänner. Das Duell in der bürgerlichen Gesellschaft*. Munich: Beck.

Großfeld, B. 1961. *Die Privatstrafe. Ein Beitrag zum Schutz des allgemeinen Persönlichkeitsrechts*. Frankfurt: Metzner.

Grossi, P. 2010. *A History of European Law*. Oxford: Wiley-Blackwell.

Günther, L. 1889–95. *Die Idee der Wiedervergeltung in der Geschichte und Philosophie des Strafrechts. Ein Beitrag zur universalhistorischen Entwicklung desselben*, vols 1–3. Erlangen: Bläsing (reprint Aalen, 1966–70).

Härter, K. 1999. 'Social Control and the Enforcement of Police-Ordinances in Early Modern Criminal Procedure', in H. Schilling (ed.), *Institutions, Instruments and Agents of Social Control and Discipline in Early Modern Europe*. Frankfurt: Klostermann, pp. 39–63.

———. 2000. 'Strafverfahren im frühneuzeitlichen Territorialstaat: Inquisition, Entscheidungsfindung, Supplikation', in A. Blauert and G. Schwerhoff (eds), *Kriminalitätsgeschichte. Beiträge zur Sozial- und Kulturgeschichte der Vormoderne*. Konstanz: Universitätsverlag Konstanz, pp. 459–80.

———. 2003. 'Zum Verhältnis von "Rechtsquellen" und territorialen Rahmenbedingungen in der Strafgerichtsbarkeit des 18. Jahrhunderts: Vagabondage und Diebstahl in der Entscheidungspraxis der Kurmainzer Landesregierung', in H. Rudolph and H. Schnabel-Schüle (eds), *Justiz = Justice = Justicia? Rahmenbedingungen von Strafjustiz im frühneuzeitlichen Europa*. Trier: Kliomedia, pp. 433–65.

———. 2005. *Policey und Strafjustiz in Kurmainz. Gesetzgebung, Normdurchsetzung und Sozialkontrolle im frühneuzeitlichen Territorialstaat*. Frankfurt: Klostermann.

———. 2008. 'Strafen mit und neben der Zentralgewalt: Pluralität und Verstaatlichung des Strafens in der Frühen Neuzeit', in G. Schlee and B. Turner (eds), *Vergeltung. Eine interdisziplinäre Betrachtung der Rechtfertigung und Regulation von Gewalt*. Frankfurt: Campus, pp. 105–26.

———. 2011. 'Die Folter als Instrument policeylicher Ermittlung im inquisitorischen Untersuchungs- und Strafverfahren des 18. und 19. Jahrhunderts', in K. Altenhain and N. Willenberg (eds), *Die Geschichte der Folter seit ihrer Abschaffung*. Göttingen: V&R Unipress, pp. 83–114.

———. 2012. 'Konfliktregulierung im Umfeld frühneuzeitlicher Strafgerichte: Das Konzept der Infrajustiz in der historischen Kriminalitätsforschung', *Kritische Vierteljahresschrift für Gesetzgebung und Rechtsprechung* 95: 130–44.

Härter, K., and B. de Graaf (eds). 2012. *Vom Majestätsverbrechen zum Terrorismus: Politische Kriminalität, Recht, Justiz und Polizei zwischen Früher Neuzeit und 20. Jahrhundert*. Frankfurt: Klostermann.

Härter, K., and C. Nubola (eds). 2011. *Grazia e giustizia. Figure della clemenza fra tardo medioevo ed età contemporanea*. Bologna: Il Mulino.

Hilgendorf, E., and J. Weitzel (eds). 2007. *Der Strafgedanke in seiner historischen Entwicklung. Ringvorlesung zur Strafrechtsgeschichte und Strafrechtsphilosophie*. Berlin: Duncker & Humblot.

Hoffmann, P. 1995. *Vergeltung und Generalprävention im heutigen Strafrecht*. Aachen: Shaker.

Holzhauer, H. 1984. 'Privatstrafe', in A. Erler, E. Kaufmann, D. Werkmüller and W. Stammler (eds), *Handwörterbuch zur deutschen Rechtsgeschichte*, vol. 3. Berlin: Erich Schmidt Verlag, pp. 1193–98.

Israel, U., and G. Ortalli (eds). 2009. *Il duello fra medioevo ed età moderna. Prospettive storico-culturali*. Rome: Viella.

Jackson, M. (ed.). 2002. *Infanticide: Historical Perspectives on Child Murder and Concealment, 1550–2000*. Aldershot: Ashgate.

Johnson, E.A., and E.H. Monkkonen (eds). 1996. *The Civilization of Crime: Violence in Town and Country since the Middle Ages*. Urbana: University of Illinois Press.

Kaspersson, M. 2003. '"The Great Murder Mystery" or Explaining Declining Homicide Rates', in B.S. Godfrey, C. Emsley and G. Dunstall (eds), *Comparative Histories of Crime*. Cullompton: Willan, pp. 72–88.

Kiernan, V.G. 1988. *The Duel in European History: Honour and the Reign of Aristocracy*. Oxford: Oxford University Press.

King, P. 1996. 'Punishing Assault: The Transformation of Attitudes in the English Courts', *Journal of Interdisciplinary History* 27: 43–74.

———. 2000. *Crime, Justice and Discretion in England 1740–1820*. Oxford: Oxford University Press.

———. 2003. 'Moral Panics and Violent Street Crime 1750–2000: A Comparative Perspective', in B.S. Godfrey, C. Emsley and G. Dunstall (eds), *Comparative Histories of Crime*. Cullompton: Willan, pp. 53–71.

Kröner, O. 1958. 'Die vorsätzlichen Tötungsdelikte in ihrer Entwicklung von der Carolina bis zum Ausgang des 18. Jahrhunderts', Ph.D. dissertation. Göttingen, Rechts- und Staatswissenschaftliche Fakultät.

Kurgan-van Hentenryk, G. 1999. *Un pays si tranquille: la violence en Belgique au XIXe siècle*. Brussels: University of Brussels.

Kurgan-van Hentenryk, G. et al. 1999. 'La violence au tribunal correctionnel de Bruxelles au XIXe siècle', in G. Kurgan-van Hentenryk (ed.), *Un pays si tranquille: la violence en Belgique au XIXe siècle*. Brussels: University of Brussels, pp. 87–105.

Lacour, E. 2000. *Schlägereyen und Unglücksfälle. Zur historischen Psychologie und Typologie von Gewalt in der frühneuzeitlichen Eifel*. Frankfurt: Hänsel-Hohenhausen.

———. 2001. 'Faces of Violence Revisited: A Typology of Violence in Early Modern Rural Germany', *Journal of Social History* 34: 649–67.

Lange, H. 1955. *Schadensersatz und Privatstrafe in der mittelalterlichen Rechtstheorie*. Münster: Böhlau.

Lindenberger, T., and A. Lüdtke. 1995. *Physische Gewalt. Studien zur Geschichte der Neuzeit*. Frankfurt: Suhrkamp.

Loetz, F. 2012. *Sexualisierte Gewalt 1500–1850. Plädoyer für eine historische Gewaltforschung.* Frankfurt: Campus.

Ludwig, U., B. Krug-Richter and G. Schwerhoff (eds). 2012. *Das Duell. Ehrenkämpfe vom Mittelalter bis zur Moderne.* Konstanz: UVK.

McMahon, R. (ed.). 2008. *Crime, Law and Popular Culture in Europe, 1500–1900.* Cullompton: Willan.

McMahon R., J. Eibach and R. Roth. 2013. 'Making Sense of Violence? Reflections on the History of Interpersonal Violence in Europe', *Crime, Histoire & Sociétés/Crime, History & Societies* 17: 5–26.

Maihold, H. 2005. *Strafe für fremde Schuld? Die Systematik des Strafbegriffs in der spanischen Spätscholastik und Naturrechtslehre.* Cologne: Böhlau.

Mantecón, T.A. 2007. 'The Patterns of Violence in Early Modern Spain', *Journal of the Historical Society* 7: 229–64.

Martschukat, J. 2006. *Geschichte der Todesstrafe vom 17. bis zum 19. Jahrhundert.* Wiesbaden: VMA-Verlag.

Miller, W.I. 2006. *Eye for an Eye.* Cambridge: Cambridge University Press.

Montazel, L. 2001. 'La peine privée en France et Allemagne (XVIème–XIXème siècles). Essai sur une notion doctrinale commune', *Ius Commune* 28: 161–202.

Mucchielli, L., and P. Spierenburg (eds). 2009. *Histoire de l'homicide en Europe de la fin du Moyen Âge à nos jours.* Paris: Édition la Découverte.

Muchembled, R. 1989. *La violence au village. Sociabilité et comportements populaires en Artois du XVe au XVIIe siècle.* Turnhout: Brepols.

Musin, A., X. Rousseaux and F. Vesentini (eds). 2008. *Violence, conciliation et répression. Recherches sur l'histoire du crime, de l'Antiquité au XXI*[e] *Siècle.* Louvain-la-Neuve: Presses Universitaires de Louvain.

Nassiet, M. 2007. 'Vengeance in Sixteenth- and Seventeenth-Century France', in S. Carroll (ed.), *Cultures of Violence: Interpersonal Violence in Historical Perspective.* Basingstoke: Palgrave Macmillan, pp. 117–28.

———. 2008. 'Survivance et déclin du système vindicatoire à l'époque moderne', in A. Follain, B. Lemesle, M. Nassiet, É. Pierre and P. Quincy-Lefebvre (eds), *La violence et le judiciaire du Moyen Age à nos jours. Discours, perception, pratiques.* Rennes: Presses Universitaires de Rennes, pp. 75–87.

———. 2011. *La violence, une histoire sociale. France, XVI*[e]*–XVIII*[e] *siècles.* Paris: Champ Vallon.

Netterstrøm, J.B., and B. Poulsen (eds). 2007. *Feud in Medieval and Early Modern Europe.* Aarhus: Aarhus University Press.

Nolde, D. 2003. *Gattenmord. Macht und Gewalt in der frühneuzeitlichen Ehe.* Cologne: Böhlau.

Nubola, C., and A. Würgler (eds). 2002. *Suppliche e 'gravamina'. Politica, amministrazione, giustizia in Europa (secoli XV–XVIII).* Bologna: Il Mulino.

Ortalli, G. (ed.). 1986. *Bande armate, banditi, Banditismo. E repressione di giustizia negli stati europei di antico regime.* Rome: Jouvence.

Piant, H. 2008. '"Car tels excès ne sont pas permis": l'injure et la résolution judiciaire dans un tribunal de première instance sous l'Ancien Régime', in A. Follain, B. Lemesle, M. Nassiet, É. Pierre and P. Quincy-Lefebvre (eds), *La violence et le judiciaire du Moyen Age à nos jours. Discours, perception, pratiques.* Rennes: Presses Universitaires de Rennes, pp. 125–36.

Pohl, S. 1999. 'Ehrlicher Totschlag – Rache – Notwehr. Zwischen männlichem Ehrencode und dem Primat des Stadtfriedens (Zürich 1376–1600)', in B. Jussen and C. Koslofsky (eds), *Kulturelle Reformation. Sinnformationen im Umbruch 1400–1600.* Göttingen: Vandenhoeck & Ruprecht, pp. 239–83.

Roth, R. 2001. 'Homicide in Early Modern England 1549–1800: The Need for a Quantitative Synthesis', *Crime, Histoire & Sociétés/Crime, History & Societies* 5: 33–67.

Rousseaux, X. 1989. 'L'incrimination du vagabondage en Brabant (14ᵉ–18ᵉ siècles). Langages du droit et réalites de la pratique', in G. van Dievoet, P. Godding and D. van den Auweele (eds), *Langage et droit à travers l'histoire. Réalités et fictions.* Leuven: Peeters, pp. 147–84.

———. 1999. 'From Case to Crime: Homicide Regulation in Medieval and Modern Europe', in D. Willoweit (ed.), *Die Entstehung des öffentlichen Strafrechts. Bestandaufnahme eines europäischen Forschungsproblems.* Cologne: Böhlau, pp. 143–75.

Rousseaux, X., and R. Lévy (eds). 1997. *Le pénal dans tous ses Etats. Justice, Etats et Sociétés en Europe (XIIe–XXe siècles).* Brussels: Faculté Universitaire Saint-Louis.

Ruff, J.R. 2001. *Violence in Early Modern Europe.* Cambridge: Cambridge University Press.

———. 2008. 'Popular Violence and its Prosecution in Seventeenth- and Eighteenth-Century France', in R. McMahon (ed.), *Crime, Law and Popular Culture in Europe, 1500–1900.* Cullompton: Willan, pp. 32–51.

Rummel, W. 1993. 'Verletzung von Körper, Ehre und Eigentum. Varianten im Umgang mit Gewalt in Dörfern des 17. Jahrhunderts', in A. Blauert and G. Schwerhoff (eds), *Mit den Waffen der Justiz. Zur Kriminalitätsgeschichte des Spätmittelalters und der Frühen Neuzeit.* Frankfurt: Fischer Taschenbuch-Verlag, pp. 86–114.

Schaffstein, F. 1987. 'Wiedergutmachung und Genugtuung im Strafprozeß vom 16. bis zum Ausgang des 18. Jahrhunderts', in H. Schöch (ed.), *Wiedergutmachung und Strafrecht.* Munich: Fink, pp. 9–27.

Schlee, G., and B. Turner (eds). 2008. *Vergeltung. Eine interdisziplinäre Betrachtung der Rechtfertigung und Regulation von Gewalt.* Frankfurt: Campus.

Schulze, R., T. Vormbaum, C.D. Schmidt and N. Willenberg (eds). 2008. *Strafzweck und Strafform zwischen religiöser und weltlicher Wertevermittlung.* Münster: Rhema-Verlag.

Schwerhoff, G. 2002. 'Criminalized Violence and the Process of Civilisation', *Crime, Histoire & Sociétés/Crime, History & Societies* 6: 103–26.

———. 2004. 'Social Control of Violence, Violence as Social Control: The Case of Early Modern Germany', in H. Roodenburg and P. Spierenburg (eds), *Social Control in Europe, Vol. 1: 1500–1800.* Columbus: Ohio State University Press, pp. 220–46.

———. 2011. *Historische Kriminalitätsforschung.* Frankfurt: Campus.

———. 2013. 'Violence and the Honour Code: From Social Integration to Social Distinction?', *Crime, Histoire & Sociétés/Crime, History & Societies* 17: 27–46.

Shoemaker, R.B. 2004. *The London Mob: Violence and Disorder in Eighteenth-Century England.* London: Hambledon.

Sieferle, R.P., and H. Breuninger (eds). 1998. *Kulturen der Gewalt. Ritualisierung und Symbolisierung von Gewalt in der Geschichte.* Frankfurt: Campus.

Smith, G.T. 2008. 'Violent Crime and the Public Weal in England, 1700–1900', in R. McMahon (ed.), *Crime, Law and Popular Culture in Europe, 1500–1900.* Cullompton: Willan, pp. 190–218.

Sonntag, E. 2005. *Entwicklungstendenzen der Privatstrafen. Strafschadensersatz im antiken römischen, deutschen und US-amerikanischen Recht.* Berlin: Berliner Wissenschafts-Verlag.

Spierenburg, P. 1991. *The Prison Experience. Disciplinary Institutions and in their Inmates in Early Modern Europe.* New Brunswick, NJ: Rutgers University Press.

———. 1996. Long-Term Trends in Homicide: 'Theoretical Reflections and Dutch Evidence, Fifteenth to Twentieth Centuries', in E.A. Johnson and E.H. Monkkonen (eds), *The Civilization of Crime. Violence in Town and Country since the Middle Ages.* Urbana: University of Illinois Press, pp. 63–105.

———. 2008. *A History of Murder: Personal Violence in Europe from the Middle Ages to the Present*. Cambridge: Polity Press.

———. 2011. 'Violence and the Civilizing Process: Does it Work?', *Crime, Histoire & Sociétés/Crime, History & Societies* 5: 87–105.

Spierenburg, P. (ed.) 1998. *Men and Violence: Gender, Honor, and Rituals in Modern Europe and America*. Columbus: Ohio State University Press.

Strafgesetzbuch für die Preußischen Staaten. Berlin 1851 (new edition 1856).

Tedoldi, L. 2008. *La spada e la bilancia. la giustizia penale nell'Europa moderna (secc. XVI–XVIII)*. Rome: Carocci.

Thauer, J. 2001. *Gerichtspraxis in der ländlichen Gesellschaft. Eine mikrohistorische Untersuchung am Beispiel eines altmärkischen Patrimonialgerichts um 1700*. Berlin: Berlin Verlag Arno Spitz.

Thome, H. 2001. 'Explaining Long Term Trends in Violent Crime', *Crime, Histoire & Sociétés/Crime, History & Societies* 5: 69–86.

Ulbrich, C., C. Jarzebowski and M. Hohkamp (eds). 2005. *Gewalt in der Frühen Neuzeit. Beiträge zur 5. Tagung der Arbeitsgemeinschaft Frühe Neuzeit im VHD*. Berlin: Duncker & Humblot.

Van der Heijden, M. 2013. 'Women, Violence and Urban Justice in Holland c. 1600–1838', *Crime, Histoire & Sociétés/Crime, History & Societies* 17: 71–100.

Vautier, S. 2008. 'Les juges et la violence quotidienne (Blois, 1815–1848)', in A. Follain, B. Lemesle, M. Nassiet, É. Pierre and P. Quincy-Lefebvre (eds), *La violence et le judiciaire du Moyen Age à nos jours. Discours, perception, pratiques*. Rennes: Presses Universitaires de Rennes, pp. 137–48.

Weinberger, B. 1996. 'Urban and Rural Crime Rates and Their Genesis in Late Nineteenth- and Early Twentieth-Century Britain', in E.A. Johnson and E.H. Monkkonen (eds), *The Civilization of Crime: Violence in Town and Country since the Middle Ages*. Urbana: University of Illinois Press, pp. 198–216.

Weisser, M.R. 1979. *Crime and Punishment in Early Modern Europe*. Hassocks: Harvester Press.

Wiener, M.J. 2004. *Men of Blood: Violence, Manliness and Criminal Justice in Victorian England*. Cambridge: Cambridge University Press.

Wittke, M. 2002. *Gewaltdelikte im Fürstbistum Münster, 1580–1620. Täter, Opfer und Justiz*. Münster: Aschendorff.

Wood, J.C. 2003. 'It's a Small World after All? Reflections on Violence in Comparative Perspectives', in B.S. Godfrey, C. Emsley and G. Dunstall, *Comparative Histories of Crime*. Cullompton: Willan, pp. 35–52.

———. 2004. *Violence and Crime in Nineteenth-Century England: The Shadow of Our Refinement*. London: Routledge.

Chapter 6

Crime in Motion

Predation, Retaliation and the Spread of Urban Violence

Richard Wright, Volkan Topalli and Scott Jacques

It has long been recognized that criminal violence is contagious; it has a tendency to spread beyond the instigating event, from person to person and from neighbourhood to neighbourhood, especially in urban areas characterized by high crime rates, poverty, social disorganization, ineffective formal social control and decaying infrastructure (Loftin 1986; Blumstein and Rosenfeld 1998; Fagan and Davies 2004; Fagan, Wilkinson and Davies 2007). Less well understood, however, are the precise mechanisms underpinning the diffusion of underworld violence.

In this chapter we argue that the contagion of urban violence arises from dynamic, recursive cycles of victimization and retaliation that occur between criminally involved individuals, embedded within facilitative sociocultural settings and circumstances. Years of talking to hardcore street offenders has taught us that such individuals, driven by intense materialistic and sensual needs, are prone to prey on fellow offenders. In turn, offender/victims are compelled to retaliate for such affronts by a street culture that lionizes and rewards violence, self-sufficiency and vigilantism on the one hand, and a mainstream culture that denies them legal recourse on the other. In the absence of intervention, these conditions are likely to result in ever-intensifying patterns of retaliation and counter-retaliation between offender/predators and offender/victims, causing the spread of violence beyond the initial affront, whereby innocent – and not-so-innocent – third parties are drawn into a widening circle of violence.[1]

To explain how this dynamic develops and how it might be disrupted, we first provide an overview of the ways in which individual patterns of thinking and behaving are shaped by *antecedent conditions* (background risk factors and participation in street culture), *instigating conditions* (a cyclical pattern of conspicuous consumption, financial desperation and violent predation that simultaneously instigates retaliation and fuels further consumption) and *encapsulating conditions* (shaped by street culture on the one hand and mainstream culture on the other). Next, we demonstrate how, unabated, these conditions may produce a cycle of self-perpetuating, recursive violence that ends only when involved individuals are successful at managing the threat of retaliation or are somehow removed from the system altogether through death or imprisonment (but see Decker and Lauritsen 2002; Jacques and Wright 2008a). As we will see, however, such drastic outcomes do not necessarily preclude the continuation of violence, and in some cases actually may intensify its spread. We therefore conclude by delineating ways in which efforts targeted specifically at particular instigating and encapsulating conditions may prevent, contain or disrupt the contagion of violence.

How Cultural Conditions and Offender Lifestyles Breed Predatory Violence

A complete understanding of how and why offenders think and act as they do demands that attention be paid to the intersection of individual-, group- and contextual-level (background, culture, situational) factors. The conditions that set the stage for recursive violence are interconnected. In describing our model of retaliation, however, we believe that it is important to start with an understanding of the macroconditions – cultural, physical, social and even historical – that incubate the various characteristics of street culture driving retaliatory behaviour at the microlevel. These conditions can be divided into three categories that, operating together, facilitate the perpetuation of violence:

- *antecedent conditions*, which make individuals susceptible to the allure of street life. These set the stage for →
- *instigating conditions*, whereby individuals who actively participate in street culture become enmeshed in patterns of conspicuous consumption that drive them to engage in predatory behaviour towards other offenders, thus setting in motion recursive cycles of retaliation and counter-retaliation. Such cycles are maintained by →
- *encapsulating conditions*, which more than any other factors make offender participation in retaliation virtually inescapable and increase the likelihood that such behaviour will spread beyond the initial offence by drawing others into violence.

Antecedent Conditions: Background Breeds Culture

Antecedent conditions – referred to by Katz (1988) as 'contemporaneous social conditions' – are those circumstances that set the stage for criminality. In public health terms they can be said to serve as the major risk factors for participation in street life and the ancillary difficulties that accrue with such participation. Street criminals do not contemplate and carry out their crimes in a vacuum; their actions are embedded in an ongoing process of human existence

(Bottoms and Wiles 1992). Both structuralist and culturalist approaches (see Jefferson 2004) serve us well in understanding how individuals live and operate in crime-ridden urban environments, and why some of them participate in a particularly intense form of street life culture that promotes retaliatory violence (Anderson 1990, 1999; Jacobs, Topalli and Wright 2000; Topalli, Wright and Fornango 2002; see also Webber 2007). As such, the impact of antecedent-level conditions on criminal decision making is best viewed through a combination of cultural and background criminological perspectives. What emerges from a combined approach is the comprehensive description of how antecedent conditions (including both demographic and cultural elements) create the circumstances that make some individuals susceptible to the temptations of retaliatory violence and less likely to participate in legitimate, mainstream behaviours and activities.

Individually and together, we have interviewed hundreds of active offenders recruited from the streets of St. Louis, Atlanta and New Orleans.[2] These cities are perennially among the most violent in America, as measured by a variety of common crime indicators such as homicide and assault. They are plagued by all the stereotypical correlates of street crime, including poverty, unemployment and underemployment, decaying infrastructure and widespread social disorganization.

Endemic to such neighbourhoods are a proliferation of common individual-level background factors related to criminality, including poor formal education, lack of family structure and weak bonds to conventional society. Escape from their crushing poverty and high mortality rates is rare, and most of those living in these environs have been exposed to these conditions from birth, knowing little else (see Garbarino et al. 1992; Bell and Jenkins 1993; Lorion and Saltzman 1993; Wilson and Daly 1997; Hoffman 2004). Foosey, an eighteen-year-old robber, indicated as much: 'I've been robbed when I was at school, been ripped off, been shot at … Hell, someone shot at my granny's house' (Brezina, Tekin and Topalli 2009: 1114).[3] Deathrow, a nineteen-year-old drug robber and carjacker from New Orleans, remarked:

> I grew up with shootin' and fightin' all over. You [referring to the interviewer's line of work] grew up with books and shit. Where I'm from you never know if you gonna live one minute to the next. It's like a war out there. People die every day. You can go to sleep and hear gunshots all night man, all night. Bullets be lying on the street in the morning. Ambulances and police cars steady riding through my neighbourhood, man. (Brezina, Tekin and Topalli 2009: 1113)

It is within this toxic milieu that *street culture* flourishes (see, e.g., Cohen and Short 1958; Wolfgang and Ferracuti 1967; Anderson 1990, 1999; Wright and

Decker 1994, 1997; Shover 1996). Street culture is characterized by, among other things, a willingness to use violence to settle differences, obtain cash and goods, and establish your reputation as a deterrent against future victimization. As J-Blue, a twenty-four-year-old drug robber and carjacker from Atlanta, noted:

> You see all this [gesturing to a row of blighted buildings with drug dealers standing in front of them]? This is where we work. You work here, you better be ready to defend your shit. This is some real competition. That dude [pointing] and that dude [pointing again] working right next to each other, see? But you know what? He will kill that other motherfucker in a quick minute if he can. He will take his shit if he can. Beat him down for it. That's how you get ahead. The only reason he don't is the other dude just as bad, just as crazy. Ain't no, let's talk it out. Ain't no 'this is fair' or 'that ain't fair' or anything like that. No. They follow that law we got down here. You need money? Beat some ass. You need to send a message? Cap [shoot] somebody's ass. Handle your business with these [gesturing to his fists] or this [gesturing to the .45 in his jacket pocket]. Take what you can. Everybody knows that around here.[4]

Street culture strongly emphasizes hedonistic pursuits (see Shover 1996), a lack of future orientation (see Brezina, Tekin and Topalli 2009) and an obsession with maintaining self-respect at all costs (see Anderson 1999). Traditional understandings of such violence-oriented subcultures hold the somewhat deterministic view that culture wholly governs behaviour. However, even the originators of such formulations support a more soft-determinist view, whereby culture interacts with situational and dispositional factors to promote rather than dictate behaviour (see, e.g., Wolfgang and Ferracuti's 1982 revision of their subculture of violence hypothesis). Recent notions of street culture go even further. For example, Anderson's (1990, 1999) more nuanced formulation of street culture is manifested in an unwritten yet universally known 'code' that governs the lives not just of offenders, but of non-offenders too. As Blue Eyes, a female pimp and burglar from Atlanta, noted:

> We have a different way of life here. Handle your own business. Don't snitch. Protect yourself. That kinda shit. Don't matter if you are a pimp like me or an old lady. Everybody knows the rules.

The 'code of the street' serves as a backdrop for all social interactions within these neighbourhoods, but allegiance to the code varies across people and thus so too does its impact on violence. Non-offenders may act 'street' when the situation demands it, and streetwise people are only variably involved in crime depending on their degree of attachment to the code. What remains constant is the extent to which poverty, unemployment and a lack of access to social services and justice produce this way of life.

In describing the functioning of street culture, Anderson (1990: 92) emphasizes the willingness of many disadvantaged young males to risk injury or even death 'over the principle of respect' (see also Katz 1988). In an environment where predation between offenders is a common (and often preferred) route to obtaining money, goods and illegal substances (see Jacobs, Topalli and Wright 2000), maintaining respect goes beyond esoteric notions of honour or self-esteem. It is the bedrock of the street offender's capacity to deter victimization. As Stub, a then forty-eight-year-old drug dealer from St. Louis, put it:

> That's very important if you gonna live that lifestyle. You need to let it be known you not gonna take no shit, you know what I'm saying? Fuck no, you would be out of business or dead, 'cause you would have people, little kids, coming up trying to rob you [thinking] he ain't gonna do nothing, he's a punk. People just know don't fuck with me [because of my] reputation – don't fuck with me 'cause they know if they fuck with me they got to kill [me], you got to kill me. (Topalli, Wright and Fornango 2002: 343)

In this sense, respect is a commodity whose value must be maintained, and retaliation serves this purpose well. This obsession with reputational factors and their concomitant deterrent value fuels the recursive violence dynamic at the heart of our discussion.

Instigating Conditions: Street Culture Fuels Predation

The antecedent conditions mentioned above set the stage for an intense form of participation in street life that Shover (1996) refers to as 'life as party', the hedonistic pursuit of good times and the concomitant lawbreaking that supports such activities (also see Wright and Decker 1994, 1997). According to Shover and Copes:

> The hallmark of this lifestyle is enjoyment of 'good times', with minimal concern for obligations and commitments external to the person's immediate social setting … Life as party is distinguished in many cases by two repetitively cyclical phases and corresponding approaches to crime. When efforts to maintain the lifestyle (i.e., party pursuits) are largely successful, crimes are committed to sustain circumstances or a pattern of activities they experience as pleasurable … By contrast, when offenders are less successful at party pursuits, crimes are committed to forestall or avoid conditions experienced as unpleasant, precarious, or threatening. (Shover and Copes 2010: 129)

This lifestyle emanates from conditions on the streets and the culture that they breed. Lacking education or employment opportunities, hardcore offenders rush headlong into hedonistic pursuits (drugs, gambling and sex) that align with the unpredictable and unforgiving nature of the streets. To illustrate, Mo, a carjacker interviewed in Jacobs, Topalli and Wright (2003: 677), described how he spent the money obtained from his crimes on drugs and partying:

> Just get high, get high. I just blow money. Money is not something that is going to achieve for nobody, you know what I'm saying? So every day there's not a promise that there'll be another [day] so I just spend it, you know what I'm saying? It ain't mine, you know what I'm saying? I just got it, it's just in my possession. It's a lot of fun. At a job you've got to work a lot for it, you know what I'm saying? You got to punch the clock, do what somebody else tells you. I ain't got time for that. Oh yeah, there ain't nothing like gettin' high on $5,000!

Most adherents to the street culture lifestyle anticipate and accept the prospect of an early death (see Brezina, Tekin and Topalli 2009), ignoring the future consequences of their behaviour and focusing instead on the immediate rewards. Such an orientation breeds fearlessness, avarice and desperation. As Chris, a twenty-year-old drug dealer and robber from Atlanta, put it:

> I swore that I wasn't gonna see 19. I swear. The way I was goin', I didn't think I was ever gonna see 19. I swear. My aunties used to always say, 'Man you gonna be dead.' Made me wanna go do some more stuff. Made me wanna go do some more bad stuff.

The resultant intensity with which many offenders pursue life as party necessitates the continuous acquisition of illicit substances and money, both of which are likely to be found in the hands of neighbourhood drug dealers.

Drug dealers make excellent targets for other offenders. To begin with, they are reluctant to go to the police when they are victimized for fear of exposing their own criminal activities (Black 1976; Wright and Decker 1994, 1997; Jacobs 2000; Jacques and Wright 2008b; Jacques 2010).[5] Moreover, such behaviour violates a central tenet of the code of the street demanding that individuals avoid contact with the police for fear of being labelled snitches (see Cooney 1998; Rosenfeld, Jacobs and Wright 2003; Natapoff 2004, 2006, 2009; Topalli 2005, 2006).[6]

Successful offender/predators are rewarded for their efforts with significant amounts of cash and drugs, which satisfy the need to keep the party going. However, the ease with which such rewards are achieved, coupled with the quantity of drugs and money obtained, may serve to distort the offender's perception of the value of their gains, encouraging them to consume and expend their resources quickly and irresponsibly. Tone, a seasoned carjacker from St. Louis, remarked:

> Just got the money to blow so fuck it, blow it [on] whatever, it don't even matter. Whatever you see you get it, fuck it. Spend that shit. It wasn't yours from the getty-up, you know what I'm saying? You didn't have it from the jump so … Can't act like careful with it, it wasn't yours to care for. Easy come, easy go. The easy it came, it go even easier. Fuck that, fuck all that; I ain't trying to think about keeping nothing. (Topalli and Wright 2013: 162)

This in turn leads to the desperate search for a means to sustain the action, which almost invariably results in another predatory crime. As such, disposable and easily replenished cash and drugs serve to fuel a self-propagating behavioural system of consumption, desperation and predation. This cycle (see Figure 6.1) instigates recursive patterns of retaliation and counter-retaliation because it encourages further offending, much or all of it directed against fellow lawbreakers. As long as this 'boom and bust' etiological cycle of criminality remains in effect, so too will additional recursive cycles of retaliation continue to emerge.

Encapsulating Conditions: How Street and Mainstream Cultures Thwart the Cessation of Violence

Conventional society and street society handle the satisfaction of grievances very differently. Victimization creates potentially severe consequences for all people, both criminal and noncriminal. These include the potential loss of resources, physical harm, and emotional and psychological stress (Topalli, Wright and Fornango 2002). To deal with the aftermath of victimization, individuals may engage in a variety of counteractive coping strategies designed to re-establish cognitive-emotional balance and/or replenish lost resources. Such strategies are geared towards restoring the individual's sense of equity, safety, comfort and

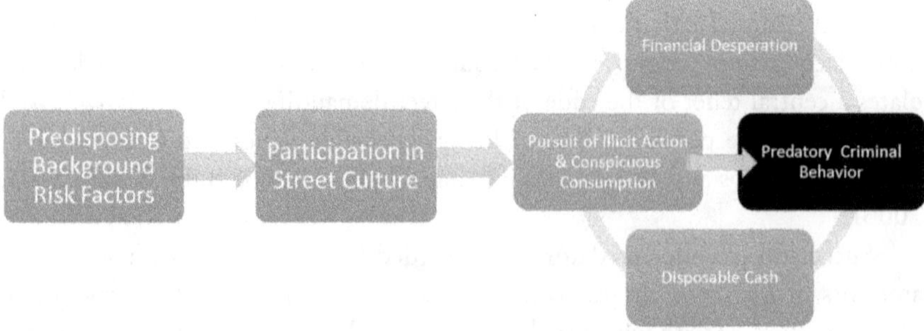

Figure 6.1 The etiological cycle of predatory crime

wealth. Mainstream society has established institutions to facilitate this restoration process: law enforcement apprehends violators, the courts judge them and the correctional system ensures incapacitation or restitution. Insurance will even provide compensation or replacement for those possessions that have been taken from the victim. Of course, this elaborate system is not designed for the sole purpose of satisfying the emotional and psychological needs of victims, but also to thwart those impulses for revenge and vigilantism that result from such feelings. To maintain social order, they allow formal systems of social control to act as proxies for victims, supplanting the pre-industrial system of justice based on self-initiated retribution and compensation (see Nisbett and Cohen 1996; Cooney 1998).

Unlike law-abiding citizens, individuals victimized during the course of illicit activities cannot easily access formal systems of social control (that is, the police), as such contact could invite legal scrutiny. Nor would law enforcement agencies necessarily want to help offenders who have been wronged. Moreover, as discussed above, street offenders must adhere to a strict code of conduct that requires them to avoid contact with the authorities lest they be labelled snitches, and to handle conflicts on their own. Stub, a seasoned veteran of St. Louis' drug-dealing scene, said the following after recounting an episode where he resisted a robbery attempt, getting shot in the process:

> Stub: See, you got to stab me or shoot me, I'm not gonna just let you take my shit because if you just take it the word on the street gonna get out [that] you can take [Stub's] shit, you know what I'm saying? … And whoever he told [about this robbery attempt], he told them that [Stub's] a strong little guy. [Stub] said no you ain't robbing me, even though I had a gun on him. After that I got out [of the hospital] for about two weeks, recuperated and got back out doing the same thing [dealing drugs].
>
> Interviewer: What about this guy [the robber] though?
>
> Stub: In so many details … he got his, he's no longer.
>
> Interviewer: He's no longer?
>
> Stub: In existence.

In explaining the motivation behind such extreme responses, Stub outlined the central tenets of the street code vis-à-vis the utility of retaliation:

> I handle my business, don't fuck with me … because I'm gonna get you, you know? See you have to realize if I didn't get back at him, you and him could say [Stub's] a punk. Everybody can go take [Stub's] shit. So, if he [the drug robber] gets hurt, everybody knew who hurt him. They

> might not have knew exactly [who hurt him] but they have an idea [that it was me]. If you handle your business you ain't got to even worry about it 'cause they'll say, 'That time [so-and-so] robbed [Stub], and shit he came up missing!' So that's gonna give them the fear right there not to fuck with you. That's very important if you gonna live that lifestyle. You need to let it be known that you not gonna take no shit. (Topalli, Wright and Fornango 2002: 342–43)

For offenders who have been victimized, then, the lack of access to formal justice provided by conventional society coupled with the disdain for formal justice dictated by street culture may serve to encourage retaliation.

How Predatory Violence Breeds Recursive Retaliation

As demonstrated above, street offenders are often motivated to target other criminals who can provide them with the means to sustain the party lifestyle promoted by street culture. The rub is that such victims cannot go to the police and thus have strong incentives to take the law into their own hands through violent retaliation, especially because they share with their attackers a subcultural perspective conducive to doing so. Offender/predators know this and have developed a repertoire of strategies designed to minimize the chances of retaliation (Jacobs, Topalli and Wright 2000; also see Jacques and Reynald 2011). First, during the offence, offender/predators may attempt to project a fearsome persona so that offender/victims will be deterred from trying to strike back. Bread, a twenty-year-old drug dealer and carjacker from Atlanta's south side, was adamant about this:

> Look, I try to scare the shit outta them. These guys livin' on the streets same as me. You got to put the fear in 'em or they will come back at you. I take it to another level man. I'm like the motherfuckin' Hulk. I lose my shit in front of 'em. Screaming, point that gun, make my hands shake, you know. When I'm through with 'em they either shakin' in they boots or pissin' in they pants. They sure as fuck ain't thinkin' about lookin' for me though.

Second, offender/predators may endeavour to mask their identities during offences so that they remain anonymous to their victims. This can be accomplished in several ways, including targeting strangers, employing disguises and not publicly discussing or displaying the proceeds of their crimes. Finally, offender/predators, recognizing that no strategy is foolproof, remain hypervigilant after their crimes lest they be caught off guard by victims seeking revenge. Taz, a twenty-eight-year-old carjacker and burglar from the west side of Atlanta, frequently targeted drug dealers and talked about how such seemingly paranoid measures were essential to survival:

> You know, I am really careful. I don't rob on the west side. I go to Lakewood or the Bluffs or downtown. I do my shit in the evening and make it so they don't look at my face, well you know, I come up behind them and shit. Stick 'em up! Or put the gun through window from behind so they ain't lookin' at my face. That kinda shit. I make 'em look at the ground and shit … When I was a young buck, I used to wear that jewelry that I got or flash that cash, or – this is real stupid – I would drive up and down Peachtree in a car I took if it was nice [shaking his head and laughing]. That's how they found my cousin, shit. So I just lay low, get rid of the car, get that money, them little dope and just chill on it. Now, when people ask where I got all my shit, my answer is this: Fuck you, what you askin' me about my business? But in the end man, it's tough you know. To keep it 100 per cent quiet? Motherfucker get robbed for his car, his dope, his cash … you better believe he motivated to get his shit back or get you in the back, know what I'm sayin'? So, you know, I'm always extra paranoid. You don't wanna be one of them sad motherfuckers got his head blowed off takin' a shit at McDonald's or something, know what I mean?

While such strategies undoubtedly can be effective, they are at best imperfect and in some cases actually may intensify victims' desire to retaliate. For example, they may be applied *incompetently* or *incompletely*, as when offender/predators let their identity leak out by confiding in the wrong person. Street offenders operate within tightly constrained spatial boundaries characterized by dense social networks, making it hard to constrain the flow of information. Once word of the offender/predator's identity is on the street, it is only a matter of time before the victim hears about it and is thus in a position to seek vengeance. Nook, a drug dealer from the south side of Atlanta, described such an opportunity:

> You know, I almost gave up on that thing [the fact that he had been robbed]. Didn't see the dude's face. Didn't see where he ran off too. Just chalked it up to the game, know what I mean? It was so frustrating man, to know somebody caught me like that and took my shit, but what could I do? Then, you know, I'm at this party and my cousin like, 'Hey Nook, you know there's another dude with the same [street] name as you?' And I'm like, 'Serious?' And she like, 'Yeah, he even got a chain like you had.' And then I'm like, 'Wait the fuck a minute. What'd it look like?' And when she told me it was that white gold colour with the little stones in it, I just knew that was my motherfuckin' chain. So now I'm excited

> and I ask her who the dude is, and she tell me she saw him at this party and he was driving around in such-and-such a car. So I investigated on it with my people, and after like three or four days, we figured that out. And the rest is like, you know, a happy ending. I got my shit back and then some … Ah man, it was so sweet! It was some punishment. It was almost worth getting robbed by that little bitch just to get his ass back!

Alternatively, retaliation threat management techniques may intensify violence by being applied *disproportionately.* This may happen when an offender/predator uses excessive force to dissuade a victim from striking back, but accomplishes exactly the opposite by making him or her madder still. A drug dealer named Gino, for example, told Topalli, Wright and Fornango (2002: 341) why he decided to escalate his response to being robbed by a friend:

> That's what really made me want to retaliate so bad because he scared me so. Real bad, yeah. Yeah mad, after I got to thinking about it I said [to myself], 'He threatened me like that? I got to get him!' But he left town on me. Now, if I would have caught him that same day, I would have killed him. I was mad, I would have killed him. I was angry with him.

In the same article, Stub, a veteran drug dealer from St. Louis, relayed similar sentiments when reflecting on how he'd been treated during his robbery: 'Now if he'd have [just] robbed me I might have said, "Fuck that little dope, I got plenty more of this shit." But when you shot me, see, you kind of took my manhood and you violated me, you know what I'm saying? That's your ass.'

Ironically, in those instances where offender/victims are successful at meting out punishment, their victimizers assume the role of victim. Retaliation is viewed as an affront, and the offender/predator-turned-victim will attempt counter-retaliation to satisfy his or her grievances. Recall, however, that the offenders and victims in these encounters share similar cultural commitments and cannot rely on the law to deter future victimization. This means, in turn, that successful victim retaliation is likely to set in motion a self-perpetuating cycle of vengeance and counter-vengeance, in which neither party is willing to call a truce. This was brought home in clear fashion by Goldie, a drug dealer and carjacker we have interviewed multiple times. Following the successful carjacking of a fellow drug dealer (during which Goldie shot the man in the leg and ran him over), Goldie himself was the victim of retaliation by his victim. We interviewed him during his recovery from multiple gunshot wounds and asked him: 'You don't feel like you all are even now? You shot him – he shot you. Why go after him?' He responded: 'It's [about] retaliation. When I feel good is when he taken care of … and I don't have to worry about him no more. Now down there [in the neighbourhood], when they hit you, you hit them back. That's how it is done there or you'll be a bitch. Everybody will shoot you up, whoop your ass. Know what I'm saying? Treat you like a punk' (Topalli and Wright 2013: 166). Detroit, a drug robber operating in Atlanta, focused on the pre-emptive deterrent value of counter-retaliation: 'Look, I robbed you, now you trying to kill me, so I gotta kill you before you kill me. If you are shooting at me, you better kill me because I'm fixing to kill you.' This is the essence of recursive retaliation, which sets the stage for the spread of violence.

Contagion

For those who see little value in the lives of street offenders, the fact that they prey on each other might not be particularly problematic. Indeed, many people probably regard offender-on-offender violence as a good thing in that it serves to remove criminals from society without the expensive or lengthy involvement of the criminal justice system (see Cohen, Miller and Rossman 1994: 74). But the fact is that oftentimes victims are unable or unwilling to exact vengeance on their own, and therefore seek to enlist the help of friends and associates (see Cooney 1998). In fact, our interviewees frequently indicate that their first response to being robbed is to gather up a 'posse' of their associates and drive around town looking for the transgressor (see Topalli, Wright and Fornango 2002). In the course of aiding the offender/victim, such individuals may develop grievances of their own or may themselves become the targets of counter-retaliation.

Retaliatory threat management techniques, of course, are in no way prosocial; they are intended merely to insulate the instigating offender from punishment. So, what happens when those techniques are successful? Unable to retaliate against the offender/predator, but still needing to recoup losses and maintain their reputation as someone who cannot be attacked with impunity, offender/victims may displace their aggression onto third parties (Topalli, Wright and Fornango 2002; Jacobs and Wright 2006). Although targeting law-abiding citizens risks police intervention and does little to restore the offender/victim's reputation as someone not to be crossed, it does allow offenders to recoup their losses with little fear of retaliation. Because non-offenders seldom retaliate in turn, the violence is finite – that is, it is unlikely to be propagated further. Where violence *is* likely to be propagated further, though, is when offender/victims target offenders other than those who victimized them. This is a popular choice among offender/victims who are unwilling or unable to strike back against the person who victimized them; it allows them not only to recoup their losses, but also serves to deter future predation by advertising their reputation for toughness. Doing so, however, carries the risk of instigating a new cycle of violence between the offender/victim-turned-predator and a new offender/victim, who is operating according to the same cultural dictates and encapsulating conditions that prompted the original affront. Almost inevitably, each new offender/victim will seek similar avenues of redress, thereby perpetuating yet more violence in neighbourhoods already plagued by high rates of crime (see Figure 6.2).

Conclusion

The analyses outlined above paint a picture of a series of dynamic interactive processes that, taken as a whole, serve not only to spread violence but also to concentrate and intensify its destructive impact. Enmeshed in self-perpetuating cycles of desperate partying that can only be maintained by regular infusions of fast cash, street offenders are in no position to move far afield to find suitable victims and are prone to prey on their fellow criminals who, owing to their own illicit activities, are unlikely to seek police help. In this way, offenders move forward in time, accumulating more and more enemies in the process, each of whom is bent on retaliation. Urban criminals are unusually provincial, tending to operate within the confines of their home turf and adjacent neighbourhoods. As a consequence, these offenders – each with his or her own ongoing history of offending and victimization – come into constant contact with one another. In such a world, frequent outbreaks of crosscutting violence and counter-violence are almost inevitable.

What might be done to break these ever-intensifying concentrated cycles of retaliatory violence? One useful approach might be to conceptualize recursive

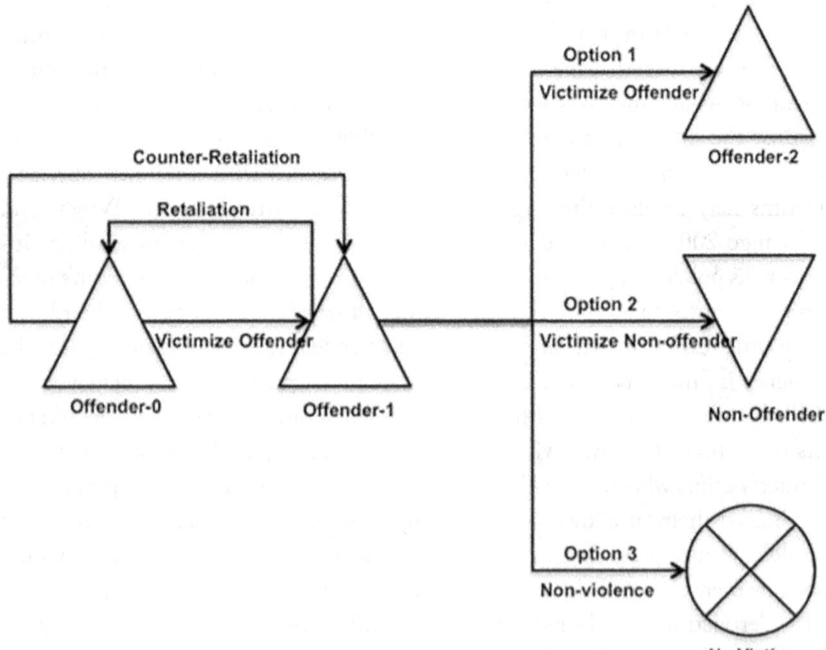

Figure 6.2 Recursion and contagion of violence

retaliation and the spread of violence in public health terms. This approach was advocated by Loftin, who, in 1985, was asked by the New York Academy of Medicine to contribute to a public health symposium on homicide:

> In epidemiology there is a fundamental distinction between infectious diseases transmitted by social contact and those that have an etiology independent of social contact. Infectious diseases are not necessarily more costly in human terms than others, but unchecked they are especially pernicious because the incidence can rise explosively (geometrically), affecting a whole population. In criminology, there is an analogous distinction between offenses that are subcultural – those that are encouraged by social contact – and those that are impulsive. My argument is that serious assaultive violence is subcultural and therefore analogous to disease. Most important, it has the potential to spread explosively in a vulnerable population. (Loftin 1986: 550; see also Patten and Arboleda-Flórez 2004)

If predatory offender-on-offender violence and its spread through recursive retaliation is viewed as a process of contagion whereby offender/predators 'infect' third-party offender/victims with violence, who in turn spread it to others, we can apply a simple disease-prevention model to understand the phenomenon. In presenting the etiological cycle of predatory crime, we demonstrated how and why offenders target other criminals for violence. These predators are the progenitors of recursive violence. In public health terms, an epidemiological investigation would designate them as the *index* or *primary* case (sometimes referred to as 'patient zero') of the affected population. Prevention models typically target index cases and their behaviour when implementing palliative or curative measures. Such models may implement primary, secondary, tertiary and quaternary measures to deal with infection and contagion. In this chapter, however, we deal with only the first two.

Primary interventions are those that occur before the person is infected and are designed to reduce or eliminate both the incidence and prevalence of a disease. For our purposes, these would include measures designed to disrupt the etiological cycle, so that offenders susceptible to its influences forgo targeting other offenders for victimization. This outcome would also prevent potential offender/victims from becoming offender/predators themselves and propagating violence to third or fourth parties. Secondary prevention occurs after an individual has been infected, but before he or she can transmit the disease to others. For our purposes, this may include strategies for preventing offender/victims from seeking direct retaliation or targeting third-party offender and non-offender victims.

To best describe how such measures can be applied to the problem of violence contagion, we draw the reader's attention to Figure 6.3, which unifies the essential components of the etiological cycle of predatory violence model (see Figure 6.1) with the violence contagion model presented above (see Figure 6.2). Connecting the two models permits us to see where the most promising primary and secondary solutions might be implemented.

We see the following promising avenues for intervention based on the above model: (1) disrupt the etiological cycle of predation by altering or eliminating the use of cash; and (2) prevent or dissuade offender/victims from seeking retaliation by removing the cultural barriers to accessing formal justice. Avenue (1) represents a primary prevention strategy, whereas avenue (2) represents a secondary intervention strategy.

Primary Prevention: Averting Retaliation by Removing Cash from the Day-to-Day Street Economy

A key causal link in the etiological cycle of predatory violence is the presence of cash. We contend here and elsewhere (see Wright and Decker 1997; Topalli and Wright 2013; Wright and Topalli 2012) that its removal through the transformation to a totally digital-based economy would significantly disrupt the ability of offenders to participate in the kind of intense partying that drives them to target other offenders in the first place, thereby instigating substantial retaliatory behaviour. The impact of cash on street corner transactions cannot be overestimated. In its absence, procuring drugs, sex and illegal goods is far more difficult because, apart from a limited amount of bartering, purveyors of these goods and services do not generally accept credit cards, checks or internet-based payments.

Cashless economies are not as far-fetched as they sound. Indeed, developed nations worldwide are rapidly approaching an era dominated by digital financial transactions (see, e.g., Garcia-Swartz, Hahn and Layne-Farrar 2006; Liao and Handa 2010). Credit card technology has made it simple for businesses to limit the amount of cash held on premises, to prohibit customers from using

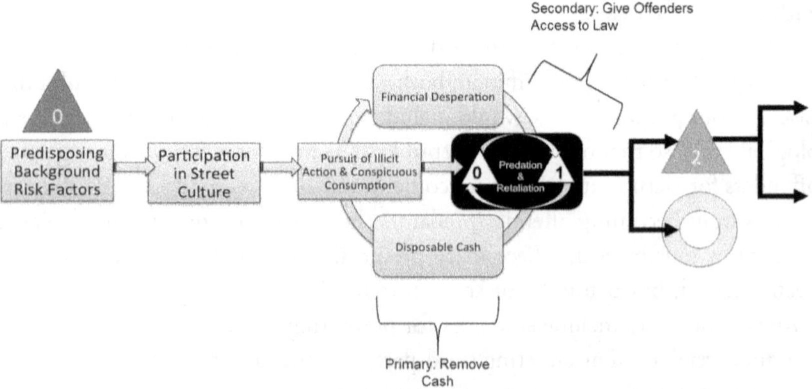

Figure 6.3 Unified model of criminality, retaliation and contagion

large denomination bills to pay for purchases and even to adopt no-cash policies. Many social service agencies have followed suit, adopting electronic debit cards in place of paper welfare checks. These initiatives foreshadow the total elimination of cash in favour of a variety of card- or internet-based methods of electronic monetary transfer. Such methods are not liquid and untraceable in the same way that cash is and leave a digital 'paper trail' that makes illicit transactions potentially far riskier. Without cash, therefore, we hypothesize that the street culture that gives rise to so much predatory street crime will be seriously undermined and that such offences will decline along with the retaliation that follows in their wake (see Wright and Topalli 2012).

Secondary Intervention: Breaking the Bonds of Encapsulation

Beyond effecting large-scale changes in the antecedent and instigating conditions that drive predatory street crime, it is worthwhile speculating about how policy might address aspects of the encapsulating conditions that prevent offenders from breaking out of ongoing recursive cycles of retaliation and counter-retaliation. Because violence has already occurred in these cases, such solutions are understood in the current discussion as forms of secondary prevention. Recall that a key reason that retaliation between offenders is recursive in that neither party is willing to call a truce. This aversion to peaceful resolution stems from two mutually reinforcing factors: first, a street culture code that requires that individuals handle their own disputes through violence; and, second, a mainstream culture that excludes offender/victims from access to the legitimate justice system. These encapsulating cultural conditions are closely interrelated. Formal legal recourse is largely unavailable to offenders in part because the street culture requires adherents to treat it with contempt, and retaliatory vigilantism is viewed as preferable to the law because offenders are treated with scorn by those who control the legal system, especially the police (Klinger 1997).

Nevertheless, it might be possible to improve offender/victims' access to legitimate legal redress, thereby reducing their motivation to take the law into their own hands. Essentially, this would require that the police and courts treat offender/victims just as they treat any other victim by encouraging them to report crimes without fear of incriminating themselves. On its face, such a solution might seem untenable. Offenders, after all, view the police with disdain, and the police traditionally want nothing to do with protecting 'criminals'. However, this dynamic may not be as clear-cut as it initially appears to be.

First, there is ample evidence that offenders are not completely averse to communicating with the police (that is, snitching) when such action suits their needs (Cooney 1998). In fact, Rosenfeld, Jacobs and Wright (2003) found that offenders frequently communicate with the police in order to take advantage of their ability to arrest, detain and prosecute rivals (see also Topalli 2005; Natapoff 2009). The police frequently respond by acting on such information without implicating or punishing the informant. Recently, efforts have been made to legitimize cooperation between those from the streets and the police via 'pro-snitching' campaigns designed to counter the street cultural push to remain silent. Police departments working with community organizations have begun to implement 'start snitching' and anti-violence campaigns to encourage residents to report crime and cooperate with police (Natapoff 2009). If, as Anderson asserts, the code of the street pervades both the offender and non-offender urban population, then it stands to reason that efforts directed towards community residents might filter back to offenders themselves, particularly if the protections of the law are made clear and reliable to such individuals. In addition, there is legal precedent for this kind of cooperation between offender/victims and the criminal justice system related to the sexual assault of prostitutes. As noted in Topalli, Wright and Fornango (2002: 349), 'it is worth recalling that one of the major accomplishments of the anti-rape movement was to get police to recognize that sex workers are especially vulnerable to rape (much in the same way that drug dealers are especially vulnerable to robbery), and that such crimes should be treated like any other sexual assault'. Some may argue that criminal/victims are undeserving of the benefits of formal justice, but we believe otherwise. Continuing to deny them those benefits leaves them with little option but to seek informal means of redress, thereby perpetuating the unchecked cycles of recursive retaliation that underpin the spread of so much urban violence.

Richard Wright is Professor and Chair of the Department of Criminal Justice and Criminology in the Andrew Young School of Policy Studies at Georgia State University, United States. He has written widely and influentially on offender decision making in real-life settings and circumstances. He was elected a Fellow of the American Society of Criminology in 2009.

Volkan Topalli is Professor of Criminal Justice and Criminology at the Andrew Young School of Policy Studies, Georgia State University, United States. His scholarly research addresses violence in urban settings, with a particular focus on the decision making of street criminals. With the support of funding from the National Science Foundation, the Harry Frank Guggenheim Foundation, the Centers of Disease Control and the National Institute of Justice, he has conducted over 300 interviews with active offenders in St. Louis and Atlanta over the past seventeen years. His research has been featured in such outlets as *Criminology*, the *British Journal of Criminology* and *Criminal Justice & Behavior*.

Scott Jacques is Associate Professor of Criminal Justice and Criminology at Georgia State University, United States. His work explores the offenders' perspective on crime and control. His coauthored book is *Code of the Suburb: Inside the World of Young Middle-Class Drug Dealers* (University of Chicago Press, 2015).

Notes

1. This chapter distinguishes between predatory and retaliatory violence. The key conceptual difference between them is that the former is primarily motivated by the desire to obtain wealth, whereas the latter is principally concerned with righting wrong (Jacques and Wright 2008b).
2. For a detailed description of our methodology and research agenda, see Wright et al. (1992); Wright and Decker (1994, 1997); Jacobs, Topalli and Wright (2000); Topalli, Wright and Fornango (2002); Topalli (2005); Jacobs and Wright (2006); Jacques and Wright (2008a, 2008b, 2011a).
3. All names are pseudonyms.
4. Throughout this manuscript, quotes appearing without reference to previous research represent original data analysed specifically for this work. The data were collected through research funded by the US National Science Foundation (Grant 0520092) and by the Georgia State University Research Foundation.
5. To be clear, not all predation and retaliation is violent (Jacques and Wright 2008b, 2011a; Jacques 2010). For example, nonviolent forms of predation and retaliation include acts of fraud and burglary primarily motivated by the desire to obtain resources or vengeance, respectively. Moreover, there are informal ways to handle victimization peacefully, such as avoidance, negotiation, informal settlement and toleration. Violence does not always beget violence. An initial offence may be nonviolent but responded to violently, just as a violent predatory act may be handled through peaceful means of social control.
6. The rules regarding snitching are not hard and fast. In their piece on street snitching, Rosenfeld, Jacobs and Wright (2003: 299) state: 'The code of the street matters for our interviewees. They cannot ignore it. It shapes world-views and provides a compelling vocabulary of motives for social action on the street. But, like all normative systems, it is not an infallible guide to behavior.'

References

Anderson, E. 1990. *Streetwise: Race, Class, and Change in an Urban Community*. Chicago: University of Chicago Press.

———. 1999. *Code of the Street: Decency, Violence, and the Moral Life of the Inner City*. New York: W.W. Norton.

Bell, C., and E. Jenkins. 1993. 'Community Violence and Children on Chicago's Southside', *Psychiatry* 56: 46–54.

Black, D. 1976. *The Behavior of Law*. New York: Academic Press.

Blumstein, A., and R. Rosenfeld. 1998. 'Explaining Recent Trends in US Homicide Rates', *Journal of Criminal Law and Criminology* 88: 1175–1216.

Bottoms, A., and P. Wiles. 1992. 'Explanations of Crime and Place', in D. Evans and N.R. Fyer (eds), *Crime, Policing and Place: Essays in Environmental Criminology*. London: Routledge.

Brezina, T., E. Tekin and V. Topalli. 2009. '"Might Not Be a Tomorrow": Anticipated Early Death and Youth Crime', *Criminology* 48: 1024–49.

Cohen, M.A., T.R. Miller and S.R. Rossman. 1994. 'The Costs and Consequences of Violent Behavior in the United States', in A.J. Reiss and J.A. Roth (eds), *Understanding and Prevention Violence: Consequences and Control*, vol. 4. Washington DC: National Academy Press, pp. 67–166.

Cohen, A.K., and J.F. Short, Jr. 1958. 'Research in Delinquent Subcultures', *Journal of Social Issues* 14: 20–37.

Cooney, M. 1998. *Warriors and Peacemakers: How Third Parties Shape Violence*. New York: New York University Press.

Decker, S.H., and J.L. Lauritsen. 2002. 'Leaving the Gang', in C.R. Huff (ed.), *Gangs in America III*. Thousand Oaks, CA: Sage, pp. 51–70.

Fagan, J., and G. Davies. 2004. 'Natural History of Neighborhood Violence', *Journal of Contemporary Criminal Justice* 20: 127–47.

Fagan, J., D.L. Wilkinson and G. Davies. 2007. 'Social Contagion of Violence', in D. Flannery, A. Vazsonyi, and I. Waldman (eds), *The Cambridge Handbook of Violent Behavior*. New York: Cambridge University Press, pp. 688–726.

Garbarino, J., N. Dubrow, K. Kostelny and C. Pardo. 1992. *Children in Danger: Coping with the Consequences of Community Violence*. San Francisco: Jossey-Bass.

Garcia-Swartz, D.D., R.W. Hahn and A. Layne-Farrar. 2006. 'The Move Toward a Cashless Society: A Closer Look at Payment Instrument Economics', *Review of Network Economics* 5: 21–40.

Hoffman, J.S. 2004. *Youth Violence, Resilience, and Rehabilitation*. New York: LFB.

Jacobs, B. 2000. *Robbing Drug Dealers: Violence Beyond the Law*. New York: Aldine de Gruyter.

Jacobs, B., V. Topalli and R. Wright. 2000. 'Managing Retaliation: Drug Robbery and Informal Social Control', *Criminology* 38: 171–98.

———. 2003. 'Carjacking, Street Life, and Offender Motivation', *British Journal of Criminology*, 43: 673–88.

Jacobs, B., and R. Wright. 2006. *Street Justice: Retaliation in the Criminal Underworld*. New York: Cambridge University Press.

Jacques, S. 2010. 'The Necessary Conditions for Retaliation: Toward a Theory of Non-violent and Violent Forms in Drug Markets', *Justice Quarterly* 27: 186–205.

Jacques, S., and D. Reynald. 2011. 'The Offenders' Perspective on Prevention: Guarding against Victimization and Law Enforcement', *Journal of Research in Crime and Delinquency* 49. doi:10.1177/0022427811408433.

Jacques, S., and R. Wright. 2008a. 'The Victimization –Termination Link', *Criminology* 46: 1009–38.

———. 2008b. 'The Relevance of Peace to Studies of Drug Market Violence', *Criminology* 46: 221–54.

———. 2008c. 'Intimacy with Outlaws: The Role of Relational Distance in Recruiting, Paying, and Interviewing Underworld Research Participants', *Journal of Research in Crime and Delinquency* 45: 22–38.

———. 2011a. 'Informal Control and Illicit Drug Trade', *Criminology* 49: 726–65.

———. 2011b. 'Ironies of Crime, Control, and Criminology', *Critical Criminology* 20: 153–67. doi:10.1007/s10612-011-9136-x.

Jefferson, T. 2004. 'From Cultural Studies to Psychosocial Criminology: An Intellectual Journey', in J. Ferrell, K. Hayward, W. Morrison and M. Presdee (eds), *Cultural Criminology Unleashed*. London: GlassHouse Press, pp. 29–40.

Katz, J. 1988. *Seductions of Crime: Moral and Sensual Attractions in Doing Evil*. New York: Basic Books.

Klinger, D.A. 1997. 'Negotiating Order in Patrol Work: An Ecological Theory of Police Response to Deviance', *Criminology* 35: 277–306.

Liao, W., and J. Handa. 2010. 'Is the Modern Economy Heading Toward a Cashless and Checkless One? Evidence from the Payments System in Canada', *IUP Journal of Bank Management* 9: 48–70.

Loftin, C. 1986. 'Assaultive Violence as a Contagious Social Process', *Bulletin of the New York Academy of Medicine* 62: 550–55.

Lorion, R.P., and W. Saltzman. 1993. 'Children's Exposure to Community Violence: Following a Path from Concern to Research to Action', *Psychiatry* 56: 55–65.

Natapoff, A. 2004. 'Snitching: The Institutional and Communal Consequences', *University of Cincinnati Law Review* 73: 645–52.

———. 2006. 'Beyond Unreliable: How Snitches Contribute to Wrongful Convictions', *Golden Gate University Law Review* 37: 107–16.

———. 2009. *Snitching: Criminal Informants and the Erosion of American Justice.* New York: New York University Press.

Nisbett, R.E., and D. Cohen. 1996. *Culture of Honor: The Psychology of Violence in the South.* Boulder, CO: Westview Press.

Patten, S.B., and J.A. Arboleda-Flórez. 2004. 'Epidemic Theory and Group Violence', *Social Psychiatry and Psychiatric Epidemiology* 39: 853–56.

Rosenfeld, R., B.A. Jacobs and R. Wright. 2003. 'Snitching and the Code of the Streets', *British Journal of Criminology* 43: 291–309.

Shover, N. 1996. *Great Pretenders: Pursuits and Careers of Persistent Thieves.* Boulder, CO: Westview Press.

Shover, N., and J.H. Copes. 2010. 'Decision-Making by Persistent Thieves and Crime Control Policy', in H.D. Barlow and S.H. Decker (eds), *Criminology and Public Policy: Putting Theory to Work.* Philadelphia: Temple University Press, pp. 128–49.

Topalli, V. 2005. 'When Being Good is Bad: An Expansion of Neutralization Theory', *Criminology* 43: 797–836.

———. 2006. 'The Seductive Nature of Autotelic Crime: How Neutralization Theory Serves as a Boundary Condition for Understanding Street Crime', *Sociological Inquiry* 76: 475–501.

Topalli, V., and R. Wright, 2013. 'Dubs, Dees, Beats, and Rims: Carjacking and Urban Violence', in D. Dabney (ed.), *Criminal Behaviors: A Text Reader*, 2nd edn. Boulder, CO: Aspen Publishers, pp. 149–69.

Topalli, V., R. Wright and R. Fornango. 2002. 'Drug Dealers, Robbery, and Retaliation: Vulnerability, Deterrence, and the Contagion of Violence', *British Journal of Criminology* 42: 337–51.

Webber, C. 2007. 'Revaluating Relative Deprivation Theory', *Theoretical Criminology* 11: 97–120.

Wilson, M., and M. Daly. 1997. 'Life Expectancy, Economic Inequality, Homicide, and Reproductive Timing in Chicago Neighborhoods', *British Medical Journal* 314: 1271–74.

Wolfgang, M.E., and F. Ferracuti. 1967. *The Subculture of Violence: Towards an Integrated Theory in Criminology.* London: Tavistock.

———. 1982. *The Subculture of Violence*, 2nd edn. Thousand Oaks, CA: Sage.

Wright, R., and S. Decker. 1994. *Burglars on the Job: Streetlife and Residential Break-ins.* Boston: Northeastern University Press.

———. 1997. *Armed Robbers in Action: Stickups and Street Culture.* Boston: Northeastern University Press.

Wright, R., S. Decker, A. Redfern and D. Smith. 1992. 'A Snowball's Chance in Hell: Doing Fieldwork with Active Residential Burglars', *Journal of Research in Crime and Delinquency* 29: 148–61.

Wright, R., and V. Topalli. 2012. 'Choosing Street Crime,' in F. Cullen and P. Wilcox (eds), *The Oxford Handbook of Criminological Theory.* Oxford: Oxford University Press, pp. 461–74.

Section IV

Faith-Based Retaliation

Spirituality and Normativity of the Retaliatory Grammar

Chapter 7

Crime and Punishment

Intentionality and Diya *in Algeria and Sudan*

Yazid Ben Hounet

This chapter focuses on *diya* (blood money) in Algeria and Sudan, a practice inscribed in the Qur^can, in various schools of Islamic jurisprudence and in some penal state laws (including in Sudan, but not in Algeria). *Diya* can be defined as a determined amount of goods or money that must be paid in the case of homicide or injury committed unjustly (sometimes intentionally) against others. It is sometimes a substitute for the talion (*qisas*), a legal and legitimate type of retaliation via violent response that we find within the *madhâhib* (sg. *madhab*), the schools of classical Islamic jurisprudence (Maliki, Hanafi, Shafii, etc.). Within these *madhâhîb* there are three categories of crime: (a) 'crimes against God (Allah)', for which there are explicit sanctions (*hudûd*) in the Qur^can; (b) sinful or forbidden behaviour or acts endangering public order or state security, for which there are local sanctions (*ta'zîr* and *siyâsa*); and offences against persons – that is, homicide and personal injury – subdivided into those requiring in principle *qisas* (retaliation of the 'an eye for an eye' type) and those requiring in principle *diya* (financial compensation or 'blood money') (Peters 2005: 7). *Qisas* existed among Arabs prior to the introduction of Islam (Tyan 1965). In the Qur^can and in Islamic norms, this practice has been recognized as a way to achieve justice, but can only be enacted against the guilty person (not against his kin) and must follow certain prescriptions (Peters 2005: 44–49). As quoted in the Qur^can (verse II, 173):

> To you who are believers the *kisas* [*qisas*] is prescribed for the slain, the freeman for the freeman, the slave for the slave and the woman for the woman; but if anyone is pardoned anything by his brother, he shall be dealt with equitably … and pay him compensation as best he can. This is an indulgence and mercy from your Lord. But he who commits a transgression after this shall be severely punished. (Schacht 1986: 177)

The Qurᶜan and schools of classical Islamic jurisprudence recognize the value of *qisas*, but also recommend forgiveness, mercy and *diya* between Muslim believers. In schools of classical Islamic jurisprudence, the right to retaliate 'can only be awarded if the killing was willful or intentional'; in other words, 'the legal effects of killing and inflicting bodily harm depend very much upon the perpetrator's intent' (Peters 2005: 43).

Many factors come into play in the practice of blood money, such as social structure and political organization. Some scholars (Schlee 2002; Drieskens 2005) have, for instance, shown the importance of a balance of power between families and clans in determining whether *diya* is applied instead of *qisas* and in determining the modalities of the compensation itself (notably the amount of blood money). In this chapter, I would like to focus on how the intentionality of homicide (or injury) is defined and, thus, how people choose *diya* as a substitute for retaliation. Indeed, the evaluation of the intentionality orients the sanction towards either *diya* or *qisas*. An ethnographic approach helps us to understand how an act is contextually defined as intentional or not. Moreover, the way to define intentionality is linked to several contextual aspects and consists of an explicit and/or implicit negotiation between the actors. First, I will briefly outline the normative aspects of *diya*, particularly in Algeria and Sudan. I will then discuss two examples that show the practical aspects that orient actors' decisions (judges or mediators) concerning the application of *diya* instead of *qisas*: both concepts are closely related since one (*diya*) may sometimes be seen as the substitution by compensation for the other (*qisas*). The analysis aims to explore two questions in particular. First, under what conditions are the circumstances of homicide (or injury) perceived to be sufficiently deviant or socially transgressive that the matter cannot be settled by *diya* and a reconciliation process, but by retaliation only? Second, how do *diya or qisas* come to be legitimized, both explicitly and implicitly?

Diya: The Normative Framework

In its most restricted meaning, more common in law, *diya* refers to compensation in the case of homicide only; compensation for injuries is more accurately called *arsh* (Tyan 1965: 350). *Diya* existed in the pre-Islamic period. It is a customary practice that has its origins in both theology and law; in the Islamic tradition, it is remembered as the compensation paid (one hundred camels) by the grandfather of the Prophet for not sacrificing his son Abdullah ibn Abdul-Muttalib (the Prophet's father), as he had originally promised to do (Chelhod 1971; Chelhod 1986: 141). In the Qurᶜan, *diya* is defined as a softening, a favour representing Allah's forgiveness and leniency regarding the rule of talion – 'an eye for an eye' (Sura II, 'The Cow', verses 178–79). *Diya* is expressly recommended in cases of unintentional murder of a worshipper by another worshipper. The conditions for setting compensation are stipulated in this case (Sura IV, 'Women', verse 92). In the *hadiths* (reports of the deeds and sayings of the Prophet Muhammad), compensation was extended to cover intentional homicide (*qatl 'amdi*). Some *hadiths* mention several forms of possible or permitted uses of *diya*, including in cases of intentional homicide – that is, murder – that the Prophet Muhammad had to judge personally (Daaïf 2006). This possibility – *diya* for intentional homicide – is accepted, but only if the victim's family (*awliyâ' al-qatîl*) forgives the murderer and accepts the compensation, which must be paid by the murderer himself and not by his clan (*'aqila*). As stated in the Qurᶜan, the concept of *diya* is connected to forgiveness, mercy and indulgence.

Diya was discussed and applied by different schools of Islamic jurisprudence, including the Maliki *fiqh* (see *al-Muwatta* of Imam Malik) used in North Africa. This practice still exists in certain regions of some Muslim countries and has been integrated into the state law of countries that have adopted shariᶜa, such as Iran, Sudan and Saudi Arabia. In these countries and elsewhere in the Muslim world, it is important to note that *diya* is discussed and re-evaluated locally among religious authority figures. For instance, in 2004, during the Doha International Conference on the Family in Qatar, Yusuf al-Qardawi pressed for gender equality in the amount of blood money to be paid for a death. Whereas the amount of *diya* for killing or injuring a woman had been half of that for a man, now the amount of *diya* in Qatari law is the same for women and men.[1]

The application of *diya* is also justified by means of custom (*'ûrf* or *adat*) in countries where shariᶜa is applied, as well as in other regions of the Muslim world where it is not applied. According to Joseph Chelhod (1986: 26), custom ('ûrf) in matters of blood money was often used by the Muslim judge (*qadi*) himself: 'Le *wergeld* lui-même n'est envisagé, par l'Islam, que d'une manière très générale … Dans un grand nombre de cas, le *qâdî* se réfère à des règles coutumières.'[2] Chelhod also explains that Yemeni custom distinguishes four kinds of homicide: accidental, by imprudence, by self-defence and with premeditation. The victim's kin has to accept compensation in the first three cases (Chelhod 1985: 157). While Chelhod makes this important distinction, he nevertheless fails to explain the criteria by which people define the intentionality of the homicide. The question is, however, central in determining when to apply blood money instead of retaliation, and thus it can lead to arguments among and pressure from the actors involved (families, judges, arbitrators, etc.). This question has also been a matter of discussion within the schools of classical Islamic jurisprudence. Jurists have focused on characteristics of the weapon (for example, whether it is sharp or not). Malikite and Shiite jurists have also taken other circumstances into consideration, such as the offender's emotional state and the relationship between the offender and the victim (for example, if there is a history of antagonism) (Peters 2005: 43). I will discuss the question of intentionality by drawing on research I have conducted in Sudan and Algeria.

Diya in Sudan and Algeria

In contrast to Algeria, Sudan – an Islamic republic – has integrated *diya* and, logically, *qisas* into its penal law. This important distinction that exists between Algeria and Sudan will allow us to broaden the comparison and give some insights into the way in which blood money is applied in Muslim societies both within and outside the courts.

Diya *in Sudan*

Diya has long been applied in Sudan within the country's different tribes.[3] In the countryside the practice still remains, for the most part, a tribal one. Indeed, the *nâzir*, *'omda* and *shaykh* (i.e., the local leaders) still manage the application of *diya* within their clan and tribes and between tribes.

Diya was incorporated into Sudan's penal code in 1983, but the actual application follows the revised penal code of 1991. This law stipulates the conditions under which *diya* is to be applied and how to determine the amount and type of *diya* that is to be paid. It distinguishes two types of *diya*: complete *diya* (for involuntary homicide) and aggravated *diya* (for murder cases in which the victim's family has forgiven the perpetrator and agreed to forgo *qisas*). It also defines the legal responsibility of the clan (*'aqila*). Article 43 of the penal code states that a judge can recommend *diya* in the following cases: (a) murder or intentional injury, if the victim or his or her legal representative waives the talion (*qisas*); (b) semi-intentional homicide or semi-intentional injuries;[4] (c) homicide or injuries caused by negligence; and (d) homicide or injuries caused by a minor or a person who is not mentally competent.

Article 45 of the 1991 penal code mentions that the people responsible for the payment of the *diya* are: (a) the guilty person in cases of voluntary homicide or injury; and (b) the guilty person and his clan (*'aqila*) in cases of semi-intentional homicide or injury or homicide caused by negligence.[5] In this article, the clan is defined as the agnatic kin of the guilty person, or his or her insurance company or agent, the persons legally responsible for the guilty person. It could also be his or her employer if the offence takes place during working hours. The amount of *diya* for homicide was fixed in 2000 at a maximum of three million Sudanese dinars (aggravated *diya*) and a minimum of two million dinars (complete *diya*) (approximately €10,000 and €6,600, respectively).[6]

These are the general stipulations. In practice, the modalities of judgment and settlement of compensation can vary. I will take here just a simple example of a homicide following a group fight that took place in Khartoum in 2007. The suspect had not been clearly identified as the murderer, but only as the owner of the knife. He was found guilty of involuntary homicide and was thus sentenced to pay the complete *diya*. Part of the amount was collected from his agnatic and uterine kin, as well as from some neighbours and friends. When his brother told me this story (January 2009), half of the *diya* had not yet been paid. Thus, the case was considered still to be pending, and violent retaliation and/or imprisonment of the perpetrator were still possible outcomes.

Diya *in Algeria*

Before the arrival of Islam, blood money did not exist in North Africa (Camps-Fabrer 1995). The Kabyles, for instance, practised the *tamegrest*, which was analogous to the talion (an eye for an eye). The practice of compensation (*diya*) is linked to the spread of Islam and the 'arabization' of North African societies. Some anthropologists specializing in North African societies have already studied *diya* cases in both Arab-speaking and Berber-speaking groups. For instance, in his book *Ritual and Belief in Morocco*, Edward Westermarck (1926: 525–26) dealt with *diya* cases (also called *diyith* in Morocco) within the framework of his study of *'ar* (literally 'shame' or 'disgrace', but the word also refers to injunctions against curses and other threats). Raymond Jamous analysed some cases of *diya* in his study of the Iqariyen, a Berber group in the mountainous Rif region of northern Morocco. He defines *diya* not as compensation for the loss of a person, but rather as the price of honour and *baraka*[7] (Jamous 1981: 87–97). These studies couple the practice of blood money with the social organization, social norms and beliefs of a given society, as they focus on the application of blood money when crimes occur in or around sacred or important places such as markets (Hart 2000: 13–15, 121–22). Thus, while the topic of blood money has been rather thoroughly discussed, the topic of intentionality related to blood money has not been addressed in much detail.

In certain regions of Algeria, and especially in the Sahara and pre-Sahara regions, *diya* is practised, with some changes that have come about as a result of interaction with the dominant state law. *Diya* is not recognized in Algerian state law; it is thus practised in parallel to state judicial processes. Among the tribes I studied in the Ksour Mountains (southwestern Algeria) and in the Khenchela Region (eastern Algeria), for instance, a large number of cases are not settled through state law procedures, but according to *diya* custom. This is principally the case when someone has been injured. In the case of homicide, the application of state law is obligatory; however, *diya* can still be applied to complement state penal law procedures, particularly if the homicide was accidental or unintentional.

The ᶜAmûr, a tribal confederation in the Ksour Mountain region whose members used to be predominantly nomadic and to some degree still are,[8] have been applying a system of *diya* since the early 1980s.[9] This date corresponds to the settlement of a large proportion of the nomads and thus to a new organization of tribal cohesion (Ben Hounet 2012a). All the tribal factions (including the inhabitants of the *qsûr* (traditional village) of Sfissifa and the families of Awlâd Ziad, a small foreign lineage recently established in the region) contribute to the blood-money payment, which was, in early 2000, 80,000 Algerian dinars (DZD) for the unintentional homicide of a child, 100,000 DZD for a woman and 120,000 DZD for a man.[10] In 2008, the price was set at 100,000 DZD regardless of the sex or age of the victim. When compared to the traditional *diya* payment of one hundred camels, this monetized *diya* (approximately equal to the value of ten sheep) is rather small and only serves to facilitate reconciliation. Each tribal faction has two *mashul* (persons responsible for the compensation) in charge of collecting money, which amounts to approximately 10,000 DZD per faction. These *mashul* are chosen on the basis of their position within their factions and their ability to reconcile people – in other words, for their diplomatic skills. In addition, the insurance company or the guilty person (when he or she has no insurance or when the insurance is not involved) has to pay an amount that corresponds to the damages established during the trial. In cases of intentional homicide, assuming that the victim's family is willing to reconcile and accept compensation, *diya* is collected from the guilty person's immediate agnatic family members only and not from all the tribes.

The charter in Appendix 1 concerns the amount of *diya* to be paid within the framework of local reconciliation practices in the Khenchela region of eastern Algeria.[11] Among the ᶜAmûr, there is no such written charter. When I met the imam of the Ben Badis mosque (the author of the charter) in Khenchela, he told me that it is not a formal charter of law (*qanûn*), but a synthesis of people's customary practices (*ᶜûrfiya*) regarding *diya* in the region. In consultation with other imams involved in local reconciliation practices, he drafted a first version of this document. This version was revised and elaborated in 2008. People can follow the recommendations in this document if they want to, but they are not obliged to; it is simply a set of guidelines based on the amounts of *diya* people in the region usually pay. This charter was eventually published in a newspaper (without the imam's agreement), which led to police accusations that he was trying to create a 'state within the state' (*dawla fi dawla*). The imam defended himself against these accusations, saying that he and the other imams had drawn up the document simply because some people were demanding excessive amounts for *diya* and that he never intended to have it published. The police response to this situation indicates that *diya* and reconciliation practices are tolerated by the Algerian state as long as they remain informal. We also observe that the imam distinguishes between *al qanûn* (rules, state law (in contrast to *shariᶜa*) and *ûrf* (custom), and thereby subtly acknowledges the authority of the state without delegitimizing the importance and reality of local reconciliation (*sulh*) and *diya* practices. He pointed this out when defending himself against the charges the police and the administration brought against him. It is also interesting that the imam did not refer to *diya* as an Islamic recommendation, but rather emphasized its customary background (*ᶜûrfiya*). This charter recommends the amount of *diya* to be paid for many categories of crime or tort (homicide, injury, rape, etc.). It also contains a distinction between intentional, semi-intentional and unintentional homicide. Because of the problems that the charter's publication caused for the imam, I was not able to work directly with him on concrete cases, but I can say that the way in which *diya* is defined and applied and the amounts of the compensation are all very similar to the application of *diya* in the region of the Ksour Mountains. The charter is nevertheless much more elaborated and includes more categories of crime and tort than can be solved through *diya* compensation and banquet ceremony in the region of the Ksour Mountains.

The people I interviewed who were involved in *diya* cases told me that contemporary *diya* practices no longer conform to *diya* as it is supposed to be according to Islamic norms and Bedouin custom. In Maliki jurisprudence and in Bedouin custom, the *diya* compensation is indeed one hundred camels for an involuntary homicide. However, the compensation payments in the region of the Ksour Mountains (Ain Sefra) and in Khenchela are clearly smaller: for example, as noted earlier, the *diya* for an involuntary homicide is approximately 100,000 DZD – the price of ten sheep. The reasons cited are the high cost of living and the fact that the guilty person or the insurance companies (most cases are accidental homicides)[12] must also pay the victim's family the damages set during the civil judgment. In addition, they have to pay the fine fixed during the penal judgment. The *diya* amount is thus a symbolic reminder of community (tribal) solidarities and pressures. According to people I interviewed, local reconciliation (*sulh*) and *diya* come to complement state law, which can be too slow and does not take into account the collective responsibility of the guilty person's group (to prevent retaliation) and of the victim's group (to retaliate). It is here that the distinction between Algerian positive law, which focuses above all on the individual, and customary practices, which deal mainly with communities and groups, becomes most pronounced. In Algerian state penal law, only adult persons are responsible for their acts. The communities, the groups they belong to, cannot be held responsible for the acts of their members. As Joseph Chelhod (1971) noted when discussing the Bedouins of the Middle East, this collective includes members of the agnatic line up to the fifth degree, the *khamsa* (the Arabic word for 'five'). But in cases of voluntary homicide among the ᶜAmûr, people talk only of persons who share the same name and not of the *khamsa*. This means that the responsible group may be larger or smaller than the agnatic family up to the fifth degree.

Questioning Intentionality

As explained above, the unintentionality of homicide is one of the conditions for the application of *diya* as opposed to *qisas*. Indeed, *diya* is for the most part recommended when the homicide is unintentional – as a result of accident, imprudence, self-defence and so forth. However, defining and determining intentionality is no simple matter, as it is directly connected to the idea of premeditation and can be influenced by a number of factors, such as the context, the actors involved, their standards, their backgrounds and the factual elements. Of course, intentionality is also not clearly defined in the authoritative texts, that is, the Qurʿan or the penal code. Classical Islamic scholars have tried to provide some guidelines on how to determine intentionality (see Peters 2005: 43), but they are limited and not necessarily followed by the different actors (judges, arbitrators, elders, notables, etc.). Below I will discuss two examples of this: the first from the Sudan and the second from Algeria.

The Sudanese Case

This case is based on the decision of a judge, handed down on 1 July 2007, following a trial that occurred in the tribunal of Khartoum North. The case involved a homicide that took place in 2005 in the Arab market in Khartoum. The accused had escaped from a psychiatric hospital and stabbed another man, who died shortly thereafter. There was no doubt that the accused had in fact stabbed the victim; rather, the purpose of the trial was to establish whether the homicide was intentional or (due to the purported mental instability of the person accused) unintentional.

Here I will highlight certain excerpts from the decision to extract the argumentation concerning the question of intentionality (see Appendix 2 for a translation of the court decision):

> the accused person used a knife that was on display [in the market] in order to stab the victim. The result was a profound injury to the thorax followed by profuse bleeding … The court concluded in this case that the accused was aware that his act would lead to death because of the use of a knife at the level of the heart (a vulnerable human organ) and at its location in the thorax.

We observe that the decision is not based on the accused's personality or his possible motivation, just as it does not focus on the fact that the weapon was not originally in the accused person's hands. More pragmatic considerations – the nature and location of the strike on the body – orient the court's decision, resulting in the 'logical' reasoning that the location of the strike indicates the perpetrator's awareness of the potential consequences of his actions.

This example shows clearly that the judges (and the courts) 'are without doubt more concerned about demonstrating their capacity to judge correctly according to the standards of their profession, the relevant formal constraints, the judicial sources on which it is based and the norms of the interpretative work that it implies, than reinforcing the Islamic legal notion that is being used' (Dupret 2011).[13]

In the case in question, the court rejected the insanity defence; the accused was judged to be mentally competent and therefore responsible for his actions, and the homicide was deemed to be culpable and 'semi-intentional'.[14] The person was put in jail and required to pay aggravated *diya* (three million Sudanese dinars, or approximately €10,000).

No attempt at reconciliation was made by the guilty party's family; in fact, they demonstrated no solidarity with the defendant and clearly expressed their lack of support in front of the judge. This led the judge to find a compromise between involuntary homicide, justified by the presumed insanity of the guilty person – which would have been interpreted as an affront by the victim's family and would force the family of the guilty person to contribute to the *diya* – and intentional homicide, which would carry the death sentence because the victim's family had shown no inclination to forgive the accused. The fact that *qisas* is inscribed in the penal law of Sudan has a direct impact on the way in which the case is judged because it gives the victim's family the opportunity to ask for a sentence commensurate with the crime, which in this case would be the death penalty. In such a context, the judge – if he is humane and sympathetic (as was the case with this judge) – has to find a compromise in order to avoid handing down a penalty he feels is too harsh.

The Algerian Case

During fieldwork in the region of Ain Sefra (Ksour Mountains) in October 2010, I was told about the murder in March 2010 of a semi-nomadic shepherd from the Lamdabih clan in which five members of the Awlad Shahmi clan (one murderer and four presumed accomplices) were implicated. Both clans belong to the ᶜAmûr tribal confederation. Three attempts at reconciliation, all led by notables of the region who had proposed *diya*, had failed. The victim's father refused to accept reconciliation between the two clans and settlement via *diya* before the judgment of the court. He wanted the court to shed light on the role played by the four accomplices in order to define the degree of complicity and premeditation of the crime, and thus the possibility of reconciliation not with the culprits, but with the clans to which they belonged. As the trial had not yet started, the conflict was still open and, in order to prevent other attacks, the tents of the guilty person's clan that had been in close proximity to the victim's clan's encampment were moved more than 100 km away. This in itself can be interpreted as a form of forced exile and thus as indirect social retaliation.

This case is similar to another one involving two homicides that occurred in 2006 and that ended in reconciliation and acceptance of *diya*. In 2006, two members of the Awlâd ᶜAbdallah faction of the Awlâd Bûbkar tribe (in the ᶜAmûr tribal confederacy) killed two members of the Lamdabih faction (of the same tribe). These were intentional homicides that followed a quarrel. The guilty persons were put in jail, but the murders led to considerable agitation within the

Lamdabih faction. The parents of the guilty persons and the members of the Awlâd ᶜAbdallah faction managed to engage in a *diya* process in order to calm the tensions and avoid vendettas against the murderers and their parents. Several *shuyukh* (notables) and *kbar* (elders) belonging to the ᶜAmûr confederacy were asked to come with the members of the Awlâd ᶜAbdallah faction to settle the dispute generated by the two homicides. After several solicitations and considerable pressure from the *shuyukh* and the *kbar*, the victims' families accepted compensation in the amount of 400,000 DZD (200,000 DZD for each victim). The money was collected by the Awlâd ᶜAbdallah faction, namely, by the perpetrators' agnatic kin. The latter, with the *shuyukh* and the *kbar*, visited the victims' families. They brought with them several sheep for the sacrifice. The meal was organized by the victims' families, and the compensation was handed over at the end of the meal. The *diya* process was closed. The penal and civil judgment took place some months later. Because the homicides were intentional, the victims' families did not request reduced sentences. The two guilty persons were sentenced to 20 years in prison and to the payment of moral damages. They are now in prison.

In these two examples, reconciliation processes were urgently undertaken immediately following the crimes in order to avoid an escalation of violence between the clans and the associated vendettas. Visits, sacrifices and collective meals are all carried out in order to mend the link that has been broken. But it also gives the victim's family the necessary time to evaluate how directed vengeance (*qisas*) or a vendetta can be carried out if such solutions are deemed better than reconciliation.

It is interesting to see the involvement of *mashul* (mediators) in these two cases. Indeed, most of the *mashul* told me that they do not involve themselves in cases of intentional homicide. Nevertheless, both cases presented here would normally be seen as intentional homicides. I would like to explain this apparent contradiction using another interpretation based on spatiotemporal conditions. Using David Delaney's concept of nomosphere, Bertram Turner (2013) shows, for instance, the impact of the spatiotemporal dimensions in a case of drunkenness and dispute that happened during the night near a village market in the Souss (Morocco). Topics of time and space, linked to law, have also been theorized in a recent volume edited by Franz and Keebet von Benda-Beckmann and Anne Griffiths (2009).

When I discussed the cases with the different *mashul*, they all indicated that the homicides took place 'in the area of Fortassa' (*mjit Fortassa*) and during the spring (*rbi'*). No one indicated to me the exact location and date, as a judge, for instance, would do. Yet this specific definition of spatiotemporal dimension is itself a way of interpreting and even justifying the degree of intentionality that one ultimately attributes to an actor. Indeed, the expression 'in the area of Fortassa' indicates that the homicides took place far away from the main town (Ain Sefra), in a space reserved for pastoralism, near the Moroccan border (and thus also a space of smuggling). The word *rbi'* indicates that the homicides took place during the spring, when nomadic shepherds are seeking pastures for their sheep, and thus a potential conflict period. In other words, the fact that the homicides took place in such a place and time implies that they are more likely to be considered semi-intentional. If they had taken place in a town or during another period, they would probably have been considered intentional and *mashul* would not have been involved in the cases.

Conclusion

These two cases show how the qualification of intentionality is evaluated. The actors are here inscribed within different logics connected first and foremost to the contexts in which the case settlements are evaluated (tribunal courts in the first case and extra-state judicial settlement in the second case). The arguments are linked to situated and specific interpretations: witnesses and forensic tests in the first case and knowledge of the spatiotemporal context in the second case.

As a result, the manner in which the choice is made between reconciliation and *diya* on the one hand and (violent) retaliation on the other hand is linked to the way in which intentionality is evaluated. The balance of power between the parties can go some way towards explaining why an offence is evaluated as intentional, semi-intentional or unintentional, and demonstrates why we must always be aware of the balance of power between the parties (see, e.g., Schlee, this volume). But it does not explain everything; in particular, it does not explain how the different actors, in context, interpret, evaluate and explain intentionality according to their own standards.

More generally, and in order to broaden the discussion, there are a number of different reasons for choosing reconciliation (*sulh*) and *diya* over retaliation. Reconciliation and *diya* can also be a matter of honour. This was the case, for instance, when a member of the Khlifi, a lineage of the ᶜAmûr, was responsible for injuring a resident of Algiers (the capital) in a car accident in 2004. The injured person had been covered by his car insurance following the accident (his insurance company then dealt with the guilty person's insurance company). Members of the Khlifi lineage went to Algiers to hand over the *diya*. The injured party was surprised because this practice (blood money) is rare among the urban residents in the northern part of the country. In this case, members of the Khlifi lineage did not give him *diya* to prevent vengeance. It was, as one of them told me, 'a matter of honour'. At that time I did not understand why it was a matter of honour, but I would come to understand it later. In fact, the Khlifi lineage is not a leading one within the ᶜAmûr confederation. Moreover, the lineage's apical ancestor had been integrated into the ᶜAmûr by alliance. This ancestor and the Khlifi lineage owe their respect within the ᶜAmûr mostly to the fact that the ancestor was a *taleb*, a religious man (but not with a prestigious ancestry), and that his descendants present themselves as religious. Thus, it would be regarded as dishonourable for them not to follow religious recommendations that, in this case, would have meant not following the practice of *diya* when it is recommended. Thus, we must also be aware of the positions of individuals and groups not only in relation to the victim's group, but also in relation to their own larger group, their own self-presentation and the variety of normative standards.

Yazid Ben Hounet is a social anthropologist, research fellow at the Centre National de Recherche Scientifique and member of the Laboratoire d'Anthropologie Sociale (CNRS – Collège de France – EHESS), France. He received his Ph.D. from the Ecole des Hautes Etudes en Sciences Sociales (Paris). His research lies at the intersection of legal and political anthropology in the Muslim context. He also undertook research in the field of kinship studies. He is the author of two books entitled *L'Algérie des tribus* (L'Harmattan) and *Parenté et anthropologie sociale* (Gingko éditeur), both published in 2009.

Notes

1. See http://www.islamonline.net/English/News/2004-12/24/article05.shtml; http://www.courrierinternational.com/article/2009/04/30/le-prix-du-sang.
2. '*Wergeld* [blood money] is only envisaged by Islam in a very general manner … In many cases, the *qadi* refers to customary rules.'
3. See, for instance, Cunnison (1972). We also found the practice of blood money among the tribes of South Sudan, such as the *cut* among the Nuer (Evans-Pritchard 1940).
4. The Criminal Act of 1991 defines three types of homicide: murder (Article 130), semi-intentional homicide (Article 131) and homicide by negligence (Article 132). For an explanation of semi-intentional homicide, see 'Sudan: The Criminal Act 1991', *Arab Law Quarterly* 9(1) (1994): 64–65.
5. In schools of classical Islamic jurisprudence, 'the basic distinction is between intentional (*'amd*) and accidental (*khata*) homicide or wounding. In addition, all schools but the Malikites recognize an intermediate category of semi-intentional homicide (*shibh 'amd*)' (Peters 2005: 43).
6. The average monthly wage is around €200 a month.
7. Blessing and beneficent force from God.
8. The ᶜAmûr comprises three tribes: the Swala, the Awlâd Bûbkar and the Awlâd Salim. Each tribe (*'arch*) is composed of factions (*farqa*). In 1957, the Swala population was 3,765, the Awlâd Bûbkar 3,908 and the Awlâd Salim 1,500 (Bison 1957: 16). There is no more recent data on tribal membership. It is therefore difficult to assess the exact number of persons belonging to these groups nowadays. However, if we take into account the proportion of the ᶜAmûr in the region where they live (the area of Ain Sefra in southwestern Algeria), we can estimate their numbers at around 40,000 – the most populous group in the southern area of the *wilaya* (region) of Naama (mainly around Ain Sefra). We can also estimate that approximately 25 per cent of the ᶜAmûr live a semi-nomadic way of life (part-time or year round) in tents (*khaima*). The number of semi-nomads has increased since independence, but not as rapidly as the settled population; see Ben Hounet (2009). On *diya* among the ᶜAmûr, see Ben Hounet (2010a, 2010b).

9. Interviews with the *mashul*, persons in charge of the compensation, conducted during fieldwork in 2008.
10. According to the law, the minimum wage is around 12,000 DZD per month (approximately €120).
11. For further elements about this charter/guideline and *diya* in Algeria, see Ben Hounet (2012b).
12. Insurance does not pay for the *diya*, but for the damages caused by the policy holders. The liability insurance functions mainly in case of accidents (such as automobile accidents).
13. Translated from the French by the author.
14. According to Articles 131/2 and 131/3 of the Criminal Act of 1991*, 131/2: 'Notwithstanding the provision of section 130 (1), culpable homicide shall be deemed semi-intentional in any of the following cases: Where the offender commits culpable homicide under the influence of mental, psychological or nervous disturbance which manifestly affects his ability to control his acts. 131/3: Whoever commits the offence of semi-intentional homicide shall be punished with imprisonment for a term not exceeding five years, without prejudice to the right of *diya* [in other words, the sentence does not compromise the victim's family's right to claim *diya*].
15. In what follows, 10,000 DZD is approximately equal to €1.

References

Ben Hounet, Y. 2009. *L'Algérie des tribus. Le fait tribal dans le Haut Sud-Ouest contemporain.* Paris: Editions L'Harmattan.

———. 2010a. 'La tribu comme champ social semi autonome', *L'Homme* 194: 57–74.

———. 2010b. 'La *diya* (prix du sang): gestion sociale de la violence et logiques sacrificielles en Algérie (Sud-Oranais)', *Annales de la Fondation Fyssen* 24: 196–215.

———. 2012a. 'Algérie: la tribu comme horizon politique', *Maghreb/Machrek* 2(212): 77–89.

———. 2012b, '"Cent dromadaires et quelques arrangements"' Notes sur la *diya* (prix du sang) et son application actuelle au Soudan et en Algérie', *Revue des Mondes Musulmans et de la Méditerranée* 131: 203–21. Retrieved 1 September 2016 from http://remmm.revues.org/7695.

Benda-Beckmann, F. v., K. v. Benda-Beckmann and A. Griffiths (eds). 2009. *Spatializing Law: Anthropological Geography of Law in Society*. Farnham: Ashgate.

Bison, L. 1957. *Monographie de l'Annexe d'Ain Sefra (mise à jour au 31 décembre 1957).* Ministère de l'Algérie, Territoires du Sud.

Camps-Fabrer, H. 1995. 'Diya', in *Encyclopédie Berbère*, vol. 15: 2367–69. Aix-en-Provence: Edisud.

Chelhod, J. 1971. *Le droit dans la société bédouine, recherches ethnologiques sur le 'orf ou droit coutumier des Bédouins.* Paris: Marcel Rivière et Cie.

———. 1985. *L'Arabie du Sud: histoire et civilisation*, vol. 3. Paris: Maisonneuve et Larose.

———. 1986. *Les structures du sacré chez les Arabes*. Paris: Maisonneuve et Larose.

Cunnison, I. 1972. 'Blood Money, Vengeance and Joint Responsibility: The Baggara Case', in I. Cunnison and Wendy James (eds), *Essays in Sudan Ethnography*. London: Hurst, pp. 105–25.

Daaïf, L. 2006. 'Le prix du sang (*diya*) au premier siècle de l'islam', *Hypothèses* 1: 329–42.

Drieskens, B. 2005. 'What Happened? Stories, Judgements and Reconciliations', *Egypte Monde Arabe* 1: 145–58.

Dupret, B. 2011. 'Introduction : Pertinence et perspectives de la référence anthropologique à la catégorie "droit islamique"', in Y. Ben Hounet and B. Dupret (eds), *Les Rencontres du CJB, n° 1: De l'anthropologie du droit musulman à l'anthropologie du droit dans les mondes musulmans*. http://www.cjb.ma/images/stories/Rencontres_CJB_1.pdf.

Evans-Pritchard, E.E. 1940. *The Nuer*. Oxford: Clarendon Press.

Hart, D. 2000. *Tribe and Society in Rural Morocco*. London: Frank Cass.

Jamous, R. 1981. *Honneur et Baraka, les structures sociales traditionnelles dans le Rif*. Paris: Maison des Sciences de l'Homme.

Malik ibn Anas. 1989. *al-Muwata of Imam Malik ibn Anas, the First Formulation of Islamic Law*, trans. A'. Abdurrahman Bewley. London: Kegan Paul.

Peters, R. 2005. *Crime and Punishment in Islamic Law: Theory and Practice from the Sixteenth to the Twenty-First Century*. Cambridge: Cambridge University Press.

Schacht J. 1986, 'Kisas [qisas]', in *The Encyclopaedia of Islam*, 2nd edn, vol. 5. Leiden: Brill, pp. 177–80.

Schlee, G. 2002. 'Régularités dans le chaos. Traits récurrents dans l'organisation politico-religieuse et militaire des Somali', *L'Homme* 161: 17–50.

Sudan: The Criminal Act 1991. 1994. *Arab Law Quarterly* 9(1): 32–80. doi: 10.2307/3381514.

Turner, B. 2013 'Religious Subtleties in Disputing: Spatiotemporal Inscriptions of Faith in the Nomosphere in Rural Morocco', in F. v. Benda-Beckmann, K. v. Benda-Beckmann, M. Ramstedt and B. Turner (eds), *Religion in Dispute: Pervasiveness of Religious Normativity in Disputing Processes*. Basingstoke: Palgrave Macmillan, pp. 55–73.

Tyan, E. 1965. '*Diya*', in *Encyclopédie de l'Islam*, vol. II. Paris: Maisonneuve and Larose, pp. 350–52.

Westermarck, E. 1926. *Ritual and Belief in Morocco*. New York: University Books.

Appendix 1

الرقم	نوع القضية	تقدير الدية وقصاصها
01	القتل العمدي	خمسون مليون سنتيم دية وعشرة ملايين للوليمة مع عدم التنازل على الدعوة القضائية
02	القتل شبه العمدي	25 مليون سنتيم دية و05 ملايين للوليمة مع تنازل الطرف المدني على الدعوة القضائية
03	القتل الخطأ الذي تتسبب فيه مختلف وسائل الاسترزاق كالمركبات بأنواعها	0- في حالة وجود وثائق المركبة ورخصتي التامين والسياقة فالدية تقدر بعشرة ملايين والوليمة بثلاثة ملايين . 0- في حالة انعدام وثائق المركبة ورخصتي التامين والسياقة فالدية تقدر ب : 25مليون سنتيم وخمسة ملايين وليمة مع التنازل عن القضية في الحالتين . 0- في حالة عودة ملكية المركبة لمؤسسة أو شركة فتتحمل هذه الأخيرة مع السائق باعتباره موظفا وذلك في حالة وقوع الحدث في أوقات العمل وبدون أي مشكل خارج القانون. أما في حالة العكس فتسقط المسؤولية على السائق لا سيما ان كان في حالة سكر.
04	القتل الخطأ باستعمال السلاح الناري في الأعراس والأفراح	0 في حالة استعمال الذخيرة الحية والأسلحة الحربية فتقدر الدية بـ25 : مليون سنتيم مع 05 ملايين وليمة والتنازل عن القضية قضائيا. 0 في حالة استعمال الذخيرة غير الحية فتقدر الدية بعشرة ملايين سنتيم وثلاثة ملايين وليمة والتنازل عن القضية
05	موت العامل _ الصانع أو المعاون -	0- في حالة وفاة عامل تم جلبه من طرف مؤسسة أو شركة فالدية تدفع من طرف الهيئة المستخدمة وتقدر بنفس دية القتل الخطأ. 0 _ في حالة عمل الضحية عند شخص عادي فلا دية عليه وهناك وليمة إكرامية . 0 في حالة وفاة مساعد الصانع أي المعاون وقد تم جلبه من طرف صاحب البيت أو صاحب الهيئة المستخدمة فان الدية على عاتق الذي جلبه لا على الصانع وهي الدية نفسها للقتل الخطأ . 0 ترتفع دية المتوفي الى 25 مليون سنتيم وخمسة ملايين سنتيم كوليمة إذا كان الضحية قاصرا دون سن 18 عاما
06	الوفاة الناتج عن لعب الصبيان	0 في حالة ما كان عمر الفاعل أقل من 12 سنة فكله قتل خطأ ومهما كانت طريقته. 0 أما إذا تعدى السن 12 عاما فعمده عمدا وخطاه خطأ
07	إتلاف وفقدان الأعضاء والأطراف	0 ان تعلق الأمر بعضو او طرف زوجي كالأرجل واليدين فالدية تقدر ب : 25 مليونا . 0 ان تعلق الأمر بعضو او طرف فردي كالجهاز التناسلي فالدية تقدر ب : 50 مليون سنتيم
08	حوادث المرور	0 في حالة وفاة سائقي مركبتين نتيجة تصادم فلا دية وتتولى الجهات القضائية القضية . 0 في حالة وفاة أحد السائقين فيتولى السائق الحي دفع دية القتل الخطأ في حالة صحة الوثائق . 0 في حالة وفاة شخص بصدمة السيارة فالدية عشرة ملايين سنتيم ووليمة بثلاثة ملايين سنتيم مع التنازل . 0 في حالة وفاة شخص دون السائقين فالمتسبب في الحادث هو من يتولى أعباء الدية السالفة الذكر مع الاستعانة بالخبرة القضائية .
09	حوادث الجروح والكسور	تدرس حسب الشهادات الطبية وتتراوح قيمة الدية ما بين مليون و37 مليون حسب الحالات المبينة أعلاه .
10	العنف العمدي _ المواجهات الجماعية	تقدر الدية بثلاثة ملايين سنتيم مع تعويض كل الخسائر إن وجدت .
11	حوادث كسور الأصابع والأضلاع من يد ورجل والف واسنان	تدرس حسب الشهادات الطبية وتتراوح قيمة الدية ما بين مليون و37 مليون حسب الحالات المبينة أعلاه . مع تحديد قيمة دية كسر السن الواحد بمليون سنتيم
12	قتل السارق وقتل صاحب البيت او المحل المستهدف	0 لا دية مفروضة عن قاتل السارق 0 دية القتل العمدي 50 مليونا لقاتل صاحب المنزل او المحل المستهدف عمدا .
13	الاغتصاب الفردي والجماعي	0 دية ثمانية ملايين سنتيم لغاصب عزباء مع الزواج بها . 0 دية 15 مليون سنتيم لغاصب عزباء رفض الزواج بها 0 دية 7ملايين ونصف مليون تدفع من طرف شخصين للعزباء في حالة اغتصابها من طرفهما 0 دية خمسة ملايين سنتيم تدفع من طرف كل شخص للضحية في حالة الاغتصاب الجماعي للعزباء 0 دية عشرون مليون للفاعل في حالة اغتصاب متزوجة او عاقدة تدفع لزوجها.
14	اللواط	0 دية 10 ملايين سنتيم للفاعل 0 دية مليونين ونصف مليون للفاعل في حالة محاولة اللواط
15	المهر	حدد مهر الزوج بعشرة ملايين سنتيم بالإضافة الى الكبش الذي يقدم لأهل العروس ليلة الزفاف

Figure 7.1 Khenchela's charter (granting of rights)

Translation

Table 7.1 Shaikh Mascûd Shîr Masâl, Imam of the Abd al-hamîd ban Bâdîs mosque in Khenchela

N°	Incident	Measure of *diya* (blood money) and its talion (*qisâs*)[15]
1	Intentional homicide	50 million DZD for the *diya* and 10 million DZD for the banquet, without renunciation of prosecution
2	Semi-intentional homicide	25 million DZD for the *diya* and 5 million for the banquet, with renunciation of prosecution
3	Involuntary homicide caused by instruments of subsistence (such as automobiles)	- If the driver has a valid automobile registration, insurance policy and licence, the recommended *diya* is 10 million DZD and 3 million for the banquet, with renunciation of prosecution - If the driver does not have a valid automobile registration, insurance policy and licence, the recommended *diya* is 25 million and 5 million for the banquet, with renunciation of prosecution - If the car belongs to a society or an organization and the accident occurred during working hours and without violation of state law (*al qânûn*), the employer and the driver, as the employee, must both contribute to the *diya*. If this is not the case, however, the driver alone assumes the responsibility, particularly if he was driving under the influence of alcohol
4	Involuntary homicide caused by weapons during wedding celebrations	- If real bullets and weapons were being used, the recommended *diya* is 25 million and 5 million for the banquet, with renunciation of prosecution - If blanks were being used, the recommended *diya* is 10 million and 3 million for the banquet, with renunciation of prosecution
5	(Involuntary) homicide of an employee, a craftsman or an assistant	- In case of homicide of an agent recruited by a firm, the firm has to pay a *diya* equivalent to the *diya* for semi-intentional homicide - If the victim worked for an individual person, there will be no *diya*. There will only be a banquet - In case of homicide of the assistant of a craftsman or an employee recruited by the owner of a corporation or of a house, the recruiter has to pay a *diya* equivalent to the one for semi-intentional homicide. The amount of *diya* would be 25 million and 5 million for the banquet if the victim is under 18 years of age
6	Homicide that occurs while children are playing	- If the child (perpetrator) is under 12 years of age, the incident is considered involuntary homicide no matter how it happened - If he is more than 12 years of age, the homicide would be judged as intentional or semi-intentional

7	Loss of a body part	- If it is a paired limb such as a hand or a leg, the recommended *diya* is 25 million - If it is an odd numbered limb/member such as the male organ, the recommended *diya* is 50 million
8	Road accidents	- If both drivers involved in a collision are killed, there will be no *diya*. The legal authority will judge the case - If only one driver is killed, the surviving one will pay *diya* for involuntary manslaughter according to the present document - In cases of vehicular homicide, the recommended *diya* is 10 million and 3 million for the banquet, with renunciation of prosecution - In case of the death of a third person (i.e., not one of the drivers), the driver who caused the fatality would pay the *diya*, with the help of legal authorities (to determine who caused the death)
9	Injuries and fractures	The *diya* is determined with reference to the medical records. It will vary from 1 to 37 million in accordance with the cases cited above (loss of a body part)
10	Intentional violence and confrontations	*Diya* would be 3 million. It would be added compensation for all the damages
11	Fractures of fingers, ribs, hands, legs, nose and teeth	*Diya* is determined with reference to medical records. It will vary from 1 to 37 million in accordance with the cases cited above. *Diya* for one tooth is 1 million
12	Homicide of a thief or of the owner of house targeted by a thief	- No *diya* for the homicide of a thief - The *diya* for the intentional homicide of the owner of a shop or a house targeted by a thief is 50 million
13	Individual and collective rape	- The rapist of an unmarried woman has to pay a *diya* of 8 million if he agrees to marry the victim - The rapist of an unmarried woman has to pay a *diya* of 15 million if he refuses to marry the victim - Two rapists of an unmarried woman have to pay a *diya* of 7.5 million each - In case of the collective rape of an unmarried woman, the rapists have to pay a *diya* of 5 million each - The *diya* for the rape of a married woman is estimated at 20 million, to be given to the husband
14	Sodomy	- The recommended *diya* is 10 million for the seducer (the active person) - The recommended *diya* is 10 million for the seducer in cases of attempted sodomy
15	Bride-wealth	The recommended bride-wealth is 2.5 million, with a ram to be offered to the bride's family on the wedding night

Appendix 2

Court Decision in Khartoum North (1 July 2007)

In the name of God, Most Gracious, Most Merciful
The decision comes down and is dated 01/07/2007. In the Arab market of Khartoum (inside the petrol station), south of the Great Mosque, the accused, Haitam O., was walking in an alley in the centre mentioned above after escaping from the psychiatric ward (*Kubar*). He met the deceased, Abderrahmane E. Seeing in him and other passers-by monsters who wanted to devour him, he took an Omani knife that was on display in the market and stabbed him in the back and then left. The victim was sent to hospital, where he died. An autopsy was ordered after the event. The accused was in a miserable psychological state and was therefore given the necessary treatment so that he could respond to the accusations against him.

He was questioned on the basis of the facts attributed to Section 130 of the Penal Code. In his testimony, he claimed that he was not conscious of his actions and he therefore could not be legally liable. The court in the ensuing discussion referred to Article 129 of the Penal Code, which reads as follows: 'Homicide is to kill a living person with or without premeditation. And murder (voluntary homicide) is to kill with the intention to kill.' As stipulated in Article 130 of the Penal Code: 'Killing [i.e., murder] is 1. to take a human life; 2. premeditation in the act of taking a life; 3. the relationship between the act and death.'

The court discussed the following points: Did the accused, Haitam O., stab the victim, Abderrahmane E? The answer was yes. The prosecution witnesses testified that they saw the victim stabbed in the back in the Arab market in the presence of the police, and that he was taken to hospital where an autopsy was ordered. The autopsy report revealed a wound in the thorax with a depth of 9 cm and a width of 1 cm on the left side. There was also damage to the diaphragm. The left ventricle of the heart was pierced. The causes of death: a wound to the heart and bleeding due to injury. Document signed by coroner Dr. Akil Ennour S. E., dated 01/07/2005.

The second point: Did the accused intend to kill the deceased? The intention is defined by section 03 of the Criminal Code and on the basis of the case against the Government of Sudan Aissa A. M. Vol. No. 72 p. 74: the accused person used a knife that was on display [in the market] in order to stab the victim. The result was a profound injury to the thorax followed by profuse bleeding … In the testimony of prosecution witnesses, they found a wound in the thorax and bleeding due to the injury. The coroner's report confirms the facts. The court concluded in this case that the accused was aware that his act would lead to death because of the use of a knife at the level of the heart (a vulnerable human organ) and at its location in the thorax.

The third point: 'Is there a relationship between the act and the death of the victim?' The answer was yes. The prosecution witnesses claimed that the victim had fallen following the injury from the knife and as a result he died the same day after the blow delivered by the accused to the victim with a sharp object (exhibit No. 2). There is no evidence that other factors have caused the death of the victim.

After it was proved that the accused committed an act punishable under article 130/2 of the Penal Code and that it was not in self-defence and he was not provoked by the victim, we move directly to discuss the paragraph about mental instability, and we ask the question: Was the accused affected by mental instability, mental or nervous to a degree such that he was unable to control his actions? The prosecution witnesses claimed that the accused at this time was psychologically unstable; his clothes were torn and dirty. This statement was confirmed by the psychiatrist, who said he [the accused] had been interned in a psychiatric hospital where he was receiving treatment before he escaped and committed the crime, and that he had been transferred from another hospital on the recommendation of another psychiatrist (Dr. A). His [the accused's] family had complained that he was violent and mentally unstable. He was also an alcoholic. He was interned on the basis of this behaviour. Initially, he mumbled at the hospital. That meant he was hearing voices. After treatment, the mumbling has stopped. There is also evidence that the accused had violence outbursts without reason. This statement was confirmed to the court by his brother, who said he and his sister had been victims of violent attacks by the accused before he was interned.

The defendant was found liable and the court rejected the hypothesis of mental instability, based on Article 2/131 of the Penal Code which defines premeditation. He was convicted under the Criminal Code of 1991.

Chapter 8

'Bewitched People and Bad Luck Everywhere!'

Disputing and Magical Retaliation in SiSwati-Speaking Southern Africa

Severin Lenart

Introduction

The old market hall at the centre of a small town in siSwati (Swazi)-speaking southern Africa[1] is the daily workplace of Nonhlanhla Dlamini.[2] She is one of several market vendors eking out a living selling fruits and vegetables in the immediate vicinity of a supermarket chain. It is about lunchtime in early September 2009 and business is going well for her. This, however, has not always been the case, as she explained to me when I met her later that day at her home in the adjacent township:

> Everything started about six months ago when I realized that something was going terribly wrong in my life. Fewer and fewer people came to my stall, and even my regular customers suddenly started to turn away from me. The other women's businesses flourished while my produce began to decay. And as if this wasn't enough, my colleagues developed a hatred for me and avoided me totally. I felt sick and developed a feeling of dizziness and vicious headaches. I was about to quit my job as a vendor! At church they told me that I had been bewitched, so they prayed for me. But I needed to know more. I decided to consult a *sangoma* [traditional healer] to find out the truth. That *sangoma* confirmed my bewitchment and identified a small bottle that was hidden under my stall at the market as the cause of my misfortune. My son was sent to take out the bottle stuffed with *muti* [medicinal and magical herbs] to bring it to the healer so that he could reverse the spell and send it back to the perpetrator. (Interview, Piggs Peak, 4 September 2009)

According to Nonhlanhla, her difficulties vanished after she had consulted the healer: her health improved, her customers returned, she earned enough money to continue her business and she was, again, respected and held in great esteem by her colleagues at the market hall. It seems as if she was satisfied with the solution to her problem through the help of the *sangoma* who had told her the cause of her misfortune. He had identified the root of her suffering within the vicinity of the market hall and made it possible for her to retaliate by sending the spell back to its perpetrator.

This chapter is concerned with such faith-based retaliatory actions. In exploring what witchcraft means for the organization of social affairs in siSwati-speaking southern Africa, I ask how people respond to the experience of injustice and conflict.[3] In this context, I discuss magical retaliation as a mode of dispute management and as a normative element of social ordering. I shall focus on disputes and contestations in the social practice of witchcraft and retaliation rather than exploring in detail the philosophical, historical and comparative dimensions of the belief in magic and witchcraft. Magical retaliation follows a logic that differs somewhat from the concept of retaliation as it is used and discussed in other contributions in this volume. Rather than solely aiming at the re-establishment of the status quo ante by retaliatory measures, magical retaliation aims to restore one's own situation by sending the evil back to its perpetrator who, in an ideal scenario, can be identified by a traditional healer. This perpetuates an imbalance characteristic of aspects of a retaliatory logic that are totally absent in other social settings (cf. Schlee and Turner 2008).

The subtle conflict that arose among vendors over competition for customers in the above example or, as Nonhlanhla interpreted it, the result of others begrudging her success can serve as an example of the many different kinds of conflicts that are often dealt with and explained in terms of witchcraft. This can occur in all aspects of life, be it in connection to business and development, farming, sport, health, neighbours or even sexual or family relationships. Witchcraft, as a cultural phenomenon and a belief realized through practice, is a lively component of worldview and religion, a system of imagination, interpretation and action. In this context, I find the definition of religion proposed by Ellis and ter Haar (2004: 14) – 'a belief in the existence of an invisible world, distinct but not separate from the visible one, that is home to spiritual beings with effective powers over the material world' – a useful starting point to understand the way in which distinctive features of religious thought influence the disputing process. Such a perspective leads us to conceptualize witchcraft as an inclusive aspect of religion that takes into consideration mystical powers and spirits when accounting for people's perceptions and experiences of social reality.

Traditional Healers, Witchcraft Belief and Discourse

When people with whom I have talked in my field sites refer to witchcraft, they seem to understand it as a broad conceptual category. They refer to the actions of people who had either inherited evil spirits from their mothers – wittingly or unwittingly – or to people who use magic formulas, spells, animals, bones and herbs with occasional assistance from traditional healers to cause harm or accumulate wealth and power. The term 'traditional healers' – 'witch-doctors' in colonial and apartheid times, as I shall explain later – comprises a number of different categories of medical and religious practitioners. In common parlance, the local siSwati and isiZulu terms *inyanga* (pl. *tinyanga*) and *sangoma* (pl. *tangoma*) are generally used to cover all traditional healers regardless of their fields of specialization. Upon further inquiry into the differentiations, one learns that people do differentiate among categories of healers: they use the term *tinyanga* or *tangoma* when referring to diviners who communicate with ancestors and other spiritual beings and who engage in the activity of drumming, and they also recognize *emagedla* (sg. *ligedla*), the local term for herbalists. For the sake of a more fluid narrative and without implying any value judgements, I shall use the term 'traditional healers' unless the context requires specification.[4]

Generally, spirits and mystical powers have constructive and destructive dimensions. Whereas witches perpetrate harm, illness and death, traditional healers act as medical or religious practitioners. The differences are not an absolute opposition between good and evil forces; rather, their boundaries are rather fluent or, as Ashforth (2005: 17) puts it: 'In the most simple terms, witchcraft is the illegitimate use of occult force; healing is its legitimate purpose.' What I want to emphasize here is the ambiguous role of traditional healers in southern Africa as healers on the one hand and powerful and feared witches on the other (Kuper 1963: 65).

Furthermore, it is important to make an analytical distinction between the *belief in witchcraft* and the *actual accusations of witchcraft* that may follow from such a belief. It is equally important to investigate both aspects, as well as their reciprocal relationship in social interaction. When dealing with the realm of religion, it is also helpful to distinguish between forms of spiritual belief and observable, analysable actions and their ramifications. Such a differentiation would enable the South African state to uphold the constitutional principle of religious freedom, including the belief in witchcraft, and still be able to intervene where there is a real risk that accusations of witchcraft may result in criminal actions such as assault, rape or murder.

Witchcraft discourses sometimes (but not always) result in violent action. While in the South African context such discourses are often interpreted as a critical commentary on the illicit accumulation of wealth and power (Comaroff and Comaroff 1999), Niehaus (2005) has convincingly demonstrated that witchcraft accusations are also often made against destitute and elderly people. Patterns of witchcraft accusations and their effects on local social structure were also a concerted focus of the Manchester School (e.g., Gluckman 1973). These authors claimed that practices of witchcraft were on the rise where traditional society was disrupted as a consequence of social, political and economic changes (Douglas 1970: xix ff.). In these studies, belief in witchcraft was interpreted as a potent force for social control. According to this homeostatic model, an increase in witchcraft accusations had to be an indication of the general breakdown of society. Many writers today maintain such a perspective (Hund 2003), while others interpret the same dynamics as a dramatic increase in 'occult economies' (Comaroff and Comaroff 1999). In any case, what is clear and important is that many people in southern Africa experience and perceive witchcraft and its related activities as being on the rise.

Muti, Zombies and Witch-Familiars

From an emic perspective, witchcraft and its ramifications are widespread, important and especially present matters in southern Africa. Simon Roberts (1979: 34) once wrote that in many societies, some degree of disharmony is inevitable because of the very beliefs of their members, and thus everyday occurrences or incidents are potential sources of conflict. Because it is popularly perceived as 'a manifestation of evil believed to come from a human source' (Kgatla et al. 2003: 5), witchcraft relates to the idea of dispute and social conflict, and therefore to redress and retaliation as well. Many people in my field site regard dealing with and settling witchcraft disputes a central function of traditional healers as well as traditional leaders such as chiefs and headmen. From a strictly legal perspective, witchcraft is excluded from these actors' jurisdiction, but in practice it has never been completely revoked from their remit (Niehaus 2001). During colonial and apartheid times, witchcraft was perceived as repugnant and superstitious by the colonizers, and even recognizing and dealing with it was considered antithetical to European traditions of due process. Indigenous forms of criminal justice such as the 'sniffing out' of witches, which is also a part of the healing process, were viewed as competing sources of power and a serious threat to colonial authority. Anti-witchcraft legislation that prohibited, among other things, the practice of witchcraft, accusations of witchcraft and the employment of so-called 'witch-doctors' was widely introduced (Niehaus 2001). Some of this legislation continues to be in force in the new South Africa to this day.

In an increasingly uncertain context of poverty, unemployment, crime and a high rate of HIV infection, many interpersonal conflicts, social and physical ills, death and material misfortune are likely to be cast in terms of witchcraft. Witches can cause all kinds of harm and sickness, and healers, on the other side, claim to be able to cure any disease and to solve nearly every physical or spiritual malady. A healer in the town of Barberton, for instance, advertises his ability to cure tuberculosis and gonorrhoea, to enlarge penises and to bring back a lost love. He further claims to work on court cases, deal with bad luck and employment problems, and he can supposedly help if a husband is stingy with money or weak in bed. To perform all of these functions, the healer primarily uses *muti*. In southern Africa, the phrase 'using *muti*' (Ashforth 2001) refers to the practice of healers and witches using herbs and other substances for both positive and negative purposes. The particular powers of *muti* vary according to a person's knowledge and method of using it. These may range from poisoning and the application of herbs to human body parts to the use of witch-familiars and zombies (see Comaroff and Comaroff 1999). *Muti* also protects houses, premises or cars when it is sprinkled over them, buried or burned, or it can turn into a huge snake when a burglar or car thief strikes. Even if a person is not suffering or experiencing misfortune, there is a lively suspicion that others might cause harm through witchcraft because witches keep a jealous watch over potentially successful people. In such instances, it is possible to seek the assistance of traditional healers or religious prophets to protect one's life and property. *Muti* can also be used for cleansing and strengthening purposes, as well as to achieve economic, social and political objectives. My informants described these methods as being incredibly complex, diverse, secret and largely inexplicable. Neither privilege nor social position nor wealth nor gender can prevent people from being accused of or afflicted by witchcraft. Almost everybody with whom I have discussed these issues was convinced that they were, to paraphrase Ashforth (2001: 217), living in a world with witches, but only the witches know how witchcraft really works. In this local conceptualization, the powers of witchcraft and witchcraft beliefs appear to be highly dynamic, multidimensional and virtually infinite in their interpretive and reinterpretive potential (Geschiere 1998; Niehaus 2005).

The Variegated Ways of 'Using **Muti***'*

In southern Africa, many accounts of *muti* point to its apparently unlimited applications, particularly in matters of intimate social relationships. A man or a woman who suspects a partner of having an affair has a great variety of solutions at his or her disposal. A substance called *likhubalo*, for instance, is said to guard a man's wife and defend his marital rights while he is working in far-off mines or plantations, as one informant elaborated:

> It makes the woman feel uneasy when another man tries to have sex with her, so she will automatically relieve herself. Another form of that, *likhubalo lenja*, tenses up a man's penis while he has intercourse with the woman. They will interlock like dogs! Only the rightful husband is able to free the culprit in order to bring him to justice. (Interview, Piggs Peak, 10 August 2009)

Substances are generally deployable through sexual intercourse, other forms of physical contact, or even mere proximity when the *muti* is placed in or around the house or where a person would have to walk over it. *Muti* can come in many different forms. Uncertainty and secrecy characterize witchcraft and the fear of it, and often make people blame illness and misfortune on witches even when there has been no face-to-face contact. In this context, younger men in particular often invoke *muti* in connection with the brewing and drinking of *umcombotsi* (traditional beer) in *shebeens* (informal drinking places). They fear being bewitched and condemned to doing dirty work without getting paid, which would result in being perceived as 'useless' in the wider society. As one informant explained to me: 'We can drink from the same bucket here but the person whose name has been called by the witch, *hawu!* The *muti* is in the bucket, we can continue drinking, no problem. We can be a hundred people but if that person who has been named drinks from it, he'll be in trouble' (Interview, Mpofu, 25 September 2009). While protection in such cases is partially possible through protective *muti*, it becomes more difficult when it comes to hovering or flying *muti*, when a witch from a distant place calls out the victim's name while blowing *muti* from his or her hand.

The same is true for the realm of dreams. Dreams are widely regarded as providing evidence of bewitchment because they shift 'cognitive processes to a paranormal mode and [provide] cryptic images of transcendent truths' (Niehaus 2005: 203–4). My research assistant, Mangaliso, complained one morning about a severe pain, as if something was stuck in his throat. He looked terrible that morning and vomited several times without any relief before we went to a herbalist to get the appropriate medicine. Mangaliso had been afflicted by *sidliso*,[5] a mode of deploying *muti* through food, although in this case it occurred in a dream. 'It happens at night', Mangaliso explained. 'It is like a nightmare. You feel, like, "I'm eating some apples!" Once you allow yourself to eat those apples, it means you eat the *muti*' (Fieldwork notes, 26 August 2009). A few days earlier, Buhle, a young woman from the neighbourhood, had asked him to no avail for a considerable amount of money. Later, she sent her son, this time to ask for bread. Mangaliso consented and handed ten rand to the boy to buy bread in a nearby shop. According to Mangaliso, however, Buhle was not interested in the bread, but rather wanted to check whether he had money. Because she did not spend the money on bread, Mangaliso in the end interpreted his suffering through *sidliso* as Buhle's revenge. He assumed that she had bewitched him for being 'stingy': he had been working with an *umlungu* (a white person, meaning myself), which is locally presumed to mean that one 'has money', yet he refused to give her money when she asked.

Narratives on witch-familiars are equally present in accounts of witchcraft. The anthropological literature describes multifarious forms of practices whereby witches deploy animals or change shapes themselves in order to carry out their dreaded deeds (Hammond-Tooke 1981). In the South African *lowveld* (the research region), witches are believed to possess or to turn into 'familiars' such as baboons, snakes, crocodiles, hyenas or birds. For example, when certain birds, most commonly owls or hamerkops, are seen in a homestead, they are thought to be carrying *muti* to cause evil or bearing the unfortunate message that somebody in the family will get sick or die. Baboons can be sent out to steal, or the witch may sit on them backwards and ride them on his or her nocturnal excursions. Baboons can also steer trucks while the driver himself or herself is asleep in the passenger seat. This image of the truck-driving baboon is a good example of the dynamism in interpretations of witch beliefs, as it reveals elements of continuity with traditional beliefs combined with significant transformations through the incorporation of modern technologies. Accounts of impregnating women from a distance by manipulating remote-controlled devices (Stadler 1996: 91) implicitly refers to another frequently occurring familiar in southern Africa, the *tokoloshe* (Hunter 1979). The *tokoloshe* is usually described as a horrible creature, a hairy old dwarf, often naked and always with extraordinarily large genitalia in the case of a male *tokoloshe* (with his penis slung over his shoulder) or enormous breasts in the case of females. The *tokoloshe* achieves invisibility by means of a magic pebble that it keeps in its mouth. Generally, the creature is mischievous, but is only malevolent when controlled by a witch. It is said that witches send them out to rape people in the vicinity or even in far-off places like Johannesburg if those people are known.

These brief accounts of witchcraft and the variegated uses and effects of *muti* show how witchcraft as a belief in mystical powers and spirits influences ideas and notions of the arrangement of social affairs. Witchcraft affects people's behaviour when they are in trouble and even when they are not, and motivates them to act or to abstain from acting in ways that either stabilize or question relations of power, depending on the situation. In this context, witchcraft and counter-witchcraft are sometimes applied as (legitimate) forms of retaliation against perceived wrongs, as in the cases of my research assistant's affliction by *sidliso* and the healer's offer to avenge Nonhlanhla's misfortune in the market hall. In what follows, I shall provide a more detailed case in which magical retaliation as part of a healing treatment was involved in a violent dispute tried in a criminal court.

Secrecy, Identification and Accusations of Witchcraft

Above I indicated that the practice of witchcraft in southern Africa is generally ascribed to malicious others who deliberately inflict suffering and misfortune upon their victims. In this regard, it is important to ask how the perpetrators can be identified, as their motives are mostly covert and secret (Lienhardt 1951: 311 ff.). The motives are secret because witches want to avoid retaliation or punishment for their evil doings, and since the modes and means are secret too, one can never really know what they are capable of; as the above examples show, witches seem to be capable of doing anything in any given situation.

Generally speaking, women, because of the social role ascribed to them in Swazi society, are more often accused of practising witchcraft than men (see Ashforth 2001: 216). While men often resort to physical violence, women, and especially elderly women, are said to use hidden actions such as witchcraft because they are too weak physically to retaliate via physical violence. The example of Buhle and my research assistant illustrates one way of identifying persons who might be capable of practising witchcraft. Mangaliso assessed the possible motives of a particular person as well as that person's potential to resort to violence, and then identified Buhle as the culprit. Even if the signs of motive appear to be conclusive, one can never be completely sure about a witch's identity unless he or she confesses to the deeds, but this very seldom happens because the perpetrator would be exposing himself or herself to potential punishment. The second common method of breaking through the secrecy of a witch is to consult a religious prophet or a traditional healer. It is not always clear from the outset that one's suffering or misfortune is caused by bewitchment; this is often only revealed upon consultation and divination, as I showed in the example of Nonhlanhla's streak of bad luck. In her case, bewitchment was first diagnosed by a prophet before being affirmed by a *sangoma*, who then revealed the perpetrator in her close proximity.

This aspect of social proximity constitutes a prominent feature of witchcraft accusations. The accused are usually found in the immediate social vicinity, which is characterized by multiplex, overlapping networks of kin and others involved with the accuser in sexual, economic and other types of relationships. Therefore, it appears that witches must know their victims. They must have knowledge about them or a substance from them in order to be able to strike. On this basis, a strong link is made between witches and kinship (Geschiere 1997), age (Stadler 1996) and gender relations (Turner 1996). The wide range of literature on these issues shows that accusations are most likely to affect fellow villagers or township dwellers, unrelated neighbours and relatives by marriage rather than consanguineal kin (Niehaus 2005: 200). As has already been pointed out, women tend to be accused of witchcraft more often than men. Studies on southern Africa suggest various explanations for this phenomenon, ranging from strong exogamy rules and virilocal residence patterns to the cultural practice of polygyny, which opens the door to accusations between co-wives (Hammond-Tooke 1974).

Envy and Jealousy

In fact, anyone can be a witch because, it is said, envy, jealousy and personal grudges motivate people to turn into witches.[6] Someone wearing nice clothes, driving a new car, drinking expensive alcohol or being in the company of an *umlungu* (a white person) can evoke such feelings, as the mother of my assistants explained during a conversation:

> If you see a neighbour's child progressing or the neighbour has a better job than you have, then you get jealous of her. Like, when your child finishes school and goes to varsity [university] – before the child starts working, she suddenly dies. She probably died in a car accident that was caused by a jealous person. People usually think they won't be hungry anymore because their children will buy groceries for them when they start working. But I am also struggling even though my children are working. Like the other day, I was in a taxi and people started gossiping. A woman complained that she doesn't have work and would need to cleanse herself where the snake is. She was referring to me because all my children are working now, some assisting you. Even now, they are jealous around here because they can see that you are with us. (Fieldwork notes, 15 May 2009)

The mother of my assistants has been running a *shebeen*, a drinking place, which is popularly known as *eNyokeni*, 'the place of the snake'. The story says that the mother keeps a snake in a big drum where she only needs to add water and sing for the snake to start producing *umcombotsi*, the traditional beer. The image of the snake actually derives from the beginnings of the settlement in this part of the township. A python supposedly had its hideout where the mother's house and the *shebeen* were built. Moreover, my assistants repeatedly told me that neighbours and friends questioned them about the *muti* they were using that made me employ them and keep returning over a long period. Such a notion never entered my mind until they mentioned it to me. My presence and our interaction sometimes even put them at risk, as was already illustrated by Mangaliso's *sidliso*, a reality I was equally unaware of prior to the event.[7] It seems as if envy was the cause of this incident, at least from Mangaliso's point of view. He assumed that Buhle tried to bewitch him because he appeared to be stingy with money since he was working with an *umlungu*. Because Mangaliso only returned to his natal village for the course of our research, he decided to refrain from any action against the suspected woman. He made it clear to me that if the circumstances had been different, he would have got 'into troubles', but that would have mired his brother, who was living in the village, in trouble. Otherwise, he claimed, he would have taught Buhle a lesson either by spreading rumours about her or by seeking assistance from a traditional healer. Spreading rumours in this incident would have been tantamount to a veiled public accusation of witchcraft, another mode of avenging a perceived wrong.

In social practice it also happens the other way around: envy and jealousy are communicated through rumours and gossip rather than by using *muti*. Both gossip and rumours thus constitute important catalysts in the processes leading to witchcraft accusations (Stewart and Strathern 2004). In addition to being dangerous psychological conditions (Stadler 1996: 93), feelings of envy and jealousy are also potent forces of social control in settings 'where everybody is increasingly out for themselves'. This situation is characteristic of southern Africa, despite the new elite's talk of *Ubuntu*, the 'African humanism'. Thornton (2005: 25) conceptualizes jealousy in a structural way, as a moral principle, a social value that helps to maintain equality, which is a principal ideological value of many African political systems. From a social perspective, equality then means that all (especially male) members of a community, by virtue of being human beings, are regarded as equal.[8] In some instances, jealousy leads to violence. This gives rise to the judicial problem of controlling or preventing this kind of violence: it challenges and can even threaten the future of democracy (Comaroff and Comaroff 2004: 535) because it is difficult to respond to without curtailing human rights and the rule of law (Ashforth 2005). Since jealousy can lead to violence and therefore constitutes a political threat, I follow Thornton (2005: 26) and conceptualize it as a political and not merely a psychological concept.

Envy and jealousy often expressed through gossip, rumours, witchcraft and accusations of witchcraft can lead, or rather aim to lead, to a levelling of social inequalities in an ideological sense, as in the case of Buhle and my assistant, who ideally should have shared his newly acquired 'wealth' with her. Hence, witchcraft and witchcraft accusations are a source of power for those who are disadvantaged and who envy the more privileged; they reveal deviations from social values and the 'wrongs' committed by the more privileged. They can also be used by the disadvantaged to try to gain the fortune of the 'wealthy' because it is often believed and communicated that the wealthy have used witchcraft to accumulate their wealth. Somewhat paradoxically, accusations of witchcraft can be used by successful people to legitimate their success (Gluckman 1973: 96). Younger, better-off people often accuse the poor and the elderly (both male and female alike) of witchcraft (Niehaus 2001: 197–98). In siSwati-speaking southern Africa, they argue that their success is proof that they do not need witchcraft. The poor, the old and 'the ugly', on the other hand, live without money, assistance or love and therefore must rely on illicit means to survive, such as sending out baboons to steal food, keeping zombies to plough fields or using *tokoloshes* for sexual gratification.

To sum up, accusations of witchcraft feature primarily in the immediate social vicinity of one's multiplex relationships with fellow village and township dwellers, neighbours and relatives by marriage rather than cognates. These relationships are usually characterized by ambiguity and inequality of wealth, success and power. Although both men and women are said to be perpetrators and victims of witchcraft and witchcraft accusations, there is a tendency for women and the elderly to be accused and identified as witches. Accusations and practices of witchcraft are believed to be caused by feelings of envy and jealousy, and are communicated to a large extent through gossip and rumours. At the same time, these feelings entail a dialectic social dimension by, on the one hand, aiming to level social inequalities in wealth and power and, on the other hand, legitimating success by accusing the disadvantaged of using illegitimate means for survival. Because the motives and actions of witches are covert and secret, traditional healers play a central role in processes leading to these accusations and in the ensuing disputes. As an elder of a rural chieftaincy put it:

> traditional healers are the ones who play a major part because very often they cause conflict between the people in our community. The healer will tell the patient that she is bewitched by somebody; for instance, the healer will point to the patient's neighbour and say that she is the one who did it. That is why people often end up having disputes, and then they come to the chief and lay a charge against each other. (Interview, eMjindini 6 May 2009.)

Viewed from the perspectives of traditional leaders, traditional healers and their clients, the question of justice in witchcraft-related conflicts thus constitutes a serious social problem. The principal question that arises, then, is how people respond to such problems. In the following I shall focus on one particular mode of dealing with the experiences of injustice and conflict pertaining to witchcraft. I explore the case of an attempted murder that was tried in the Barberton regional court and that revealed a dimension of magical influence in the course of the trial. Rather than focusing on the actual criminal court hearing, the discussion here turns mainly on the accusations of using *muti* and the practices of traditional healing.

Thabiso and the Demons

The story[9] starts at the end of 2009 in Extension 11, a notoriously dangerous part of the township of Barberton. One day Thabiso visited his mother's house to attend a ceremony for his sister's deceased baby. The following morning, a young man whom Thabiso only knew by sight asked Thabiso to accompany him to his house in order to help him carry some things. On their way, Thabiso told the young man that, strangely enough, he had dreamed about him. This dream turned out to be advance notice of what he would live through in the coming months and years. On their way to the young man's house, they were called upon by neighbours to enter their homestead. Thabiso hesitantly acquiesced despite an uneasy premonition. He ended up being right and as soon as he entered the premises, he was grabbed and held by two men and a woman, while a fourth man stabbed him with a knife. The young man he had accompanied hit him with a wood block, while one of the two others initially holding him hit him over the head with a hoe and severely injured him. Now something happened that apparently seriously affected his future recovery. The woman started collecting

Thabiso's blood in a bowl. He then passed out and only after a close friend of his came running was he taken to hospital where, after about three weeks, he came to his senses. He was discharged two months later, but because of his grievous head injuries he could hardly walk or even wash himself. His sister cared for and supported him for several months in another part of the township before he moved back to his mother's house in Extension 11. Soon after being discharged from the hospital, rumours started circulating about the young man who had asked Thabiso to accompany him. Apparently, he used to be the partner of Thabiso's former girlfriend, with whom Thabiso had a three-year-old son. It seems, then, that the attempted murder was motivated by jealousy, though this has been never fully proved. The perpetrators – three brothers and their sister – were taken into custody, charged with attempted murder and assault, and released on bail set at 1,500 rand per person. However, the other young man involved was never arrested or subpoenaed to appear in court. On their return from custody, a street committee led by the ward councillor successfully lobbied to have the perpetrators and their family removed from the vicinity. Trying to find shelter in other parts of the township as well as in a rural chieftaincy proved to be a luckless undertaking because local people and the chief vehemently refused to accommodate them. With the help of the local municipality, they finally moved to a farm about 30 km from town.

About half a year later, something happened that made Thabiso seek out traditional healing in addition to medical care. As he tells the story:

> One day I wanted to take a bath in the morning. When I started to brush my teeth something just entered my mouth. It was like the wind because I couldn't see what it was. I couldn't see that thing which then forced its way down to my stomach. I was supposed to die immediately, but I was strong and fought against it. But the *emalumbo* [demons] were already inside me. About two weeks later they attacked me for the first time – my hand, actually the whole of my left side, started shaking, aching and my hand then swelled so big that you can't even imagine it. I am always thinking about dying when that happens. (Interview, eMjindini, 16 September 2011)

His mother then took him to a nearby Jericho church, where religious prophets told him that the mother of the perpetrators was attacking him with evil spirits in order to kill him before he could bring the case to court. Apparently, she had been consulting a number of traditional healers and was trying to kill him by using *muti*. For that reason, Thabiso consulted five different healers in the township, all of whom tried to help him but failed. The sixth one he consulted lived in a rural chieftaincy and was recommended by an acquaintance whose relative had been successfully cured by this herbalist. Thabiso was given various sorts of medicine to drink, to lick, to bathe in, to blow and to burn. It seemed as if he responded well to the treatment, but there were still times when the evil spirits attacked him. In order to protect Thabiso from these spirits, which the herbalist claimed was very difficult because the perpetrators had taken Thabiso's blood to make the *muti* stronger, he suggested performing a ritual. Because the perpetrators performed their dreaded deed at a graveside next to a river to obtain the strongest possible *muti*, the counter-attack, according to Thabiso's healer, needed to be performed in a similar setting. The perpetrators had used a *muti* called *vuka*, that is, 'to wake up', where they mixed *muti* with human bones to awaken a random ancestor who would then call Thabiso to join him in his grave. In order to perform the counter-attack, we went to a river where Thabiso was first cut with a razor and then he was completely buried in a symbolic grave with only his face, which was covered with a red cloth, remaining exposed. By mixing potassium permanganate, a strong oxidizing agent, with glycerine and various secret herbs, the healer performed the retaliatory act of sending the evil spirits back to those who created them. The grave served as a kind of trap for the spirits that had attacked Thabiso, and some of his blood was left behind in order to make the spirits smell it and assume that he was dead. Through the *muti*, the spirits then apparently return with more power to those who initially created them and cause to happen to them whatever was intended to happen to the victim. After the symbolic burial, Thabiso had to be cleansed with steam in order to be strengthened and protected from the spirits while the spirits were still busy performing their duties at the symbolic graveside. On the same day, we also went to another healer, this time a *sangoma*, a diviner, who was guided by various spirits to 'sniff out' the evil from Thabiso's body. The *sangoma* further diagnosed a *tokoloshe* that had been performing its mischievous deeds not only with Thabiso but also with his whole family.

With all these treatments, Thabiso hoped to be spared from the evil spirits' attacks and to be physically and psychologically strong enough to face his assailants in court. Certainly he was only willing to attend the hearings with additional support in the form of *muti* from his traditional healer, which he hoped would help him win the case easily. Thabiso went to court eleven times from early 2010 until the final verdict at the end of January 2012. In one of our regular email conversations, he informed me about the 'unsatisfactory' decision of the judge: the man who stabbed him was sentenced to five years in prison; the one who wounded him with the hoe also received a five-year sentence; the woman who took his blood received a five-year sentence, but with three years suspended and the option of paying a 2,000 rand fine in lieu of serving the remaining two years in prison; and the fourth defendant received a five-year suspended sentence. A few days later, I received an email from Thabiso's sister commenting on the judgment:

> At least it was better than nothing because if they'd all gotten off it would have been very painful for us because they deserved to be punished. But one of these good days they are going to suffer the consequences. Hope the Lord will be on our side. I also told Thabiso not to worry too much because at least they got something to take home as a punishment. (Email, 2 February 2012.)

As we can see from this comment, the question of justice was of decisive importance, not only for the victim but also for his family. With the final judgment, the violent conflict came to an end as far as the criminal court procedure was concerned. Justice in this case, however, appears to be multidimensional and required alternative mechanisms to be gained. With the attacks of evil spirits allegedly sent by the perpetrators' mother, the conflict widened its scope to include the world of magic and witchcraft, which necessitated the involvement of a different kind of expert. Due to his sickness, Thabiso consulted traditional healers, who then offered the possibility of retaliatory justice as part of the treatment, as Ashforth (2005: 248) also notes in his study on spiritual insecurity in Soweto: 'most traditional healing is premised upon the promise that the "evil forces" dispatched by a witch to cause harm and death will be returned to the perpetrator to hoist him with his own petard'. Justice in this case builds on the principle of retaliation, a reciprocal relationship between different actors that demands an appropriate reaction in response to any kind of action. In southern Africa, reaction in the form of magic is widely acknowledged as a legitimate form of defence or punishment. The specific nature of magic retaliation is more than re-establishing the status quo ante by retaliatory measures, that is, it is more than just getting even. It is a logic of retaliation that includes self-defence or self-healing where an imbalance continues. It is about restoring one's own situation by transferring the evil back to its sender. Thabiso's healing can only be successful if the attacking spirits are turned back on to the malefactor who dispatched them. Whether this has actually occurred in this case cannot be determined yet, because this promise depends on the success of the treatment. At the time of writing, Thabiso was still going through some difficulties with occasional spirit attacks, though less frequently than before. It is a matter of time because different powers of different actors are fighting against each other, and nobody can actually say when it is going to be over.

The healing process also involved the practice of *kufemba*, the 'sniffing out' of witchcraft substances from Thabiso's body by a *sangoma*. As I have mentioned above, this practice is prohibited in South Africa under the contentious Witchcraft Suppression Act, but this legislation clearly contradicts social reality in this case because the practice constitutes an integral part of the treatment whereby the *sangoma* communicates with the spiritual domain of ancestors and other spirits, indispensable forces for physical and spiritual recovery. However, it vividly shows the practical ways in which people affected by witchcraft adapt to and deal with their specific circumstances.

Conclusion

In this chapter I have discussed witchcraft as a belief that motivates social action in disputing processes. Based on examples from siSwati-speaking southern Africa, I have explored the ways in which witchcraft informs the organization of social affairs and have asked how people respond to the experience of injustice and conflict pertaining to the problem of witchcraft. I have demonstrated that witchcraft intrinsically informs people's perception of reality and that witchcraft as a religious belief in mystical powers and spirits is highly dynamic and virtually limitless in its interpretive potential. Witchcraft actually only depends on the powers and knowledge of those applying it. The ethnographic examples presented show how retaliation as a mode of dispute management is invoked in various scenarios. The roles that traditional healers play in this regard turn out to be ambiguous and multilayered. On the one hand, healers act as medical and religious practitioners in the fields of herbalism and divination; on the other hand, they are often feared as powerful perpetrators of malicious acts. Because they are able to identify and penetrate the secrecy of witches, they take a front seat before, during and sometimes even after a dispute has entered the legal arena. Traditional healers promise justice as part of the treatment when their clients have been harmed or have experienced misfortune. They offer retaliation by turning attacking spirits back on to the malefactor who had originally dispatched them. This is an understanding of justice that builds on relations of reciprocity between different actors while getting rid of whatever it is that causes social conflict.

I presented the case of the market vendor who was confronted with a fellow vendor's apparent attempt to ruin her business by using *muti*. Once the cause of her misfortune was identified, the healer offered to avenge the personal attack by sending the spell back to its perpetrator. Feelings of envy also seemed to be the driving force behind the retaliatory magic applied in the case of Buhle and Mangaliso. According to Mangaliso's account, he had been afflicted with *sidliso* in a dream. He ascribed this mode of deploying *muti* to a young woman who had asked him for money, a request he refused to grant. The third example, that of Thabiso, involved a tragic assault and attempted murder, and reveals the different dimensions that disputes in siSwati-speaking southern Africa may entail. On the surface, it might appear as if this case had only one dimension, the procedure within the criminal justice system. This is what we would know if we only studied the court records. Empirical research, however, revealed that there is another dimension to the case, namely a second attack and its subsequent counter-attack, this time through supernatural retaliation by sending spirits. This dimension does not replace the criminal procedure in the state court as such; it complements the official state-based legal system and extends the scope and the exploration of the conflict to the invisible in our visible world.

Severin Lenart has worked as a social anthropologist in research and conflict management. He studied social and cultural anthropology, African and conflict studies in Vienna and Utrecht, and conducted extensive fieldwork in South Africa and Swaziland. He was a doctoral fellow at the International Max Planck Research School on Retaliation, Mediation and Punishment at the Max Planck Institute for Social Anthropology and received his Ph.D. from the Martin Luther University Halle-Wittenberg. He further engaged in conflict transformation and worked as a mediator in social housing programmes in Vienna, Austria. Currently he is an advisor for indigenous rights and conflict transformation to a social development organization in the Philippines.

Notes

1. The title of this chapter is taken from a traditional healer's advertising slogan in Paarl, South Africa.
2. The informants' names are all pseudonyms. Fieldwork in South Africa and Swaziland as part of my doctoral research (Lenart 2012a, 2012b, 2013a, 2013b, 2013c) was made possible scientifically and financially by the Max Planck Institute for Social Anthropology, Halle (Saale) and the International Max Planck Research School on Retaliation, Mediation and Punishment (IMPRS-REMEP).
3. Witchcraft is used here as a translation of local terms concerned with magic. The sociological distinction between sorcery and witchcraft made by Evans-Pritchard (1937) appears not to be very useful in the southern African context because, as Kapferer (2006: 12–13), drawing on Douglas (1970), argues, 'witchcraft rather than sorcery appears to be the dominant form [in southern Africa], and this appears to be associated with social forces, for example, that encourage movement and the regular break-up and formation of new settlements; fairly weak social boundaries crossed by kinship ties that articulate diverse localities; and little in the way of powerfully socially differentiated hierarchies'. Moreover, people hardly ever refer to sorcery and do not make an analytical distinction between witchcraft and sorcery. They either use local terms such as *butsakatsi* or the English term 'witchcraft'.
4. The designation 'traditional' in the term 'traditional healers' does not refer to a static and bounded, normatively defined and constrained category in the sense of a timeless, unchanging tradition. Rather, it connotes an image of continuity with the past that nonetheless allows for constant innovation, flexibility and adaptation in the context of the present.
5. *Sidliso* can be translated as 'poisoning'. It is derived from the verb *kudlisa*, meaning 'to cause or help to eat', from *kudla*, 'to eat'.
6. The notions of envy and jealousy have assumed an important generational dimension in many southern African settings (Stadler 1996).
7. Doing ethnography in such contexts shows that anthropologists clearly influence and shape local discourses and practices. This is well known among social scientists, but nonetheless deserves to be regularly brought to our attention.

8. However, this does not necessarily imply that all individuals have equal access to resources such as rights. Here the principle of respect comes into the picture. The notion of respect characterizes different relationships between men and women as well as between chiefs and their 'subjects', and acknowledges individual status, charisma and spiritual power that may then in certain instances lead to privileged access to resources (see Thornton 2005).
9. See Lenart (2013c) for an ethnographic photo essay of this case.

References

Ashforth, A. 2001. 'On Living in a World with Witches: Everyday Epistemology and Spiritual Insecurity in a Modern African City (Soweto)', in H.L. Moore and T. Sanders (eds), *Magical Interpretations, Material Realities: Modernity, Witchcraft and the Occult in Postcolonial Africa.* New York: Routledge, pp. 206–25.

———. 2005. *Witchcraft, Violence and Democracy in South Africa.* Chicago: University of Chicago Press.

Comaroff, J., and J.L. Comaroff. 1999. 'Occult Economies and the Violence of Abstraction: Notes from the South African Postcolony', *American Ethnologist* 26: 279–303.

———. 2004. 'Policing Culture, Cultural Policing: Law and Social Order in Postcolonial South Africa', *Law & Social Inquiry* 29: 513–45.

Douglas, M. 1970. 'Introduction: Thirty Years after Witchcraft, Oracles and Magic', in M. Douglas (ed.), *Witchcraft, Confessions and Accusations.* London: Tavistock Publications, pp. xiii–xxxviii.

Ellis, S., and G. ter Haar. 2004. *Worlds of Power: Religious Thought and Political Practice in Africa.* London: Hurst.

Evans-Pritchard, E.E. 1937. *Witchcraft, Oracles and Magic among the Azande.* Oxford: Clarendon Press.

Geschiere, P. 1997. *The Modernity of Witchcraft, Politics and the Occult in Postcolonial Africa.* Charlottesville: University Press of Virginia.

———. 1998. 'Globalization and the Power of Indeterminate Meaning: Witchcraft and Spirit Cults in Africa and East Asia', *Development and Change* 29: 811–37.

Gluckman, M. 1973. *Custom and Conflict in Africa.* Oxford: Blackwell.

Hammond-Tooke, W.D. 1974. 'The Cape Nguni Witch Familiar as a Mediatory Construct', *Man* 9(1): 128–36.

———. 1981. *Boundaries and Belief: The Structure of a Sotho Worldview.* Johannesburg: Witwatersrand University Press.

Hund, J. 2003. 'African Witchcraft and Western Law – Psychological and Cultural Issues', in J. Hund (ed.), *Witchcraft Violence and the Law in South Africa.* Pretoria: Protea Book House, pp. 9–39.

Hunter, M. 1979 [1936]. *Reaction to Conquest: Effects of Contact with Europeans on the Pondo of South Africa.* Cape Town: David Philip.

Kapferer, B. 2006. 'Introduction. Outside All Reason: Magic, Sorcery and Epistemology in Anthropology', in B. Kapferer (ed.), *Beyond Rationalism. Rethinking Magic, Witchcraft and Sorcery.* Oxford: Berghahn Books, pp. 1–30.

Kgatla, S.T., G. ter Haar, W.E.A.V. Beek and J.J.D. Wolf. 2003. *Crossing Witchcraft Barriers in South Africa: Exploring Witchcraft Accusations: Causes and Solutions.* Utrecht: Utrecht University.

Kuper, H. 1963. *The Swazi: A South African Kingdom.* New York: Holt, Rinehart and Winston.

Lenart, S. 2012a. 'Practices of Local and Transborder Governance: Locality and Boundaries in eMjindini/Barberton, South Africa', *Ethnoscripts* 14: 59–84.

———. 2012b. 'From Truth Seeking to Verdict in Mozambique: A Comment', *Recht in Afrika* 1: 97–103.

———. 2013a. 'Chiefs and Witches in a Gendered World: Legitimacy and the Disputing Process in the South African Lowveld', Ph.D. dissertation. Martin Luther University Halle-Wittenberg, Halle (Saale), Germany.

———. 2013b. *The Complexity of the Moment: Picturing an Ethnographic Project in South Africa and Swaziland, Vol. I: Photo Essays and Fieldwork Reports, 2007–11*, Field Notes and Research Projects IV.Halle (Saale): Max Planck Institute for Social Anthropology, Department 'Integration and Conflict'. http://www.eth.mpg.de/3346015/fieldnotes_series.

———. 2013c. *The Complexity of the Moment: Picturing an Ethnographic Project in South Africa and Swaziland, Vol. II: Photo Essays and Court Cases, 2007–11*, Field Notes and Research Projects V. Halle (Saale): Max Planck Institute for Social Anthropology, Department 'Integration and Conflict'. http://www.eth.mpg.de/3346015/fieldnotes_series

Lienhardt, G. 1951. 'Some Notions of Witchcraft among the Dinka', *Africa: Journal of the International African Institute* 21: 303–18.

Niehaus, I. 2001. 'Witchcraft in the New South Africa: From Colonial Superstition to Postcolonial Reality?', in H.L. Moore and T. Sanders (eds), *Magical Interpretations, Material Realities: Modernity, Witchcraft and the Occult in Postcolonial Africa*. New York: Routledge, pp. 184–205.

———. 2005. 'Witches and Zombies of the South African Lowveld: Discourse, Accusations and Subjective Reality', *Journal of the Royal Anthropological Institute* 11: 191–210.

Roberts, S. 1979. *Order and Dispute. An Introduction to Legal Anthropology*. Harmondsworth: Penguin.

Schlee, G., and B. Turner (eds). 2008. *Vergeltung: Eine interdisziplinäre Betrachtung von Rechtfertigung und Regulation von Gewalt*. Frankfurt: Campus.

Stadler, J. 1996. 'Witches and Witch-Hunters: Witchcraft, Generational Relations and the Life Cycle in a Lowveld Village', *African Studies* 55: 87–110.

Stewart, P.J., and A. Strathern. 2004. *Witchcraft, Sorcery, Rumors, and Gossip*. Cambridge: Cambridge University Press.

Thornton, R.J. 2005. 'Four Principles of South African Political Culture at the Local Level', *Anthropology Southern Africa* 28: 22–30.

Turner, V.W. 1996 [1957]. *Schism and Continuity in an African Society: A Study of Ndembu Village Life*. Oxford: Berg.

Section V

Retaliation in Negotiations and Organizations of Social and Political Orders

Chapter 9

Forum Shopping as Retaliation in Disguise

How Nomadic Fulbe Condemn Retaliation and Forum Shopping, But Practise Them Anyway

Albert K. Drent

Introduction

This chapter deals with both norms and actual practices of dispute management by nomadic Fulbe in the Far North Region of Cameroon. I call these cattle herders 'nomadic' (as opposed to 'sedentary') because they move with their cattle the whole year round, carrying their huts and households with them. They are all Muslims, although their ancestors tend to be less strongly associated with the nineteenth-century Fulbe-led jihad movements and precolonial Fulbe state formation than those of the present-day 'sedentary' Fulbe.[1]

The disputes I will focus on are more specifically those involving homicide among nomadic Fulbe, offences that are largely neglected in the Fulbe literature. After describing the normative way of dealing with such manifestations of violence, I will illustrate why retaliation is strongly disapproved of, both normatively and in practice. In spite of their identification with Islam, nomadic Fulbe in the Far North Province categorically reject *diya* ('blood money') as a proper way to deal with homicide. This is all the more remarkable since in the literature one can find many examples of Islamic pastoral groups applying *diya* to settle cases of homicide.

Involving external authorities is also not socially accepted in cases of intragroup homicide. Nevertheless, drawing on data collected between January 2009 and February 2010 among different sections of nomadic Fulbe, notably Jafun and Wodaabe, I will show that grievances related to intragroup homicide were in fact addressed through an endless process of forum shopping among external authorities.

How nomadic Fulbe pastoralists reconcile their culturally inscribed avoidance of retaliation, revenge and punishment with a penchant for extensive forum shopping will be the main question that this chapter tries to answer. In order to do this, I will start by introducing one of the main cultural determinants of behaviour for nomadic Fulbe: *pulaaku*.

Dispute Settlement and *Pulaaku*

When nomadic Fulbe talk about disputes in interviews and during actual arbitration sessions, the word *pulaaku* frequently comes up. This term is explicitly used to evoke qualities such as self-control and restraint, which should ideally be exercised by Fulbe in their interaction with others, especially in front of other Fulbe. To live up to the ideal of *pulaaku* means that:

> one must continually demonstrate in public … that one is stronger than one's needs, one's discomforts and one's impulses. Emotions and needs are points of weakness for the FulBe[2] because in their experience it is through these qualities that one is dependent on nature and dependent on other people, and this is an unpleasing fact. The ideal the FulBe strive to represent is that of a person who transcends all physical and emotional determinants. (Riesman 1992: 202)

Those who fail to embody this ideal in public are particularly liable to bring shame not only upon themselves, but also upon the other Fulbe who are closely identified with them, such as close kin. In everyday life, the fear of *semteende* – public shame associated with not upholding the behaviour expected by other Fulbe – is indeed a powerful determinant of behaviour for Fulbe.

However, the ability to display the qualities that are highly valued among Fulbe such as self-control, restraint and other norms less directly related to dispute settlement but also associated with *pulaaku* is recognized as age-dependent. Young men under the age of thirty-five are not yet regarded as social adults. They are thus not expected to uphold the behaviour required by *pulaaku* as strictly as older men. These young men often leave the main pastoral work to younger brothers under twenty years of age while they themselves meet with age mates, hang around in the surrounding villages and have affairs with already betrothed or married women. In bars they frequently drink too much beer and openly brag about how they boldly stole a cow or conquered a woman the previous night. As such, it is not surprising that among young men, especially in this age between about twenty and thirty-five, alcohol, competition for women's favours and theft frequently result in fights with lethal outcomes.

However, as they are not considered social adults, these young men do not yet have to bear full responsibility for their wrongdoings. Part of this responsibility is assigned to their fathers or to other close kin (such as paternal uncles) who are already considered elders. These older kin are also responsible for repairing the social relations that have been damaged by the deeds of their sons (or agnatic nephews) and for the payment of compensation in connection with material damage and treatment of physical injuries. When the police catch these young men, their fathers usually try to bail them out as soon as possible to avoid bringing further shame to the family.

The ideal approach to dealing with tensions between families caused by the shameful behaviour of their sons is for the adults of the families to sit together and try to reconcile their differences. However, if they cannot manage by themselves, they should as the next step inform their political leader(s) (*ardo* (sg.), *arbe* (pl.)) and give him/them the opportunity to call a meeting of elders. During these meetings, the elders try to restore their unity as Fulbe by explaining how *pulaaku* has not been respected in the behaviour of the conflicting parties. Compensation for damage can be proposed in such meetings, but it should be kept low to show the goodwill of both parties to settle and to reconcile. In all cases, the disputing parties are urged not to repeat the same 'problematic' behaviour in the future. The aggrieved person(s), in turn, should be satisfied with the arbitration; they should refrain from making demands for compensation beyond that recommended during the meetings of elders, and especially from taking other forms of revenge. When one of the parties violates these norms of *pulaaku*, it is considered shameful behaviour in the eyes of the (Fulbe) public.

Being Fulbe versus Being Muslim

Islam is, along with *pulaaku*, another important frame of reference for the behaviour and identity of nomadic Fulbe pastoralists. Thus, nomadic Fulbe of the Far North Region sometimes mention the concept of *diya* – the Arabic term for blood money – in cases of homicide-related compensation. This is a form of compensation calculated with reference to the *shariᶜa* and a list of fixed tariffs for the killing of persons belonging to particular sex and age categories.

Fulbe, however, refer to *diya* in a very different way from that generally found in the literature about *shariᶜa* and Islamic pastoralists.[3] Most Nomadic Fulbe in the Far North only have rudimentary knowledge of the Qurᶜan because their mobile lifestyle does not allow them to go to Qurᶜan school.[4] Due to this, and because in Cameroon *diya* is officially forbidden by state law, nomadic Fulbe are mainly aware of the existence of *diya* because they share the area with another group of nomadic Islamic cattle herders, Shuwa Arabs. The latter are reputed to be better educated in religious matters than nomadic Fulbe, despite the fact that many aspects of their livelihoods are similar. Both groups frequently interact in the bush and at markets, and they pray in the same mosques. Consequently, intermarriages between nomadic Fulbe and Shuwa Arabs have become increasingly common, and economic ties through cattle-rearing activities between members of the two groups have increased over the years as well. Finally, spending the days in the same villages in the shade of the same trees results in strong friendships between members of these groups. However, in spite of the increasing interconnections between these groups in many domains of life and the observation that both Shuwa Arabs and nomadic Fulbe refer to their Islamic identity in all aspects of life, nomadic Fulbe stress that their approaches to conflict settlement are very different. They describe Shuwa Arabs as hot-tempered and prone to immediate, often violent, retaliation. Nomadic Fulbe also refer to this difference, in spite of the similarities, in order to illustrate the contrast between the normative public behavioural codes of the two groups and the uniqueness of the restraint expected from Fulbe.

Specifically with regard to homicide settlements, nomadic Fulbe point out that, in contrast to themselves, the Shuwa Arabs practise *diya.*[5] This practice among Shuwa Arabs was brought to my attention by a nomadic Fulbe pastoralist, who told me the following story:

> Around the year 2000 a quarrel between two young Fulbe from two different nomadic factions ended in the death of one of them. The family of the victim reported the homicide to the district police commander as well as the district head, who both came to conduct their investigations. They found that the killer had already fled to Nigeria, and they closed the case.
>
> Soon after the departure of the state authorities, elders representing the kin of the victim and the kin of the killer gathered in order to try to restore the damaged relations between the two factions. The oldest brother of the victim worked as a herdsman for a rich elder of the Shuwa Arabs who, because of his high socio-economic status among both Shuwa Arabs and Fulbe, had come as one of his main representatives in the negotiations.
>
> The Shuwa Arab was one of the first to speak, and he demanded that the kin of the killer give seventy head of cattle for the loss of their son. This was, according to logics of shariᶜa law, the amount of *diya* that should be paid in compensation for the homicide of a young man among the Shuwa Arabs. The family of the killer, however, refused to pay this.

Despite the increasing interconnectedness between Fulbe and Shuwa Arabs, and although nomadic Fulbe admire the Shuwa Arabs for their superior understanding of the Qurᶜan, they explained that they still disapprove of *diya.* In cases of homicide between nomadic Fulbe, elders instead urge the family of the victim to trust in the long-term providence of Allah and not to give in to emotional short-term satisfaction through immediate revenge or material compensation. They insist that it is up to Allah to give life and to take life. The killer will not escape from the Almighty and will have to justify his behaviour to Allah eventually.

They furthermore insist that, in this world, Fulbe should uphold their unity as Fulbe and their difference from other groups, expressed most notably through the notions of *pulaaku* and *semteende* (the shame felt when one does not uphold the ideal of *pulaaku*). The elders thus urge the victim's family to follow the way of *pulaaku* by showing patience and enduring the suffering caused by their loss (*munyal*), and to let Allah take care of it. The elders do comfort the kin of the victim by arguing that even in this world there will be justice in the long term. If a Fulbe member of a certain faction kills a member of another Fulbe faction, one day in the future the roles will inevitably be reversed, and this open account will be settled.

My informant, who was one of the elders present at the meeting supporting the kin of the victim, illustrated this point by explaining to the Arab Shuwa elder how Fulbe should behave in case of a homicide:

> Young men kill each other, but among us Fulbe we have never asked for blood money [*ceede mbar'hoore*, the Fulfulde equivalent of *diya*] … If Fulbe enter a fight they will fight, but if a person is killed, it is [the will of] Allah. Since the time of our ancestors there has never been *diya* between us. Even if a bull of one man kills the bull of another man, there is no grievance. If the horse of one man kills the horse of another man, you do not pay. Between us it is like that. Accidents happen. You give a cow, you take a cow, you will still have to eat, you will still have to drink [i.e., life continues]. This is the way of *pulaaku*. People sit down and cry but wait until the final day for Allah to do justice.[6]

In the perception of the Fulbe, *diya* not only amounts to an expression of the value of a life in monetary terms – it is even considered the implicit transformation of human life into a commodity. They thus associate compensation of the *diya* type with greed, and tend to use this term metaphorically to bring shame upon community members who, at least in the eyes of the kin of the killer, try to get an unfairly large compensation settlement for costs incurred following a homicide. According to the ideal of *pulaaku*, compensation should not exceed the actual expenses incurred by the bereaved family for the transport of the victim to a medical facility, the (unsuccessful) treatment of his or her physical injuries in that facility and the costs associated with his or her funeral.[7] This form of compensation, which functions as symbolic reparation for the damaged relations, should in principle merely enable the victim's family to recover the procedural costs directly related to the death of their kin, and is locally referred to as *ceede wahalaaje*.

Accusations of *diya* between Fulbe thus have nothing to do with the compensation for homicide as described in *shariʿa*, on which the claim of seventy head of cattle by Shuwa Arabs is based. They are merely normative accusations of greed and personal gain. The family of the killer often cleverly exploits the potential public shame involved in these accusations (*semteende*) as a form of social pressure and leverage in negotiations in order to keep the victim's kinsmen's claims for compensation to a minimum.

These accusations of *diya*, combined with the low level of compensation and the elders' demand to refrain from retaliation, in practice often leave grievances and tensions unresolved. Close young paternal kin of the victim, who are not yet expected to behave according to *pulaaku*, generally express these unresolved tensions through threats of revenge. The fathers of both the killer and the victim are thus wary of impulsive actions by these young men, over whom they have little control. Moreover, the father of the killer has the additional concern that the killer will probably be arrested and imprisoned if he stays around.

To avoid these escalations, the father of the killer usually sends his son into exile, providing him with part of the herd to which he is entitled. The killer will live with relatives across the national border for about a decade, which allows emotions on the part of the family of the victim to cool down. Moreover, because the police commander and district chief are generally replaced after some years, the risk of state prosecution will most likely have subsided after a decade. This more or less forced temporary exile is at the same time a form of 'punishment' for the killer and his father in and of itself. The latter loses the labour and the company of his son, while the son loses the direct material and moral support of his father.

Local Traditional and State Authorities

When norms of *pulaaku* are respected in dispute settlement, neither the so-called traditional territorial authorities originating from other (ethnic) groups nor the state authorities have an active role in settling conflicts between nomadic Fulbe. One of the reasons why nomadic Fulbe are ambivalent towards state authorities is that state law does not simply focus on compensation, but also on punishment. This model of justice is largely opposed to that advocated by *pulaaku*, which rather privileges dispute management as a process oriented towards forgiveness and reparation of damaged social relations. Moreover, deprivation of liberty is one of the most feared punishments for nomadic Fulbe, not least because the living conditions in prisons in Cameroon clearly reduce life expectancy.

Problems 'originating in the bush' should thus be settled 'in the bush'. This principle applies to both intragroup cattle theft and homicides, that is, crimes committed within the nomadic Fulbe community. It is especially disapproved of socially and in practice to seek the involvement of external authorities in homicide cases because a dead person cannot be brought back to life. However, it is rather well accepted to do so in connection with cattle theft, but only as a last resort to regain a stolen animal.

When nomadic Fulbe involve external authorities, they usually start with the involvement of the local 'traditional' territorial authorities from neighbouring sedentary groups who are 'the fathers of the land' and 'auxiliaries' of the state administration. According to state law, the competences of 'traditional' chiefs are limited to civil cases requiring 'traditional' knowledge. These include, for example, disputes concerning divorce, inheritance and property boundaries between farmers. The traditional chiefs should, however, delegate criminal cases like theft and physical violence to state authorities. In their own words, traditional authorities recognize that they should refer to the police if 'blood has been shed'. However, they do not always do so. This is especially true among administratively higher-ranking chiefs, that is, first-degree chiefs who are still highly respected among their subjects. If traditional chiefs do deal with cases of bodily harm, such as that which may occur as a result of fistfights or robberies, they are expected to report their arbitration to their local traditional superior, the local commander of the police or the district chief. If the commanders of the police and/or the district chief agree with the decision of a traditional chief, the case will be closed after these state authorities have received their 'financial share' of the arbitration.

Nomadic Fulbe feel that 'traditional' territorial authorities are more competent in reaching correct verdicts than both their own elders and representatives of the state administration. This is because most high-ranking chiefs are Muslims who can make the parties take an oath on the Qur^can to find out the 'truth', which the state administration cannot do. In practice, traditional authorities also have the power to enforce their decisions, which nomadic elders seldom have.

Over the last two decades, however, the state administration has become increasingly involved in dispute settlement 'in the bush'. This evolution has been partly promoted by the process of administrative decentralization that started in the 1990s, during the course of which large departments became increasingly subdivided into smaller administrative units, each with its own district chief and police station.

A second reason for the increased involvement of external authorities in the bush is that litigants are not the only actors to pursue their own interests. Authorities too may have their own goals and see dispute settlement as an occasion to pursue their own rivalries or economic interests. In practice, they often have more to gain from the perpetuation of a conflict than from its resolution (Moritz 2006). In local jargon, the quest for personal gain by authoritative figures is called 'eating' and thus is famously referred to as 'politics of the belly' (Bayart 2006 [1989]).

For the above reasons, many authorities are shopping for cases just as much as litigants are shopping for dispute settlement forums (Benda-Beckmann 1981), and it is therefore ever harder 'to settle problems in the bush'. Many nomadic Fulbe to whom I talked complained that even if they wanted to negotiate without the intervention of a third party, a neighbour would have already noticed the affair and informed a chief. Local witnesses often reported disputes to these authorities in order to establish privileged relations with them as personal informants or to intentionally damage one of the parties involved. In many cases, officials were in some way already involved before a litigant had the time to actually decide which forum he wanted to present his case in, or indeed if he wanted simply to negotiate directly. This tendency has grown even more prevalent now that mobile telephone networks reach the most remote areas in the bush.

For the public, it is often not clear whether one of the disputing parties has indeed brought the case to the chief himself without informing the elders, which would be shameful behaviour according to *pulaaku*, or whether the chief has heard about the dispute and has summoned the parties in order to 'eat from them'. For the most part, I found that the wider public would give the disputing parties the benefit of the doubt and would remark cynically that the 'chiefs had been eating again'. Nomadic Fulbe thus share the belief that their illiteracy makes them vulnerable to abuse by state officials, whom they accuse of using them as 'milk cows', in reference to the large herds of cattle that they maintain.

It would, however, be misguided to regard the Fulbe simply as victims in this process. Successful litigation depends largely on the skills of the litigants to approach the right persons and pay the right amounts of money. Nomadic Fulbe are reputed to be quite generous when it comes to giving 'gifts' to authorities in order to assure favourable judgments in court trials. Most other groups cannot compete with such 'gifts' because they do not possess the wealth (in cattle) that nomadic Fulbe have, and thus often lose in litigations with Fulbe.

Case: Leaving the 'Way of *Pulaaku*' to Engage in Forum Shopping

After this brief presentation of the norms that nomadic Fulbe strive to follow and the sociolegal setting, I will now present a rather extensive case that evolved over the course of several years. This case started with the theft of a knife, but escalated dramatically until most observers could no longer make head or tail of it. However, most nomadic Fulbe suspect that it is in fact about homicide. It is a notorious case among nomadic Fulbe in the Far North because, although *pulaaku* seemed to be respected at the start, the case eventually degenerated into a neverending process of forum shopping. The case will thus show how *pulaaku* is continuously renegotiated between conflicting parties and the public through a continuous reframing of the dispute within the sociolegal context of the state. I will first introduce the main actor in this case, Issa, and will shortly describe how I found out about this case and the way in which I have proceeded to investigate it.

I met Issa, a nomadic Fulbe Jafun cattle owner, for the first time in his camp south of Lake Maga in February 2009. On his own initiative, he eagerly told me that he had been the victim of cattle theft a year and a half earlier. He listed all the authorities he had visited thus far to get the stolen cattle back, but to no avail. He also showed the documents he had gathered during the course of his judicial forum shopping, although he could not read them himself because they were written in French. In some of these documents there was not only a complaint of cattle theft, but also of homicide. I did not ask Issa about the latter during our first meeting, expecting him to mention the accusation of homicide during future interviews that I would conduct with him in the following months. Issa did not, however, volunteer this information, so in February 2010, I finally confronted him with my awareness that the case involved much more than just cattle theft. He seemed a little shocked that I knew about the homicide and hesitantly admitted that the theft and the homicide were somehow related. Yet, he remained reluctant to speak candidly about this connection, for reasons that I will discuss after having presented the whole case, reconstructed with the help of Issa, his opponents and other sources, including 'traditional' and state authorities.

On a night in September 2007, Issa's son, Oumarou, was herding the cattle when thieves assaulted him and stole a cow and her bull calf. In the battle with the thieves, he also lost his knife. Because of the darkness and the surprise attack, Oumarou had not recognized the thieves.

During a wedding in a neighbouring camp in around March 2008, Oumarou noticed that a young nomadic Fulbe, Abdoulaye, was carrying the stolen knife. They had a fight and Oumarou regained his knife. Back home, he showed it to his father, Issa, and told him how he had found it. Four days later, Abdoulaye came with two other youngsters to Issa's camp and, under some pretext, lured Oumarou away. In the bush, Abdoulaye and his friends tied Oumarou to a tree and tortured him, inflicting grave injuries to his genitals. Issa, who went after Oumarou as soon as he heard that he had left with Abdoulaye, found his son in agony, trying to drag himself back home. His son refused to tell him what had happened. After Issa had brought his son home, he returned to the bush to look for traces of the perpetrator who had wounded his child. The trail eventually led to Abdoulaye, who proceeded to provoke Issa by describing how he had abused his son.

Although he was furious, Issa controlled himself and went to the camp of Abdoulaye's father, Moumini, who was not there that night. Issa went back again the next day, but claims that Moumini refused to talk to him about the incident between their sons and the insults he had endured. Eight days later, Issa's son died.

Issa did not inform the political leader of his faction of the suspect circumstances of his son's death. He probably felt that the way in which his son had been tortured was too shameful to be openly revealed in front of a meeting of elders.[8]

Moreover, Issa explicitly stated that he did not bring the case to the attention of the chief of Guirvidig either, in whose administrative territory he was staying when his son passed away. This canton chief belonged to the Musgum ethnic group. According to Issa, other people had gossiped about what had happened between his son and the son of Moumini, and that this was how this chief heard about the case. By insisting that he did not go to the chief to complain about the death of his son, Issa was demonstrating that he had observed the restraints prescribed by *pulaaku*. He also implied adherence to the injunction that one should ideally refrain from involving external authorities from ethnic or subethnic communities other than one's own.

On 17 May 2008, the aforementioned Musgum chief summoned both Issa and Moumini to explain what had happened. While recounting the hearing, Issa led me to understand that he had upheld the ideal of *pulaaku* with regard to the homicide. He stated that what had happened between their sons was something that could not be undone and that raising the issue with the Musgum chief would not bring back his son. However, at the same time, he argued that it was not shameful to want to recover one's stolen cattle and that, following the norms of *pulaaku*, one indeed had the right to pursue someone for theft. He thus explained to the chief the connections he had made between the incident involving his and Moumini's sons, the lost knife and the stolen cattle.

Moumini, however, denied that either he or his son was involved in the cattle theft of which Issa accused them. The chief urged Moumini to back up his assertion by taking an oath on the Qurᶜan, and Moumini did so, swearing that neither he nor his son was guilty of the acts of which Issa accused them. After this oath taking, the chief declared that he was free to go.

This case took another important and unexpected turn around October 2008, when Issa saw in a foraging herd the bull he believed the son of Moumini had stolen. The youngsters leading the herd told him that it belonged to their father, a nomadic Fulbe called Saidou, who had bought the bull in the rainy season that year. Issa demanded that the bull be given back to him on the spot, but the youngsters refused to give it to him and threatened to beat him up. Infuriated, Issa went again to the Musgum chief of Guirvidig to file a new complaint. The chief sent a messenger to summon the youngsters, who contacted their father, Saidou.

Saidou came to the Musgum chief in the first week of November with two elders from his faction. Issa, who attended the meeting as well, had brought with him a sedentary Fulbe, Mahmadou, who was his regular host (*beero*)[9] in Guirvidig and had a good relationship with the chief. During the meeting, Issa announced that he not only wanted the bull back, but also its mother, which had been stolen on the same occasion. He thus asked Saidou to reveal both the name of the seller and that of the market official who had acted as intermediary between him and the seller.

Saidou stated that he did not know the name of either of these two persons and that the official transaction papers had been destroyed by water in the rainy season. The Musgum chief of Guirvidig then told Saidou that because he could not show the papers, he had to give the bull back to Issa and pay him 60,000 FCFA (€92), a sum of money equivalent to the expenses that Issa claimed to have made up to that point to find his bull.

Issa was disappointed that Saidou had denied knowledge of the cattle theft and had not denounced Abdoulaye. Because of this, Issa was reluctant to take the bull back and suggested that if Saidou had not stolen the bull, then they had a common interest in this case. Both of them had 'lost' something: in the case of Saidou, it was the money he paid for the bull that now had to be given back; in the case of Issa, it was the stolen bull's mother. Both of them also knew that the name of the seller was necessary if they were to have any chance of regaining what had been 'taken' by others. Saidou, however, continued to maintain that he did not remember who the seller was. After a while, and once it had become obvious that neither disputant would change his stance, Mahmadou, Issa's host in Guirvidig, decided to intervene. He urged Issa to settle his dispute with Saidou and invoked *pulaaku* to convince him to accept the decision of the chief of Guirvidig. Not accepting the decision of the chief and the advice of his own representative would have amounted to willingly escalating the case, as well as showing disrespect to the elders, both of which would have been instances of shameful behaviour. Socially speaking, Issa had no choice but to accept the bull and agree to stop demanding that Saidou find the mother cow.

However, Issa claimed that another incident occurred the same evening that compelled him to reopen the case. The sons of Saidou had been drinking and when they saw Issa on his way to the mosque, they 'insulted and threatened him'. Issa was infuriated by this new offence and went back to the Musgum chief of Guirvidig the next day to tell him what had happened and that he no longer agreed with the verdict. He now claimed both the bull and its mother from Saidou.

Saidou was already on his way back to his camp when the chief of Guirvidig called him on his phone and summoned him to return. The chief asked him to swear on the Qurʿan this time that he had purchased the bull legally. Because Saidou blamed Issa for putting shame on him for no reason, the chief also asked Issa to swear that the bull in the herd of Saidou was really his. Issa, however, refused to take an oath on the holy book. He explained to me that, first, he felt it was useless to take an oath only about the bull because what he really wanted was to get its mother back as well. He was persuaded that the quest for the mother cow would prove the involvement of Moumini's and/or Saidou's children in this theft. Second, he was of the opinion that 'oath taking should not be taken lightly' and that Saidou and Moumini should also have taken it more seriously than they did. However, Issa's refusal to swear on the Qurʿan was interpreted negatively by the chief of Guirvidig, who then decided that Saidou could keep the bull.

Three weeks later, Issa went to the police brigade in the district capital, Maga, to file a complaint against both Moumini's and Saidou's sons for the theft of his cattle. Issa knew that the truth-confirming function of oath taking on the Qurᶜan was not recognized by state law and that the police would conduct their own investigation. He accompanied the police officials to Guirvidig, where they discussed the affair again with the Musgum chief. The officials then arrested one of Saidou's sons in his father's camp on suspicion of theft, and summoned Saidou and two faction elders. Saidou now involved Ibrahima, a sedentary Shuwa Arab who had a large network of connections among influential authorities throughout the entire Far North Region. Saidou gave Ibrahima about 100,000 FCFA (€154) to distribute on his behalf in order to free his son and make the police 'lose' the case in the proverbial 'bottom drawer'. Issa returned to the police station three times, but the commander always told him that Saidou had not come. The third time, the commander told him that he had freed Saidou's son due to lack of evidence. In the meantime, the rainy season had started and, as the roads were washed out and the village was no longer accessible, Issa was forced to drop the case for a while.

In December 2008, in the following dry season when the roads were passable again, Issa filed a complaint with the prosecutor in Yagoua, the town close to his rainy season area, naming both Moumini and Saidou as responsible for the actions of their children. He got in contact with an attorney through Mahmadou, his host in Guirvidig.

In his complaint against Abdoulaye, Issa not only mentioned the cattle theft, but also the stolen knife and the death of his son, knowing well that state law (as opposed to *pulaaku*) did allow one to press charges for homicide. He also demanded that Abdoulaye's father, Moumini, whom he reproached for not having taken responsibility for the wrongdoings of his son, pay him compensation of 6,000,000 FCFA (€9,230) for the medical expenses for his son Oumarou, the costs of the litigation before the 'traditional' authorities and interest.

Before seeing the prosecutor, Moumini, who had realized that Issa would not drop the case, decided to send his son with some cattle to relatives in Chad in order to avoid further escalation and get him out of reach of the Cameroonian police. Moumini filed a counter-complaint of harassment against Issa with the same prosecutor in Yagoua as well. Without mentioning Issa's accusation concerning the death of his son, Moumini claimed that Issa was harassing him without cause, as he had already acquitted himself by swearing on the Qurᶜan that he was not involved in the cattle theft.

In addition, Moumini went to the 'traditional' Fulbe chief of Kolara, the village in whose administrative territory both Issa and Moumini used to spend the rainy season. This chief is influential among nomadic pastoralists because he often represents the nomads when they have problems with the state authorities. The chief summoned both Issa and Moumini and pressured Issa to drop the charges against Moumini. During this meeting, Moumini successfully invoked *pulaaku* to shame Issa into following the chief's advice. Issa acquiesced because he did not want to bring shame upon himself and had an interest in staying on good terms with this chief. However, Issa also revealed to me that he never intended to let Moumini's son get away with the theft. For the time being, however, he considered it judicious first to pursue the case against Saidou and then take up the case against Moumini again.

The first time Moumini visited the prosecutor in Yagoua, he also ran into Saidou, who had been summoned the same day. The prosecutor told Saidou that Issa had filed an accusation of cattle theft against him and his sons in which he claimed 600,000 FCFA (€920) for expenses and interest. Saidou once again enlisted the help of Ibrahima, the sedentary Fulbe, to whom he gave 300,000 FCFA this time (€462) to distribute between the prosecutor and other people of the court in order to encourage them to drop the case.

Saidou's strategy was apparently successful. The prosecutor summoned Issa five more times to confront Saidou, but Saidou never showed up and was apparently not reprimanded in any way for his truancy. Travelling about 300 km each time to the prosecutor's office took its toll on Issa. Moreover, every time he was absent from his camp, thieves would sneak in and steal cattle from him at night. He believed that Ibrahima, the intermediary of Saidou with the administration, was informing the thieves when he was not present so that they could steal from him.

Disillusioned after his fifth visit to the prosecutor, Issa decided to file a new complaint, this time with the commander of the police in the regional capital, Maroua. Being illiterate, he had received the name of a contact person in Maroua, who became his intermediary with the administration and to whom he gave money to distribute among influential persons. Despite Issa's initial doubts, this intermediary did a rather good job. Indeed, in March 2009, Saidou and the two competing leaders mentioned above[10] were publicly arrested at a market, a fact that soon became known by all nomadic Fulbe and constituted a public humiliation for Saidou and the Fulbe elders concerned.

For his part, Saidou showed the police commander in Maroua the document written by the Musgum chief of Guirvidig attesting to the fact that he had already taken an oath on the Qurʿan in regard to this same case. The commander took some police officials with him to accompany Issa and Saidou to the chief in Guirvidig to hear his version of the story. They also went to the police commander in Maga, the district capital where Issa had filed an earlier complaint against Saidou as well. Issa stated that they spoke in French, which he did not understand. At the end, the commander told him they would continue to investigate the case and would contact him again in three weeks.

The three weeks passed, but Issa had not yet heard anything from the police commander at the time I left the research area in February 2010, five months after his first meeting with that official. At that time, Issa believed that Ibrahima had again distributed money for Saidou among the authorities in order to obstruct the legal procedures. Issa, however, told me that he would continue to pursue the case against Saidou and was even willing to bring it to the attention of the governor of the Far North Region if necessary. However, he was unsure what his next step should be and asked me where he should go next in the state hierarchy. Saidou and the two notables of his faction who had been arrested by the police, for their part, claimed that Issa wanted 'war' and that they too would not give up.

Public Shame and Honour at What Price?

The huge expenditures both by the plaintiff and the accused in this case illustrate that for nomadic Fulbe in the Far North Region of Cameroon, the main rationale behind forum shopping is not a financial one.[11] Rather, the infliction and avoidance of public shame seems to be the central motivation behind this forum shopping.

Lund (1999) discusses a comparable phenomenon in which shame and what appears to be economic irrationality go hand in hand in trials about cattle theft between Fulbe in Burkina Faso. In his attempt to explain why in these contexts Fulbe are often willing to spend much more money in bribes than the animal is actually worth, Lund writes that animal theft was a cause of dishonour, but only:

> If the theft was discovered … Or rather, if the attempt was unsuccessful, for someone who had stolen an animal to be made to hand it back would be a severe humiliation and the shame would be acutely felt. If, on the other hand, he [the thief] were able to hold on to the animal despite facing some sort of formal trial the man would earn a formidable reputation, while the dishonour and shame would fall on the head of the unlucky owner. The latter would be seen as unable to fend for himself, and as lacking the influence to make the authorities enforce his rights. (Lund 1999: 585)

Public shame thus plays a crucial role in these conflicts. While pursuing other nomadic Fulbe for homicide is strongly disapproved of and is shameful in the eyes of the public, pursuing other nomadic Fulbe for cattle theft can even increase honour. As Issa was well aware of these facts, he strategically chose to reframe his grievances about the homicide of his son and relate them to cattle theft in order to make his claims socially acceptable. The accusations of cattle theft allowed him to act upon the real grievance he held against Moumini and Saidou, that is, their refusal to repair the damaged relations between their families after the (supposed) homicide and, second, their unwillingness to take responsibility for the irreverent behaviour of their sons towards him after this incident.[12]

But it was not only the motivations and framing of this dispute that changed during the process; the intended outcome of the process changed as well. Issa's initial goal might effectively have been punishment and financial compensation when he started to shop in external juridical forums. However, when grievances and frustrations accumulated in the course of his forum shopping, he no longer aimed at punishment by state institutions or at material compensation. Rather, the conflict now turned out to be about the legal procedure itself – that is, for Issa, it became a contest in manipulating the authorities to achieve his own goals. Forum shopping itself started to take on aspects of revenge through harassment and public humiliation in a game of bribing the authorities.

One could say that the lack of efficiency and transparency of the Cameroonian justice system allowed Issa to inflict shame on his opponents and at the same time increase his own reputation by fending for himself. He showed his capacity to manipulate the authorities for his purposes, while at the same time following 'legal rules and processes'. The very fact that Moumini was summoned by higher-ranking state authorities and that Saidou was arrested by the police inflicted public shame and material damage on them, and served as a form of revenge for the disrespect and financial losses Issa himself had suffered.

Rather than understanding this as shameful behaviour on his part, Issa presented his actions (and their consequences) as just compensation for all the problems he had encountered as a result of Moumini's and Saidou's deviations from the norms of *pulaaku*. The facts that he had sold twelve head of cattle since the start of this ordeal to finance his forum shopping and that a final verdict still seemed far away one and half years later only seemed to motivate him even more. He proudly told me that he received little economic support from his faction (because most of its members lived in Nigeria), especially when compared to his opponents, who had many kin in the region. He found it especially important to demonstrate that in spite of this difference in wealth and support, he was a strong person whom 'you could not disrespect' without repercussions.

By reframing his grievances about the death of his son as a quest for his cattle, Issa aimed to transform a potentially shameful endeavour into a quest for honour in the eyes of the public, much as Lund (1999) observed among Fulbe in Burkina Faso.

Forum Shopping and Shameful Behaviour: The Public Decides!

Previously I noted that one should avoid involving external authorities in dispute settlement because doing so could be perceived as shameful in the eyes of fellow Fulbe. As I have already noted, if one nevertheless opts for this approach, one should ideally not do it before having first sought the arbitration of the political leader(s) of one's faction(s).

In Issa's case, shame turned out to be a double-edged sword. Because of the shameful nature of the torture of his son, which allegedly led to his death, Issa could not present the case in front of a public hearing of his elders. It would be impossible to explain this without bringing public shame upon himself. However, in order to avoid shameful behaviour in the eyes of the public for not having consulted the elders, Issa was careful to insist that the traditional chief of Guirvidig had summoned him and that he had not gone to the authorities on his own initiative. This was plausible, as the authorities do indeed often shop for conflicts to pursue their economic interests. Issa also insisted that before the chief he explicitly stated that his son could not be brought back, so he was not interested in bringing charges for homicide. He was thus careful to make a distinction between the homicide and the cattle theft.

Once Issa started to shop in external juridical forums, however, he could adopt different framings of the conflict, and we have seen that his claims, discourses and motives were continuously redefined and adapted to fit the specific normative framework of each forum. The framings also evolved when his grievances increased during the course of the conflict with each new complaint and each successful rebuttal of the complaint by the other party (see also Felstiner, Abel and Sarat 1980–81).

Different framings of the dispute in different forums thus existed next to each other at the same moment in time. Issa had to maintain a verbal formulation and reasoning that continued to separate the case of homicide from the case of theft for his fellow Fulbe in order to avoid public shame. He even managed to do this in front of me. However, in the written complaints to the police commander and the prosecutor, he not only described the cattle theft but also explicitly connected it to the alleged homicide and the costs incurred following up on the homicide. That the homicide was his main motivation also became clear through his claims: compensation claimed from Saidou in the letter to the prosecutor was one-tenth of the damages he was trying to claim from Moumini, whose son had allegedly killed his son. The compensation demanded by Issa from Moumini thus reflected much more than the procedural costs for the homicide and the loss of his cattle, and in fact looked more like compensation for the loss of his son – in other words, a form of blood money, the highly frowned upon *diya*.

Although Issa was not directly accused of claiming *diya*, he was in the end reproached for a lack *pulaaku* by other nomadic Fulbe. Even those nomadic Fulbe he moved with during parts of the year urged him to drop the case because he had already shown a lack of restraint and let the conflict escalate way too far for the loss of one bull calf. Saidou, for his part, stated that Issa was instigating a 'war' between their factions and that he was ruining them both. He did not understand why Issa was harassing him so much over a bull he claims to have purchased legally.

Issa's obsession with pursuing Moumini and his son Abdoulaye had aroused attention among all nomadic Fulbe, and the real reason for this obstinacy – that is, the homicide – had become an item of gossip circulating through the marketplaces in Guirvidig and its surroundings. Nomadic Fulbe who belonged to factions other than Issa's told me that everybody knew that Issa's son had always suffered from internal bleeding because he had frequent bloody noses. They shared the belief that the illness associated with these bleedings was the real cause of Issa's son's death.

On top of bringing shame upon himself by disrespecting the norms of *pulaaku* in the eyes of his fellow Fulbe – the very thing he had tried to avoid from the start – nomadic Fulbe also considered Issa irrational because he was squandering his cattle for no valid reason. Issa learned the hard way that there is a fine line between fending for oneself and madness, though this no longer seemed to bother him at this stage of the conflict.

Shifting Behaviour out of the Realm of *pulaaku* by Including Sedentary Fulbe

Although in the end Issa was not able to avoid public shame, in other cases I found that nomadic Fulbe did manage to involve external authorities, claim enhanced compensation and avoid public shame at the same time. I will end this discussion with such a 'success story' in which the kin of the victim did manage to gain larger than expected compensation by involving external actors without being accused of shameful behaviour or of exacting *diya*. This serves to illustrate another potentially successful strategy Fulbe can use to bypass the strict requirements of *pulaaku*.

In 2006, a young nomadic Fulbe Jafun severely wounded a young nomadic Fulbe Sallube. The victim was brought to Guirvidig, to the house of the cattle owner for whom he worked as a herdsman, after which they brought him to the hospital in the next biggest town. The father of the perpetrator came to Guirvidig to hear how the wounded young man was doing and to reconcile with the kin of the victim. The Musgum chief of this village, who had already heard of the case, immediately summoned the father of the young Jafun. The chief told him that he would not intervene; blood had been shed, so it was outside of his competence. He was even willing not to report the case to the police and to leave it instead to the nomadic Fulbe themselves to settle.[13]

The injured man died the same day and, as his father had passed away, it was his older brother, Aliou, who was responsible for settling the case with the father of the killer. Because it was a Friday, Aliou and the father of the killer coincidentally met in the homestead of the local imam. The imam, a sedentary Fulbe, took it upon himself to assist in the negotiations. He told them that they were both sons of Allah and that a member of the Jafun had now killed a member of the Sallube, but that one day, maybe in a hundred years, a member of the Sallube would kill a member of the Jafun. Given this, the brother of the victim should not demand a large compensation payment, but should wait for Allah to do justice. The brother of the victim accepted the words of the imam and demanded 100,000 FCFA (€154) for the costs of transportation to the hospital, the medical treatment and the funeral, which the father of the killer paid him on the spot. Apparently, the imam had convinced the disputing parties to settle according to *pulaaku*.

After that, Aliou visited the cattle trader for whom he worked as a hired herdsman. This sedentary Fulbe told him that he had settled too easily, noting that the father of the killer was a rich cattle owner and that Aliou should claim compensation for the loss of his brother's labour power[14] as well. He thus pushed Aliou to go back to the homestead of the imam, where the father of the killer was still staying, to renegotiate the compensation payment up to 800,000 FCFA (€1,230), instead of the initially agreed-upon 100,000 FCFA.

Confronted with this new demand, the father of the killer asked Aliou if he was now requesting blood money (*diya*) for the homicide of his brother. Aliou said that it was not *diya*, but that he simply wanted fair compensation. The father of the killer told him that if he truly was not demanding *diya*, then they needed to go to the Musgum chief of Guirvidig and ask him to act as witness for the money transaction. The brother of the victim baulked at this proposal and suggested asking the imam to fulfil that role on the spot. However, the imam refused, saying that the police commander should handle settlements involving that kind of money. Moreover, no meeting of elders had been held to discuss the compensation. The father of the killer then proposed going to the police, which the brother also vetoed. The father of the killer finally suggested going back to the 'bush' and calling a meeting of the elders so that the brother of the deceased could justify to them why he wanted 800,000 FCFA for the homicide.

The father of the killer thus hoped that Aliou would renounce his demand. A public request for this kind of money for the homicide of his brother would be considered shameful behaviour in the eyes of their fellow Fulbe, who would definitely interpret his demand as *diya* – in other words, as an attempt to 'sell' his brother. The father's strategy seemed to work because Aliou left again without further claims.

Aliou had, however, not abandoned his claims. He returned to his employer for support. This sedentary Fulbe, who had rather good connections with the administration, took the case to the police commander in the regional capital Maroua, who summoned the father of the killer. The police held him in custody for two days and made him pay an undisclosed amount of money to bribe his way out. The commander shared this money with the Fulbe employer who, in turn, shared some of what he got with the brother of the deceased man. The father of the killer then received a paper stating that the case had been decided. After that, the paternal uncle of the killer gave a bull and 20,000 FCFA (€31) as late compensation for the funeral rites in order to symbolically restore the relations between the families of the disputing parties.

Other Fulbe I spoke to were of the opinion that the state authorities had heard about the case and 'eaten' as usual, but that no *diya* had been paid to the brother of the victim. According to them, the very fact that the family of the killer had paid for the funeral was a sign that the case had indeed finally been resolved according to *pulaaku*, that the disputing parties had repaired their damaged relations and that there was no shame on any of these parties.

The brother of the victim, Aliou, legitimated the involvement of the police by saying that if the father of the killer had really been willing to reach a just agreement from the start, the state authorities would not have had to intervene. He also stressed that it was not he but his employer, the sedentary Fulbe, who had taken the affair to the state authorities, and if we wanted further information, we would have to refer to his employer.

In this case it is clear that Aliou, the brother of the victim, just like Issa, aimed for a much larger compensation settlement than that which is normally given in a case of homicide when the litigants actually settle the dispute 'in the bush' and according to the norms of *pulaaku*. Aliou did not seem, at first glance, to actually behave in conformity with these norms. However, in contrast to Issa, other nomadic Fulbe did not reproach him for having displayed shameful behaviour. Aliou had managed to shift the responsibility for his actions to another level, making use of the construction of differences between subethnic groups. As previously noted, the person who helped Aliou get an 'enhanced compensation' in connection with the homicide of his brother was a sedentary Fulbe, someone belonging to the historical, wider ethnic group of which nomadic Fulbe also feel part. However, nomadic Fulbe categorically assert that sedentary Fulbe have a weaker sense of *pulaaku* than themselves. This alleged tension between similarity and difference was drawn on by Aliou to shift his behaviour outside the framework of *pulaaku*. Instead of blaming him for a lack of *pulaaku*, in the opinion of his fellow nomadic Fulbe Aliou had not really done anything wrong by involving a sedentary Fulbe. Yet, had he involved a non-Fulbe instead of a Fulbe from another group as his representative, he would have risked censure.[15] By stressing this point, nomadic Fulbe chose to give more weight to their similarities with sedentary Fulbe and the fact that this person was an important cattle owner who had many connections with nomadic Fulbe. However, by virtue of his otherness, a sedentary Fulbe was not socially obliged to uphold *pulaaku* as strictly as members of the in-group of nomadic Fulbe would be expected to do in the same situation.

In Issa's case, however, we have seen that the opposite can happen as well. Instead of circumventing the restrictive norms of *pulaaku* by involving sedentary

Fulbe and engaging in forum shopping, nomadic Fulbe can just as well involve sedentary Fulbe *chiefs* as a way of reintroducing the norms of *pulaaku* and getting out of ongoing forum shopping. Because of their customary status, chiefs still respect *pulaaku* much more than ordinary sedentary Fulbe. Moreover, sedentary Fulbe chiefs are in a much better position to impose their arbitration because, as has been discussed earlier, they have much more power of enforcement than the nomadic Fulbe elders. In the case of Issa, this occurred notably when Moumini managed to involve a 'traditional' authority from a sedentary Fulbe group. He was well respected by most nomadic Fulbe and asked Issa to refrain again from prosecuting Moumini. Out of fear of the consequences of disobeying this influential chief, Issa thus abandoned his forum shopping against Moumini.[16]

Conclusion

In this chapter, I have stressed that retaliation and *diya* are strongly disapproved of by nomadic Fulbe in the Far North Region of Cameroon, both normatively and in practice. In these cases, the threats of escalation of violence are largely buffered by members of older generations who are responsible for repairing the damaged relations between families. Fathers of killers, for example, take it upon themselves to send their sons across national borders in order to avoid further provocation that could result in an escalation of violence and revenge.

Furthermore, we have shown that intragroup homicides are contexts in which it is especially frowned upon, both culturally and in practice, to pursue the offender in other juridical forums. However, I have also shown that in spite of this, grievances often do persist in the aftermath of intragroup homicides and that the prosecution of a killer's paternal kin does occur. The initial motivations for forum shopping often shift over time and increasingly focus, for some, on the restoration of honour and, for others, on the bestowal of shame. In the course of this evolution, the forum shopping itself can indeed become more and more about either social compensation or revenge, and less and less about either financial compensation or obtaining justice in legal terms through adjudication from state authorities.

The cases presented in this chapter illustrate that although forum shopping can become very costly in financial terms, the greatest perceived cost for Fulbe plaintiffs turns out to be the risk of committing shameful behaviour in the eyes of fellow Fulbe. To avoid this, it becomes judicious to reframe grievances related to homicide in terms of cattle theft, especially in a pastoral community whose members have a strong attachment to their cattle. But whatever rhetoric one uses to reframe one's grievances, there is still the risk of being accused of deviating from the norms governing dispute settlement as soon as that rhetoric becomes implausible to other ingroup members. Thus for nomadic Fulbe, convincing the wider public that they themselves act according to *pulaaku,* while blaming the opposing party for not doing this, becomes a central part of the conflict.

Finally, we have observed a strategy to shift behaviour outside of (or back into) *pulaaku* through the inclusion of sedentary Fulbe representatives. Sedentary Fulbe, with whom nomadic Fulbe share many affinities, are nevertheless recognized as different, notably in the way they refer to *pulaaku* and, in the case of chiefs, their ability to enforce decisions. Exploiting this tension between ethnic similarity and difference turns out to be a successful way to bypass the strict norms of *pulaaku* while avoiding shame in the eyes of fellow nomadic Fulbe.

In a society in which overt retaliatory rhetoric is largely lacking in connection with intragroup homicide, grievances can often not be expressed. However, the presence of other normative forums (even if they are reputed to be unreliable) as well as the presence of other (related) groups offer outlets for these grievances. If one is willing and able to invest a lot of money in forum shopping, one can retaliate through a 'game' of afflicting and simultaneously avoiding shame. This tactic can be effective if one continuously reframes the dispute to conform to the different normative frameworks, while at the same time remaining within the boundaries of acceptable behaviour in the eyes of one's own group. In the end, it is up to the public to judge who has been most adroit at this 'game' of disguising retaliatory practices, a game that can most probably never be won, but can certainly be lost in dramatic fashion.

Acknowledgements

The fourteen-month field research on which this chapter is based was carried out within the framework of a Ph.D. project for the International Max Planck Research School on Retaliation, Mediation and Punishment (REMEP) and was financed by the Max Planck Institute for Social Anthropology, Halle (Saale), Germany. I would like to thank the latter institution for its support. I am also particularly grateful to Martine Guichard, Mark Moritz and Bertram Turner for their comments and suggestions on earlier versions of this chapter.

Albert K. Drent has studied anthropology and ecology. He has an interest in interdisciplinary research and has subsequently carried out research for the Development Sociology and Resource Ecology Departments of the Wageningen University, the Netherlands, the Conflict and Integration Department of the Max Planck Institute for Social Anthropology, Germany, and the Preventive Veterinary Medicine and Anthropology Departments of Ohio State University, United States. His main research topics are 'natural resource management', 'land rights', 'conflict', 'pastoralism' and 'space'.

Notes

1. This rudimentary description is an oversimplification, but it suffices for the purposes of this chapter. For ethnographic descriptions of these groups, see the main classic works on nomadic Fulbe (Stenning 1994 [1959] and Dupire 1996 [1962]). See also Burnham 1996; Schlee and Guichard 2007.
2. 'Implosive consonants' that are pronounced as glottal occlusions preceding the consonants b, d and y (Noye 1974: 8) are often indicated using the capital letters B, D and Y. In the rest of this chapter I will not make this distinction and will use lower case b, d and y to refer to both normal and glottal variants.
3. For studies dealing with *diya* in other Islamic contexts, see, for example, Peters (1967); Peters (2005); and Schlee and Turner (2008). See also the chapters by Ben Hounet, Schlee and Stahlmann in this volume.
4. Sedentary Muslims often criticize this lack of education, which is especially evident in the pronunciation and mastery of prayers, which Nomadic Fulbe mainly learn from their parents.
5. According to state authorities, *diya* is forbidden in Cameroon.
6. Interview with Amadou, Fulbe elder, Lahaye, December 2009.
7. If the victim is killed on the spot and therefore requires no medical attention, his or her family should only demand compensation for the expenses related to the funeral.
8. Some sources reported that Abdoulaye tortured Oumarou by hitting and squeezing his testicles with his herding staff. The human genitals, however, are deemed *semteende* – shameful to talk about in public. Therefore, this crime could not be dealt with in a public hearing.
9. Nomadic Fulbe have privileged personal relationships with certain villagers, mostly sedentary Fulbe. When the nomads are in the village, they stay in the house of these hosts and are taken care of by them. These hosts also often represent the nomads before the 'traditional' authorities of the village in cases of dispute.
10. These two leaders had indeed both supported Saidou during the hearing with the Musgum chief of Guirvidig.
11. Issa had already sold twelve head of cattle to finance his pursuit of justice, and yet the end of the case seemed further away than ever when I left the field in February 2010. Moreover, Saidou had already invested far more in bribes than the 600,000 FCFA Issa originally wanted from him.
12. Although the self-control and restraint associated with *pulaaku* did not allow him to openly show strong emotions, Issa had difficulty controlling himself when he described his grievances to me during an interview.
13. The Musgum chief just demanded a small monetary compensation for the favour of not reporting the case to the state authorities and to buy the goodwill of the police commander of the Maga district so that he would not pursue the case.
14. However, the formulation of this claim is indeed reminiscent of *diya*.
15. As, for example, in the case of the involvement of the Shuwa Arab elder discussed in the section entitled 'Being Fulbe versus Being Muslim' above.
16. However, Issa confided to me that once his case against Saidou was finished, he intended to resume the case against Moumini. In the dry season of 2012, however, the case against Saidou abruptly came to an end when he was killed in a conflict with fishermen in Chad. When I met Issa again in March 2013, he said he wanted to file a new complaint against Moumini and asked me to assist him because he felt that I was familiar enough with the case to do so. I politely refused.

References

Bayart, J.-F. 2006 [1989]. *L'état en Afrique: la politique du ventre.* Paris: Fayard.

Benda-Beckmann, K. v. 1981. 'Forum Shopping and Shopping Forums: Dispute Processing in a Minangkabau Village in West Sumatra', *Journal of Legal Pluralism* 13(19): 117–60.

Burnham, P. 1996. *The Politics of Cultural Difference in Northern Cameroon.* Edinburgh: Edinburgh University Press.

Dupire, M. 1996[1962]. *Peuls nomads. Etude descriptive des Wodaabe du Sahel nigérien.* Paris: Karthala.

Felstiner, W.L.F., R.L. Abel and A. Sarat. 1980–81. 'The Emergence and Transformation of Disputes: Naming, Blaming, Claiming…', *Law & Society Review* 15(3–4): 631–54.

Lund, C. 1999. 'A Question of Honour: Property Disputes and Brokerage in Burkina Faso', *Africa: Journal of the International African Institute* 69(4): 575–94.

Moritz, M. 2006. 'The Politics of Permanent Conflict: Farmer–Herder Conflicts in Northern Cameroon', *Canadian Journal of African Studies/Revue Canadienne des Etudes Africaines* 40(1): 101–26.

Noye, D. 1974. *Course de Foulfouldé; dialecte Peul du Diamaré Nord-Cameroun.* Maroua: Librairie Orientaliste Paul Geuthner.

Peters, E.L. 1967. 'Some Structural Aspects of the Feud among the Camel-Herding Bedouin of Cyrenaica', *Africa* 37(3): 261–82.

Peters, R. 2005. *Crime and Punishment in Islamic Law: Theory and Practice from the Sixteenth to the Twenty-First Century.* Cambridge: Cambridge University Press.

Riesman, P. 1992. *First Find Your Child a Good Mother: The Construction of Self in Two African Communities.* New Brunswick, NJ: Rutgers University Press.

Schlee, G., and M. Guichard. 2007. 'Fulbe und Usbeken im Vergleich', in *Max Planck Institute for Social Anthropology Report/Bericht 2007 – Abteilung I: Integration und Konflikt.* Halle (Saale): Max Planck Institute for Social Anthropology, pp. 11–53.

Schlee, G., and B. Turner. 2008. 'Rache, Wiedergutmachung und Strafe', in G. Schlee und B. Turner (eds), *Vergeltung: eine interdisziplinäre Betrachtung der Rechtfertigung und Regulation von Gewalt.* Frankfurt: Campus, pp. 49–67.

Stenning, D. 1994 [1959]. *Savannah Nomads: A Study of the Wodaabe Pastoral Fulani of Western Bornu Province Northern Region, Nigeria.* Münster: Lit.

Chapter 10

Customary Law and the Joys of Statelessness

Somali Realities beyond Libertarian Fantasies

Günther Schlee

Some writers have presented 'stateless'[1] Somalia as a model for the region or even for humankind in general.[2] These ideas have to do with a perception of customary law – an idealized perception, perhaps – which, in turn, is associated with statelessness or remoteness from the state, a condition in which elders or other 'traditional' community leaders take the place of the policeman, the attorney, the judge and the prison when it comes to dealing with issues of retaliation, compensation and mediation. Before we address the case of Somalia, let us first take a brief look at the history of this cluster of ideas.

Summarizing and reflecting on earlier work, in 1967 Christian Sigrist wrote a book called *Regulierte Anarchie* ('Regulated Anarchy'), a term that goes back to Max Weber (1956 [1921–22]: 678). It also echoes the phrase 'ordered anarchy' used by Evans-Pritchard (1940) to refer to the balanced opposition produced by the segmentary lineage system among the Nuer of southern Sudan. If one Googles 'ordered anarchy' today, one finds many entries that have nothing to do with Africa. It has become a catchphrase for discourses related to radical liberalism and the minimal state. Some of the ideas in circulation can be located on the lunatic fringe of the far right, while others have quite a respectable ancestry. After all, it was Mahatma Gandhi who said that 'the ideally nonviolent State will be an ordered anarchy. That State will be best governed which is governed the least' (quoted in Chakrabarty 2006: 138). Other varieties of anarchism or libertarianism are not necessarily pacifist or nonviolent. Below we shall see that writings about Somalia resonate with political ideologies that have evolved in a Western and, most pronouncedly, in an American context.

First, however, some clarifications are needed about customary law in those cultural settings that have served as models for Western dreams about ordered anarchy. The non-Islamic Nuer are the paradigmatic case for this kind of social order, but legal systems based on the absence of central rule and the absence of professional judges can also be found in many Muslim groups. All these systems share certain core features: retaliation between the conflicting parties or negotiations about compensation to avoid violent retaliation; collective allocation of liability; and collective payment and distribution of compensation. In other words, reprisals were taken by groups against groups, and compensation was demanded, paid and received collectively, albeit unequally distributed, with the size of shares dependent upon a party's degree of closeness to the perpetrator or victim. This state of affairs resonated with colonial practices of enforcing compensation or collective punishment.[3]

Customary Law and *Sharīᶜa*

As almost all Somali are Muslims (with the same variation in religiosity as in the rest of the world) and as Islamic law is part of the legal discourses we are going to examine, we have to look at customary law not just in its relation to state law, but also in relation to the *sharīᶜa*.

Another way to speak of the relationship between custom and *sharīᶜa* is to speak of its relationship to Islam, since *sharīᶜa* claims to be based on revealed religion, human reasoning based on the principles of revealed religion, and God-given mental gifts. This gives it religious legitimacy and makes it the standard against which laws, customs and practices of non-Islamic origin need to be measured with regard to their degree of conformity to Islam. The core of this idea pre-dates the revelation of the Qurᶜan in the seventh century. This 'relationship between custom and religion is as old as religion itself. One of the primary goals of religion, in the Abrahamitic prophetic tradition, is to combat the erroneous practices and customs that conflict with its core principles and teachings' (Shabana 2010: 2).

In Muslim societies, the entire body of legal traditions generally referred to as customary law is known as *adat*. No Muslim or group of Muslims, however, can maintain that *adat* represents the highest form of law. Priority must be given to the *sharīᶜa*; otherwise one would call one's legitimacy as a Muslim into doubt. A society that perceives itself as Islamic almost by definition has to base its legal system on the *sharīᶜa*, the law derived for the most part from the Qurᶜan and the *sunna*, the traditions of the sayings and doings of the Prophet. Therefore, at least in theory, *adat* needs to be given a place that clarifies its relation to the *sharīᶜa*. This relationship, briefly put, is that *adat* can be applied only where it does not contradict the *sharīᶜa*.[4]

This can be illustrated by matters of marriage and divorce. While the *sharīᶜa* provides clear rules about the kinds of relatives that can marry one another and the kinds that cannot, and specifies the rules of maintenance, inheritance and divorce, it does not specify marriage rituals. This leaves space for the practice of local customs, which proliferate throughout the Islamic world. In one place we find mock abductions, while in another the bride is bedecked with an abundance of golden ornaments; there may be singing and dancing, or not. In the majority opinion in Islamic countries, all this is permissible because the *sharīᶜa* does not specify otherwise and does not forbid any of these practices. However, for the sake of completeness, one may add that there is a minority opinion that rejects anything vaguely reminiscent of a ritual that is not supported by evidence from the *sunna* testifying that the Prophet and his companions had engaged in such a practice. Obviously, the rule 'Do only what the Prophet did' is more restrictive than the alternative rule of 'You may do anything the Qurᶜan or the Prophet have not forbidden'. When applied to legal matters, only the latter leaves room for varying *adat* practices.

There is a narrower and a wider sense in which the term *sharīᶜa* is used. The narrow sense has just been described: the domain in which the *sharīᶜa* is explicit leaves little room for legislation by humans because God has already legislated, and here *sharīᶜa* is followed to the letter. In practice, this domain is often coterminous with family law.[5] In the wider sense, the *sharīᶜa*, which etymologically refers to a straight or correct 'path', comprises the entire Islamic way of life. It makes no distinction between ritual and other practices. For example, the minutest details of precisely when and how to pray are regulated by the *fiqh ul-ibadat*, the jurisprudence of acts of worship. (Believers can, of course, also address God in free speech, but that is mostly done after the ritual prayers or independently of them.) The marriage rituals mentioned above, in contrast, are not a matter of *sharīᶜa*, but rather of *adat*. *Sharīᶜa* furthermore regulates how and when to fast, what and even how to eat (not more than one bite at a time). There are also rules (although not mechanically applicable ones, because they require political assessment) about from where to flee (*hijra*), namely from a place where Islam is oppressed and one cannot fulfil one's obligations as a Muslim, and when to wage war (*jihad*).[6] A full enumeration is impossible; suffice it to say, therefore, that *sharīᶜa* in the wider sense permeates the entire lives of Muslims and their communities. The legal system of any Islamic country thus has to claim to be based on the *sharīᶜa*, although in practice this may mean a rather general inspiration by the *sharīᶜa* and the avoidance of contradiction, while the details of legislation have been left to humans. Reports in Western media that the *sharīᶜa* has been 'introduced' in a particular Muslim country, frequent as they may be, are therefore nonsensical. There can be no Muslim or group of Muslims that does not claim to (wish to) follow the *sharīᶜa* already, because that would place them outside the fold of the Islamic *umma*. Therefore, the *sharīᶜa* cannot be 'introduced' in Muslim countries. What we do find is more or less liberal and more or less restrictive interpretations and applications of the *sharīᶜa*.

This relationship between *sharīʿa* and *adat* may be quite obvious to educated Muslims and scholars of Islam, but this does not mean that it has been so clear to all actors on the ground at all times. Rural Somali, for example, believing their *adat* law (*xeer* in Somali) to be the divine law, may not always have perceived the difference between the two and, given the extent of the mixture between the two in their actual workings, the distinction is not easy. In some areas, Somali may persist in making this equation. In such a case, *adat* reflects popular beliefs about the *sharīʿa*, a kind of folk version of the *sharīʿa* whose adherents are unaware of the purer and more text-based version of the *sharīʿa* in existence elsewhere.[7] Le Sage (2005: 14) assumes that Islamic law in one form or another has been present in Somalia, but that it had been incorporated into *xeer*. He speaks of 'Islamic law as a separate, but complementary system to modern judicial institutions' (it is unclear whether he intends to include *xeer* under this rubric) only in the context of the colonial and postcolonial state. In conflict settlement, Islamic sheikhs played a subordinate role:

> Somali sheikhs and religious leaders, known as *wadaad* and *ulema*, did not play a direct role in Somali political affairs, which were the domain of elders. Rather, they undertook *qadi* or judicial functions, including the conduct of marriage rites and divorce proceedings, and at times they supported the efforts of elders to promote peace between warring clans. However, according to Lewis, 'they do not themselves settle disputes, or judge between disputants, for this is the work of elders in council, and of informal courts of arbitration'. (Le Sage 2005: 16 f., citing Lewis 1999 [1961]: 217)

After clarifying the relationship between religious law, customary law and the different kinds of authority, we now proceed to the role of these in dealing with bodily harm and homicidal violence. The *sharīʿa* has a clear notion of guilt and punishment, including capital punishment. But it also stresses patience and forgiveness, though tied to strict conditions like acceptance of guilt, remorse and the promise not to relapse, and therefore leaves room for the group of a perpetrator and the group of the victim of a violent transgression to negotiate and reach a peaceful agreement through compensation and forgiveness. In practice, as we shall see from our Somali examples, the strict conditions that the *sharīʿa* has attached to forgiveness then tend to be somewhat softened, and the guilty party, if in a strong negotiating position, gets away with a lot. In other words, a large domain that would be subjected to penal law in Western countries (where the state is obliged to persecute certain crimes irrespective of the wishes of the victims) can be left to the parties concerned. Therefore, homicide and violence against human beings in general are often a matter of *adat*.[8] Not only has the *sharīʿa* left this room to *adat*, but colonial states and modern states whose legal heritage comprises a mixture of Western law of colonial introduction and other forms of law have done the same. The news that a matter is dealt with by the elders may have led attorneys and the police to abstain from investigation.[9]

The transfer of a matter from the domain of determining guilt and imposing punishment to that of mediation and negotiation has implications for the normative dimension. Establishing guilt is no longer the primary concern. The death of a person is a damage that needs to be paid for. Whether the death was accidental or planned is of secondary importance.

An alternative explanation for blood money (to it being compensation for a loss) is that it serves to prevent legitimate revenge killings. Both aspects may, in fact, be involved when it comes to explaining why negotiations are initiated in a given case and are not in another. But the fact that blood money, perhaps with a discount, also needs to be paid in the case of accidental killings, which would not – or not legitimately at least – lead to revenge killings, or in the presence of mitigating circumstances such as passion shows that its primary function is compensation for a loss. The basic principle in the context of killing a person seems to be 'a life for a life': the life of the killer or one of his kinsmen is taken in revenge, or a value is attributed to the life of the victim in the form of blood money, a life-equivalent, so to speak. This principle would imply that if the perpetrator were killed, no compensation to the family of the victim would be paid as the loss to the family of the perpetrator would cancel out the loss to the family of the victim – although in practice only in cases of extremely hostile intergroup relations would a loss to the other side be perceived as a gain for one's own side. If relations that, prior to the homicide, had been closer and friendlier need to be re-established, then even in the event of the perpetrator's death, transactions to alleviate the victim's family's loss might still take place. I have no Somali example to illustrate this, but to explain the general logic of this in an Islamic framework, Sudanese examples may do. Asad reports a case of homicide among close clansmen in a leading segment of the Kababish Arabs of northern Kordofan at a time when homicide was dealt with by the Sudanese state. The murderer was hanged, but compensation – which was called *tardia* to avoid the word *diya*[10] (which could not be paid because the killer had been hanged) – was nevertheless paid (Asad 1970: 112 f.). From the Humr Baggara Arabs further south, Cunnison reports a case in which the hanging of the murderer did not soothe the anger of the relatives of the victim, and the perpetrator's group continued to fear retaliation (Cunnison 1966: 175, 184). Both stories illustrate the importance of *diya* as compensation for the loss of life, not just as a means to avert revenge.

Where this logic of compensation for a loss dominates, moral aspects such as premeditation, malice or selfish motives – precisely those that would establish the act as a crime in a system of penal law – can in some cases be taken into account as aggravating circumstances that make forgiving more difficult and therefore drive up the amount to be paid as compensation. In other cases, motivations and guilt seem to play no role. Mediation and compensation do not re-establish a moral order or enforce 'law' and they are not meant to conform to lofty ideas of justice or to please higher authorities like God or the state. They are a form of bargaining about what to pay for damage. Apart from an assessment of the damage, in these systems of mediation, considerations such as the wealth of the perpetrators and their ability to pay or the position of the victim (who may or not have been the 'breadwinner' of a family or household) may come in before degrees of 'guilt' are discussed, if indeed they are discussed at all.

As in all bargaining situations, the parties may have unequal bargaining power. To understand the potential inequalities of the parties, one has to understand the logic of such negotiations about homicide or bodily harm according to *adat* procedures. The logic of compensation is based on that of retaliation. The primary purpose of compensation is to avoid retaliation. There is local variation within the Islamic world in terms of the degree to which third parties, that is, elements of the wider society, can oblige the conflicting parties to enter into negotiations about compensation at all. Among Somali, negotiations about compensation will not even be initiated if the aggrieved party prefers to retaliate. The role of mediators and impartial authorities seems to be much lower than, for example, in the Sudan. Often no one will step in between the parties, and the perpetrator's group may ask for negotiations in vain. This means that a group that feels strong enough to avenge the death of any of its members can do so. Its strength would also deter the groups of the victims of their revenge from retaliating in turn. In other words, a group that is strong enough to do so can kill with impunity. This is an entirely different logic from the one of punishment, where a collective that has established a rule punishes a breach of the rule rather than leaving the matter to the parties concerned (King 1980).[11]

While the literature about Sudanese Arabs is replete with examples of the initiative being taken out of the hands of the concerned parties, of members of the victim's group being tied to trees to prevent them from taking revenge (Cunnison 1966: 175), and of the importance of leaders and mediators (Asad 1970: 172; Cunnison 1966: 154ff) and their moral authority (Cunnison 1966: 159, 179), the literature on Somali and my own observations indicate that there is rather little to restrain the victim's group from pursuing the violent option[12] and that the two parties are left very much to their own devices to find a nonviolent arrangement or not.

Let us now turn to the dynamics generated when the violent option is left open. Lewis describes ordinary violence among Somali in the late colonial period, long before violence escalated into civil war. The symbol of war then was not the Kalashnikov, but the wooden trough that nomads carried around in order to distribute water to their camels at water holes. Precedence at water holes was a cause of quarrels, not just because of the competition for water (of which there may still be enough after an hour or two), but because dry season pastures could only be used from strategic water points. Therefore, the exclusion of rivals from water was also a way to get rid of them in the competition for pasture. In the process of chasing rivals from a water hole, often one or two of them were killed.

Imagine a group of contestants belonging to a large *diya*-paying group. A *diya*-paying group would normally be defined in terms of shared patrilineal descent, although smaller groups might enter into contractual relationships with distantly related groups to share in joint defence and *diya* payments.[13] A large *diya*-paying group in which every male member only has to pay a small amount as his contribution to the blood money might just pay the compensation and regard the effect of having deterred competing users from a water hole to be worth the price. A wealthy and numerically strong group would, however, also have military muscle. If the other group is no match for them, they might decide that although they could easily afford to pay compensation, they do not actually feel like doing so. If they think that their opponents will not dare to retaliate, there is no need to mollify them by paying compensation, despite the fact that doing so might be recommended by custom. To follow norms may be a good thing, but to show that one has the power to break norms may also be quite useful in a violent and insecure environment. It would, however, be interesting to know more about the long-term costs of such breaches of the norm. They must be reflected in the reputation a group has in the eyes of a wider public. What if the tide turns and in a future conflict configuration, those who are now strong and arrogant find themselves on the losing side?

If negotiations are initiated – and this may still be the more frequent case in relatively peaceful periods and in the case of negligible power differentials – it can happen not only in a stateless setting or one that is remote from statehood, but even where statehood is involved or 'in the shadow of the state' (Spittler 1980). To avoid police interference, the stronger group might be persuaded to engage in negotiations over *diya*, but it would clearly have the stronger bargaining position and would get a discount.

Sometimes governments take 'customary law' into their own hands, which of course raises the question of what remains 'customary' about it. Hoehne (2011: Chapter 6) discusses recollections of the establishment of colonial rule in Somaliland, where the British clearly enforced, and thereby changed, customary law. To maintain peace in the absence of an agreement between the elders, the district commissioner would send police officers to collect animals for compensation payments. 'Even several decades after the fact, some Somali remembered this forcible collection of huge amounts of livestock with anger' (Hoehne 2011: 234).

In reference to the state of affairs in the Buuhoodle area of Somaliland in 2004, Hoehne (2011: 297) notes that, in addition to collecting animals for compensation, the police would sometimes 'cooperate with the traditional authorities in capturing culprits in the area'. If representatives from the perpetrator's group decide to enter into negotiations with the victim's group, they might wish to apprehend the culprit. Normally it would be the brother or another close relative who would do this, as a close relative of a culprit is most likely to be shot in revenge by the group of the victim and least likely to be shot by the perpetrator. Therefore, he has the greatest incentive to catch the perpetrator and hand him over to the elders, and the least risk in doing so. However, this may not always work out and the police may be called in to assist. Clearly, there is a great deal of variation in the combinations of state and nonstate forms of law enforcement.

But let us return to the workings of *xeer* in a case in which a stronger group and a weaker group are left alone with each other, without any police around and no outside observer apart from the anthropologist. Without going into detail,[14] let me briefly describe blood-money negotiations that I witnessed between a numerically and militarily strong group and a much weaker group in northern Kenya. A herd-boy from the stronger group had raped and badly cut up a herd-girl from the weaker one. The two groups quickly reached an agreement that the damage amounted to the value of five camels. But then 'forgiveness' and 'brotherliness' entered the debate. Representatives of the stronger group reminded the members of the weaker one that if the roles had been reversed, that is, if a member of the weaker group had raped one of the daughters of the stronger group (something none of them presumably would have dared to do), they would be too poor to pay the full compensation: 'Imagine if one of you had killed one of us. Would you be able to pay the whole amount of 100 camels?'[15] Appeals were made to the magnanimity of the weaker group: 'Be like brothers to us, forgive us!' In the end, only one camel was paid. The relationship between the two groups was not close enough for the magnanimity or the 'brotherliness' of the weaker group ever to be rewarded, no matter how needy or helpless they might become. The appeal to 'brotherliness' was just a rhetorical device used by the stronger group to reduce the compensation payment. In the unlikely event that a member of the weaker group had inflicted a comparable damage on the stronger group, revenge presumably would have followed immediately unless full compensation was paid.

Of course, the culprit was not to be seen. In the entire discussion, his identity was not even disclosed apart from the admission that he did belong to the stronger group. This shows that notions of guilt or individual accountability were entirely alien to these procedures. It further shows that authors who romanticize traditional law as a form of justice – such as Michael van Notten, who we shall discuss below – have succumbed to some basic misunderstanding. It is a bargain whose outcome is largely determined by the differential in bargaining power. Justice may come in as a rhetorical device, but its role is marginal. Keeping the identity of the perpetrator hidden is something completely alien to the *sharīʿa*, which starts with establishing individual responsibility and brings in forgiveness as an option only *after* the establishment of individual guilt. This example thus also illustrates the degree to which practices in the name of customary law can deviate from the prescriptions of *sharīʿa.*

Stateless Somalia as a Model for the Rest of the World

All this leads us to a rather ambiguous perception of customary law that provides some channels for regulating and avoiding violence, but does not necessarily lead to a just result. This perception differs radically from an idealizing strain of writing that has gained quite some currency, even in the case of Somalia. The idea of a social order without a state, of a primordial form of justice that does not need police and prisons, seems to fascinate a Western public that is influenced by Rousseau, romanticism and Foucault, and that tends to adhere to or at least likes to toy with the anarchist and communitarian ideals that play such a limited role in their own states and societies.

The idea that Somalia, undoubtedly the largest chunk of inhabited territory on earth without a functioning state, can serve as a model for the rest of the world has been taken up by a number of commentators, ironically by some and without irony by others. A film that I came across on the Internet may serve as an example of the ironic or satirical treatment of Somalia as a model for the rest of humankind.[16] The short film, in the style of a promotional advertisement for tourism in Somalia, parodies the libertarian or 'minimal state' approach of some elements in the American Right. It depicts a couple on holiday who are shocked when they realize that the pleasant American beach they find themselves on is a 'public beach'. Fleeing the public domain, statehood and 'socialism' in the United States, they are encouraged by the narrator to go to Somalia, the 'libertarian paradise', where they encounter unlimited freedom from statehood. Using the imagery of the chaos of the civil war in Somalia, the film satirically praises Somalia as the materialization of the dream of the American Right: everyone has the right to bear arms or, rather, everyone actually does bear arms; the state is absent, freedom is complete. The ultimate symbol of the couple's self-reliance and freedom to take their own risks is that the woman catches cholera, a fact she mentions nonchalantly to her partner as they dance on the beach. The brief film ends with the image of the happy couple on a Somali beach with the rusting hulk of a shipwreck in the background, as the voiceover intones: 'Come to Somalia, because government isn't the solution to our problems, government is the problem … and now you have cholera.'

The same argument of the advantages of statelessness has been taken up without irony by Michael van Notten (2005).[17] As the title of his book, *The Law of the Somalis: A Stable Foundation for Economic Development in the Horn of Africa*, clearly indicates, he advocates Somali law as a model to be emulated. He describes Somali law as 'natural' because it is not given by a state institution (statutory law); rather, it has developed along with the behaviour it regulates and is therefore customary. He laments the transition from customary to statutory law that has taken place in most of the world with the development of statehood: 'most nations in the world today are based on statutory law, or legislation. Statutory law is designed by politicians, whereas customary law consists of the rules that judges discern in the customary behaviour of people' (van Notten 2005: 3).

This is a central point in van Notten's reasoning and the starting point of his argument. Empirically, however, the statement that customary law merely describes what has developed naturally, without intentional lawmaking, can be questioned. Among the Rendille, non-Muslim neighbours of the Somali who are even less influenced by writing and statehood, there are legislative processes at work in what everyone would regard as 'customary law'. In recent decades, in the period when I was a frequent visitor among them, they abolished the custom of *sabade*, which delayed the marriage of a certain category of girls by one age-set cycle of fourteen years. These girls, the daughters of one of three age-sets that form a generation, had to wait an extra fourteen years until they could marry, and then they often remained childless or just had one or two children (Schlee 1979: 147, 1989: 180). The Rendille also abolished discrimination against a despised caste whose very name was so scorned that it could not be mentioned and that I therefore referred to in my earlier work as 'K', the first letter of that name (Schlee 1979: 194 f.). In both cases, meetings of elders were held (the kind of people van Notten calls 'judges') and it was decided to pray to God to accept these changes.

The idea behind this is surprisingly theocratic for such an egalitarian society. Custom (*huggum*) has been there 'since people came out [of the ground]', which is as close to the concept of creation as Rendille beliefs get. Having been there since the beginning, it must have been established by God (*Waakh*). To change or deviate from a custom might disturb the order of the world and lead to drought, famine and the infertility of she-camels and women. This danger is also brought about by minor deviations. Sometimes meticulous attention is paid to the correct performance of rituals. For example, circumcisions are usually performed in the same kind of place and in the same social setting as the circumcisions of the father and the grandfather of the initiate had been. However, if the outcome is bad, if the circumcised boy gets a bad infection or even dies, then the ritual may be changed at the next occurrence, such as when it is time for the next members of that family or lineage to be circumcised. Such changes may also occur for reasons of convenience, for example, if the original variant of the ritual is too arduous to be performed or if certain paraphernalia cannot be procured. If everything then goes well, this is taken as an indication that something must have been wrong with the original ritual and that God has shown his consent for the new version. So the Rendille idea of customary law, in full agreement with the anthropologist's analysis of it, does not at all approximate to van Notten's idea of natural law. Van Notten insists that natural law evolves as a pattern of behaviour; it is not made, but is rather a description of behaviour. Rendille customary law, on the other hand, is not perceived as natural, but as given (by God). It can be discussed and deliberately changed (whereupon God's consent is requested), and God's will can be found out by trial and error, another form of conscious deliberation.

The natural order of things for van Notten is a kind of capitalist paradise without statehood. While for social romantics and socialists, the original order was one based on the absence of private property and their ideal was to return to that state of affairs, for van Notten, the original, natural order of things and his ideal of a future society is based on property and non-intervention by anything like a state. He is a capitalist anarchist or 'libertarian', as such people have come to be called in America. Wrongdoings should be dealt with through a type of insurance that would pay the damages after a negotiated deal, not by the state meting out punishment. He perceives such insurance in the *diya*-paying groups,[18] the clan segments or contractual alliances of such segments that share in raising blood money or in joint defence among the Somali. Every Somali belongs to such a group. As McCullum observed in the introduction to van Notten (2005: xi f.): 'Consequently a victim seldom fails to receive compensation, even if his or her rights are violated by children or by adults who are penniless, mentally ill, or have fled abroad.'

This description ignores the fact that victims may fail to get compensation for other reasons, for example, if the clan of the perpetrator feels strong enough not to pay compensation, as the cases we have cited above illustrate. Another aspect of the 'freedom' of the strong and the 'tolerance' they enjoy is described by van Notten with approval:

> Further evidence of the Somalis' tolerant view is the fact that people are free to settle their cases outside the customary law. The need for this occurs, for instance, when the family of a murdered person refuses to accept the customary 100 camels but is willing to settle for, say, 130 camels. Such a deal (*xeer jajab*) is not prohibited, but it cannot create a precedent under the customary law. (Van Notten 2005: 37)

This brief quote calls for a number of clarifications:

(1) Is it really 'outside' of customary law if people make use of the space provided by it? Analytically this may be problematic, but the Somali expression *xeer jajab* ('breaking the customary law') concurs with van Notten's interpretation that here we are dealing with something that is outside of or against the law.

(2) Next a note about terminology. To speak of 'murder' entails attribution of guilt and a moral judgement, contrary to the spirit of the law of retaliation and compensation, and also contrary to what van Notten tries to explain. It makes little sense to insist (as van Notten rightly does) that Somali law is compensatory and is concerned with damage, not with guilt, but then to speak of murder, which is a highly guilt-laden term that stems from penal

law. What van Notten means is 'a person who has been killed', not necessarily 'a murdered person'. Murder is a very special kind of killing, defined by premeditation, malice, base motives and other such indicators of 'guilt'.

(3) What kind of family does van Notten believe to be capable of demanding and receiving compensation that is higher than the customary one? Certainly not a weak one. Such settlements, called *xeer jajab* ('breaking of the law') by van Notten's interlocutors, to the extent that they actually occur, corroborate our findings about the influence of power in Somali jurisdiction. While our own case history from northern Kenya has demonstrated that the weaker group does not succeed in getting a verdict that entitles it to the full amount of customary compensation, what van Notten reports about *xeer jajab* implies that the stronger group does not even have to content itself with the full compensation, but can demand more.

(4) What does van Notten mean when he says that such cases do not establish a precedent? If they happen, they can serve as a model of behaviour for others. If they happened often enough, payments in excess of, or short of, the customary sum of one hundred camels would become part of the usual practice. The rule would then change from one hundred camels being the prescribed compensation for the killing of a man to one hundred camels being a rough estimate or recommendation for the purposes of orientation, while strong groups (whose threat to retaliate in case no compensation agreement could be reached) could in fact demand more and weaker groups would have to be content with much less. Special arrangements could be made between specific clans, and the victim's relatives could appeal to certain principles, such as having to pay more for a cruel killing or for killing an outstanding personality. But whatever the degree of formalization of such changes, the mere fact that habitual practices develop out of a power differential means that any case can provide a precedent to any following case.

Van Notten's account is rich in acute observations about Somali laws and persuasive in its generalizing description, but completely blind when it comes to how power-sensitive Somali laws are in actual practice. His account is fraught with Western notions of law, like the formal equality of the contestants. One example is his description of divorce: 'The divorce is final when one spouse says three times, "'I divorce you"' (van Notten 2005: 60). It is well known that the *shariʿa* (not the customary law/*adat*/*xeer*, which van Notten here believes he is discussing) gives the husband the right to divorce his wife in this way. If the wife says the same thing to the husband, it has no legal effect.[19] The symmetrical treatment van Notten accords to husband and wife ('spouses') and the universalist assumption about the formal equality of legal subjects are not shared even in theory by the body of law that he discusses. In the *shariʿa*, men and women have different rights and duties. In the Somali *xeer*, there is clearly an ethos of equality among men, with even a small boy being counted as a man. For anyone who has observed a discussion among Somali, it is clear that considerations of seniority, status and etiquette matter much less to Somali than to their pastoralist neighbours (the Boran, Rendille, Maasai, etc.). Every Somali tends to be as loud and assertive as any other. But in practice, as we have seen, it is not equality but the differential in wealth and firepower that to a large degree determines the outcome of the proceedings.

It is clear that numbers matter a great deal in this power game. As early as 1961, Lewis (1999 [1961]) pointed out that branches of a clan with slower demographic growth form alliances and combine into *diya*-paying groups with smaller lineage groups of other clans, in breach of the logic of the segmentary lineage system, which would posit that forms and degrees of mutual assistance reflect genealogical proximity.[20] Van Notten manages to describe the advantages of belonging to a larger group quite correctly, but the idea that these advantages might result in a distortion of justice does not seem to occur to him at all:

> Small families tend to ally themselves with other small families or to team up with an existing larger family. There are two reasons for this. One is the obligation of its members to be insured against any liability they might incur under the law. The larger the family, the less each has to pay in event one of them is convicted of a crime. The other reason is that enforcement is the responsibility of the family of the victim. The larger the family, the more able-bodied men there will be and the easier the enforcement. (Van Notten 2005: 68)

The terms 'crime' and 'convicted' are somewhat inappropriate here, since they stem from penal law and not from the logic of damage and retaliation/compensation. If the group of the perpetrator is strong enough to refuse payment or if the group of the victim feels strong enough to seek revenge, there will be no negotiations or the negotiations will be aborted and no settlement will be reached. There will be no 'crime' and no 'verdict'. The alternative is not 'guilt' or 'acquittal', but 'deal' or 'no deal'.

Van Notten, however, seems to maintain the idea that, somehow, justice in harmony with Western ideas about crime and punishment is achieved by Somali law. There is an idealizing ring to his description: 'In case of murder [again, his term], the law stipulates that, if the murderer is not apprehended quickly, the family of the victim is free [but are they also able?] to kill someone of equal stature in the murderer's family. Consequently, murderers are usually arrested by their own family' (van Notten 2005: 100).

Are they? This is, of course, an empirical question. No doubt, in some cases perpetrators of homicide may be arrested by their own people to avert worse consequences. But if that were the general rule, how could that be reconciled with

Lewis' description of strong *diya*-paying groups being able to afford to kill one or two rival herders at a water point to scare away competitors? They certainly would not arrest any killers who have acted with their tacit approval or even reveal their identities. They might leave the identity of such killers undisclosed, as the 'stronger group' in my northern Kenyan example left that of the rapist.

Under the heading 'Law is Maintained at a Low Cost', van Notten describes another advantage of the Somali system:

> Occasionally judges [elders, *odeyaal*] receive gifts from their clients [*sic*]. The same is true of policemen [armed clansmen]. This obviates the need for taxation and destruction of wealth associated with Western-style governments. (Van Notten 2005: 101)

This tells us more about the author, obviously an anti-statist libertarian akin to the present 'Tea Party' movement among U.S. Republicans, than about the Somali. We also fail to learn anything about the quality of verdicts and law enforcement facilitated by such low-cost mechanisms as personal gifts by interested parties. The paragraph reminds me of a saying I heard in neighbouring Kenya: 'Why hire a lawyer if you can buy a judge?'

Van Notten has made his observations in a corner of Somalia that was relatively untouched by the civil war, namely Awdal in the northwest (or, as the separatists in power there would insist, Somaliland). The problem of whether the law of compensation can also be applied to the many dead in modern gun battles or whether the scale and anonymity of these killings transcend the capacity of this form of law is not addressed by van Notten,[21] probably because it did not occur in his area. Furthermore, van Notten aims at describing a system he perceives as 'natural'; he therefore ignores recent influences of modern governments or development agencies (including non-governmental organizations (NGOs)). My criticism therefore also takes up the older literature or examples from areas relatively remote from the forces of modernity. To criticize his findings by contrasting them with evidence from settings that have been more exposed to these forces would be a kind of an anachronism, a mistake in the choice of timeframe. My intention here is to reveal flaws in his reasoning, not to assert that he is no longer up to date. This does not mean that van Notten's sources or the material I use for criticizing him are primordial in any way or untouched by modernity. It is difficult to assess the effects of colonial attempts to codify customary law, anthropological writings that describe it, or the periods in which there was a more or less functioning statehood in all or parts of Somalia and customary law coexisted with bodies of law of English or Italian origin. All I claim here is that van Notten seems to have focused on what appeared traditional to him and that, for the sake of fairness, I have used examples from contexts that looked relatively traditional to me in order to criticize him.

The State of Law in Somalia

The discussion of van Notten in the previous section may have had something artificial about it. Although it drew on empirical examples (both his and mine), there was a selectivity involved in the focus on traditional forms of law. In a way, it was a thought experiment exploring the logic of retaliation and compensation, and whether or not it leads to results that are compatible with normative ideas like equality before the law. In this section, we abandon such theoretical ambitions and try to give a more purely descriptive overview of the forms of law actually found in Somalia and their interaction with each other. We also change the perspective from that of the actors and their incentives and disincentives to a systematic overview with some 'top-down' elements. We move from the perspective of local elders to that of international observers and agents of intervention. We are going to have a look at the situation of law in Somalia as a whole, fictive as this entity might be without any political cohesion. It goes without saying that such an overview cannot be complete, even if the security situation in Somalia were more conducive to research on the ground. Where the data permit, we shall also illustrate the interaction of different kinds of law with case histories, abandoning the perspective of the broad overview and tying the discussion back to the first part of this chapter. It goes without saying that such sporadically available case histories are not representative, but merely glimpses at some of the many different things that are going on.

An overview of the forms of law found in Somalia will normally start with an enumeration of different such forms: *xeer*, *sharīʿa*, common law, Italian law, Indian law and so on. Such a long list of different kinds of law should, however, not let us overlook the most important feature of the legal situation in Somalia, which is the absence of law in many places at many times. A huge amount of injustice has occurred that has never been dealt with in the framework of any kind of law. Impunity is an enduring problem, as is the continuing arbitrary violence that results from the expectation of future impunity. What can be said about *xeer* is that, in spite of its shortcomings and its susceptibility to power differentials, it compares favourably with the total absence of statutory law. The Islamic courts in Mogadishu, which expanded their domain to much of southern Somalia in 2006, were set up to secure life and business in a situation that until then had been marked by anarchy. The main promoters and sponsors of these courts were businesspeople, not radical scholars, who perceived the *sharīʿa*, and not the different local versions of *xeer* or the various bodies of law of colonial origin, as the shared legal tradition upon which all Somalis would be able to agree. This development needs to be seen against the background of the absence of law. Unfortunately, this attempt to rebuild a legal order from below was shattered by the Ethiopian–American intervention of December 2006, which led to the radicalization of its remnants and a deepening of the Somali crisis (Schlee 2009:

168). Only months after the Ethiopian–American intervention, Samatar (2007) and Barnes and Hassan (2007) made quite clear that this intervention was a setback. These authors, far from being Union of Islamic Courts (UIC) supporters, are critical of internal factionalism within the UIC and accuse it of alienating large parts of the Somali population with its restrictions on media and entertainment, and the imposition of a rigorous Islamic lifestyle, along with other shortcomings and political blunders. But both of these sources insist that what came after was worse. Samatar speaks of a declining security situation; Barnes and Hassan (2007: 151, 157) noted that even then, retrospectively, the rule of the Islamic Courts appeared as a 'golden age' to many Somali.

After mentioning the negative case – the absence of statutory law – we now proceed to the different kinds of law that do exist and their modes of integration or coexistence. The institutionalization of different kinds of law applicable to different people and different situations goes back to the colonial period of Italian rule in the south and British rule in the north. According to Le Sage, in British Somaliland:

> The 1898 Principal Order-in-Council recognized that Somali were bound by customary law. The 1937 Kadis Court Ordinance and the 1947 Subordinate Court Ordinance recognized the application of *sharīʿa* to issues including marriage, divorce, family relationships, personal material responsibilities, and inheritance. By contrast, cases in which the British administration held particular interest were subject to the jurisdiction of the Common Law, Somaliland Ordinances, applicable UK laws, and the Indian Penal Code, as applied by the high court and district courts. (Le Sage 2005: 17)

In the southern part, which was first an Italian colony and then a United Nations trust territory under Italian administration, the Italian penal and civil codes were introduced. Matters of family and inheritance among Somali were dealt with by *qadi* courts, while other disputes among Somali were handled by the elders, who applied *xeer*. The fact that cases of homicide are a matter for *sharīʿa* courts is a development of the stateless period after the breakdown of the state in 1991. In this period, the family of a victim of homicide may have had the option of appealing to the elders and having the matter regulated according to customary law, or taking it to a *sharīʿa* court.

I owe the following case history from 2005 in the area around Huddur in southern Somalia to Jutta Bakonyi.[22] The case starts with a man killing his wife. Among Somali, wives continue to belong to their families of origin. Only their offspring belong to the clan of the father or the clans of the respective fathers, as the case may be. Therefore, the clan that had suffered damage was that of the woman's father, and he himself was the person most immediately concerned.

Her father rejected compensation. He was living in Kenya in an urban setting and might not have had much use for camels. He insisted on the application of the *sharīʿa*. The verdict was that he was given the right to execute the killer. By the time that the verdict was passed, he had returned to Kenya. In his stead, his son, the brother of the victim, executed the culprit publicly with a pistol. Some bystanders thought that this course of action was a bit harsh, since the victim was 'only' a woman. Had compensation been paid, it would have been (assuming payment of the standard rate) fifty camels rather than one hundred. These bystanders commented: 'If the *xeer* has different rates for male and female victims, how can the punishment according to the *sharīʿa* be the same?' These comments ignored the different logics we have just explained. The *sharīʿa*, when applied to homicide, prescribes *diya* in the case of manslaughter and accidental killings and recommends it in the case of intentional homicide. Thus, in the case of intentional homicide, it provides two options: compensation or punishment. The logic of compensation leads to one set of consequences, the logic of punishment to another. Compensation requires different payments for people assumed to be of different value. The logic of punishment, on the other hand, establishes a crime and then punishes the crime. And a murder is a murder, whether of a man or a woman or an important or an unimportant person. However, in the perception of these bystanders, the two kinds of logic have somehow got mixed up.

Compensation payments are pervaded by the spirit of equality, with some qualifications. We have seen that they are not always agreed upon, since people may prefer revenge or are in no position to prevent revenge from taking place. We have also seen that they can be higher or lower according to the respective bargaining power of the groups in dispute, or because of locally contracted agreements between specific clans. But what I have not come across is a case in which, say, two men of the same group were killed in the same incident and 120 camels were paid for one of them and only eighty for the other. Here certainly the ethos of equality would prevail. The reactions to the execution just described point to such ideas of equality. If there is a customary rate for killing a woman and if it is half as much as that for a man, how is it possible that the consequences of the killing are so much harsher if the *sharīʿa* is applied?[23]

However, the idea of equality (which in the Somali case is not universal, but is subdivided into gender categories: all men are equal to all other men and all women are equal to all other women) that pervades the domain of compensation does not extend to cases of revenge. Here clearly there are victims who are worth more and victims who are worth less. An important man needs to be killed to avenge the death of another important man. Hoehne describes a case in which a *caaqil*, a clan leader, was killed to avenge the death of a rich businessman (Hoehne 2011: Chapter 6). The two were considered of equal importance to their respective communities, and the *caaqil* was genealogically close to the alleged killers of the businessman.

The present situation in Somalia is enormously complex and the security situation is not conducive to field research. My account of legal options is therefore restricted to some general remarks and some isolated local observations; it cannot cover all of Somalia with the same level of detail.

On the whole, one can say that the breakdown of the Somali state, unsurprisingly, has led to a reduced role of the state courts and the Western bodies of law they apply. One can expect the two other forms of law, *xeer* and *shariᶜa*, to fill the gap. The balance between the three can be expected to differ between the parts of the country where rudimentary forms of statehood have been re-established (Somaliland and Puntland) and those areas (much of south-central Somalia) where this is not the case, but this is mere speculation. Among the latter, one must distinguish between areas under the control of the Shabab, a radicalized offshoot of the Islamic court militias, and those where other militias or local elders have some kind of control. This is not a zero-sum game in the sense that one form of justice replaces another, and the total amount of justice dispensed remains the same, since the total domain of regulation may be shrinking. Part of the regulation gap left by the state (to the extent that the state was a regulating agency and not just of the predatory kind) may not have been taken over by other forms of regulation, but by lawlessness. Particularly in the south, which was overrun by fighters from other parts of the country, actors 'felt less accountable for atrocities committed against the local communities', as Hoehne explains (2011: 242), and:

> the control over rich farmland, harbours, and airstrips allowed militia-leaders and warlords to finance their fighting independently from traditional authorities and even against them and the local communities. Attacks on traditional leaders became common in the south after the fall of the government in 1991.[24]

Even where state-run courts are in existence, one can say that they are underfinanced (UNDP 2001: 176; Schlee 2006: 153), corrupt and discredited. With reference to southern Somalia, Le Sage states:

> The legacies of Siad Barre's[25] rule remain to this day, including public perceptions that the judiciary system is a tool in the hands of governing elites and their clan patrons to promote personal interests, repress opposition leaders and groups, dispossess non-governing clans and non-elites of their land and property, and otherwise dominate other clans. (Le Sage 2005: 21)

In civil matters, even in Somaliland, where both options are given, people often prefer *shariᶜa* courts in urban settings for reasons that have nothing to do with the content of the law, but rather with the working of the courts. Simply put, *sharīʿa* courts are faster than the state courts; one does not need to pay bribes to expedite matters or to avoid having to wait for years or forever for a verdict. In many matters of life and business, it is better to get the second-best verdict and then to move on with life than to have a prolonged unsettled dispute (Schlee 2006: 153). In rural settings, councils of elders provide a service similar to the faster and cheaper option.

At present, depending on the security situation and access, development agencies, NGOs and diaspora-sponsored educational institutions have greater or lesser influence on the development of law in different parts of the country (Hoehne 2010a, 2010b; Hoehne and Ibrahim 2014). Rules and regulations about retaliation and compensation can change under the influence of external factors like international 'peace processes' and development interventions. In what follows, I draw on discussions I have had in the Huddur region (Bay) in southern Somalia about innovations in the field of compensation rates.

Deviations in *diya* payments from the standard rate of one hundred camels for a man in the Huddur region seem to follow a different pattern from elsewhere. According to Contini (1971: 79), the *diya* rates fixed by *xeer* vary:

> depending on whether the groups concerned are on generally friendly or unfriendly terms and other factors. For instance, between groups closely related by lineage, compensation is often increased to an amount in excess of the standard rate to discourage bloodshed.[26]

This logic appears to be widespread in Somalia. Hoehne (2011: Chapter 6) likewise describes how in some volatile areas in the east of Somaliland in the 1990s, compensation was raised by clan-to-clan contract to 130 camels for the death of a man in order to discourage killing. In the Huddur area, the opposite seems to be the case. Groups with whom there are special *xeer* agreements regarding *diya*, that is, neighbours and friends, get a discount. Here the same spirit of 'brotherliness' that we encountered in a somewhat perverted form in our initial northern Kenyan example seems to prevail.

I had the opportunity to visit Huddur in 2004 as a consultant for the Improvement of Farming Systems Project (IFSP) of the GtZ, the German Association for Technical Cooperation (now GIZ, German Association for International Cooperation). While the big, internationally sponsored peace conference in Nairobi (2002–4) was still ongoing (Schlee 2006),[27] the GtZ logistically facilitated a local peace conference and seminars in which village representatives discussed matters of traditional law. The extent to which changes or proposed changes to customary law were 'donor driven' is difficult to ascertain, but there does not seem to have been an overall bias to make the Somali law softer or more 'humane'. In fact, some aspects of it became more severe.

Reduced *diya* rates (below the normal one hundred camels for the killing of a man and fifty for a woman) by bilateral contractual (*xeer*) agreement were under discussion. By *xeer*, the local clans of Huddur District, broadly classified as Rahanweyn, paid twenty-seven camels to each other for fatalities of both genders. This applied to Hadama, Loway, Leisan, Jirom, Harin, Garwaale, Macalimweyne, Reer Dumal, Wanjeel and Ashraaf. With each of the three independent *diya*-paying groups of the neighbouring Auliyahan (< Ogadeen < Darood),[28] the Hadama had an agreement to pay forty-four camels (twenty-two for a woman). Therefore, the lowest rates were within the Rahanweyn cluster, turning the logic cited by Contini upside down. Within Hadama, however, the rates were higher (thirty-two and sixteen) than interclan payments within the Rahanweyn cluster (twenty-seven and twenty-seven) as far as men were concerned (the more frequent case). The reason given for this, which is quite consistent with Contini, was that the higher rate is to discourage internal killings (Schlee 2004b: 17). It was then proposed by a local peace conference at Wajiid that all these rates should be changed to the standard one hundred camels (fifty for women), which is the default option – in other words, the rate valid in the absence of special agreements. In addition, 50 million Somali shillings were to be paid as a fine, mixing the ideas of compensation and punishment. This proposal was backed by the authority of the Ashraaf, with their religious prestige and their power to curse others. However, at the time of my research there, it had still not been signed by the parties concerned. The idea behind this proposal was to discourage killings rather than to give discounts for killing to those with whom one had closer relations (Schlee 2004b: 17).

By March 2004, the peace conference in Nairobi had been dragging on for a year and a half, and its outcome had become more uncertain than ever. People in Somalia could not wait for the uncertain results of the peace process at the national level, but had to focus on organizing their lives at the local and the regional levels, from the grassroots up.

At the workshop in Huddur that I witnessed, the community of the village of El Lehele took over government functions. Community leaders had put a re-examination of *xeer* on the agenda. They documented it on flip charts with the help of the facilitating staff members and they found fault with parts of it. As such, they engaged in a process of legislation. To cite just one example: traditionally, the owner of a fenced field had the right to kill a trespasser whom he found on his land and whom had left the fence behind him open, not caring about possible damage by livestock that might then invade the field. It was now decided by majority vote that such a person should not be killed, but fined a three-year-old camel bull. Any damage to the crops that was subsequently caused by livestock would not have to be paid for by that person, but by the owner of the livestock. The suggestion that all or half of this damage should be paid for by the person who left the fence open was rejected. In the same spirit, the law of adultery (*xeerka gogoldhaafka*) was revised. The right of a husband to kill a lover caught with his wife was replaced by the right to demand compensation in the form of a camel bull of three years of age.

The method employed in these debates was a rather elaborate form of casuistry. People constructed imaginary cases and discussed the positions of the various characters involved in these fictive case histories. Many of the participants in the discussion seemed to be natural lawyers. All of this was legislation. It happened with the help and under the eyes of a foreign agency in the middle of a conflict that was part of a global power game.

Conclusion

This chapter has served two purposes, namely to clarify the logics of 'punishment' and 'negotiation' as an alternative to retaliation, and to describe the interaction of different kinds of law in the present situation in Somalia. In the first part, I have concluded that the logic of negotiation, which is dominant in customary law, does not lead automatically to justice in the sense of an enforcement of norms agreed on by a community against strong and weak players alike. In the second part, I have tried to overcome the dichotomy of customary law and *sharīʿa*, and have depicted the interaction of these two with each other and with other forms of law. I have provided an overview, far from complete but showing a lot of variation, of the actual situation in the field of law and conflict regulation in Somalia. Some case histories allowed me to continue the exploration of different logics of regulation begun in the first part, but with the influence of the state (or its remnants) being taken into account. I also considered the global dimension, particularly international discourses and the influence of the diaspora.

If there is one general conclusion to be drawn from this chapter, it is that justice is not a matter to be left to negotiations between conflicting parties. Such negotiations tend to be compromises and tend to favour the stronger party in a variety of ways, one of which is simply that the weaker party wants to avoid further beating. It is one of the classical functions of statehood (although in practice it may just be part of an idealized image of the state) that it provides justice for all on the basis of equality. However, to at least approach this ideal of justice, the normative dimension needs to be brought in one way or another, be it by social pressure from observers, by religious authorities or by some other outside force beyond the parties concerned. In the case of Somali customary law, these outside forces do play a role, and the normative dimension is not absent. But on the whole, these forces are very weak and, despite all their best intentions, there is a marked tendency for the stronger side to win. We can also point to the fact that older Somalis have experienced both statelessness and more or less successful forms of statehood, and can compare the two. In some cases they may come to the conclusion that if stateless periods or regions in Somalia are compared with times and places where statehood was a bone of contention, the absence of the state was often the lesser of two evils. What is often forgotten in descriptions about the stateless state of affairs is the absence of drama in everyday life. People make arrangements with each other and a kind of normalcy develops (Ciabarri 2010). Indicators of health, nutrition and other measures of the quality of life can be higher than in a situation where one is exposed to a predatory state that does not deliver anything in exchange for what it takes or in a setting of violent conflicts over the state as a resource (Leeson 2007). In the long run, however, statelessness does not appear to be a solution that appeals to many Somalis.[29] The reason for this is simply that in a world of nation-states, it is very difficult not to belong to one such state. People want travel documents, they need a recognized jurisdiction to be creditworthy and to be able to engage in anything other than illegal or informal kinds of business, and they want to extend these activities beyond Somalia and Somali networks. Most Somalis would prefer to be ordinary citizens of an ordinary state, not only for the reasons that derive from the above comparison of forms of law and forms of the administration of justice, but for many other practical reasons as well.

Günther Schlee is one of the founding directors of the Max Planck Institute for Social Anthropology in Halle, Germany. Prior to this appointment, he was until 1999 Professor of Social Anthropology at the University of Bielefeld. He conducted fieldwork in Kenya, Ethiopia and Sudan, and was a guest lecturer in Padang (Sumatra) and at the Ecole des Hautes Etudes en Science Sociales in Paris. Currently, he is one of the spokespersons of the International Max Planck Research School on Retaliation, Mediation and Punishment and co-chairs the Centre for the Anthropological Studies on Central Asia with Peter Finke at the University of Zurich. His main publications include *Identities on the Move: Clanship and Pastoralism in Northern Kenya* (Manchester University Press, 1989) and *How Enemies are Made: Towards a Theory of Ethnic and Religious Conflict* (Berghahn Books, 2008).

Notes

1. To what extent the various parts of Somalia are actually stateless and to what extent their social reality is influenced by former statehood, existing rudiments of statehood or the expectation of future statehood will be discussed below.
2. A much shorter version of this chapter has been published in the *Journal of Eastern African Studies* (Schlee 2013). I thank all those who have commented on that earlier version of this chapter or on any of the stages it has gone through, including Markus V. Hoehne, Adano Wario Roba and the participants of the REMEP retreat in Bad Lauterberg in 2010. The present version has greatly profited from comments by Bertram Turner and Brian Donahoe.

3. Anderson (1986) describes how representations of the moral economy of the Kalenjin cluster in western Kenya, which tolerated or encouraged cattle raids, served to justify British colonialists' collective punishment measures. He also describes how these ideas became obsolete and these instruments inefficient when stock theft became a nontribal, commercialized form of organized crime.
4. Where local *adat* rules clearly contradict the *sharīʿa* (according to more widely accepted interpretations), local defenders of *adat* often deny this and claim that their local practices are compatible with *sharīʿa* or even part of it. Salim explains for Aceh, Indonesia that proponents of *sharīʿa* frequently emphasize that 'adat must not contradict the dictates of shari'a', although the post-tsunami recovery process and the increased demand for adjudication may have relaxed this attitude (Salim 2015). However, custom has not just been a potential source of deviation to be tolerated to different degrees according to circumstances; it has also had and continues to have a formative influence on *sharīʿa* itself. Indeed, custom is one of the sources of *sharīʿa*. And 'although custom traditionally ranks as one of the lowest sources of Shariʿah' (Amien 2011: 127), it has exerted influence on *sharīʿa* in multiple ways. There are affirmative references to customs and common practices found to be good in the Qurʿan, and the interpretations of the Qurʿan, the *sunna* and Islamic legal reasoning have also derived some of their principles from customary practice (Shabana 2010; Amien 2011). From this literature, we can conclude that there are multiple interactions between custom and *sharīʿa* on the normative level. The picture becomes even more complex if we look at actual practice. In Morocco, *adat* is claimed to be compatible with national interpretations of the *sharīʿa* and defended against transnational movements that also claim to be based on the *sharīʿa*. In Indonesia, many local and ethnic forms of *adat* have found their own arrangements with Islam (Benda-Beckmann, F.v., K. v. Benda-Beckmann and Turner 2007: 28–29).

   Moroccan interpretations of the *sharīʿa* are based on the Maliki school of law (*madhab*), while the transnational competitors (Salafi) follow the Hanbali school (Turner 2006: 115). It is the Maliki school that has had an assimilating influence on Moroccan varieties of *adat* for centuries (Turner 2006: 110). In much of the rest of the world of Sunni Islam, the differences between the different *madahib* (plural of *madhab*) do not figure prominently in modern Islamist discourses.
5. Family law is, however, not the uncontested core domain of *sharīʿa* in all Muslim societies. Among the Minankabau of Western Sumatra, matriclan exogamy and matrilineal inheritance are enforced as part of *adat* law, despite obvious contradictions with the *sharīʿa*. It is no surprise that this is a contested matter between the defenders of local law and the protagonists of globally unifying tendencies within Islam.
6. *Jihad* is conditional on Islam having suffered oppression and a number of other factors, like competent leadership and prior mobilization that would present the possibility of a victory, conditions that clearly are not given in the case of the activities of many modern self-styled jihadists. See ʿUthmaan dan Fodio (ʿUthmaan ibn Fudi) (1978 [1806]) who, in turn, cites a vast body of Islamic scholarly opinion. The argument has been summarized by Schlee (2002a: 210–13).
7. On purity, see Schlee (2009: Chapter 10).
8. The extent to which these matters are subject to *adat* rather than to *sharīʿa* can be shown by their variation from one setting to another. The general rule for Somali is one hundred camels for the death of a man and fifty camels for a woman, but the rule is subject to variation, as will be discussed below. The Somali rule resonates with the figure of one hundred she-camels that the Kababish Arabs of Sudan remember having paid in precolonial times (Asad 1970: 108). Further south, for the Humr, a branch of the Baggara Arabs, Cunni-

son mentions sixty head of cattle (Cunnison 1966: 174). But for non-Humr, different rates were agreed on by collective deals: seventy-one head of cattle with the Rizeigat; thirty-three head with the Nuba of Kadugli and the Hawazma (Arabs); fifteen head with Nuba from western Kordofan; a monetary payment of £60 with Hamar, etc. (Cunnison 1966: 102).

9. Regarding Erigabo in Somaliland, Hoehne (2017) reports that state-appointed judges there stress the important contributions of traditional (*xeer*) to handling the vast number of cases, particularly of homicide. In Kenya there was an initiative, now aborted, by members of parliament, provincial governments and community leaders to standardize blood money for the pastoral groups of the north and east. This was in response to a situation in which killings went completely uninvestigated and unpunished because they were part of a 'war'. Officially Kenya has never acknowledged that it is not in control of its entire territory and that some of it is in a state of war (Schlee and Shongolo 2012: 35 f., 118 f.).
10. *Diya* is the Arabic term for *wergild*, blood money or compensation. The Somali term is *mag*.
11. On the logic of punishment and the history of this idea, see also Albrecht (2008) and Härter (2008).
12. In theory, there is no obligation to accept a peaceful settlement among Sudanese Arabs either: 'The acceptance of blood money … is always optional' (Asad 1970: 107).
13. This pattern of subunits of different major units combining with each other against other subunits of their own major units is quite pervasive in Somali affairs. The parties in the Somali civil war that started in 1991 are made up of alliances of subclans of different clans, reminiscent of the old type of *xeer* (here in the sense of 'contractual') alliance across clan divisions (Schlee 2002b). Luling (1997, 2006: 478) likewise makes it clear that clanship does not determine which alliances political leaders conclude, although it does limit their options.
14. I have described this case in greater detail elsewhere (see Schlee 2002b: 260; Schlee and Turner 2008: 64).
15. The customary compensation for causing the death of a male member of another group is one hundred camels unless a different figure has been agreed upon through a prior contractual arrangement.
16. See *Huffington Post* (2009).
17. A reviewer of an earlier version of this chapter suggested that reference to van Notten was not necessary because he is not to be taken seriously. I disagree. His writings betray much knowledge about Somali. I am not going to criticize him for lack of knowledge, but rather for some fundamental misconceptions. He also needs to be taken seriously because of his marked and enduring presence in Somali studies. Leeson (2007) and many others cite him approvingly. The book has also quite a presence in book stores in Africa. In Nairobi it was one of very few books I found on Somalia.
18. This comparison is not far-fetched. One can describe any traditional *diya*-paying group as a kind of insurance. Apart from that, there are also formal, modern companies in the Islamic world that offer insurance against *diya* (Husni et al. 2014).
19. Wives have other ways to get rid of their husbands. Some sheikhs in northern Kenya are known to be easily convinced that absent husbands have not supported their wives for more than six months and then issue certificates of divorce. This is not meant as an attempt to harmonize the *sharīʿa* with Western ideas of gender equality. The *sharīʿa* clearly assumes that the rights and duties of the two genders are quite different. However, this does not have to work to the disadvantage of women. The blatant discrimination against women in many Islamic countries cannot be assumed to be an effect of the application

of the *sharīʿa*. More often, it is the breach of the *sharīʿa* rather than the *sharīʿa* itself that negatively affects the situation of women in the Muslim world. If Muslim men paid the maintenance they owe their wives (or daughters or sisters, as the case may be) and if the latter actually received half of a man's share in cases of inheritance, as they should, on the whole, women should be the wealthier of the two genders. They are maintained by others and therefore can save or invest whatever they inherit. That this is not the actual gender distribution of wealth shows the extent to which the *sharīʿa* is violated.

Women and the *sharīʿa* are a much-debated issue and an ideological minefield. This issue cannot be adequately dealt with in a footnote of a chapter on a different topic. The few remarks I have made are just meant to prevent some of the most common misunderstandings.

20. In an earlier chapter (Schlee 2002b), I take this finding up and show how the pattern of alliances of subclans of different clans persists in modern Somali internal fighting and politicking. Even the holders of the apparently most arbitrary power (the 'warlords') are limited in their options for recruiting followers by the logic of clanship (Schlee 2004a). The difference to the classical model of the segmentary lineage system lies in the fact that the logic of 'mechanical solidarity' with those who are genealogically closer against those who are genealogically more distant does not extend necessarily to higher levels of segmentation because alliances between subclans of different clans who fight jointly against other such subclan alliances comprising members of their own clans are quite common. This, however, does not in any way diminish the importance of patrilineal descent for military recruitment and joint defence; it only distinguishes between different levels of segmentation. Authors who interpret this position as implying that 'the segmentary lineage system blindly dictate[s] Somali social and political allegiances' (Little 2003: 163) or who think that Lewis and I have given too much primacy to segmentary kinship (Bradbury 2008: 14) have missed this point. The importance of the segmentary lineage system for Somali is hard to overemphasize, but, of course, one also has to consider those of its workings that are specific to Somali, and not simply apply models imported from other groups (e.g., from the Nuer, Arabs or Pashtuns).
21. In Western law as well, killings in war are not a matter of penal law unless human rights have been abused, as in massacres of civilians, and even then it is selectively applied, with trials against the winning side being rare.
22. Oral communication.
23. The *sharīʿa* recommends compensation and reconciliation without, however, specifying the amount, which is therefore a matter of local custom and varies accordingly. Collections of *ahaadith* (sayings and doings of the Prophet, plural of *hadith*) that claim otherwise tend to be from relatively recent collections and enjoy little supraregional authority. What is meant here by application of the *sharīʿa* is the insistence on the punishment it provides, not the forgoing of punishment it recommends.
24. Hoehne here refers to Human Rights Watch (1995) and Reno (2003: 22–32).
25. Siad Barre was the last president of the whole of Somalia. He was toppled in early 1991 and eventually left for Nigeria, where he died in 1994.
26. Contini cites Lewis (1999 [1961]: 161) in this context.
27. In retrospect, the peace process can now definitively be declared a failure.
28. The sign '<' stands for 'subgroup of'.
29. What Leeson neglects in his comparison is that statelessness may describe the political situation within Somalia, but when it comes to economic measures, the impact of remittances from the Somali diaspora is considerable. Often these stem from welfare payments by states in other parts of the world. The beneficial effects of these transfers cannot be

counted among the advantages of statelessness because they originate in statehood, especially the welfare state (see Hoehne 2011: 445).

References

Albrecht, H.-J. 2008. 'Strafrecht und Strafe: Belastung oder Entlastung?', in G. Schlee and B. Turner (eds), *Vergeltung: Eine interdisziplinäre Betrachtung der Rechtfertigung und Regulation von Gewalt.* Frankfurt: Campus, pp. 127–48.

Amien, W. 2011. 'Review of: Ayman Shabana: Custom in Islamic Law and Legal Theory. The Development of the Concepts of 'urf and' adah in the Islamic Legal Tradition', *Journal for Islamic Studies* 31: 122–37.

Anderson, D. 1986. 'Stock Theft and Moral Economy in Colonial Kenya', *Africa* 56(4): 399–416.

Asad, T. 1970. *The Kababish Arabs: Power, Authority and Consent in a Nomadic Tribe.* London: Hurst.

Barnes, C., and H. Hassan. 2007. 'The Rise and Fall of Mogadishu's Islamic Courts', *Journal of Eastern African Studies* 1(2): 151–60.

Benda-Beckmann, F. v., K. v. Benda-Beckmann and B. Turner 2007. 'Umstrittene Traditionen in Marokko und Indonesien', *Zeitschrift für Ethnologie* 132: 15–35.

Bradbury, M. 2008. *Becoming Somaliland.* London: Progressio.

Chakrabarty, B. 2006. *Social and Political Thought of Mahatma Gandhi.* London: Routledge.

Ciabarri, L. 2010. *Dopo lo Stato: Storia e antropologia della ricomposizione sociale nella Somalia settentrionale.* Milan: Franco Angeli.

Contini, P. 1971. 'The Evolution of Blood-Money for Homicide in Somalia', *Journal of African Law* 15(1): 77–84.

Cunnison, I. 1966. *Baggara Arabs: Power and the Lineage in a Sudanese Nomad Tribe.* Oxford: Clarendon Press.

Evans-Pritchard, E.E. 1940. *The Nuer: A Description of the Modes of Livelihood and Political Institutions of a Nilotic People.* Oxford: Oxford University Press.

Härter, K. 2008. 'Strafen mit und neben der Zentralgewalt: Pluralität und Verstaatlichung des Strafens in der frühen Neuzeit', in G. Schlee and B. Turner (eds), *Vergeltung: Eine interdisziplinäre Betrachtung der Rechtfertigung und Regulation von Gewalt.* Frankfurt: Campus, pp. 105–26.

Hoehne, M.V. 2010a. 'Diasporic Engagement in the Educational Sector in Post-conflict Somaliland: A Contribution to Peace-Building?', *DIASPEACE Working Paper No. 5.* https://jyx.jyu.fi/dspace/bitstream/handle/123456789/36879/DIASPEACE_W%3E%20P5.pdf?sequence=1

———. 2010b. 'Diasporisches Handeln in Bürgerkrieg und Wiederaufbau: Beispiele aus Somalia und Somaliland', *Friedens-Warte* 85(1–2): 83–103.

———. 2011. 'Political Orientations and Repertoires of Identification: State and Identity Formation in Northern Somalia', Ph.D. dissertation. Halle (Saale): Martin Luther University Halle-Wittenberg.

———. 2017. 'One Country, Two Systems: Hybrid Political Orders (HPOs) and Legal and Political Friction in Somaliland', in O. Zenker and M.V. Hoehne (eds), *The State and the Paradox of Customary Law in Africa.* London: Routledge.

Hoehne, M.V., and M.H. Ibrahim, 2014. 'Rebuilding Somaliland through Economic and Educational Engagement', in L. Laakso and P. Hautaniemi (eds), *Diasporas, Development and Peacemaking in the Horn of Africa.* London: Zed Books, pp. 53–76.

Huffington Post. 2009. 'Somalia Libertarian Paradise', Video Clip. Retrieved 13 June 2010 from http://www.huffingtonpost.com/2009/05/06/somalia-libertarian-parad_n_197763.html.

Human Rights Watch. 1995. 'Somalia Faces the Future. Human Rights in a Divided Society'. Retrieved 24 November 2010 from http://www.hrw.org/reports/1995/somalia.

Husni, A.B.M., A.F. Omar, M.N. Alias and M. al-Adib Samuri 2014. 'The Role of Insurance in Place of Aqilah in Paying Blood Money Resulting from Accidents: An Analytical Study', *Social Sciences* 9(1): 58–64. doi:10.3923/sscience.2014.58.64.

King, C.J. 1980. 'A Rationale for Punishment', *Journal of Libertarian Studies* 4(2): 151–65.

Le Sage, A. 2005. 'Stateless Justice in Somalia: Formal and Informal Rule of Law Initiatives', *Henri Dunant Centre of Humanitarian Dialogue, Report,* July 2005.

Leeson, P.T. 2007. 'Better off Stateless: Somalia before and after Government Collapse', *Journal of Comparative Economics* 35(4): 689–710.

Lewis, I.M. 1999 [1961]. *A Pastoral Democracy: A Study of Pastoralism and Politics among Northern Somali of the Horn of Africa.* Oxford: James Currey.

Little, P.D. 2003. *Somalia: Economy without State.* Oxford: James Currey for the International African Institute.

Luling, V. 1997. 'Come back Somalia? Questioning a Collapsed State', *Third World Quarterly* 18: 287–302.

———. 2006. 'Genealogy as Theory, Genealogy as Tool: Aspects of Somali "Clanship"', *Social Identities* 12(4): 471–85.

Reno, W. 2003. 'Somalia and Survival in the Shadow of the Global Economy', *Queen Elisabeth House Working Paper No. 100.* Oxford: University of Oxford.

Salim, A. 2015. *Contemporary Islamic Law in Indonesia: Shari'ah and Legal Pluralism.* Edinburgh: Edinburgh University Press

Samatar, S.S. 2007. 'The Islamic Courts and Ethiopia's Intervention: Redemption or Adventurism?' Talk given at Chatham House, London, 25 April 2007. Retrieved 30 November 2010 from http://www.chathamhouse.org.uk/research/africa/papers.

Schlee, G. 1979. *Das Glaubens- und Sozialsystem der Rendille. Kamelnomaden Nordkenias.* Berlin: Dietrich Reimer Verlag.

———. 1989. *Identities on the Move: Clanship and Pastoralism in Northern Kenya.* Manchester: Manchester University Press.

———. 2002a. 'Les Peuls du Nil', in Y. Diallo and G. Schlee (eds), *L'ethnicité peule dans des contexts nouveaux.* Paris: Karthala, pp. 207–23.

———. 2002b. 'Regularity in Chaos: The Politics of Difference in the Recent History of Somalia', in G. Schlee (ed.), *Imagined Differences: Hatred and the Construction of Identity.* Hamburg: Lit, pp. 251–80.

———. 2004a. 'Taking Sides and Constructing Identities: Reflections on Conflict Theory', *Journal of the Royal Anthropological Institute* 10(1): 135–56.

———. 2004b. 'Conflict Analysis in Bakool and Bay, South-Western Somalia'. Report on a two-week consultancy in the framework of the conflict resolution and reconciliation component of the Improvement of Farming Systems Project (IFSP), Bay and Bakool Region, 3–17 March 2004. Halle (Saale): Max Planck Institute for Social Anthropology.

———. 2006. 'The Somali Peace Process and the Search for a Legal Order', in H.-J. Albrecht (ed.), *Conflict and Conflict Resolution in Middle Eastern Societies – Between Tradition and Modernity.* Berlin: Dunker & Humblot, pp. 117–67.

———. 2009. *How Enemies are Made.* New York: Berghahn Books.

———. 2013. 'Customary Law and the Joys of Statelessness: Idealised Traditions versus Somali Realities', *Journal of Eastern African Studies* 7(2): 258–71.

Schlee, G., and A.A. Shongolo. 2012. *Pastoralism and Politics in Northern Kenya and Southern Ethiopia*. Woodbridge: James Currey.

Schlee, G., and B. Turner. 2008. 'Rache, Wiedergutmachung und Strafe: Ein Überblick', in G. Schlee and B. Turner (eds), *Vergeltung: Eine interdisziplinäre Betrachtung der Rechtfertigung und Regulation von Gewalt*. Frankfurt: Campus, pp. 48–67.

Shabana, A. 2010. *Custom in Islamic Law and Legal Theory: The Development of the Concepts of ʿurf and* ʿ ādah *in the Islamic Legal Tradition*. New York: Palgrave Macmillan.

Sigrist, C. 1994 [1967]. *Regulierte Anarchie*. Hamburg: Europäische Verlagsanstalt.

Spittler, G. 1980. 'Streitregelung im Schatten des Leviathan. Eine Darstellung und Kritik rechtsethnologischer Untersuchungen', *Zeitschrift für Rechtssoziologie* I: 4–32.

Turner, B. 2006. 'Competing Global Players in Rural Morocco: Upgrading Legal Arenas', *Journal of Legal Pluralism* 53–54: 101–39.

UNDP. 2001. *Human Development Report, Somalia 2001*. Compiled by M. Bradbury, K. Menkhaus and R. Marchal. United Nations Development Programme. Retrieved from http://hdr.undp.org/sites/default/files/somalia_2001_en.pdf.

ᶜUthman dan Fodio, Osman dan Fodio (ᶜUthman ibn Fudi). 1978 [1806]. *Bayaan wujuub al hijra ᶜalal-ᶜibaad wa bayaan wujuub nasbi al-imaam wa iqaamati al-jihaad*, ed. and trans. F.H. al Masri. Khartoum: Khartoum University Press and Oxford University Press.

Van Notten, M. 2005. *The Law of the Somalis: A Stable Foundation for Economic Development in the Horn of Africa*, ed. by S.H. McCullum. Trenton, NJ: Red Sea Press.

Weber, M. 1956 [1921–22]. *Wirtschaft und Gesellschaft*. Tübingen: J.C.B. Mohr.

Section VI

Travelling Models of Retaliation

Postconflict Scenarios in International Law and on the Ground

Chapter 11

Retaliation in Postwar Times

An Analysis of the Rhetoric and Practices of Retaliation in Bamyan, Afghanistan, 2009

Friederike Stahlmann

In Bamyan, as in many other parts of Afghanistan,[1] retaliation is the dominant concept of dispute management. As such, it spells out local criteria of justice and peace, and provides for a procedural model to achieve these aims. Justice and peace are, per definition, ideal scenarios, which are, if ever, almost never completely realized anywhere or at any time. The degree to which and the conditions under which models of dispute management are able to serve these aims are highly contingent upon the sociolegal and political environment. The following analysis will contribute to an understanding of retaliation by discussing an Afghan model of retaliation under the specific conditions of a postwar setting. After a short introduction to Bamyan, I will introduce this local model of retaliation in its ideal-typical form. The analysis that follows will trace the main effects of postwar conditions on the realization of this model and will discuss their impact on the proclaimed aims of retaliation to serve justice and peace. To do so, I draw on the rhetoric and practices of retaliation as I encountered them in the city of Bamyan in 2009.[2]

The chapter will demonstrate that, under the conditions provided by this postwar setting, it is virtually impossible to realize the aims of justice and peace. It also shows how these conditions turn the very means that ought to serve justice into a means of injustice, and retaliation itself into a threat rather than a chance to achieve security and peace.

The Setting: Postwar Bamyan, 2009

The city of Bamyan is the provincial capital of Bamyan Province, located in the central highlands of Afghanistan. Like most parts of Afghanistan, Bamyan has a decades-long history of civil and regional wars.[3] These wars and the many regime changes that have occurred in their wake have caused extraordinary suffering through mass killings, lootings and large-scale physical destruction of homes, belongings and infrastructure. They have also had a considerable impact on a more structural level: socially, people's individual war biographies have created relationships that are shaped by guilt and victimhood, and often follow group lines based on ethnic or sect affiliation, as well as new markers of identity such as war-party membership or shared experiences of flight and exile. From both political and legal perspectives, the wars have caused severe ruptures, as every regime provided for its own legal order and power arrangements that advantaged those bearing certain markers of belonging, and disadvantaged others through partisan ruling and partisan 'justice'.

Since 2002, Bamyan has been spared any warlike events. By 2009, state institutions supported by (international) non-governmental organizations ((I)NGOs) and New Zealand troops allowed for a state of physical and material security that was, compared to other areas of Afghanistan, extraordinarily stable. This security permitted people to work their fields, get married and send their children to school, and allowed me to share in people's lives, witness their disputes and follow them through their dispute management. In general, it gave the overall impression of a situation that is usually described as 'postwar reconstruction'.[4]

However, the past wars and regime changes very clearly reverberate in the present and continue to shape life in manifold ways. Many of the past institutions and networks of power continue to exist, and the current plurality of legal, political and social arrangements largely represents remnants of the various past regimes. The past wars also affect the present through the inferences people draw from past experiences, which in turn inform their evaluation of the present and their expectations for the future. When referring to the relevant environment for disputing in general and retaliation in particular, I draw on these emic perceptions because they underlie both interpretations of dispute management and the decision-making processes that it entails.[5] In general, these emic views betray a pervasive sense of unpredictability and uncertainty in all relevant matters of life, and anticipation of yet another regime change and thus further insecurity to come, all of which relativizes the official image of a healthy postwar reconstruction situation.

A Local Model of Retaliation

The following section introduces the norms of how disputes ought to be managed and settled as I encountered them in Bamyan. The accounts I gathered in this regard depict retaliation as the only model that can possibly satisfy individuals' needs in gaining justice on the one hand, and provide the necessary means to ensure fair and lasting settlements on the other hand.

Applicability

The local model of dispute resolution in Bamyan conforms to the definition of retaliation underlying this volume: it regulates and settles disputes between nominally equal parties through compensatory or violent responses to harm, and is based on the principle of reciprocity. A number of local terms are used to discuss retaliation in Bamyan, the most formal of which are *enteqam* (retaliation) and *enteqam gereftan* (to retaliate). More colloquial expressions that refer to the same principle are 'settling accounts', 'getting even' and 'making up for harm one caused'. The most common way of discussing retaliation, however, is through reference to *kina*, which is 'the urge and will to gain satisfaction'. *Kina* is the driving force that shapes the disputing relationship and bears great emotional value. It must be distinguished from *bohs*, which describes the immediate fury a person feels after an offence or trespass has occurred.

Limiting retaliation to nominally equal parties excludes disputes where the state is involved as a party. Otherwise, most social constellations can be handled under this order, despite recognized social inequalities, such as that between men and women. This is due to the local system of legal representation, which designates the hierarchically highest men of a household to take responsibility for harm that children or women of the household have caused or endured. In cases of marital disputes, for example, the wife's family of origin provides for the woman's representation against the husband. Thus, formally, only men figure as disputing parties.

This general retaliatory model applies to all kinds of disputes regarding substantial matters. Within this model, there are internal distinctions between types of harm, which necessitate different retaliatory responses. How these different types of harm are locally defined and translated into claims for satisfaction will be discussed in the following section.

Different Kinds of Harm, Different Needs for Satisfaction

According to the local model of retaliation in Bamyan, the main distinction between kinds of harm is between material and bodily harm on the one hand and 'social harm', which is harm to the social status of a person, on the other hand.

Gaining satisfaction for material and bodily harm tends to be relatively easy, as it can be done through compensation for damage to a given good based on the principle of reciprocity. For damage to be considered compensable simply by replacing the value of the damaged good, the victim and all relevant audiences need to interpret the offence as unintentional. For that, the acknowledgment of the aggrieved person's right, the acknowledgement of responsibility for having caused harm and the willingness to make up for it must be voluntary and expressed immediately and publicly. This public acknowledgment is crucial because any infringement upon rights challenges the social status of the injured party, as social status is in part delimited by the rights one claims and defends. Therefore, any kind of harm – whether committed intentionally or not – is automatically interpreted as a challenge to the victim's social status until that status has either been reaffirmed by the perpetrator through public confession, a show of respect or, in extreme cases, self-humiliation, or reclaimed by the victim through an act of retaliation. As long as this social status has not been re-established in one way or the other, the parties are in a state of dispute with each other.

Cases where there is an apparent trace of intentionality or where the alleged perpetrator refuses to publicly acknowledge responsibility and remorse constitute social harm because the social status of the victim is not only temporarily called into question, but is also intentionally challenged. In terms of retaliation and the need for satisfaction, such social harm is taken into account in addition to material or bodily harm. Social harm may also be caused independently of material or bodily harm by any deed that, in the perception of the victim, calls his social status into question, such as defamation, a groundless claim to something the victim believes is his, or any other offence to his reputation or honour. This social status is a personal matter of pride (*qeirat*) and honour (*nang*), but also concerns the relationship between the disputing parties and, even more importantly, one's absolute standing in the wider community. Measures to gain satisfaction for social harm are therefore not only directed at the offending party, but also address the community at large. The community in turn makes the resulting social status of the offended party dependent on his motivation to take whatever measures are necessary to gain satisfaction, as well as on his practical ability to realize it. Both motivation and ability matter, but for different reasons: motivation demonstrates the victim's claim to a right and thus to a certain status. It is this that matters most in terms of reputation and honour. The motivation to defend one's rights through bravery and courage proves pride (*qeirat*), which is regarded a crucial element of a man's honour (*nang*). A man without pride and thus honour would be less likely to be entrusted with a woman for marriage, accepted as a trustworthy partner for business or taken seriously when he gives advice, to name just a few consequences. While *qeirat* socially matters on its own account, it is the ability to defend one's rights that determines whether one may practically regain the enjoyment of an entitlement and deter other potential perpetrators by establishing the precedent that offenders will suffer and pay for any kind of harm committed.

In sum, there are three major kinds of interests in retaliation that need to be fulfilled in order to achieve satisfaction of *kina*: the emotional interest to get even in terms of suffering; the economic interest to be compensated for damage (in case of material or bodily harm); and the social interest to reaffirm and keep one's social status as a rights-bearing subject of honour.

Victims' Responsibilities and Powers

The pursuit of retaliation places a huge responsibility on injured parties to defend their rights and status, but it also gives them considerable powers and wide leverage to do so. First, there is no normative requirement to realize the execution of satisfaction all by oneself. It is perfectly legitimate to engage a third party to acknowledge one's right, organize compensation and arrange a plea for forgiveness by the offender. Second, local norms do not set any time limit on the settling of accounts. Satisfaction need not be achieved immediately; it may be gained in twenty, forty or even eighty years. Retaliation, I was told, is a dish best served cold. With regard to the terms of honour, the victim merely has to let the relevant public know that he is determined to gain satisfaction at an opportune moment. Third, victims are allowed to pursue their satisfaction by whatever means available, including self-executed violence such as poisoning the opponent, burning down his house or destroying his reputation by creating rumours. Such measures have the advantage of being cheap in a material sense. While appeals to institutions and third parties generally require a considerable investment of time and material and social resources, such self-executed measures are open to anyone, independent of economic means or access to networks of power. However, such measures alone do not directly lead to material compensation – killing a murderer cannot compensate for the murdered person in material terms. That such measures are part of the repertoire of retaliation mechanisms underlines the relative importance of emotional and social interests in gaining satisfaction. Ideally, the chosen method not only causes counter-harm to the offending party, but also serves to re-establish or increase the victim's economic status at the cost of the perpetrator. The support needed for the enactment of such solutions ought to be provided by solidarity groups on both sides. Such groups also have the responsibility to even out differences in power between the parties. But the main incentive to reach such compensatory nonviolent settlements and deter trespass in the first place is the very threat of possible and legitimate violent responses by the victim.[6]

Ensuring Reciprocity

These far-reaching victims' rights are depicted as necessary to provide the opportunity to gain satisfaction for practically weaker parties. The only normative limit on these rights is reciprocity, which circumscribes the limit of appropriate response. The all-decisive question is why victims should stick to this limit. The threat of legitimate violence already poses an incentive for perpetrators to acknowledge the rights of the victim, take responsibility and agree to compensation. The more forcefully the realization of satisfaction is conducted, the greater the chances that it will be taken seriously, allow for satisfaction and serve as an effective deterrent. The threat of violence that goes beyond the acknowledged limits of reciprocity, though illegitimate, might increase the victim's potential gains, but it also carries the threat that the dispute will escalate.

Taking the retaliatory model as a whole into account shows why escalation is not in the victims' interests. First, if the measures are regarded as excessive by the opponent, these can open up a new account. Exaggerated violence might thus backfire and create a new counter-risk, with the newly offended party able to exercise all the legitimate powers of retaliation that were just described. One interest in de-escalation and in not leaving the other party unduly humiliated or damaged is therefore to avoid creating an enemy. Second, the norm that satisfaction ought to be gained on the basis of reciprocity is also relevant in relation to the wider community and potential solidarity groups. While crossing the legitimate limit of reciprocity might prove to be an effective deterrent, as others would generally be reluctant to offend those who are known to have an exaggerated response, the price of overstepping the bounds would be social exclusion, including exclusion from public decision making and social networks, and the ensuing lack of social support in times of need, such as when one is looking for jobs for oneself or one's family members. One immediate consequence would be the loss of solidarity-based support in the process of disputing. The public encourages proof of *qeirat* through positive reputation, but the public also has an interest in settlement in order to avoid the risk of a dispute escalating and moving up to a larger social scale. The audience's interference indicates that the measures taken were sufficient proof of pride and that in terms of honour, it is time to agree to *islah* – settlement based on the readiness to accept pleas for forgiveness and to give up part of the possible gains in the name of peace. Once forgiveness is genuinely sought by the offending party, it is seen as shameful not to accept it, and anyone who rejects it is considered *binang* (without honour).

Settling Accounts Permanently

How the making up for harm is conducted is open to direct interparty negotiation, but is more likely to be achieved through mediation. As soon as a settlement is agreed upon and forgiveness is granted, it is the duty of the parties to honour the settlement, end the disputing relationship and draw no further consequences from the offence. However, given everyone's experience that actual forgiving is harder than merely uttering the words, those who try to resolve disputes strive for settlements that deter both parties from future aggression even if they are not truly emotionally satisfied. The best settlement arrangements thus bind the parties to future peace for as long as any lingering *kina* about a perceived unfair settlement might last, that is, at a minimum, as long as the parties live, but theoretically as long as the memory of the offence lasts. In Bamyan, the most prominent model for ensuring such a settlement is to give a bride to the injured party, a tradition called *bad*.[7] The bride strengthens the receiving family by bearing children for them; in the case of homicide, she also in this way replaces the men that were lost. She can also serve as leverage for the receiving party, as her brothers and father would not want to put her wellbeing at risk by engaging in future acts of aggression. If there are doubts that the victim will truly be satisfied with this arrangement, the mechanism is to promise a newborn girl as a future bride. In this case, the victim will not attack for the roughly thirteen years it takes for her to reach the age of marriage because he does not want to jeopardize the handover of the future bride. Furthermore, the wider community is responsible for watching over the whole process, sanctioning trespass of its reciprocal limits, providing for neutral third parties to broker settlements and making sure that outcomes are honoured. Anyone with possible influence on one or both of the parties has the duty to support them in their search for a solution that will satisfy open accounts and allow the parties to close them successfully and irrevocably.

Postwar Effects on Realizing Retaliation

In the last section I have traced the major characteristics of what is deemed necessary and right regarding the management and settlements of disputes. The realization of this model, like any other model of disputing, depends on the social, political and legal environment disputing parties find themselves in and react to (Benda-Beckmann 2003). This section will trace the major effects of the specific postwar environment on the conditions that need to be met in order to make this model of dispute resolution work.

Problems of Proof

In order to be successful in closing open accounts satisfactorily, the first condition is agreement about what actually happened. Establishing such facts requires agreed-upon rules of factfinding and evidence. My informants claimed that the social proximity in which people live in principle provides for sufficient publicity of relevant knowledge in order to establish such facts. I observed that even such personal matters as agreement on bride prices are known to a considerable public. However, relying on public knowledge to establish the veracity of accusations of trespassing or individuals' claims to rights and entitlements in disputes is a much more challenging matter. Disputes about entitlements to land may serve as an illustration of these difficulties. The formal method for deciding on the entitlement to a piece of land, I was taught, is to ask the immediate neighbours, who are not only expected to know the borders but should also be informed about transactions concerning fields adjacent to theirs. However, this method of rights protection now faces a major problem, because civil war party leaders used large-scale illicit appropriation and redistribution of land to reimburse fighters. Those who are neighbours and should serve as neutral witnesses are therefore often considered parties to the dispute themselves, and their testimonies are thus regarded as untrustworthy. It is generally believed that witnesses are easy to buy, which points to relatively weak social control exercised over witnesses. But even with those witnesses whose reputations cannot be called into question and whose testimonies are therefore beyond reproach, there are practical problems that stem from the past: the many regime changes and civil war periods have forced virtually everyone to flee from their land at some time or another. This means that with regard to local affairs, there are gaps in every person's memory, no matter how trustworthy and detailed it might otherwise be. Disputes are often precisely about these times of exile, as these were also times of large-scale illicit appropriation.

Migration also causes additional problems: land transactions are often made far away from the land in question and without the knowledge of those who have remained behind. For example, I came across a case in which a man who had lived in Australia returned to Bamyan and claimed that he had bought a field five years earlier from its known owner, who had also emigrated to Australia. How can one be sure that he actually speaks the truth and has the right to claim the land from the former owner's cousin, who has been using it for the last twenty-five years? In this particular case, the former owner had died in the meantime and prior to his death had not been able to maintain contact with his remaining relatives in Bamyan because of the lack of an adequate communications infrastructure in Bamyan. This returnee now has a contract signed by the former owner and witnesses who are not known in Bamyan. The cousin doubted the authenticity of the contract because he knew that the former owner was illiterate. The returnee started getting impatient and defensive, and pointed out that it was highly likely that a person who had migrated to Australia to conduct business would have learned how to read and write. In any case, it was impossible to verify the signature.

This is only one example of a general problem of documentation. Many documents that could serve as proof of entitlements of whatever kind are lost, again due to typical war-related causes such as looted homes and scenes of hurried flight. Registries are not a reliable source for verifying claims either, not only because they were not maintained for large spans of time, but also because most past and present regimes demanded exorbitant fees for the registration of transactions. Failing to register in order to avoid paying these fees might make the transaction invalid in state legal terms, but the local perception of rightfulness in selling or buying does not depend on registration with the state. Given the lack of legitimacy that these civil war regimes had among large portions of the population, it is even more understandable that many people could not or would not want to engage with these power holders, and avoiding doing so was an acceptable practice for many local residents. While it is often difficult enough and sometimes impossible to prove the validity of a single transaction that happened under such extraordinary circumstances, disputes tend to develop their own history of harm, claims, counter-harm and counterclaims, and create along with these many relevant facts (Benda-Beckmann 2008: 142 ff.). These are difficult to trace and agree upon under the best of conditions. Without agreed-upon and trustworthy means to gather the necessary information, the facts of a dispute and the process of establishing those facts remain very easy to challenge on procedural grounds when the results are not favourable to one of the parties concerned.

Unsettled Normative Plurality

Agreeing on the relevant facts of a dispute is only the first prerequisite for the possibility of successful settlement. Next, the parties must agree upon the norms by which to judge these facts, to establish that a certain action indeed constitutes harm, and to determine who is the victim and who is the perpetrator. Here again, the past casts its shadows onto the present: every former regime enacted a different legal framework, and every group of migrants returned to their homelands with their own legal experiences and repertoires that they had become accustomed to while in exile. These different legal orders provide for different allocations of rights and responsibilities, and have very different understandings of what counts as relevant harm. However, legal pluralism in and of itself does not necessarily lead to legal uncertainty. What creates uncertainty in this setting is a lack of predictability and, consequently, a lack of reliability regarding the norms which the other party, relevant audiences and institutional actors are going to apply in any given situation.

However, even where only one set of relevant norms comes into play, past wars cause practical problems. One such problem is that past and current war party allegiances create collectives in which individual responsibility is not clearly demarcated. Many people joined not just one but several war parties over the course of time, thereby making it possible, in theory at least, for virtually everybody to have claims and open accounts against almost everyone else. The previous or current regime's appropriation and granting of land to supporters – an act that the previous owners of the land regard as theft – may again serve as an example of the problems associated with allocating responsibility. It is difficult to predict whether the previous users will blame the regime, the current users or both. This uncertainty regarding who holds *kina* against whom is further increased by the local application of the concept of collective responsibility. Based on this concept, one may carry grief and *kina* against another for the latter's belonging to a certain collective such as an ethnic group, or for being a returnee or a former member of a war party, or for the religious education one received, or for possessing any one of a number of other markers of identity. All of these collectives bear guilt for past crimes. The collective aspect of guilt also applies to families – a son might be held responsible for an offence committed by his father and might not even know why or what the original offence was.

If the parties can, despite these problems, agree on the basic facts, the definition of harm and the attribution of legal responsibility, the norm of reciprocity still requires that an agreement be reached on the scale for both material and immaterial compensation (Turner and Schlee 2008: 12). Value, however, is subjective, and since it is unlikely that two opposing parties will agree on this subjective value, the scales necessary to measure just compensation should be agreed upon and established by the community prior to and independent of the current case. Given both a highly fragmented society and an institutional environment that is shaky in terms of normative legitimacy and unable to mediate a socially binding renegotiation of such scales, it becomes quite easy for one party to publicly argue against and reject a compensation offer without being challenged. A decision might be taken by some legal institution based on executive power, but that does not necessarily solve the problem between the parties, the assessment of unsettled accounts or all its possible consequences. As a local elder noted:

> There will be peace in cases where two persons have a legal problem and both parties come to an agreement. If one side agrees, but the other side doesn't and feels he isn't able to assert his rights, we can't call it peace. It doesn't matter how many times elders make a judgment, the parties will continue to be in conflict with each other.

The importance of mutual agreement for settlements to be viable applies not only to retaliation, but to other kinds of disputing processes as well. Retaliation, however, with its emphasis on personal acknowledgment of satisfaction, highlights both the importance of mutual agreement and the challenges of realizing it.

A case involving *bad* – the tradition of giving a daughter for marriage in order to facilitate dispute settlement – will serve as an example illustrating how the legal changes of the past continue to affect disputing parties in their efforts to reach agreements and settle accounts. One day, an elderly man approached me in the market seeking my advice. Many years earlier, he explained, an unfriendly relationship between two neighbouring families had escalated, leaving several people on both sides injured and one man dead. The Taliban controlled the area at that time, but involving them was regarded as risky because the outcome was unpredictable. The parties agreed that my informant would give his newborn daughter as a wife (when she became older) to the brother of the victim. In this way, the dispute was kept rather quiet and small-scale, and the involvement of the Taliban was thus avoided. However, the current regime set out to end this settlement tradition and punish forced marriages. The man who made the initial agreement was now dependent on his daughter's voluntary acquiescence to the marriage. In the event, the girl refused, and her father found himself on the horns of a dilemma. The would-be husband threatens him with death if the agreement is not honoured and makes it clear that he is not willing to accept any other terms of settlement, while the state threatens the man with imprisonment if the agreement was honoured. This case shows how the legal changes of the past are inscribed into the disputes' histories and remain relevant. It also shows how difficult and sensitive attempts to reach settlements can be.

Lack of Trust in the Protection of the Limit of Reciprocity and the Sustainability of Results

The above description of the local model of retaliation reveals that the realization of justice and peace in practice relies on a public composed of solidarity groups, a neutral wider public and neutral third parties. These actors are meant to encourage and support victims in their quest for satisfaction, to ensure the limits of reciprocity in doing so, and to encourage, enable and protect fair and lasting solutions. Their role is to support *qeirat* (pride) to the extent of reciprocity and encourage *islah* (willingness to settlement) when this level has been reached. To do so, they need to put some power behind the concept of reputation. This power lies in a wide range of measures of social control, especially those of social inclusion or exclusion, through which the differences in power between the parties may be balanced. The task of balancing the parties' asymmetric power becomes even more important when one takes into consideration the lack of agreement on the normative basis for defining the scope of legitimate interests as well as reciprocity, as discussed above. In order to accomplish this task in a satisfying manner, external actors must be regarded as willing, able and reliable to do so by the disputing parties.

Gaining this trust is complicated by the lack of agreement on relevant norms. The problem is further exacerbated by what appears to be only marginal public concern with both addressing acts of injustice and maintaining reputations. The reasons for this are multilayered, but a core element is the relativization of immorality and even outright trespass based on the extraordinary injustices people have experienced. I once had dinner with a family that was involved in a dispute, and the talk turned to this lack of public concern. The day before, I had witnessed a meeting of the democratically elected village council, comprised of a range of socially respected and relatively powerful men. When I asked why they could not execute or initiate social sanctions, I was laughed at: 'You were sitting with murderers yesterday. And you are sitting with a murderer now. What does lack of appropriateness matter? We suffer from it, we can judge it, but applying sanctions to all bad behaviour? How should that work?' The shared guilt and, I would suggest, the crimes people have witnessed and suffered from seem to put injustice into a perspective that renders the enactment of social sanctions somehow hypocritical.

This lack of concern and the subsequent lack of will to exercise social control have severe consequences at all stages of a dispute – from the public acknowledgement of an infringement of rights to the social protection and thus sustainability of settlement agreements. Not only do stronger parties have no incentive to agree upon anything less than the maximum possible gain, but there are also no social incentives to honour an agreed-upon settlement. No perpetrator can be certain that the granting of forgiveness, which is part of a settlement agreement and implies that the victim waives the right to a legitimate counter-attack, will actually be honoured by the victim. Any past dispute might re-erupt at any time. Settlements thus tend to be hardly more than temporal statements of strength, but cannot possibly be regarded as justice or peace. This puts everyone at risk because, after decades of civil war, almost no one can claim to be without guilt. The public lack of interest in reputation that follows from a lack of concern for others' behaviour supports nonviolent responses to harm because it diminishes the need to socially defend one's status through a violent counter-attack. This approach is reinforced by public fear of any outbreak of violence, which is based on the countless experiences of uncontrolled and unlimited violence. Many cases were cited as daunting examples of the escalation potential of unrestrained violence. The most prominent concerned a village not far from the centre of Bamyan city, which was inhabited mainly by two families sharing a common ancestor. These two families had been caught up in an uncontrolled *kina*-driven escalation of violence, leaving between forty and 160 people dead (the number differed depending on whom I asked). The death toll, I was told, was so high because the families had allied themselves with opposing civil war parties. Whether these war parties had an interest in causing this escalation or the disputants were using the war parties' power to turn the dynamic to their own advantage I do not know, but here it does not matter much. What matters is that the war parties were present and that they played an active role in the escalation. 'And now', they said, 'look, all these people killed, the young ones, the educated ones, even women! Many women lost their husbands, lost their sons and even babies'.

Such experiences and the subsequent fear of escalation raise the question of why such escalation was not inhibited by neutral third parties. When I asked surviving inhabitants of the village why the mullahs, who are usually listed among those who should function as neutral third parties, did not facilitate the cessation of violence between the two families, they laughed and said that the mullahs themselves had started the killing. I then inquired if there had been no elders who could have negotiated a stop to this. 'Yes, they have elders', they responded. 'They are elders, but they are all murderers. And who should stop them?' Without such control, any act of violence indeed threatens to start an uncontrolled process of escalation. The current fear and disapproval of privately executed violence is further seconded by the state, which tries to realize its claimed monopoly on violence through criminal prosecution. Sanctions for violence per se seem to be a peace-supporting policy. And, indeed, given the gravity of past crimes, the number of unsettled disputes and the social proximity of perpetrators and victims, the rate of assault and especially murder is surprisingly low.[8] But escalation only becomes a risk when a victim responds violently to an injustice. Sanctions for violence thus tend to discourage the response to a trespass rather than the trespass itself. This does contain escalation, but it does not contain injustice. On the contrary, it tends to increase injustice because potential perpetrators have little to fear in terms of consequences.

Without the threat of violence, the possibility for victims to enter into negotiations with a chance for justice would have to come from elsewhere. If the general public is not ready to sanction injustice, the question becomes whether neutral third parties will fulfil their mandate to mediate and encourage fair solutions, and thus provide a forum where victims can satisfy *kina*. Given that there seems to be no agreement on what is right or wrong, where the limits of reciprocity are or what fair settlements would look like, true neutrality is difficult to achieve. But this lack of agreement is something any mediator tends to face to some extent under any circumstances. However, the description of mullahs and elders as murderers points to another problem with neutrality, namely a past of active, partisan participation in large-scale crimes. This is predominantly a question of age, because those who are now at the age where they could be considered respected elders or established mullahs were young men during the war and, as such, were part of active, partisan fighting. Given the collective responsibility for crimes and thus also collective *kina*, it does not matter much whether a given individual is known to bear personal responsibility or not.

The following vignette will serve as an example of how this collective *kina* can reverberate on attempts to reach settlements. An elderly man told me in considerable fury that a judge had found him guilty of cutting his neighbour's trees and that this judgment had not been fair. I asked him if he had not been the one who had cut the trees. 'No, no, it was me', he replied. I then suggested that perhaps the trees had actually belonged to him. 'No, they were his, and I cut them', he acknowledged. He also told me that the compensation sum the judge had ordered him to pay was appropriate. Seeing that I was puzzled, obviously unable to understand the injustice in the decision, he explained: 'You see, it was not the decision itself, but his [the judge's] motivation. He wanted to make a Hazara pay for the destruction of the old Tajik bazaar. He has *kina* and he would have made me pay even if I had not cut the trees. He is Tajik.' Hazaras and Tajiks, as the two largest ethnic groups in Bamyan, were often on opposing sides during the civil wars. That he apparently afforded the judge no possibility of proving his legitimacy by delivering a substantially fair judgment shows how important the perception and delegitimizing effect of unsatisfied *kina* can be. The recent past of civil wars not only burdens people with guilt and victimhood, but also deprives any kind of potential third party of the possibility of gaining legitimacy based on neutrality.

The fear of escalation and the little concern that is granted to matters of injustice further deprive the weaker party of support from solidarity groups. These groups ought to form whenever support is necessary and thus should help create a practical balance of power. However, solidarity in disputing not only means taking sides with one party, but also necessarily implies taking sides against the other party. Without the checks and balances that are necessary to make the disputing process predictable, taking sides is a dangerous undertaking, and it becomes even more so when one allies oneself with the potentially weaker party. Even if violence is practically contained for the moment, the widely shared anticipation of a near collapse of this current state order and a return to some kind of civil war means that the risk of violence is only temporarily contained.

As a consequence of the lack of support both for the defence of rights and for satisfying results of disputing, any kind of settlement becomes a voluntary task, but this only tends to happen when both parties' power is already quite balanced and if their primary interest lies in an immediate settlement. These cases exist, but whenever victims are relatively weak, they tend not to confront the perpetrator or, if they do, they have to expect that the power differential will force them to waive their rights in part or in whole. In cases in which a partial waiving of rights by both parties would be part of a just settlement, people's anticipation of the future may lead to a lack of willingness to compromise. The expectation of fundamental sociopolitical changes soon to come makes it seem a bad investment to pay now for what might be gained for free, or at least more cheaply, in the near future. This not only applies to relatively more powerful parties, but also to relatively weaker ones. After all, even a current negative power balance could soon be inverted. However, the mere hope for future justice cannot make up for suffering from and frustration with current injustice. In any case, this strategy to wait is only open to parties that can afford to wait. If the right under dispute concerns the field that a family needs in order to survive the next winter, waiting is not an option and the family's position in negotiations is further weakened by the other party's ability to wait.

Conclusion

I was told time and again that retaliation is the only way to satisfy needs and fulfil the interests people have in disputing, and that it was the only disputing model that could possibly provide for justice as well as peace. But I was also told on a daily basis that now there is no chance for either justice or peace, and that the needs and interests of disputing parties cannot be met in a satisfactory manner by any type of dispute resolution. Many of the reasons for this that I have described here are not merely hindrances to the realization of retaliation as a successful and satisfying mode of dispute settlement; they similarly hamper justice in other forms and institutions. I could have, for example, written a very similar account of the difficulties the courts experience in fulfilling their mandate and gaining legitimacy. The analysis of retaliation is particularly interesting, though, for a number of reasons, foremost among them being that retaliation reflects the criteria of justice held by people rather than legal professionals or institutional actors. These criteria express what is needed on an interpersonal level for both justice and peace, and thus tell us more about the success and failure of dispute management than any court file ever could. Retaliation further reveals that both justice and peace-making efforts are dependent upon the social aspects of long-term legal care and the necessary conditions for this long-term care and protection – above all social cohesion and accountability. The reasons why retaliation is currently doomed to fail highlight how detrimental the effects of repeated fundamental sociopolitical change are and how devastating the overall uncertainty about the future can be to the chances of achieving any kind of justice or peace, even in such small-scale problems as an interpersonal dispute over a piece of land. All this negatively affects more than just the realization of retaliation, as is demonstrated by the aforementioned case of the judge whose decision, despite being substantively correct, was nevertheless perceived as 'winner's justice'. But the wars might have had their most detrimental impact on the concept of retaliation, with its considerable reliance on social powers for the administration of justice on the one hand and its supreme significance in normative regards on the other hand. The above discussion of criteria that would have to be fulfilled to realize retaliation satisfactorily has shown that the conditions created by the civil wars have turned retaliation from an option for relief and satisfaction into a risk and threat in its own right. This has consequences for the assessment of the model of retaliation itself. Quotes by elderly men on the practical realization of retaliation succinctly expressed this threat and its potential dimensions:

> Retaliation made brothers kill each other. This is why retaliation is bad – it is war, it makes war. You are from Germany; you also had war, you know.
>
> Retaliation is not a way out of trouble but a way in.
>
> You cannot trust retaliation, it is bad, it causes harm and loss.
>
> Look what the wars did. All these killings! Retaliation makes war and more war.

People's overall experience is that retaliation has not only been unable to resolve the past large-scale patterns of guilt and victimhood that are the result of decades of civil and regional wars; attempts to address smaller-scale interpersonal injustices via retaliation may also reactivate war-related group formations and thereby create the threat of potentially uncontrollable violence. The continuation of past injustice, of guilt and victimhood, the assessment of continuing systemic injustice and a rule of might rather than of law, and the constant fear of escalation all lead to a perceived continuation of past wars. In and even through disputing, it seems, the wars continue.

When trying to get even can only go wrong and where the protection of the limit entailed in reciprocity fails, as people's experiences suggest it often does, those who attempt retaliation find themselves attracting suspicion and reproach rather than support in their efforts to resolve disputes: 'They say they just want retaliation, but the only thing they really want is to create trouble.' In this light, it is not surprising that I did not find anyone who explained his own disputing strategies and actions as *enteqam* or *kina*, the terms most commonly used to refer to retaliation. What I encountered were assessments of the actions of others as retaliation. But contrary to the conceptual rhetoric about retaliation, these were not made in a respectful tone, but rather reproachfully, applied to situations and actions that were perceived as unfair or only became explainable through an 'old' and 'out-of-place' (*bijai*) *kina* of others. *Kina*, with its potentially collective character and open timeframe, thus served people as an explanatory tool to make sense of circumstances that were difficult to bear, highly unfair and in many ways hard to grasp. The relative lack of development aid and its unfair distribution, discriminatory employment schemes and administrative decisions, unjust pricing politics in the market and, finally, yet importantly, the wars themselves were all regularly explained as having their causes in various cycles of *kina* and failed attempts at retaliation.

This leads disputing parties into the dilemma of being emotionally, economically, socially and normatively bound to retaliation, all the while recognizing that, for the moment at least, it can provide neither satisfaction nor peace, and in fact can even pose a threat. I encountered several local responses to this dilemma, the most radical of which was to drop the concept of retaliation altogether and replace it with unconditional forgiveness. However, although this proposal was prominent, it does not solve the problem of how to meet the emotional needs and material interests that retaliation ought to serve. Options that attempted to address parts of the problem included delegating all of the responsibility for dispute management to state institutions, closing the timeframe for dispute management, and overcoming feelings of past guilt and victimhood by externalizing responsibility for past wars and projecting it onto external forces. As interesting as these compromises are as creative adaptations of a disputing model to extremely difficult circumstances, in practice they only seemed to work where both parties had an immediate interest in settlement. Apart from the fact that they could not address the need for emotional and material satisfaction, such agreements were, just like the overall circumstances, not expected to be reliable or trustworthy, at least not in the long run. What is left is hope, as weak as it may be, for some better future. In the interest of justice and peace, this is a hope for retaliation to meet conditions under which it can serve as a solution rather than a threat.

Friederike Stahlmann is a Ph.D. candidate at the Max Planck Institute for Social Anthropology, Halle, Germany. She is a member of the International Max Planck Research School on Retaliation, Mediation and Punishment and of the Centre for the Anthropological Studies of Central Asia (CASCA). She holds MA degrees in the study of religions, peace and conflict studies (Philipps University Marburg) and international and comparative legal studies (SOAS, University of London).

Notes

1. See, e.g., Steul (1981).
2. I thank the Max Planck Institute for Social Anthropology, Halle (Saale), Germany and the International Max Planck Research School on Retaliation, Mediation and Punishment for intellectual and financial support.
3. On the specific regional history, see, e.g., Ibrahimi (2009). For a general overview of recent Afghan history, see, *inter alia*, Maley (2002).
4. For an impression of this official etic perception, see the compilation of news releases about Bamyan on the homepage of the United Nations Assistance Mission in Afghanistan (UNAMA 2012). For a critical discussion, see Suhrke (2007).
5. For the temporal-sensitive understanding of agency, see Emirbayer and Mische (1998).
6. See also Turner (2007: 107) on the importance of this threat to maintaining order.
7. Smith and Manalan (2009: 45) note that this is a rare and unusual practice in Bamyan. I came across several cases from the past, but what makes it 'prominent' is how often it is used to explain the logic of retaliation. Both supportive arguments and the critique of its unintended consequences seem to be rather widespread (see, e.g., Schlee and Turner 2008: 52 f.).
8. There was not a single case of intentional homicide in Bamyan city – neither in court nor even in rumour – in the entire time I was there.

References

Benda-Beckmann, K. v. 2003. 'The Environment of Disputes', in W. van Binsbergen (ed.), *The Dynamics of Power and the Rule of Law: Essays on Africa and Beyond.* Münster: LIT, pp. 235–45.

———. 2008. 'Streit ohne Ende', in J. Eidson (ed.), *Das anthropologische Projekt.* Leipzig: Universitätsverlag, pp. 133–49.

Emirbayer, M., and A. Mische. 1998. 'What is Agency?', *American Journal of Sociology* 103(4): 962–1023.

Ibrahimi, N. 2009. 'At the Sources of Factionalism and Civil War in Hazarajat', *CSRC Working Paper Series* 2(41). Retrieved 1 September 2016 from http://www2.lse.ac.uk/internationalDevelopment/research/crisisStates/Publications/wpPhase2/wp41.aspx.

Maley, W. 2002. *The Afghanistan Wars.* New York: Palgrave.

Schlee, G., and B. Turner. 2008. 'Rache, Wiedergutmachung und Strafe: Ein Überblick', in G. Schlee and B. Turner (eds), *Vergeltung, eine interdisziplinäre Betrachtung der Rechtfertigung und Regulation von Gewalt.* Frankfurt: Campus, pp. 49–67.

Smith, D.J., and S. Manalan. 2009. *Community-Based Dispute Processes in Bamiyan Province.* Kabul: Afghanistan Research and Evaluation Unit. Retrieved 1 September 2016 from http://www.areu.org.af/Uploads/EditionPdfs/940E-Community-Based%20Dispute%20Resolution%20in%20Bamyian%20CS%202009.pdf.

Steul, W. 1981. *Paschtunwali. Ein Ehrenkodex und seine rechtliche Relevanz.* Wiesbaden: Franz Steiner.

Suhrke, A. 2007. 'Reconstruction as Modernisation: The "Post-conflict" Project in Afghanistan', *Third World Quarterly* 28(7): 1291–1308.

Turner, B. 2007. 'Imposing New Concepts of Order in Rural Morocco', in K. v. Benda-Beckmann and F. Pirie (eds), *Order and Disorder: Anthropological Perspectives*. Oxford: Berghahn Books, pp. 90–111.

Turner, B., and G. Schlee. 2008. 'Einleitung: Wirkungskontexte des Vergeltungsprinzips in der Konfliktregelung', in G. Schlee and B. Turner (eds), *Vergeltung, eine interdisziplinäre Betrachtung der Rechtfertigung und Regulation von Gewalt*. Frankfurt: Campus, pp. 7–47.

UNAMA. 2012. 'Advanced Search Results Bamyan'. Retrieved 23 March 2012 from http://unama.unmissions.org/Default.aspx?tabid=1778&Search=Bamyan.

Chapter 12

The International Criminal Court Reparation System

Punishment, Retaliation, Restoration

Pietro Sullo

Introduction

The perpetration of mass atrocities necessarily implies a distortion in the social order of the victimized community.[1] The research field known as 'transitional justice' has highlighted that an impressive variety of strategies has been elaborated in different ages and different human contexts in order to cope with the legacy of gross human rights violations (Kritz 1995; Teitel 2000). However, despite the efforts of researchers from diverse backgrounds, we still do not know much about how victims, perpetrators, bystanders and rescuers can live together in postviolence settings where mass atrocities have been committed (Fletcher and Weinstein 2002). The main aim of this chapter is to show how international criminal justice, which is becoming increasingly victim-oriented, complements punishment mechanisms with victim-oriented retaliatory measures such as reparations to redress mass atrocities. In this chapter, I use the term 'retaliation' to refer to the wide range of responses, including compensation and other forms of reparation, triggered by behaviours perceived as deviant or socially aberrant. The range of legitimate retaliatory reactions to violent behaviour has evolved in parallel with the emergence of the sovereign state's monopoly on violence. Outlawing revenge mechanisms, the Leviathan has imposed state-sanctioned jurisdictional responses to crime, limiting the scope for violent reaction to criminal offences to self-defence (Alessi 2002; Simma 2008).[2] As a consequence, the right to compensation has replaced the right to legitimate retaliatory violence. Similarly, in the international legal order, largely based on the logic of retaliation, reprisal and reciprocity (Simma 2008: 1–5), the use of armed force, originally admitted in various forms including wars of aggression under the Westphalian system, has been progressively restricted. The room for violent responses falling under the umbrella concept of retaliation is consequently limited to individual and collective self-defence in international relations. This development is mirrored by a body of provisions, including the 1928 Kellogg–Briand Pact,[3] the binding norm of *jus cogens* entrenched in Article 2.4 of the United Nations Charter, which prohibits the use of force to solve international disputes,[4] and the Rome Statute of the International Criminal Court (ICC), which, after the 2010 review conference held in Kampala, was amended to criminalize the offence of aggression.[5]

The emergence of individual criminal responsibility for international crimes was a particularly slow process. In Western societies, blanket amnesty has long been the rule in the aftermath of conflicts culminating in atrocities, as the telling example of Athens in the fifth century BC illustrates (Elster 2004: 3–23). In fact, the idea that a conflict had to end with a blanket amnesty remained unchallenged until the nineteenth century. As Nicole Loraux's famous studies on Athens's amnesties in the fifth century BC have pointed out, the obligation to forget the abuses regarding the dictatorship of the 'Thirty Tyrants' was enforced by sentencing to death those who violated the prohibition against recalling past violence (Loraux 1997; see also Elster 2004: 3–23). With the Nuremberg trials, a new and diametrically opposite principle was asserted – namely, the duty to prosecute international crimes. Important steps on this path were represented by the Treaty of Versailles signed after the First World War. Article 227 of the Treaty stated that:

> The Allied and Associated Powers publicly arraign William II of Hohenzollern, formerly German Emperor, for a supreme offence against international morality and the sanctity of treaties. A special tribunal will be constituted to try the accused, thereby assuring him the guarantees essential to the right of defence … The Allied and Associated Powers will address a request to the Government of the Netherlands for the surrender to them of the ex- Emperor in order that he may be put on trial.

Furthermore, pursuant to Article 228 of the Treaty: 'The German Government recognizes the right of the Allied and Associated Powers to bring before military tribunals persons accused of having committed acts in violation of the laws and customs of war.'

Nowadays, the duty to prosecute mass atrocities is well established under international law (Orentlicher 2007), despite several instances of general amnesties adopted by regimes that wanted to grant themselves immunity (Huyse 2003). In the case of international crimes as well, the criminal punishment remains the main instrument for coping with instances of radical evil. While Hannah Arendt asserted that radical evil 'exploded the limits of the law', international lawmakers have nevertheless tried to subject it to legal precepts.

One of the main assumptions underpinning the establishment of international criminal law is that genocide, crimes against humanity and war crimes have a peculiar nature and differ from ordinary crimes, as they embody greater potential to destroy the social order. Some offences are labelled 'crimes against humanity' because they not only target the direct victims, but all of humankind. A further distinguishing characteristic is the fact that while common crime is usually the result of deviant behaviour, international crimes are generally the consequence of collective conduct driven by conformity with accepted mass behaviour (see Drumbl 2007: 3–14). Finally, mass atrocities are usually marked by a great distance, if not a total lack of relationship, between the victim and the perpetrator, a relationship that restorative approaches to justice try to re-establish (Groenhuijsen and Pemberton 2011). Nonetheless, because they are influenced by a pattern deeply rooted in the Western legal tradition, the adjudication mechanisms for both ordinary and international crimes share several features, including reliance on the same penalties, mainly incarceration. Moreover, both are grounded in the concept of individual criminal responsibility, regardless of the collective nature of the conduct leading to the commission of international crimes (Drumbl 2007).

Mass atrocities, despite their acknowledged gravity, have gone unpunished more often than ordinary crimes. This deeply frustrates the efforts carried out by national and international actors to set up mechanisms aimed at preventing, repressing and punishing international crimes. To address this phenomenon, in recent years scholars have tried to further develop a criminology, penology and victimology of mass atrocities.

This chapter focuses on the right to reparation in international law, with a particular emphasis on the reparation scheme provided for by the founding legal instruments of the International Criminal Court. It shows how such a reparation scheme marks a shift towards a restorative approach, where reparations are victim-oriented measures and not a form of punishment for the perpetrators, as they had been according to the statutes of the two United Nations (UN) ad hoc tribunals for the former Yugoslavia and for Rwanda. When reparation orders are issued by the ICC, two formally equal subjects (whose relationship is, however, normally marked by a strong imbalance in power), namely the victim and the perpetrator of an international crime, become the protagonists in a retaliatory action mediated through a body endowed with international legal personality. The consequences that such an action can have on the victim–perpetrator relationship and for the social order of the beneficiaries' communities are at the moment unpredictable for two reasons: first, because the ICC has delivered only two reparation decisions (in the *Lubanga* case), which have not yet been implemented (Sullo 2014 and 2017);[6] and, second, because the previous practice of international and hybrid tribunals in the realm of reparation is extremely poor. Hence, the unknown risks connected with the implementation of reparation measures must be duly taken into account.

The ICC Reparation Model: Key Features and Challenges

Scholars and practitioners are well aware that even though consolidated in international law, the right to reparation is rarely implemented (De Greiff, 2014). Reparations for gross human rights violations are an exception in both national and international criminal justice systems (Sarkin 2005). Teo van Boven has stressed that:

> Large categories of victims of gross violations of human rights, as a result of the actual contents of national laws or because of the manner in which these laws are applied, fail to receive the reparation which is due to them. Limitations in time, including the application of statutory limitations; restrictions in the definition of the scope and nature of the violations; the operation of amnesty laws; the restrictive attitude of courts; the incapability of certain groups of victims to present and to pursue their claims; lack of economic and financial resources: the consequence of all these factors, individually and jointly, is that the principle of equality of rights and due reparation of all victims are not implemented.[7]

The notion of reparation has significantly evolved in recent decades under international law. The principle that states have to provide reparations to other states to redress wrongful acts they have committed is undisputed under international law. It is confirmed by the 2001 International Law Commission Draft Articles on Responsibility of States for Internationally Wrongful Acts (Articles 31 and 34–37; see Sullo and Wyatt 2014). The primary function of reparations in international law is the re-establishment of the situation that would have existed if an international wrongful act had not been committed. The forms that such reparations may take are various. Initially framed as a duty and conflict resolution mechanism between sovereign and equal subjects of international law, namely states, reparations have gradually become an instrument to redress deviant behaviour by a state against its citizens. The European and the inter-American human rights courts have developed a sophisticated jurisprudence on this matter. Moreover, through the legal mechanisms establishing the ICC, the principle that perpetrators of international crimes have to compensate and, possibly, repair the harm inflicted on victims is gradually being consolidated. Particularly within the discourse surrounding transitional justice, reparations are seen as a promising victim-redress mechanism targeting a wide gamut of needs of victims in conflict and post-conflict contexts. There is a variety of legal sources in which the right to reparation can be anchored, including binding international law and soft law. Similarly, the claim to reparation can be the result of a tribunal decision, of national legislation or decree, or of the recommendations of a truth commission. Within this textured framework, the unique features of the ICC reparation system distinguish it from its precursors. The aim of this chapter is to shed light on both the challenges faced by the ICC and the new opportunities offered by the Rome Statute in the field of reparations as an emerging modality of retaliation. Procedural aspects, although relevant, fall outside the scope of this chapter.

The goals of international criminal law are manifold: retribution, deterrence, prevention, expressivism (Drumbl 2005: 592–93), contribution to social peace and, as some argue, reconciliation.[8] Given the collective nature of most international crimes, usually committed by groups or by state actors, and the consequent collective nature of the corresponding patterns of victimization, some legal scholars argue that: 'Individualizing victims would push aside the predominantly collective character of the crime and would mean a selection of individual victims from the collective of victims that is necessarily arbitrary' (Dwertmann 2010: 33). However, other scholars argue that individual victims' interests fall within the protection shield provided by international criminal law (Dwertmann 2010; see also Bassiouni 1988: 181, 186; Triffterer 1999). The Rome Statute constitutes a watershed in this regard, granting victims of crimes falling within the jurisdiction of the ICC the right to participation, protection and reparation. My argument is in line with Ewa Dwertmann's assertion that international criminal law is concerned with both the interests of individuals and of humanity as a collective (Dwertmann 2010: 36).The centrality of the reparation system designed through the Rome Statute has already been emphasized by the jurisprudence of the ICC. In *The Prosecutor v. Thomas Lubanga Dyilo*, Pre-Trial Chamber I has in fact affirmed that 'the reparation scheme provided for in the Statute is not only one of its unique features. It is also a key feature. In the Chamber's opinion, the success of the Court is, to some extent, linked to the success of its reparation system'.

Even if not fully corroborated by practice, the ICC reparation mechanism has generated enthusiasm among scholars and human rights activists. The dual objective pursued by the ICC, namely punishing perpetrators and repairing, to the possible extent, the harm inflicted on victims, mirrors the slow evolution of international justice adopting a more reparative and victim-centred model. As a consequence, the ICC has also spawned new studies concerning the criminology and penology of mass atrocities. The reparation system provided for in the Rome Statute marks a shift from the approach adopted by the International Criminal Tribunal for Rwanda (ICTR) and its sibling, the International Criminal Tribunal for the Former Yugoslavia (ICTY), both of which limited redress opportunities to restitution. While reparations under the statute of the ICTR were included in the part devoted to punishment, in the Rome Statute they are listed under Part VI, 'The trial', indicating that the rationale underlying reparative measures is not punitive and that the Anglo-Saxon idea of punitive damages cannot be applied to the ICC reparation system. Moreover, it is interesting that the reparation mechanisms of the ICC are to some extent firmly in the victims' hands. The Rules of

Procedure and Evidence of the Court in fact allow victims to request that the judges not make a reparation order.[9]

The main rules on reparation provided for in the Rome Statute are Articles 75 and 79. Article 75 endows the Court with the power to award reparations – which include, but are not limited to, restitution, compensation and rehabilitation – even where the victim has not filed an application. Article 79 establishes the Trust Fund for Victims (TFV), which is associated with the ICC. The creation of the TFV associated with a court endowed with reparation powers has great potential. At the same time however, it raises practical and theoretical challenges that need to be addressed in order to allow the TFV to smoothly complement the work of the ICC. Moreover, challenges faced by the ICC in the realm of reparations are not confined to its cooperation with the TFV. As a global criminal tribunal, the ICC will focus only on a handful of major cases. Consequently, large numbers of victims of international crimes will be out of the reach of its reparations model. This raises the question of the extent to which (if at all) the complementarity principle also applies to the reparation system of the ICC. This issue is paralleled by the strain inherent in the effort to provide reparations in the context of international criminal law. In this realm, an undeniable tension exists between the principle of individual penal responsibility and the collective nature of the conduct leading to the commission of international crimes.[10] The state, as a collective, is in fact often responsible for these offences. The ICC, however, is not endowed with the power to recognize the responsibility of states and to make reparation orders against them. Finally, despite its limited scope, the ICC will be tasked with providing reparations to a multitude of victims, probably putting to the test the Court's capabilities and resources.

From Retribution to Restoration

Nowadays, scholars, governments, non-governmental organizations (NGOs) and international institutions are increasingly interested in investigating the role of reparations programmes in enforcing the rule of law, respect for human rights and reconciliation processes in postviolence settings where transitional justice mechanisms are adopted (de Greiff 2008: 5–13). Reparations efforts, as a key element of comprehensive transitional justice strategies mirroring contemporary developments of international law,[11] have become a crucial instrument for addressing human rights abuses and represent a textured and promising mechanism to deal with the past. A variety of measures have been conceived in response to the chilling volume of atrocities and violations of fundamental rights that occur during conflicts and under authoritarian regimes. They encompass criminal prosecution, truth-telling mechanisms, institutional reforms, vetting strategies, local justice mechanisms and reconciliation efforts. A clear understanding of the need to link different justice initiatives involving the victims themselves in designing holistic strategies to redress past abuses has emerged, as exemplified by former UN Secretary-General Kofi Annan's 2004 report on the rule of law and transitional justice in conflict and post-conflict societies. Annan pointed out that: 'Where transitional justice is required, strategies must be holistic, incorporating integrated attention to individual prosecutions, reparations, truth-seeking, institutional reform, vetting and dismissals, or an appropriately conceived combination thereof.' Within this comprehensive policy, we must be aware of the particular role that reparations can play. As Pablo de Greiff, a leading authority in this field, has highlighted: 'While prosecutions and to some extent vetting are, in the end, a struggle against perpetrators, and truth-seeking and institutional reform have as their immediate constituency society as a whole, reparations are explicitly and primarily carried out on behalf of victims. Hence, in terms of potential direct impact on victims at least, they occupy a special place among redress measures' (de Greiff 2008: 2–3). Retaliatory nonpunitive measures such as reparations addressing deviant behaviour are not a novelty of our time. In fact, it is the retributive paradigm and the focus on the perpetrator that are relatively new in the realm of criminal justice. Ancient societies acknowledged reparations to victims of a criminal offence as a central feature of the justice mechanism. In precolonial African communities, devices such as the Rwandan *gacaca*[12] or the Ugandan *Mato-Oput* awarded compensation to the victims of crimes as an essential step towards the re-establishment of harmony within the community. The mechanisms leading to the dispute settlement were firmly in the hands of the injured party. In fact, 'at the origin of criminal law victims were essential for the initiation of criminal prosecutions' (Zappalà 2005). The Anglo-Saxon justice system also recognized the role of some form of reparation in criminal justice (McCarthy 2009: 252). The emergence of the state's monopoly on the administration of justice marked a shift from a harmony-oriented approach to a more punishment-centred focus.[13] The legitimacy of private revenge as a retaliatory action in response to crime has been called into question and restricted to specific privileged categories by the modern state (Alessi 2002). When the latter fully emerges as the sole subject of sovereignty *superiorem non recognoscens*, it also becomes the only actor endowed with the right to punish and pardon (Alessi 2002). This development, culminating in the age of codifications in the eighteenth and nineteenth centuries, had a significant impact on the role of victims in the criminal trial. In modern Westernized criminal justice systems, the victim and perpetrator are, to some extent, separated, and the trial takes place to satisfy the interests of the society as a collective rather than the injured party (McCarthy 2009: 252). In the retaliatory logic that has replaced the individual violent response through a state-sanctioned reaction, the role of the victim has often been marginalized. While in the civil law tradition a role for victims in criminal proceedings survived thanks to the *partie civile* being allowed to ask for compensation within the proceedings, in common law systems the criminal trial and the civil litigation – the only locus where victims are entitled to claim reparations – were clearly separated. However, in the light of reparative justice theory, a reversal has been observed starting in the 1960s, when a more restorative approach to justice emerged that paid increasing attention to the role of victims in international proceedings. Reparative theory argues that:

> An exclusively adversarial trial leading to the custodial punishment of a perpetrator is seen as a wholly inadequate response to this harm. It is argued that modern legal systems industrialize the process of criminal justice, classifying and packaging conduct into generalizable categories that enable the defendant to be expediently processed. This tendency, it is contended, introduces an unhelpful degree of abstraction and depersonalizes the justice process by distancing the parties to the conflict from one another. (McCarthy 2009: 352)

According to Antoine Garapon what distinguishes retributive justice from restorative justice is in the fact that, while the former, being centred on the punishment of the offender, is past-oriented, the latter, aimed at the reconnection of the link between victim and perpetrator, is future-oriented (Garapon 2005). The UN Economic and Social Council's Basic Principles on the Use of Restorative Justice Programmes in Criminal Matters (2000) stress that restorative and retributive approaches to justice are not in a mutually exclusive relationship. On the contrary, restorative programmes can complement retributive justice.[14] This means that while punishment remains one of the cornerstones of the criminal justice system, a restorative approach to criminal justice provides the victim, the perpetrator and the community where the crime took place with new opportunities. This happens on a voluntary basis, as the agreement of the interested parties is normally a *condicio sine qua non* for participation in restorative programmes. The programmes themselves are marked by significant differences as to their level of formality, their relationship with the criminal justice system, the involvement of legal counsels, criminal justice officers, victims, state agencies and their focus on the rehabilitation of the offender (Sullo 2016). Common features of these programmes are the involvement of the victim, the perpetrator and the affected community, the possibility to ask questions, provide answers, express emotions about the offence, make and receive reparations and apologies, restore the relationship between victim and offender, and reach closure with regard to the dispute (Sullo 2016). The increasing awareness of the culturally determined perspectives of Western criminal justice systems, coupled with the challenges posed by the purely retributive approach in contexts marked by large-scale violence, has pushed lawyers and researchers from other fields to seek new complementary dimensions of justice. Examples of a restorative approach to justice are victim–offender mediation, family group conferencing, victim–offender reconciliation programmes and peace circles. The European Council Framework decision in March 2001 established that European Union countries had to introduce restorative justice measures by 2006. Consequently, some European countries have already adopted restorative measures, for instance, by introducing mediation officers in national prisons.[15] In parallel, restorative, mediation- and reconciliation-oriented aspects of traditional justice systems rooted in customary law in Africa, Asia and South America remain very much in the spotlight nowadays (Huyse 2008). The construction of a victim-friendly justice model culminated in the adoption in 1985 of the UN Declaration of Basic Principles of Justice for Victims of Crime and Abuse of Power.[16] Because this document is referred to by the drafters of the Rome Statute, it has to be duly taken into account when interpreting the ICC founding legal instrument. The 1985 Declaration refers to victims of crime under national legislation, stressing their need for state restitution, compensation and assistance. The scope of the definition of victim in such a context is particularly interesting for our purposes:

1. 'Victims' means persons who, individually or collectively, have suffered harm, including physical or mental injury, emotional suffering, economic loss or substantial impairment of their fundamental rights, through acts or omissions that are in violation of criminal laws operative within Member States, including those laws proscribing criminal abuse of power.
2. A person may be considered a victim, under this Declaration, regardless of whether the perpetrator is identified, apprehended, prosecuted or convicted and regardless of the familial relationship between the perpetrator and the victim. The term 'victim' also includes, where appropriate, the immediate family or dependants of the direct victim and persons who have suffered harm in intervening to assist victims in distress or to prevent victimization.

This definition has strongly influenced the definition of 'victim' in the legal instruments of the ICC. The latter, with its aforementioned paradigm shift towards restorative models, provides victims with significant participatory (Smith Cody, Stover, Balthazard and Koenig 2015; Pena and Carayon 2013) rights as well as with the right to claim adequate redress measures.

The ICC Reparation System

The ICC reparation scheme is legally unique. The ICC has jurisdiction to award different forms of reparation to victims pursuant to Article 75(2) of the Rome Statute, thereby addressing a lacuna in the ICTR and ICTY Statutes.[17] The opportunities for victims to participate as such in proceedings before the ICTY and the ICTR were extremely limited.[18] Article 24(3) of the ICTY Statute and Article 23(3) of the ICTR Statute limit themselves to the possibility of providing property restitution to the victims of the offences falling within their jurisdictions.[19] A restitution order, however, has not been delivered by either of the two ad hoc tribunals. Common Rule 34 of the ICTY and ICTR Rules of Procedure and Evidence envisages the possibility of providing the victims with counselling and support 'in particular in cases of rape and sexual assault'. According to Anne-Marie de Brouwer (2005: 283):

> this approach is based on the idea that the Tribunals first and foremost were established to punish alleged perpetrators of serious violations of international humanitarian law and that the rights of the accused, to a fair and expeditious trial, need to be safeguarded in this process.

De Brouwer (2005: 285) furthermore notes that the prosecutor would already be protecting the interests of the international community, and therefore also those of the victims, when prosecuting the alleged perpetrators.

The concept of 'victim' adopted under the legal instruments of the ICC is crucial in order to clarify who is entitled to claim reparation awards. Under Rule 85 of the ICC Rules of Procedure and Evidence:

> (a) 'Victims' means natural persons who have suffered harm as a result of the commission of any crime within the jurisdiction of the Court;
> (b) Victims may include organisations or institutions that have sustained direct harm to any of their property, which is dedicated to religion, art, or science or charitable purposes, and to their historic monuments, hospitals and other places and objects for humanitarian purposes.

The ICC's definition of victim encompasses both natural and legal persons, but, contrary to the 2005 UN Basic Principles, it does not expressly acknowledge collective victimization (REDRESS 2011: 15). Indirect victims such as immediate family members or dependants of the direct victim, as well as those who tried to prevent the victimization, may also be granted victim status before the ICC. The ICC has established that 'the harm suffered by indirect victims must arise out of the harm suffered by direct victims, brought about by the commission of the crimes charged'.[20] This implies that persons who have suffered harm as a result of the conduct of the direct victims (a relevant instance for the ICC would be that of forcibly conscripted child soldiers) are not categorized as indirect victims. This decision has attracted a good deal of criticism (Spiga 2010; Sullo 2014). The harm suffered by natural persons must be personal harm, that is, the applicant must have personally suffered the harm.[21] Harm has been interpreted to include physical or mental injury, emotional suffering, economic loss or substantial impairment of fundamental rights.[22]

The reparation regime of the ICC laid down in Articles 75 and 79 of the Rome Statute is further elaborated in rules 94–99 of the Rules of Procedure and Evidence. The ICC can pass an order awarding reparations on the basis of the conviction of the accused. Moreover, the ICC legal instruments provide for a broad system of reparation that allows reparative measures to be claimed at any stage in the trial, including the investigation, pretrial and trial stages. An interpretation of the term 'reparation' that is in line with the van Boven/Bassiouni principles and with the UN's Basic Principles of Justice for Victims of Crime and Abuse of Power (1985) is consistent with the drafting history of the Rome Statute. The Rome Statute and the Rules of Procedure and Evidence however, have left unaddressed several substantial and procedural issues regarding the ICC reparation pattern. Pursuant to Article 75(1) of the Rome Statute, for instance: 'The Court shall establish principles relating to reparations to, or in respect of, victims, including restitution, compensation and rehabilitation.'[23] Article 21 of the Rome Statute assists in addressing the gaps in the Court's Statute by clarifying what are the normative provisions to be applied by the ICC in its decisions. According to Article 21(1), the Court shall apply:

> (a) in the first place, this Statute, Elements of Crimes and its Rules of Procedure and Evidence; (b) in the second place, where appropriate, applicable treaties and the principles and rules of international law, including the established principles of the international law of armed conflict; failing that, general principles of law derived by the Court from national laws of legal systems of the world including, as appropriate, the national laws of States that would normally exercise jurisdiction over the crime, provided that those principles are not inconsistent with this Statute and with international law and internationally recognized norms and standards. The Court may apply principles and rules of law as interpreted in its previous decisions. The application and interpretation of law pursuant to this article must be consistent with internationally recognized human rights, and be without any adverse distinction founded on grounds such as gender as defined in article 7, paragraph 3, age, race, colour, language, religion or belief, political or other opinion, national, ethnic or social origin, wealth, birth or other status.

Because the ICC is a treaty-based body, Articles 31 and 32 of the Vienna Convention on the Law of Treaties have to be applied when dealing with interpretative issues. Accordingly, its drafting history is a 'supplementary means of interpretation' of the Rome Statute. The first decisions of the ICC have confirmed that both the application and interpretation of law 'must be consistent with internationally recognized human rights' (Dwertmann 2010: 6–7).

Even though the Rome Statute affirms that the 'Court shall establish principles relating to reparations to, or in respect of, victims, including restitution, compensation and rehabilitation', several aspects surrounding the legal nature and the objectives of the principles, as well as the organ competent to establish them, are not clarified in detail. However, the draft history and the location of Article 75 in the Rome Statue seem to suggest that the competent organs are the Trial Chambers or the Chambers in general (Dwertmann 2010: 46–47). Article 75 also leaves unresolved the issue of whether the principles on reparation should apply as general principles or only on a case-by-case basis through the jurisprudential activity of the ICC. Both scenarios offer advantages and challenges. Establishing general and abstract principles would provide the Chambers with guidance and would encourage consistency in decisions. On the other hand, it is very difficult to foresee in advance in abstract terms all the possible cases and circumstances where reparations are due. In my opinion, the wording of Article 75 suggests that the principles should be of an abstract nature and that the ICC should orient its jurisprudence on reparation on the basis of these principles. The practice of the ICC, however, seems to suggest that it does not share this interpretation, as was confirmed by President Sang-Hyun Song's statement in May 2011.[24] The Assembly of States Parties (ASP) expressed its criticism of the ICC's approach during its Tenth Session, where it requested the Court 'to ensure that Court-wide coherent principles relating to reparations shall be established in accordance with article 75, paragraph 1, based on which the Court may issue individual orders for reparations'.[25]

The ICC finally shed light on the issues surrounding reparation principles on 7 August 2012. On this date, Trial Chamber I of the ICC issued the 'Decision Establishing the Principles and Procedures to be Applied to Reparations' with regard to the situation in the Democratic Republic of Congo (DRC) in the case of *The Prosecutor v. Thomas Lubanga Dyilo* (case no. ICC-01/04-01/06). In this decision, the Chamber clearly stressed that the validity of the principles it has established and of the suggested approach to the implementation of reparations was limited to the *Lubanga* case, and highlighted both general and case-relevant purposes of reparations. The former are obliging 'those responsible for serious crimes to repair the harm they caused to the victims and enable the Chamber to ensure that offenders account for their acts' (*Lubanga,* Decision on Reparations, paras. 64–65). Reparative objectives pertaining to the *Lubanga* case are to 'relieve the suffering caused by these offences; afford justice to the victims by alleviating the consequences of the wrongful acts; deter future violations; and contribute to the effective reintegration of former child soldiers'. Moreover, in the opinion of Trial Chamber I: 'Reparations can assist in promoting reconciliation between the convicted person, the victims of the crimes and the affected communities (without making Mr. Lubanga's participation in this process mandatory).' Further clarification by the ICC Trial Chambers of the very meaning of the term 'reconciliation' in this and similar contexts would be very useful.[26] To the best of my knowledge, the ICC has not shed light on either the meaning of the term or on how a reconciliation process should be conducted between individuals convicted by the ICC and their victims. As a result, the role that reparative measures might play in the dynamics of reconciliation between victims and perpetrators of international crimes remains partially unclear. Trial Chamber I has decided not to limit reparations to the victims who have either participated in the *Lubanga* case or applied for reparations. The Chamber has also stressed that the ICC has to ensure that reparations are awarded on a nondiscriminatory and gender-sensitive basis, prioritizing the needs of the most vulnerable victims. The Trial Chamber emphasizes that the principle of the best interests of the child entrenched in the Convention on the Rights of the Child has to guide the reparation decisions of the ICC. Consequently, the Chamber has established that reparation proceedings, and reparation orders and programmes in favour of child soldiers, should guarantee the development of the victims' personalities, talents and abilities to the fullest possible extent and, more broadly, should ensure the development of respect for human rights and fundamental freedoms. For each child, the measures should aim at developing respect for their parents, cultural identity and language. Former child soldiers should be helped to live responsibly in a free society, recognizing the need for a spirit of understanding, peace and tolerance, showing respect for equality between the sexes and valuing friendship between all peoples and groups.[27]As to the modalities of reparations, the ICC has clarified that the list included in Article 75 of the Rome Statute is not exhaustive. The conviction of the accused individual and the sentence of the ICC are also to be considered forms of reparation for the victims.[28] Moreover, the ICC is allowed:

> to institute other forms of reparation, such as establishing or assisting campaigns that are designed to improve the position of victims; by issuing certificates that acknowledge the harm particular individuals experienced; setting up outreach and promotional programmes that inform victims as to the outcome of the trial; and educational campaigns that aim at reducing the stigmatisation and marginalisation of the victims of the present crimes. These steps can contribute to society's awareness of the crimes committed by Mr Lubanga and the need to foster improved attitudes towards events of this kind, and ensure that children play an active role within their communities.[29]

It is important to highlight that because he is indigent, however, Mr. Luabanga was not the recipient of a reparation order issued by Trial Chamber I.

Trial Chamber I also decided that reparation awards appropriate for the victims of sexual and gender-based violence should be delivered, stretching the reparations award beyond the charge brought against Mr. Lubanga.

Finally, Trial Chamber I has stressed that reparations should mirror customary practices of the local culture.[30] This was confirmed in the Appeals Chamber (AC) judgment on the appeals against the Decision Establishing the Principles and Procedures to be applied to reparations. Addressing a lacuna in the Rome Statute, which does not clarify which organ of the ICC is tasked with monitoring the reparation process, Trial Chamber I has affirmed that this responsibility falls within the functions of the judiciary.[31] This conclusion is based on Article 64(2) and (3)(a) of the Rome Statute. Trial Chamber I has also ruled that reparations in the *Lubanga* case have to be dealt with mainly by the TFV, which has to determine the most suitable forms of reparations with the help of a group of experts in the fields of child soldiers, violence against minors and gender issues appointed by the TFV itself. The TFV is to be 'monitored and overseen by a differently composed Chamber'.[32] The Appeals Chamber's judgment of 3 March 2015 on reparation confirmed the award of redress measures exclusively on a collective basis. The high number of victims was a crucial factor influencing the adoption of reparations on a collective rather than an individual basis. The AC, however, amended the decision on reparation adopted by TC I stressing that despite his condition of indigence Mr. Lubanga was due to contribute to reparations awarded to his victims. Consistently with this assumption, the reparation order by the AC has directly targeted Mr. Lubanga. According to Stahn, 'This reading of Article 75 is a clear victory for victims who sought express judicial acknowledgement of accountability, independently of the perpetrator's indigence. It strengthens the expressivist dimensions of ICC reparations which are of key importance, in light of the limited resources of the Trust Fund' (Stahn 2015). Crucial to define the extent and modalities of the retaliatory logic underlying the ICC mandate was also the decision by the AC regarding the reparation of sexual violence in Ituri. Because Mr. Lubanga was not convicted for such a crime, the AC, unlike TC I, decided that no reparative measures were due for sexual crimes. In other words, and against the opinion expressed at previous stages also by the TFV, the AC established that a reparation order is limited by the criminal charge. The AC also required the TFV to draft a plan for collective reparations to be submitted by 3 September 2015. The plan elaborated by the TFV was considered inadequate by Trial Chamber II, which is monitoring the implementation of the reparations in the *Lubanga* case. Trial Chamber II required the TFV a new plan by the end of 2016. The plan was finally approved only on 21 October 2016. Four years after the conviction of Mr. Lubanga the victims of his crimes have not yet received any form of reparation.

The basic legal instruments of the ICC also refrain from shedding light on the legal nature of the reparation principles. Consequently, it has to be established whether they are binding and, if so, upon whom, and whether they have external or internal relevance only. Moreover, the applicability of the complementarity principle to the reparation mandate of the ICC is also disputed.[33] The Rome Statute does not spell out what such a principle means in respect of reparations.[34] Finally, it is crucial to stress that the *travaux préparatoires* of the Rome Statute require interpreting the content and scope of reparations in line with the 1985 Victims Declaration and the 2005 Basic Principles (Dwertmann 2010: 50–51). If we assume that the reparation principles will have external relevance, what actors are they going to target? Answering this question is crucial in order to understand what actors are involved in the retaliatory dynamic between victim and offender after the perpetration of international crimes. Despite the fact that a crime within the jurisdiction of the ICC can imply both individual criminal responsibility and state responsibility, the Court cannot make reparation orders against states. Efforts in this direction were not successful at the Rome Conference where the ICC Statute was adopted.[35] In any case, active cooperation from states will be crucial in ensuring that the ICC can fulfil its reparation-related mandate properly. Consequently, despite the fact that it has jurisdiction only over natural persons,[36] the question arises whether the ICC can target states through its reparations principles (Dwertmann 2010: 52–53). Reading Article 25(4)[37] of the Rome Statute in conjunction with Article 75(6)[38] and in the light of the principle of complementarity, it seems that there would be sufficient room for the ICC to stress states' responsibility to provide reparations within the framework of the reparations principles.[39] There is, however, no consensus on this point among legal scholars. On the one hand, it seems clear that the ICC cannot establish principles concerning reparations binding on states. On the other hand, this does not expressly preclude the ICC from addressing states with non-binding recommendations on reparations. The most auspicious approach towards reparations for the ICC might be engaging states in a dialogue over reparations, as states might be interested in complementing the Court's tasks in this regard (Dwertmann 2010: 54–56). As mass atrocities are usually committed with the consent of states, it seems reasonable to hold them accountable for their deeds and involve them in the victim–perpetrator dynamics.

The Trust Fund for Victims (TFV)

As mentioned earlier, the TFV was set up in 2002 by the Assembly of States Parties to the Rome Statute. It is an autonomous body supervised by a Board of Directors and is tasked with complementing the reparation mandate of the ICC. Article 75 of the ICC Statute states that: 'Where appropriate, the Court may order that the award for reparations be made through the Trust Fund provided for in article 79.' According to Article 79 of the Rome Statute, the TFV is established:

> for the benefit of victims of crimes within the jurisdiction of the Court, and of the families of such victims. The Court may order money and other property collected through fines or forfeiture to be transferred, by order of the Court, to the Trust Fund. The Trust Fund shall be managed according to criteria to be determined by the Assembly of States Parties.

The Rules of Procedure and Evidence also include important details concerning the *modus operandi* of the TFV. In particular, rule 98 establishes that:

> The Court may order that an award for reparations against a convicted person be deposited with the Trust Fund where at the time of making the order it is impossible or impracticable to make individual awards directly to each victim. The award for reparations thus deposited in the Trust Fund shall be separated from other resources of the Trust Fund and shall be forwarded to each victim as soon as possible. The Court may order that an award for reparations against a convicted person be made through the Trust Fund where the number of the victims and the scope, forms and modalities of reparations makes a collective award more appropriate. Following consultations with interested States and the Trust Fund, the Court may order that an award for reparations be made through the Trust Fund to an intergovernmental, international or national organization approved by the Trust Fund. Other resources of the Trust Fund may be used for the benefit of victims subject to the provisions of article 79.

The ICC is entitled to award both individual and collective reparations and the role of the TFV concerning group reparations seems to be particularly relevant. On the basis of the aforementioned legal instruments, it is possible to identify two key tasks of the TFV: first, to implement the ICC reparation award; and, second, to conduct assistance activities targeting the communities affected by the crimes (rule 98 of the Rules of Procedure and Evidence). The wording of Article 75(2) does not clarify what exactly is meant by the statement in rule 98.3 of the Rules of Procedure and Evidence, which states that: 'The Court may order that the award for reparations … be made through the Trust Fund.' In particular, it is not clear whether the ICC, when ordering reparations measures, can use the 'other resources' of the TFV mentioned in rule 98, namely the voluntary contributions of states. Several legal scholars interpret this in the negative, citing the lack of provisions regulating such a power of the Court in respect of the TFV in the ICC legal instruments.[40] However, no legal instruments of the ICC prevent the TFV from deciding to complement the reparations awarded by the Court using its own resources. Article 56 of the TFV regulations is clear in this regard:

> The Board of Directors shall determine whether to complement the resources collected through awards for reparations with 'other resources of the Trust Fund' and shall advise the Court accordingly. Without prejudice to its activities under paragraph 50, sub-paragraph (a), the Board of Directors shall make all reasonable endeavours to manage the Fund taking into consideration the need to provide adequate resources to complement payments for awards under rule 98, sub-rules 3 and 4 of the Rules of Procedure and Evidence and taking particular account of ongoing legal proceedings that may give rise to such awards.

Pre-Trial Chamber I, however, has not followed this scholarship, stressing in the *Lubanga* case that 'the responsibility of the Trust Fund is first and foremost to ensure that sufficient funds are available in the eventuality of a Court reparation order pursuant to Article 75 of the Statute'.[41] This approach was endorsed by Trial Chamber I in its Decision establishing the principles and procedures to be applied to reparations with regard to the situation in the Democratic Republic of Congo. Trial Chamber I has established that: 'In circumstances when the Court orders reparations against an indigent convicted person, the Court may draw upon "other resources" that the TFV has made reasonable efforts to set aside.'[42] This view was not shared by the Appeals Chamber, which in the judgement on appeal against the reparation decision of the Trial Chamber I has recognized the TFV's discretion as to whether or not to use its 'other resources' to finance reparation.[43]

The TFV provides humanitarian assistance to individuals and communities irrespective of any finding of individual criminal responsibility of a defendant. Pursuant to rule 50, it has to ask for the permission of the Chambers to start activities connected with its second mandate. It seems clear that the harms to be redressed by the TFV are physical, psychological or material. The TFV has conducted recovery activities targeting victims in Uganda and the Democratic Republic of Congo, and plans to start new projects in the Central African Republic. The intervention of the TFV is based on the so-called livelihood assessments, which are 'necessary for identifying the needs of victims and designing the subsequent and appropriate interventions to address the impact of victimization' (McCarthy 2009: 268).

Conclusion

Concepts such as reciprocity, retaliation and reprisal have played a major role in the creation, observance and sanction of international law (Simma 2008: 1–5). However, the mere logic of reciprocity, including the possibility of violent retaliation against the perpetrator of mass atrocities, is not contemplated under current international criminal law.

Reparations under the ICC system are not subjected to the logic of punishment, but rather to that of restorative retaliation. This allows the ICC to intervene through unprecedented modalities in the victim–offender relationship. The victim-oriented mandate of the ICC is comprehensive and innovative. Victims, when their interests are affected, can participate in ICC proceedings in order to protect their physical and psychological wellbeing as well as their dignity and privacy. Pursuant to the Rome Statute, victims can present their views and concerns at appropriate stages of the proceedings. Consequently, victims can participate in criminal proceedings with a view to claiming damages (REDRESS 2011: 1). Within its unique legal framework, the ICC enjoys considerable latitude in shaping the reparation principles it is mandated to establish. International human rights law provides the ICC with guidance when it faces this daunting challenge. Victims of the crimes adjudicated by the ICC however have so far not received any reparation award. In particular child soldiers victimized by Lubanga are waiting for reparations after his conviction.

Reparations for vulnerable groups in particular will require special attention from the ICC. Given the cases currently before the ICC, gender-sensitive and child-focused measures are critical to ensuring that the reparation awards will meet the real needs of the most vulnerable victims. Taking into account the scope and extent of any damage, loss or injury, the ICC may award reparations on an individualized basis or, where it deems it appropriate, on a collective basis, or both. Clarifying the meaning and role of the 'complementarity' principle in respect of reparations is important if the ICC is to fulfil its reparation-related mandate. In particular, it would be useful to clarify the role of states parties to the Rome Statute in awarding reparation measures in order to understand to what extent they can contribute to retaliatory dynamics, which might have a considerable impact on the victim–perpetrator relationship. It also remains to be seen whether and how the ICC will be able to face a potentially very large number of applications for reparations and whether it will be able to abide by the principle of 'do no harm' when performing such a task. Previous experience in the realm of redress measures adopted in conflict and postconflict settings shows that the impact of reparations on the social order of the targeted communities can be divisive if these measures are not consistently adopted and implemented according to a nondiscriminatory rationale. Wisely, Trial Chamber I in the *Lubanga* case has stressed that reparations should mirror local customary practices (§ 82). The reparation decision delivered in the *Lubanga* case by the ICC also includes an interesting (but quite superficial) reference to how reparations can contribute to the logic of retaliation and the reshaping of identities and relationships within the communities affected by the crimes adjudicated. In the opinion of Trial Chamber I: 'Reparations can assist in promoting reconciliation between the convicted person, the victims of the crimes and the affected communities (without making Mr Lubanga's participation in this process mandatory).' Unfortunately, the ICC does not venture to make any suggestions as to how such a reconciliation process should be operationalized, nor it elaborates on the risks connected with establishing reparation policies in the heart of Europe for the benefit of remote communities about which not much is known in The Hague.

Instances where the borders between the victim and the perpetrator blur, such as those involving child soldiers as in the *Lubanga* case, will work as a crucial litmus test to assess the ICC reparation system in the near future. Bearing this in mind, it is interesting to notice that both direct and indirect victims, such as relatives and dependants of the direct victims, are entitled to apply for reparations, but not the victims of the victims, namely, in the *Lubanga* case, the victims of the child soldiers (Sullo 2014). It is possible that within their communities the latter are perceived as both victims and perpetrators, while their victims are perceived simply as victims. It is difficult to predict what the consequences of the ICC reparation order will be in the affected communities, but it is possible to foresee that awarding reparations to perpetrators of mass violence such as child soldiers without implementing redress measures for their victims might trigger mixed feelings. The situation might be even more complicated in the light of the selectiveness of the approach of the prosecutor, which had severe consequences for the crimes prosecuted before the ICC and the reparations provided for their victims.[44] So far in fact cases before the ICC concern exclusively African countries. As a consequence of this policy South Africa is considering to quit the ICC.[45] It remains to be seen whether the ICC Prosecutor will broaden the scope of action of the Court and consequently expanding the possibility to award reparation beyond Africa.

The recent accession of the Government of Palestine to the Rome Statute for instance might open up a scenario including both new challenges but also new possibilities for the ICC. The preliminary examination by the ICC Prosecutor Fatou Bensouda regarding alleged crimes committed in the Palestinian Occupied Territories puts the Court to the legitimacy test while simultaneously providing it with the opportunity to establish itself as an impartial, unbiased adjudicatory body. After the conviction of Lubanga for crimes against the children of the DRC, the children of Gaza are waiting for a restorative intervention by the ICC to give them back a 'life project'.[46]

Pietro Sullo, Ph.D. Scuola Sant'Anna, Pisa, was Director of the European Master's Program in Human Rights and Democratization organized by the European Inter-University Centre for Human Rights and Democratization (EIUC) in Venice from 2013 to 2015. Previously, he has worked at the Max Planck Institute for Comparative Public Law and International Law in Heidelberg, Germany, as a senior researcher coordinating the Doctoral International Max Planck Research School on Retaliation, Mediation and Punishment. He was a consultant for the Libya Constitution Drafting Assembly on human rights and transitional justice in 2015 and has worked for different international NGOs. In 2016 he has conducted a study on the EU asylum *acquis* for the UN High Commissioner for Refugees, Regional Representation for Western Europe, Brussels, Belgium. His main areas of expertise include EU and international human rights law, transitional justice, international criminal law, constitution-building processes and international refugee law.

Note

1. The views expressed in this chapter are solely those of the author. The usual caveats apply.
2. As Simma has noted (2008: 1): 'particularly in criminal law, retribution (in a wide sense of the term) has been taken out of the hands of affected individuals or groups and has been brought into relationship with other principles'.
3. The Kellogg–Briand Pact was an international agreement whose adherents promised not to resort to war to resolve 'disputes or conflicts of whatever nature or of whatever origin they may be, which may arise among them'.
4. Article 2.4 of the UN Charter reads as follows: 'All Members shall refrain in their international relations from the threat or use of force against the territorial integrity or political independence of any state, or in any other manner inconsistent with the Purposes of the United Nations.'
5. The Rome Statute of the International Criminal Court, agreed upon by the Assembly of the States Parties to the International Criminal Court in 1998 and entered into force on 1 July 2002, is the basic legal document establishing the ICC. For the crime of aggression, see Articles 8 and 15 of the Rome Statute.
6. *The Prosecutor v. Thomas Lubanga Dyilo* (case no. ICC-01/04-01/06) was the first case adjudicated by the ICC. Three decisions were delivered during the first instance trial: on 14 March 2012 (judgment), on 10 July 2012 (sentence) and on 7 August 2012 ('decision establishing the principles and procedures to be applied to reparations'). On 14 March 2012, Lubanga, a former rebel leader active in the Ituri Province of the Democratic Republic of Congo, was found guilty under Articles 8(2)(e)(vii) and 25(3)(a) of the ICC Statute of the war crimes of enlisting and conscripting children under the age of fifteen and using them to participate actively in hostilities from 1 September 2002 to 13 August 2003. On 10 July 2012, he was sentenced to a total of fourteen years in prison. On 1 December 2014, the Appeals Chamber confirmed the verdict and declared Lubanga guilty. The Appeals Chambers also confirmed the sentencing decision. On 3 March, the Appeals Chamber delivered a judgment on the appeal against the Trial Chamber's Decision Establishing the Principles and Procedures to be applied to reparations. The Appeals Chamber amended the Trial's Chamber order for reparation and instructed the ICC TFV to draft an implementation plan by 3 September 2015. The appeal against the Trial's Chamber order for reparation was lodged by both Lubanga and of the victims' legal team.
7. Study Concerning the Right to Restitution, Compensation and Rehabilitation for Victims of Gross Violations of Human Rights and Fundamental Freedoms, Final Report submitted by Mr Theo van Boven, Special Rapporteur, UN Doc. E/CN/4/Sub.2/1993/8, para. 124.
8. See also in this regard Resolution 955/1994, in which the UN Security Council (UNSC) affirms to be: 'Convinced that in the particular circumstances of Rwanda, the prosecution of persons responsible for serious violations of international humanitarian law … would

contribute to the process of national reconciliation and to the restoration and maintenance of peace.'

9. On this point, see rule 95(2) of the ICC Rules of Procedure and Evidence, which allows victims to refuse reparation awards: 'If, as a result of notification under sub-rule 1: (a) A victim makes a request for reparations, that request will be determined as if it had been brought under rule 94; (b) A victim requests that the Court does not make an order for reparations, the Court shall not proceed to make an individual order in respect of that victim.'
10. On this point, see Dwertmann (2010: 4–5).
11. These developments culminated in the adoption by the United Nations General Assembly of the Basic Principles and Guidelines on the Right to a Remedy and Reparation for Victims of Gross Violations of International Human Rights Law and Serious Violations of International Humanitarian Law (2005), a soft-law instrument corresponding to the current state of the art of international law regarding reparations.
12. Rwanda's *gacaca* courts have recently attracted a significant amount of scholarly research. On this point, see Drumbl (2007); Clark (2011); Bornkamm (2012); Sullo (2012 and 2014).
13. On this point, see Bassiouni (2003: 65 ff. and 97 ff.), cited in Dwertmann (2010: 14).
14. The Basic Principles on the Use of Restorative Justice Programmes in Criminal Matters do not provide a definition of restorative justice. The very meaning of the concept is in fact debated. Some definitions concentrate on procedural aspects. Marshall (1999), for instance, affirms that: 'Restorative Justice is a process whereby parties with a stake in a specific offence resolve collectively how to deal with the aftermath of the offence and its implications for the future.' Other definitions are more outcome-oriented. According to Bazemore and Walgrave (1999), for instance: 'Restorative Justice is every action that is primarily oriented towards doing justice by repairing the harm that has been caused by the crime.'
15. On this point, see http://www.restorativejustice.org/prison/09examples/belgium, retrieved 1 September 2016.
16. The declaration was adopted by General Assembly Resolution 40/34 of 29 November 1985.
17. It is worth noting that the older international criminal tribunals, Nuremberg and Tokyo, also did not provide for any procedural rights for victims. On this point, see van Boven (1999: 77–89).
18. Even though victims are not allowed to participate in the proceedings before the two UN ad hoc tribunals, Anne-Marie de Brouwer (2005: 286) observes that 'three situations of "victim participation" before the Tribunals deserve to be mentioned: (1) victims "participating" in the trial proceedings through victim impact statements submitted by the Prosecutor to the Chamber; victims "participating" in the trial proceedings through *amicus curiae* intervention; and (3) victim "participation" by addressing the Prosecutor directly'. In these cases, however, the victims have no direct, individual right to participation.
19. See Article 24(3) of the ICTY Statute and Article 23(3) of the ICTR Statute: 'In addition to imprisonment, the Trial Chambers may order the return of any property and proceeds acquired by criminal conduct, including by means of duress, to their rightful owners.'
20. Redacted version of 'Decision on "Indirect Victims"', *The Prosecutor v. Lubanga, Situation in the DRC*, ICC-01/04-01/06-1813, T. Ch. I, ICC, 8 April 2009, paras 49 and 52.
21. Judgment on the Appeals of the Prosecutor and the Defence against Trial Chamber I's Decision on Victims' Participation of 18 January 2008, *The Prosecutor v. Lubanga, Situation in the DRC*, ICC-01/04-01/06-1432, A. Ch., ICC, 11 July 2008, paras 32 and 38.

22. Decision on Victims' Participation, *The Prosecutor v. Lubanga, Situation in the DRC*, ICC-01/04-01/06-1119, T. Ch. I, ICC, 18 January 2008, para. 92.
23. The term 'to, or in respect of, victims' in Article 75(1) seems to refer to the next of kin of victims. In a footnote in the report of the Working Group on Procedural Matters at the Rome Conference, it was clarified that: 'Such a provision refers to the possibility for appropriate reparations to be granted not only to victims but also to others such as the victims' families and successors. For the purposes of interpretation of the terms "victims" and "reparations", definitions are contained in the text of article 44(4) of the Statute, article 68(1) and its accompanying footnote, the Declaration of Basic Principles of Justice for the Victims of Crime and Abuse of Power (General Assembly resolution 40/34 of 29 November 1985, annex) and the examples in paragraphs 12 to 15 of the revised draft basic principles and guidelines on the right to reparation for victims of gross violations of human rights and humanitarian law' (E/CN.4/Sub.2/1996/17). See footnote 5 to Article 73 on Reparations to Victims in the Report of the Working Group on Procedural Matters, A/CONF.183/C.1/WGPM/KL.2/Add.7 (13 July 1998).
24. On this point, see REDRESS (2011: 24): 'This is unfortunate, and as explained below, REDRESS' view is that Court-wide reparations principles should be prepared and agreed in advance of the first reparations proceedings. These will be essential to ensure certainty and consistency as a general principle of law. The dangers in not establishing an adequate basis upon which decisions are made before the first case are clearly demonstrated in the unfortunate experience of the ECCC. In addition, Court-wide principles are necessary for the purposes of internal preparation, intra-organ coordination and the preparation of external stakeholders.'
25. Resolution ICC-ASP/10/Res. 3, adopted by consensus at the 7th plenary meeting, 20 December 2011.
26. Despite the frequent reference to reconciliation in conflict and postconflict settings, the concept lacks a precise and shared definition. On this point, see David Bloomfield, *On Good Terms: Clarifying Reconciliation*. Berghof Report No. 14 (October 2006), pp. 4-5 available at http://image.berghof-foundation.org/fileadmin/redaktion/Publications/Papers/Reports/br14e.pdf, retrieved 10 March 2015.
27. Ibid.: 73–74.
28. Ibid.: 80.
29. Ibid.: 80.
30. Ibid.: 82.
31. Ibid.: 85.
32. Ibid.: 86.
33. Unlike the ICTR and the ICTY, based on the principle of primacy, the ICC is a tribunal of last resort and has jurisdiction over international crimes only if national states are unwilling or unable to investigate or prosecute. Whether such a principle also applies to reparations remains unclear, as this issue is not addressed in the legal instruments of the ICC.
34. Dwertmann (2010: 49) holds that: 'It could be considered advantageous for victims if the complementarity principle would not apply, so that in cases such as those where there is unwillingness to provide reparations on a national level, the reparation principles according to Art. 75 might contribute to the legitimacy of victims' claims for reparations.'
35. Interestingly, the Preparatory Committee Draft Statute included a rule establishing that: 'The Court may also [make an order] [recommend] that an appropriate form of reparations to, or in respect of, victims, including restitution, compensation, rehabilitation, be made by a state]: [if the convicted person is unable to do so himself/herself; [and – if the

convicted person was, when committing the offense, acting on behalf of that state in an official capacity, and within the course and scope of his/her authority]]; c) [in any case other than those referred to in subparagraph b), the Court may also recommend states grant an appropriate form of reparations to, or in respect of, victims, including restitution, compensation and rehabilitation]' (see Article 73.2 of the Report on the Establishment of an International Criminal Court, Draft Statute and Final Act, UN Doc. A/Conf.183/2/add.1 (1998)). During its tenth session, the Assembly of the States Parties also addressed the issues surrounding states' involvement in reparations by stating that 'as liability for reparations is exclusively based on the individual criminal responsibility of a convicted person, under no circumstances shall States be ordered to utilize their properties and assets, including the assessed contributions of States Parties, for funding reparations awards, including in situations where an individual holds, or has held, any official position'.

36. See Article 1 of the Rome Statute.
37. Article 25(4) of the Rome Statute reads as follows: 'No provision in this Statute relating to individual criminal responsibility shall affect the responsibility of States under international law.'
38. Article 75(6) of the Rome Statute reads as follows: 'Nothing in this article shall be interpreted as prejudicing the rights of victims under national or international law.'
39. Dwertmann (2010: 54) concludes: 'Thus, there may be sufficient legal basis for the Court to remind states to comply with their legal obligations to award reparations to victims as a primary or secondary responsibility as a part of the reparations principles established pursuant to Art. 75(1).'
40. For example, Colin McCarthy (2009: 266) asserts that: 'The absence of provisions in either the Rules or the Trust Fund Regulations provides strong indication that Article 75(2) does not, in fact, confer such a power upon the Court. This is especially telling given that if the Court were to seek to utilize Trust Fund resources to supplement a reparations award, a mechanism would surely be needed to ensure adequate consultation between the Court and the Trust Fund prior to such an award being made … while the Trust Fund is a useful means by which the Court can distribute reparations from a perpetrator, the Court cannot *require* the Trust Fund to provide reparations from resources not derived from the perpetrator.'
41. Decision on the Notification of the Board of Directors of the Trust Fund for Victims in accordance with Regulation 50 of the Regulations of the Trust Fund, 11 April 2008, ICC-01/04-492, p. 7.
42. See Decision No. ICC-01/04-01/06, at p. 89.
43. See judgment on the appeals against the 'Decision Establishing the Principles and Procedures to be applied to reparations', ICC-01/04-01/06-3129, 7 August 2012, http://www.icc-cpi.int/iccdocs/doc/doc1919024.pdf (retrieved 1 September 2016), at 7: 'The determination, pursuant to regulation 56 of the Regulations of the Trust Fund, of whether to allocate the Trust Fund's "other resources" for purposes of complementing the resources collected through awards for reparations falls solely within the discretion of the Trust Fund's Board of Directors.'
44. The limited scope of the charge against Lubanga triggered criticism among victims, human rights activists and scholars. ICC Prosecutor Luis Moreno Ocampo, despite allegations of a wide range of crimes committed by Lubanga, including the killing of peacekeepers and rape, decided to focus only on the recruitment of children, the crime for which evidence was abundant. Despite the efforts of victims' legal representatives to amend the charge to include at least sexual crimes, a well-known plague marking the conflict in Ituri, the prosecutor remained exclusively focused on child soldiers. As the Trial Chamber I (**TCI**)

reiterated in the *Lubanga* judgment: 'Not only did the prosecution fail to apply to include rape and sexual enslavement at the relevant procedural stages, in essence it opposed this step. It submitted that it would cause unfairness to the accused if he was tried and convicted on this basis' (Judgment, § 629).

45. See Al Jazeera, South Africa to quit the International Criminal Court, http://www.aljazeera.com/news/2016/10/south-africa-formally-applies-quit-icc-media-161021044116029.html (retrieved 21 October 2016).
46. The Inter-American Court of Human Rights in its case law has established that compensative measures have to be financially assessed against a parameter related to the so- called *proyecto de vida* (life project) of the victim; see for instance Inter-American Court of Human Rights, Case of Tibi v. Ecuador, Judgment of September 07, 2004; Case of Maritza Urrutia v. Guatemala, Judgement of 27 November 2003; Case of Mirna Mack Chang v. Guatemala, Judgement of 25 November 2003.

References

Alessi G. 2002. *Il Processo Penale, Profilo Storico*. Bari-Rome, Italy: Laterza.

Bassiouni, C.M. 1988. 'The Protection of "Collective Victims" in International Law', in C.M. Bassiouni (ed.), *International Protection of Victims*. Toulouse: Érés Publishers, pp. 181ff.

———. 2003. 'The Philosophy and Policy of International Criminal Justice', in L.C. Vorah, F. Pocar, Y. Featherstone, O. Fourmy, C. Graham, J. Hocking and N. Robson (eds), *Man's Inhumanity to Man*. The Hague: Kluwer Law International, pp. 65–126.

Bazemore, S.G., and L. Walgrave (eds). 1999. 'Restorative Juvenile Justice: In Search of Fundamentals and an Outline for Systemic Reform', in L. Walgrave and S.G. Bazemore (eds), *Restorative Juvenile Justice: Repairing the Harm of Youth Crime*. Monsey, NY: Criminal Justice Press, pp. 1–14.

Bloomfield, D. 2006. 'On Good Terms: Clarifying Reconciliation', in *Berghof Report No. 14*. Berlin: Berghof Research Center for Constructive Conflict Management.

Bornkamm, P.C. 2012. *Rwanda's Gacaca Courts: Between Retribution and Reparation*. Oxford: Oxford University Press.

Clark, P. 2011. *The Gacaca Courts, Post-genocide Justice and Reconciliation in Rwanda: Justice without Lawyers*. Cambridge: Cambridge University Press.

De Brouwer, A. 2005. *Supranational Criminal Prosecution of Sexual Violence: The ICC and the Practice of the ICTY and the ICTR*. Antwerp: Intersentia.

De Greiff, P. 2008. *Rule-of-Law Tools for Post-conflict States, Reparations Programmes*. New York and Geneva: Office of the United Nations High Commissioner for Human Rights.

———. 2014. 'Report by the UN Special Rapporteur on the Promotion of Truth, Justice, Reparation and Guarantees of Non-Recurrence', UN Doc A/69/518. Retrieved 24 October 2016, http://www.ohchr.org/EN/Issues/TruthJusticeReparation/Pages/Index.aspx.

Drumbl, M.A. 2005. 'Collective Violence and Individual Punishment: The Criminality of Mass Atrocity', *Northwestern University Law Review* 99: 539–610.

———. 2007. *Atrocity, Punishment and International Law*. Cambridge: Cambridge University Press.

Dwertmann, E. 2010. *The Reparation System of the International Criminal Court: Its Implementation, Possibilities and Limitations*. Leiden: Brill.

Elster, J., 2004, *Closing the Books: Transitional Justice in Historical Perspective*. Cambridge: Cambridge University Press.

Fletcher, L.E., and H.M. Weinstein. 2002. 'Violence and Social Repair: Rethinking the Contribution of Justice to Reconciliation', *Human Rights Quarterly* 24(3): 573–639.

Garapon, A. 2005. *Crimini che non si possono né punire né perdonare*. Bologna: Il Mulino.

Groenhuijsen, M., and A. Pemberton. 2011. 'Genocide, Crimes against Humanity and War Crimes: A Victimological Perspective on International Criminal Justice', in R.M. Letschert (ed.), *Victimological Approaches to International Crimes*. Cambridge: Intersentia, pp. 9–34.

Huyse H. (ed.). 2008. *Traditional Justice and Reconciliation after Violent Conflict: Learning from African Experiences*. Stockholm: International Institute for Democracy and Electoral Assistance.

Huyse, L. 2003. 'The Process of Reconciliation', in D. Bloomfield, T. Barnes and L. Huyse (eds), *Reconciliation after Violent Conflict*. Stockholm: International Institute for Democracy and Electoral Assistance, pp. 19–33.

Kritz, N.J. (ed.). 1995. *Transitional Justice. How Emerging Democracies Reckon with Former Regimes, Vol. 1: General Considerations*. Washington DC: United States Institute of Peace.

Loraux, N. 1997. *La Cité divisée, l'oubli dans la mémoire d'Athènes*. Paris: Payot.

Marshall, T.F. 1999. *Restorative Justice: An Overview*. London: Home Office, Research Development and Statistics Directorate.

McCarthy, C. 2009. 'Reparations under the Rome Statute of the International Criminal Court and Reparative Justice Theory', *International Journal of Transitional Justice* 3: 250–71. doi:10.1093/ijtj/ijp001.

Orentlicher, D. 2007. '"Settling Accounts" Revisited: Reconciling Global Norms with Local Agency', International Journal of Transitional Justice 1(1): 10–22.

Pena, M., and G. Carayon. 2013. 'Is the ICC Making the Most Out of Victims Participation?', *International Journal of Transitional Justice* 7(3): 518–35.

REDRESS. 2011. *Justice for Victims: The ICC's Reparations Mandate*. Retrieved 1 September 2016 from http://www.redress.org/downloads/publications/REDRESS_ICC_Reparations_May2011.pdfX.

Sarkin, J. 2005. 'Reparations for Gross Human Rights Violations as an Outcome of Criminal versus Civil Court Proceedings', in K. De Feyter, S. Parmentier, M. Bossuyt and P. Lemmens (eds), *Out of the Ashes*. Antwerp: Intersentia, pp. 151–89.

Simma, B. 2008. 'Reciprocity', in R. Wolfrum (ed.), *Max Planck Encyclopedia of Public International Law*. Oxford: Oxford University Press. Retrieved 1 September 2016 from http://opil.ouplaw.com/view/10.1093/law:epil/9780199231690/law-9780199231690-e1461?rskey=9MMOYO&result=1&prd=EPIL.

Smith Cody, S., E. Stover, M. Balthazard and A. Koenig. 2015. 'The Victims' Court? A Study of 622 Victim Participants at the International Criminal Court', Human Rights Center, University of Berkely, School of Law.

Spiga, V. 2010. 'Indirect Victims' Participation in the Lubanga Trial', *Journal of International Criminal Justice* 8(1): 183–98.

Stahn, C. 2015. 'Reparative Justice after the Lubanga, Appeals Judgment on Principles and Procedures of Reparation'. Retrieved 12 October 2016 from http://www.ejiltalk.org/reparative-justice-after-the-lubanga-appeals-judgment-on-principles-and-procedures-of-reparation/.

Sullo, P. 2012. 'When Hurbinek Survives. Transitional Justice and Children's Rights: Lessons Learnt from Rwanda', in I. Derluyn, C. Mels, S. Parmentier and W. Vandenhole (eds), *Re-member: Rehabilitation, Reintegration and Reconciliation of War-Affected Children*. Antwerp: Intersentia, pp. 127–51.

———. 2014. 'Lubanga Case', in R. Wolfrum (ed.), *Max Planck Encyclopedia of Public International Law*. Oxford: Oxford University Press.

———. 2016. 'Restorative Justice', in R. Wolfrum (ed.), *Max Planck Encyclopedia of Public International Law*. Oxford: Oxford University Press.

———. 2017. 'The ICC as a Transitional Justice Actor. New Space for Victims?', in Gabriella Citroni (ed.) *Diritti Umani e Diritto Internazionale*, Special Issue on Transitional Justice. Bologna: Il Mulino.

Sullo, P., and J. Wyatt. 2014. 'War Reparations', in R. Wolfrum (ed.), *Max Planck Encyclopedia of Public International Law*. Oxford: Oxford University Press.

Teitel, R.G. 2000. *Transitional Justice*. New York: Oxford University Press.

Triffterer, O. 1999. 'Preliminary Remarks – The Permanent International Criminal Court – Ideal and Reality', in O. Triffterer (ed.), *Commentary on the Rome Statute of the International Criminal Court – Observers' Notes, Article by Article*. Oxford: Hart Publishing, pp. 17–50.

Van Boven, T. 1999. 'The Position of the Victim in the Statute of the International Criminal Court', in H. von Hebel, J.G. Lammers and J. Schukking (eds), *Reflections on the International Criminal Court: Essays in Honour of Adriaan Bos*. The Hague: T.M.C. Asser Press, pp. 77–90.

Zappalà, S. 2005. *La Giustizia Penale Internazionale*. Bologna: Il Mulino.

Conclusion

Retaliation in Specific Spheres of Effectiveness

Bertram Turner

Introduction

One driving force behind this collective volume was the strong desire on the part of the representatives of the disciplines united here to come up with a comprehensive volume for use in a variety of disciplines, as well as for a wider public, that addresses the commonalities and differences of the various research agendas on a universal human condition. The interest was especially strong among representatives of criminal legal studies and criminology, who were already in cooperation with psychologists and social anthropologists. In this sense, the volume is already the outcome of a transdisciplinary research project. The breadth of disciplines was then further enriched to include perspectives from a number of other related research areas. It is therefore this very transdisciplinarity that is not only the volume's greatest strength, but also its very *raison d'être*. It is precisely the tension between common themes and strands connecting the chapters on the one hand, and the apparent incongruence of the central arguments and approaches on the other hand, that we want to identify and begin to work through; this is the transdisciplinary debate we want to *initiate* with this volume, and the very fact that some contributors have referred to both disciplinary overlaps *and* discrepancies gives me reason to hope that the volume will do exactly what we want it to do. Indeed, the process of coming to grips with these challenges has already greatly enriched my own reflections.

The aim of the introduction, which is admittedly written at a certain level of abstraction, was to put the research approaches of a number of disciplines in a broader (but still well-defined) context. In the more theoretically oriented Introduction, I was sparing with empirical illustrations and have, where appropriate, referred the reader to the chapters where these more 'abstract' points are illustrated with concrete data and analyses. The Introduction is therefore intended to lead into the main themes addressed in the volume, while the individual chapters illustrate those main themes in greater detail. This concluding chapter returns to the more theoretical arguments brought forward in the Introduction and uses them to inform an exploration of the thematic fields into which the book is divided.

Thus, the Introduction and this concluding chapter are designed to serve as bookends that hold together the six sections of the volume; they identify and address cross-references that may help the reader better understand the ways in which retaliation operates in specific contexts.[1] The Introduction's focus was on the theoretical and methodological embeddedness of the concept of retaliation, while this conclusion outlines the respective sections' conceptual environments using, to the extent possible, the individual chapters to help define the boundaries between them.

Plurality, Disciplinary Expertise and Fields of Interest

Experiencing Retaliation: Psychic Dispositions, Emotions, Representations and Remembering

The first section of this collection establishes a common point of departure for a renewed analysis. Emotional aspects of retaliation pervade all the chapters in the volume; however, they are most explicitly addressed in the first section (Gollwitzer and Sjöström; Bies and Tripp). In a word, these chapters assert that retaliation is not the outcome of irrationality. The desire for revenge that may arise after any experience of injustice, co-occurring with rage, grief and despair and, finally, the feeling of satisfaction that may be associated with an act of retaliation are all motivational forces that are profoundly inscribed in the concept of retaliation. We learn that the maintenance of individual emotional balance requires an expression of the desire to retaliate. It seems to be a basic human need to have some explanation for the intense feelings one has when personally involved as a damaged or injured party. In a way, retaliation opens an avenue to the claim to respectful treatment. Moreover, an incentive to act against injustice may be felt even if there is no direct personal involvement. In the psychological literature, the perpetrator's acknowledgement of responsibility and his or her subsequent apology are recognized as quasi-universal prerequisites for the injured party to move beyond the desire to respond in kind and to accept compensation (see, e.g., Scheff 1994; Murphy 2003; Gollwitzer 2005; Paul 2005; Yoshimura 2007). This entails that a (potential) retaliator also disclose his or her identity.

The entertainment value of retaliation in popular culture has much to do with its capacity to appeal to the emotions. The violent option in particular, whether acknowledged as legitimate or suppressed by a controlling agent, attracts attention beyond the circle of directly involved individuals and prompts feelings of excitement, while the exercise of violence itself is quite often regarded as emotion-driven. In contrast, coming to terms with conflicts through endless negotiation processes is rather unspectacular. The latter fact hints at a reverse connotation, namely that retaliation also provides directives for the channelling and containment of these emotions. Most important here are temporal and spatial restrictions that are imposed on the exercise of the right to retaliate. According to many local and religious normative orders, the exercise of a reaction that mirrors the initial offence is considered acceptable only for a period immediately following the retaliation-provoking act. During this period, most often some few days, retaliatory acts are believed to be dominated by emotions, which entails a preference for immediate payback. This might correspond to a state that, according to Bies and Tripp (this volume), is characterized by depleted emotional self-control. Once this initial period ends, during which a perpetrator is detained or goes into exile to deprive the victim of the opportunity to retaliate, emotions lose their legitimating immediacy and the option of a retaliatory act committed 'in the heat of the moment' (see Bies and Tripp, this volume) is replaced by the requirement to regulate the conflict through other means.[2]

This is only seemingly a contradiction to all the representations in the mass media, according to which retaliatory relations between parties may be sustained over generations. All the while, emotions are said to be kept simmering constantly over a low flame. As has been briefly outlined in the Introduction regarding empirical data and a possible discrepancy between the involved actors' rhetoric and the actual quality of their relationship, negotiations in retaliation matters often do not reach a conclusive agreement and, as long as the dialogue continues, the potential for violence is kept under control.

Psychological and Economic Analyses of Crime and Deviance

There is, to delineate the second field of studies, increasing sensitivity in jurisprudence and legal studies to the human desire to retaliate (Darley 2009). Findings coming out of the engagement with retaliation are, however, by no means homogeneous, and the conclusions reached in one discipline can stand in sharp contrast to some of the unquestioned 'certainties' put forward by other disciplines. For example, from an anthropological point of view, there is no obvious inherent conjunction between the concepts of retaliation and punishment. Only by means of secondary rationalization and in the light of the state's exclusive right to inflict punishment has retaliation become associated with the realm of sanctions.[3] Thus, the basic intention behind retaliatory practices – namely to prevent one party in a relationship from using a transgression to gain an advantage over the other party – becomes loaded with an additional charge that may also be characterized as a form of rebalancing, but with a different impetus (e.g., Aladjem 2008).[4] The state's monopoly on legitimate violence can also lead to a situation in which the aspect of group solidarity may fade into the background, and can imbue the social exclusion and reintegration of responsible individuals during the process of conflict settlement with quite different qualities and consequences.

In fact, when the state is put at the centre of analysis, retaliation is likely to be associated with the concept of punishment in its retributive aspects, which connotes a distinction between legitimate and illegitimate punishment.[5] A decisive mark of distinction in this context is the insight in social sciences that the option to break out of cycles of violence constitutes an essential component of any retaliatory logic. For this reason, we have decided to focus on the relationship between retaliation and punishment in a number of chapters in this volume.

The punitive aspects of the concept of retaliation play an important role not only in the state's monopoly on the jurisdiction of punishable offences, but also in social life. Whether individual or collective, initiatives to balance situations perceived as wrong almost always depend on a logic of retribution. In various social contexts, the punitive aspect of retaliation is foregrounded. There are even revenge handbooks and websites to help people who feel they have been humiliated or mistreated retaliate against, for instance, an ex-partner or an unfair superior.[6] Bashing on the Internet, the public exposure of an offender and anonymous avenging are well-established social strategies.[7] These examples demonstrate how the previously accepted calculus of retaliation seems to be transforming. As will be addressed in more detail below, in sociopolitical theory building, retaliation was seen as part of a causal nexus involving societal concepts, and could be used to distinguish between collective and individualizing forms of sociopolitical organization. The concept of retaliation, with its emphasis on attributing responsibility to collectives for individual acts, was considered proof of the collective character of a society, whereas the practice of holding an individual actor alone liable for his or her individual actions was considered proof of a more complex, individualized form of societal organization. In the first case, the concept of retaliation involves at least two solidary groups opposing each other. The retaliatory logic in such a constellation compels both perpetrator(s) and retaliator(s) to identify themselves, close ranks and confess responsibility for what they did or intended to do.

In societies that are considered to be individualized, on the other hand, anonymity or the disavowal of responsibility on both sides seems rather typical, which makes it necessary to profoundly revise what the social working of retaliation may entail. One consequence of anonymity in diversified modern societies is that the chance for neutral intervention in the retaliatory conflict – usually a given under less individualizing social conditions – is challenged. If the retaliatory relationship between individuals is kept under the radar of formal justice as, for instance, in competition or interpersonal conflict in the workplace, mediation does not come up and third parties cannot intervene, especially if the anonymity of a reaction can be assured. When, for example, a bystander witnesses a deviant act, 'retaliatory anonymity' involves extracting that person's social commitment or civic duty to intervene from the institutional arrangements in which retaliation is embedded. This poses a challenge to all attempts to connect retaliatory claims with third-party intervention and mediation for any conflictive constellation, from the grassroots levels all the way up to international crisis scenarios.

What the chapters in this volume show, however, is that both aspects of retaliation – its formative power on group solidarity and the individual anonymized desire to retaliate – may occur in any given societal formation, despite retaliation's hypothesized role as a proxy measure for specific types of social and political organization. Both aspects may even be interwoven. As regards the aspect of solidarity, one difference is that in individualized societies, people in a variety of different forms of relationship with the respective parties may be mobilized to take one's part, while in less individualized societies, it is the protagonists' kin who are expected to take sides.

Reconsideration of the concept takes place at various scales, from victim–perpetrator constellations at the level of individual actors to efforts initiated and undertaken by global governance institutions to come to terms with situations of mass atrocities, unrestricted use of violence, genocide and state injustice. Criteria of belonging and of inclusion and exclusion make a difference in the assessment of an individual's guilt and responsibility. At the same time, the relationship between the victim and the perpetrator of a crime as described in state law is being contested.[8] The state's perception of the public interest in criminal prosecution, as well as the subordinate role the victim is given as a joint plaintiff in claiming his or her rights against the perpetrator, are challenged by alternative models such as *restorative justice*. These models implicitly borrow aspects from the repertoire of retaliation, as in the perpetrator–victim reconciliation model, but they fail to take into account all of the consequences that may result from their implementation.[9] Simultaneously – and sometimes seemingly by the same actors – harsher punishments are demanded, often referring to the seriousness of a crime. From a legal–philosophical point of view, these relations between retaliation, revenge, justice and state penal practices demand a critical reassessment (see, e.g., Sarat 2002a; Carmichael 2003; Murphy 2003; Miller 2006).

Crime, Punishment and Encounters between Formal and Informal Normativities

The fact that the definition of retaliation includes the right or the obligation to exercise reactive violence constitutes a fundamental normative principle. In one way or another, every given normative order of a social formation and any reasoning on justice with respect to the use of violence refers to it. In modern jurisprudence, retaliation is acknowledged as a basic principle in legal theory (Kelsen 1982 [1940]), while its practice is legitimized only to the extent that the state employs it in its exercise of sovereignty. In the modern state, violent retaliation, like all recourse to violence, is subordinate to the rule of law. Some strands of research in the social sciences have used the state concept as a template in order to carve out the specifics of the social workings of retaliation. Moreover, it is important to recognize that the political organization of a society reflects its position towards retaliation. This does not necessarily affect all aspects of retaliation, but in a society that claims to organize itself as a liberal democracy, for example, the model of state organization affects all violence-based considerations because it entails the partial transfer of individual retaliatory rights and duties to the state as part of the state's monopoly on legitimate violence. So, within the framework of a state, the right to retaliation may be limited by state laws and subordinated to state sovereignty. Beyond that, recourse to violent retaliation is considered illegal.[10]

If we leave this reference to violence out, the state and its laws are not a means to suppress retaliation as a basic motivation for individual decision making and they cannot eliminate retaliation from the repertoire of reactive options of people who feel injured. Individuals' retaliatory strategies in face-to-face situations – 'getting even' in interpersonal relations – usually escape the attention of the state judiciary if they are not considered criminal offences. In criminal legal studies and criminology, it is asked what role the concept of retaliation plays in social control and the maintenance of order. Moreover, criminologists explore to what extent the concept of retaliation may serve as a means of legal or illegal deterrence or enhance alliance building and the negotiation of solidarities (Jacobs and Wright 2006; Garot 2009).

Therefore, within a state order, the actors' contemplations of reaction to a challenge may always include the option of retaliation. Individuals and groups may thus develop it into an argument justifying violence or even execute it – legitimately or illegitimately.[11] The superordinate law of the state materializes in central institutions that distinguish it from other normative orders and means of conflict regulation. Moreover, the day-to-day conflict management in any given state – that is, between individuals, within or beyond the framework of internal social differentiations – mostly takes place in the shadow of formal justice systems and state institutions. That means that for the vast majority of conflicts, including those for which formal regulation is available, formal justice systems usually only provide no more than a frame of reference. This creates room for manoeuvre. In this strategic plurality, retaliation is one of the motivations that inform actors' decisions.

Under conditions of complex plural legal configurations, the question arises: in what way and by whom are relations of retaliation legitimized? Competing models may co-exist that refer to different types of law, such as state law, international or transnational law, religious and customary law. The simultaneous normative effectiveness of competing models of retaliation has generated increasing public interest in recent times due to intensifying circumstances such as the mobility of templates and people.

A second cluster of topics within the field of law and crime associates retaliation with violent crime, crime prevention, punishment and its possible alternatives. It also includes the motivations for deviant behaviour as well as the potentials either for controlled and limited violence or an uncontrolled escalation of violence into criminal activity. These topics have encouraged our endeavour to bring these three strands together. A historical perspective, as exemplified by Härter's chapter in this volume, helps us understand the jurisprudential interpretation of retaliation that references normative ordering, punishment and the institutionalization of law (Kelsen 1982 [1940]).

Faith-Based Retaliation: Spirituality and Normativity

This section focuses on the reinvigoration of retaliation as a religious dogma and a tenet of faith. Certain concepts of retaliation, while now firmly integrated in the scientific discourse, were originally conveyed (and continue to be conveyed) as religious messages, a circumstance that endows them with a certain spiritual stability. Some crucial elements of these have taken hold in secularized moral concepts and have even entered into state-supporting ideologies. As mentioned above, these processes have accelerated in recent times, leading to an increasing 're-enchantment' of various spheres of life, the realm of law included. Religious legitimization (endorsement) or limitation (restriction) of retaliation, the compulsory duty to execute it, or its ban in favour of a tenet of forgiveness and reconciliation in the shape of penitence, atonement or absolution are all ideas that affect social practices. Apparently, no religion can do without a concept of retaliation and a term for it (Kelsen 1982 [1940]). This involves actual doctrines of causality which find expression in an allocation of responsibilities between religious and secular authorities. The symbolic representations of retaliation in depictions of Nemesis, the goddess of rightful wrath, of the Erinyes of the ancient world, and of the contemporary *nemesis divina*, the revenge of God, illustrate the belief in numinous intervention in worldly conflicts, especially when a profane balance of interests is not achieved.

Reference to retaliation in the three grand monotheistic religions – Judaism, Christianity and Islam – has attracted a great deal of attention in recent times. Contributing to this interest is an ever-increasing emphasis on the obligation to exercise retaliatory violence. In various circumstances and concrete cases, from disciplinary measures within the family to the War on Terror, actors legitimize recourse to violence as a religious duty that reflects a basic principle of divine justice.

At a procedural level, profane negotiations of retaliatory claims are often embedded in religious contexts in general. The involvement of supplementary measures and ritual acts, such as the symbolic death of the perpetrator in a homicide case, is often considered necessary to bring about a conclusive settlement. Other measures may rehabilitate the responsible party after compensating the victim's party. Aspects of purification play a role in the process of retaliation and connect legitimate secular claims to a spiritual foundation.[12]

Some religious convictions draw a direct link between mortality and the religious duty to retaliate. Upon a relative's death, the descendants have to determine who is to be made responsible for the death irrespective of the cause of death.[13] The bereaved may suspect manipulation of the supernatural via magic or witchcraft (see Lenart, this volume), even in cases of natural death, and act accordingly.[14] If this duty to retaliate is not fulfilled or if respect for the deceased is not demonstrated, his or her spirit cannot find peace and will haunt the relatives because they failed to retaliate.

Of all the occidental academic disciplines, it is probably Christian theology that has had the strongest influence on the discourse of retaliation. The formative force of the Old Testament rule to abide by retaliation reached far beyond Christian teachings and can hardly be overestimated. However, biblical writings contain a number of contradictory points on the matter. On the one hand, there is the famous *talion* ('an eye for an eye, a tooth for a tooth …', Ex. 21:23–25), which emphasizes a duty of retaliation. On the other hand, there is also the mention of asylum cities where people who committed unintentional manslaughter could seek refuge from legitimate vengeance, a concept that does not seem to be consistent with the intransigent notion of retaliation emphasized elsewhere in the Old Testament (Turner 2005). In one passage, compensation in place of violent retaliation is strictly forbidden (Num. 35:31–34), and elsewhere a killer, namely Cain, is 'marked' by Yahweh to protect him from being put to death. In short, such contradictions pervade the history of retaliation to this day (for further details, see Koch 1972; Turner and Schlee 2008).

The message from the New Testament seems to be in direct contradiction to this notion, as it exhorts one to love one's enemy and espouses forgiveness instead of retaliation (e.g., the injunction to 'turn the other cheek'; see Mt. 5:38 f.; 18:23–35). However, this is placed within a judicial context with reference to state jurisdiction, judges and prisons. This ambivalence has pervaded theology over the centuries, with the spectrum of assertions about retaliation being used to legitimate quite different concepts and practices. This holds true not only for Christian theology, but also for other religions and their sacred scriptures, in which retaliation is seen as a technique that allows the involvement of non-human actors in mundane affairs and is associated with notions of a balancing justice.

Evangelical mega-churches, for instance, place God's imminent apocalyptic retaliation at the centre of their call for personal repentance and purification. A reward in the afterlife is promised for behaviour and good deeds that please God, while bad deeds lead to divine retaliation in the form of eternal damnation. Divine punishment is not limited to the afterlife; direct punishment by God in the worldly life is also part of religious soteriology. This belief in God's retaliation indirectly legitimizes similar worldly treatment of sinners by believers.

In the same vein, unexpected or unpredictable occurrences, disasters and catastrophes are perceived as divine or supernatural acts of retaliation. This perspective in a way privileges the idea of a direct divine or supernatural involvement in mundane affairs over the vision of a judging and punishing impartial superior being withdrawn from earthly concerns.[15]

In the Islamic tradition, *talion* is mentioned as divine law for the descendants of Israel, but not explicitly for the Muslim community. On the other hand, the concept of *qisas* – balancing justice (see Ben Hounet and Schlee, both in this volume) – is laid down in the Qurᶜan, which stipulates the right of the relatives of a murdered individual to insist on capital punishment for the perpetrator or, to be more merciful, the right to claim compensation. Indeed, the scriptures recommend restricting the exercise of the right. Moreover, for all other cases, involuntary homicide included, *diya* – a form of monetary or in-kind compensation – is prescribed (Schacht 1986; see also Drent and Ben Hounet, both in this volume). All in all, the many and varied references to retaliation in the Qurᶜan and the *sunna* provide for Muslims no less need for exegesis than the biblical texts for Christians.

It follows from the foregoing that religion and law overlap with respect to retaliation. Legal and religious aspects of retaliation may interact in various ways. The devolution of retaliatory claims to state authorities under the rule of law, for instance, at least concerning the legitimate reaction to a violent act, manifests itself in the form of punishment and deterrence, but does not necessarily include the aspect of compensation for damage or injuries suffered. This may well create tensions with religious interpretations of the concepts (see, e.g., Aladjem 2008). As a consequence, the state's monopolistic claim on the execution of violence on the one hand and the religiously protected rights of the individual to retaliate on the other can come into conflict at various levels of jurisdiction. The criminal law system of the Republic of Iran, which is informed by notions of Islamic law, may serve as an example here. According to its provisions, the relatives of a victim of violence play a vital role in the penal process of a case.[16]

Cases of female mutilation as revenge, for instance, may be treated under religiously oriented state jurisdiction, as the story of the Iranian woman Ameneh Bahrami shows. This case, which attracted international attention, revolves around a young woman who had been blinded and disfigured by a rebuffed suitor, and demanded that the man be blinded as punishment. An Iranian state court agreed to the revenge demands, in accordance with the Islamic legal principle of *qisas* (retaliation), but Bahrami forgave the man at the last moment.[17] In this example, the state judiciary, through its courts, acts in compliance with a religious legal interpretation of the principle of retaliation. This specific Islamic regulation concedes an enormous amount of decisional power to the victim.

Retaliation in the Negotiation and Organization of Social and Political Orders

As an intermediate result, we may state that Christian theology, history and jurisprudence are disciplines that have laid the groundwork for further qualified reasoning on retaliation, while psychological disciplines have shown the concept's origins in human nature. All this presents a challenge to the social scientific analysis of retaliation, and especially to the anthropology of law and of political and social structure.

The study of retaliation in social anthropology resonates with this multidisciplinary polyphony, and it may serve as a common thread through the discipline's own early history as well. The abundance of incoherent data with which the young discipline was confronted in the nineteenth century necessarily led to a typological and systematized consideration of the concept. Missionaries, colonial officials, early travellers and ethnographers found evidence all around the world for the universality of a principle that they knew from biblical and historical writings and their own life experiences. And it was believed that it would be possible to track down its 'archaic' traits in contemporaneous local practices.

At that time, social anthropology was expected to make its contribution to the project of the universal history of humankind and to take a leading role in the concert of disciplines. Research tasks allocated to anthropology in the disciplinary division of labour led, from the nineteenth century onwards, to a focus on the early phases of sociocultural development as postulated in the evolutionary scheme that was prevalent at that time. According to this scheme, traits from the different consecutive phases in the unilinear evolution of civilization were imagined to be embodied as 'survivals' in extant 'primitive' societies. In the search for the origins of social formations and their political and juridical organization, anthropology's task, derived from the predetermined dogma of jurisprudence and historical sciences, was to determine the transition phase leading from unrestrained private retaliation or revenge under pre-state conditions to the establishment of a controlled penal system embedded in the judiciary of a political state order that is based on the monopoly of power (Tuori 2015). This is not the place to repeat the criticisms of the evolutionary model, with its naïve concept of constant and unilinear progress and its ahistorical drawbacks. It will suffice to emphasize that, according to this simple Eurocentric scheme of constant forward progress of civilization, a steady decrease in the exercise of violence was postulated.[18] In fact, it has become an acceptable convention in the social sciences even to the present day to conceptually reduce retaliation in conflictive relations to a 'dysfunction of archaic law' (Luhmann 1985), a quasi-automatic violent reaction that is associated with excessively high costs.[19]

However, empirical evidence shows that increasing social complexity apparently does not entail a decline in reactive violence. There is no indication of an attenuation of the efficacy of the retaliatory principle that can be attributed to the project of modernity. In effect, anthropologists were asked to identify an ideal-type that could serve as a link in human evolution to document a state of affairs typical of nonstate societies. The colonial situation even led to increased interest in settings where state intervention presumably did not exist or did not play a role.

The focus on the effectiveness of retaliatory logic beyond state legal systems opened the door to conceptual conjunctions that are less evident within a given state order. The critical reconsideration and systematization of ethnographic data on retaliatory relations and their interdependence or co-occurrence with other social phenomena suddenly proved to be especially relevant. As a result, social anthropological studies, especially those of law and conflict, began to engage in extensive research on the dialectic relationship between concepts of retaliation and forms of social and political organization. It was the model of segmentary societies in particular that showed great promise in unpacking the social workings of reciprocity in the realm of law and the regulation of deviance and crime. Segmentary societies are characterized by egalitarian structures of opposed segments based on kinship relations. Constant checks and balances exist between segmentary units in all spheres of life, in the form of competition and of an elaborate system of challenges and responses, triggering processes of fusion and fission at all levels of segmentation. This type of sociopolitical organization is also called acephalous or egalitarian, and is assumed to be the *locus classicus* of a genetic combination of retaliation with a political order and a kinship system.[20] In such societies, the concept of criminal liability applies to a great extent to segmentary collectivities, in reference to which individuals are believed to act. This implies that the regulation of disputes does not take place in a situation of pure anarchy, nor is it done through the simple rule of 'might makes right'. Rather, in conflict situations, there are groups or constellations of groups with solidary members facing each other, who, by way of negotiations, decide on potential courses of action ranging from escalation to compromise. They also have to take the prevailing opinion of non-involved members of the society into account.[21]

In the logic of unilinear cultural evolution, this model was regarded as the missing link between (an imagined) unordered retaliation at the most primitive stage of human evolution and the civilizing state. Egalitarian societies, as an evolutionarily intermediate stage, were presumed to operate with a pure and unaltered version of regulated retaliation to deal with imbalances in social relations. In simple terms, retaliation was regarded as the model of criminal law inherent in segmentary societies and that has been abolished with the establishment of state structures.

It is from this angle that, over the course of time, the field of research developed in various directions. Studies on segmentary societies concentrate on Sub-Saharan Africa, the Middle East and North Africa (MENA) and the Mediterranean. In the literature on retaliation in African societies, the interest continued to be directed towards the relationship between the use of violence, social structure and political legitimacy (Otterbein 1997), especially with respect to emerging forms of political stratification. To this web of relationships was added a classification of societies according to their prevailing mode of production, especially as herders or farmers, positing criteria such as mobility and sedentarism as determinants of the respective mode of retaliation (e.g., Peters 1967). Such differentiation was and is taken up in evolutionary psychology and behavioural sciences, where an 'ecology of revenge' was postulated on the basis of types of livelihood (e.g., Figueredo et al. 2004).[22] In my view, however, there is no evidence that mobility or sedentarism has a significant impact on preferences for violence- or compensation-oriented approaches.

The search for congruities within the MENA/Mediterranean cluster (Black-Michaud 1975), in contrast, led to the conceptualization of a particular type of segmentary organization called honour societies. Honour was introduced as a concept to deal with the constant exchange of challenges and responses among equals. This constant threat to balance was understood as competition in the accumulation of honour as social capital. As a shifting and unstable parameter in the relationship between individuals as members of different groupings in society, it was supposed to help explain the interaction between nominal equality in social status between those groupings and their de facto inequality in economic and political power. What have been foregrounded in this literature are logical inconsistencies in the association of retaliatory reciprocity with notions of nominal equality between opposed parties. Although parties are considered equal in reciprocal exchange relations, of which retaliation is but one, the same parties may differ in terms of economic and political power. Moreover, they also differ internally, and these internal differences (such as the gender biases inherent in male responsibility for the female embodiment of family honour) may affect the postulated equality between parties.

Another aspect of the action–reaction interplay takes centre stage. In honour societies, the rhetoric of retaliation also includes the mandatory reaction to a challenge that is not necessarily regarded as an injustice. The main point is that such challenges may also generate an imbalance of honour assets between nominally equal units normally represented by male individuals.[23] Here, reciprocity-oriented rebalance is suspended and appropriateness of response is understood as the necessity to always outdo the challenge in a game of one-upmanship. Honour societies thus cannot be said to represent the pure type of egalitarian organization of the political realm, and it has become clear in such societies that equity with regard to one quality or characteristic does not necessarily entail equality in every respect (Schneider 1971).

The creeping inclusion of stratified and hierarchically organized societies in the anthropological research on retaliation has widened the scope and highlighted the discrepancy between the abstract principle of retaliation, which assumes nominal equality, and the realities of life. The focus was redirected to the impulse to 'get even' in stratified, gender-biased or patriarchal societies, or in cases in which actors distance themselves from their social embedding when dealing with an imbalance and reacting to an action. This also implies that one must shift attention away from collectivities as agents and towards individuals. Finally, this different focus sheds light on the assessment of social distinctiveness as a condition determining the turn from compensation-oriented retaliation towards violence and escalation. With an increasing interest in industrialized societies, urban culture, global processes, and governance and statehood, research in the anthropology of law, disputing and conflict has taken into account the interplay of, on the one hand, codes of retaliation between solidary groups and, on the other hand, individual retaliatory agency in individualized heterogeneous industrialized societies (see, e.g., Aase 2002). The widening of the focus in anthropological research has also amplified the explanatory power of the concept of retaliation.

Travelling Models of Retaliation: Postconflict Scenarios in International Law and on the Ground

In order to provide for the wider framework of the social working of the principle of retaliation, in this section I trace the concept's recent career from the focus on industrialized societies and the nation-state to the transnational scale. With regard to international criminal law, I furthermore discuss retaliation in connection with the challenge of balancing or restoring order and of establishing peace. Two chapters in this collection reflect quite different aspects of retaliation in postwar settings: one, written by the anthropologist Friederike Stahlmann, describes the atmosphere of mistrust and devalued tradition in postwar Afghanistan; the other, written by the legal scholar Pietro Sullo, addresses the discourse within international criminal law on retributive justice and its effectiveness in dealing with crimes against humanity.

I see these chapters as embedded in a thematic field that addresses the ways in which the different layers of the concept of retaliation sketched out in the introduction coalesce, and how the resulting composite versions, which owe their existence to specific circumstances, are translated in the process of scalar interaction. Those components of the concept of retaliation that are not incorporated into the formal justice system or operate under its radar, notably those involving violence, are banned and rendered illegal by the rule-of-law approach at the national scale. This ban has rendered retaliation 'invisible' or withdrawn from the agenda of legal reasoning and ordering. However, the concept of retaliation has resurfaced at the transnational scale in all its complexity by virtue of the simple fact of its existence, effectiveness and explanatory power.

The debate in international criminology on human security, crimes against humanity and the 'responsibility to protect' (R2P; see International Commission on Intervention and State Sovereignty 2001; Glanville 2011) provides another strand of research on retaliation in scalar arrangements. International laws, transnational templates issued by global governance institutions, religious normativity and local normative orders converge when crimes against humanity have to be addressed in postcrisis situations. Global players interact with local institutions, procedural hybrids are created, and rituals as supporting measures based on local knowledge but adapted to serve higher ends of a nonlocal perception of justice are introduced. Such processes and dynamics of scalar interpenetration prompt us to rephrase some of the crucial research challenges. Upscaled local notions of retaliation are retranslated in the production of transnational templates and the setup of institutional formats for dealing with serious incidents such as violations of human rights, crimes against humanity, cases of state injustice, mass violence, genocide and war crimes. In the field of human security and crimes against humanity, notions of retaliation crop up in connection with restorative justice models, reconciliation councils, peace arrangements, and international criminal courts and tribunals. However, it is not always clear to what extent the actors involved in such scenarios – the injured parties, the perpetrators, the external interveners, etc. – were prepared to make best use of the option inherent in the concept of retaliation, namely, the option to transform the potential for violence into a potential for compensation (Roche 2004; Palmer, Clark and Granville 2012). Retaliation as an issue has come to the fore in various postconflict scenarios that have triggered international intervention and, as Pietro Sullo's contribution to this volume shows, may appear closely connected to the retributive aspects of international criminal justice.[24]

Earlier studies have already shown the predominant role of retributive aspects such as revenge in the renegotiation of social order in postconflict societies. In the eyes of the victims, reconciliation and the search for justice cannot be separated from the desire to retaliate. Perpetrators themselves may accept the transformative power of retaliation as a pathway to their societal reintegration. Moreover, locally established and formalized models of conflict settlement provide for the claim to retaliation where it appears to be an indispensable component of renewing societal balance and calculating the costs of doing so. There is, of course, always the danger that the injured party will resort to violence as a legitimate response. It is not my aim to argue away the existence of this danger. Instead, I want to show that it is precisely this option that provides the premise for self-incrimination of a perpetrator. The offended party's right to violence and the perpetrator's recognition of the facts pave the way for the transformation of claims to legitimate violence into claims to material compensation. However, there is no guarantee that the model will always work exclusively nonviolently.

This uncertainty about the violent option often leads to a clash between two opposing tendencies. One is the juridical process concerning extreme violent events between large population groups. Such a setting may be situated within a state or may cross state boundaries and involve transnational organizations and be subject to internationally accepted legal standards. The other tendency involves the return to local traditions and methods of conflict regulation in order to achieve acceptance and sustainability for a negotiated arrangement among the concerned population. The latter tendency attempts to take into account beforehand the expectation that after the cessation of hostilities, the victims will first claim the right to retaliate.[25]

To give an example of the prominent position of the discourse on retaliation, let me point out the work of the South Africa Truth and Reconciliation Commission from 1995 to 1998. Richard Wilson's powerful description emphasizes the vital importance of retaliatory claims within the reconciliation process in South Africa after the end of the apartheid system. In the tribunals, it became evident that the victims of the system did not content themselves with identifying the responsible persons and accepting apologies; they demanded retaliation against the perpetrators. Making the wrongs public and payment of compensation was deemed insufficient. The process of dealing with the apartheid past was adjusted accordingly on the local level and thus was in sharp contrast to the official public discourse on reconciliation (Wilson 2001, 2002a, 2002b).

Similar statements are true for Rwanda, Burundi, Sierra Leone, Somalia, the Sudan, and other crisis areas in Africa and Latin America.[26] At the transnational scale, the transformation processes that the principle of retaliation is producing under altered social and political circumstances most likely affect the functioning of modern instruments of international crisis management. Such instruments, while quite often suppressing retaliation claims, nevertheless stand in their shadow. Those tasked with implementing transnational crisis management often experience the 'agency' of retaliation as a threat rather than as an opportunity for reconciliation; they consider it too risky to engage in the local logics of retaliation and therefore neglect the transformative capacity of retaliation. Yet, such logics of international post-disaster interventionism generally do not reflect realities on the ground. They seem consistent with human rights standards, but reduce retaliation to the Old Testament logic of the talion, the consequential and inevitable violent response. This alone makes it worthwhile to study the entire spectrum of reciprocity-oriented strategies for conflict regulation in order to learn about the alternatives that the concept of retaliation may offer to the presumed automatism of violent action–reaction schemes. It is crucial to target the turning point in the spectrum of reactions that range from violence to compensation. I do not advocate a blind and unreflective acceptance of local models in dealing with postwar scenarios. However, experience in this area has shown that the subtleties of local understanding are key to an efficient postconflict intervention.[27]

Sensitivity to local perceptions in truth and reconciliation commissions has also become an issue at the global scale for the International Criminal Court in The Hague.[28] It also informed the work of the two international courts, the International Criminal Tribunal for the Former Yugoslavia and the International Criminal Tribunal for Rwanda, as has become evident in the increased protection of victims who have been exposed to violent threats in response to their testimonies.[29] Dealing with crimes of such dimensions in the recent past has revealed the persistence of old and unsatisfied retaliation claims. The actual eruption of events was in many cases triggered by age-old debts and the collective memory of retaliation claims that sometimes reached back to time immemorial.[30] To lay the past to rest, then, means to put diachronic events into one context and to devise a tenable and future-oriented regulation. Cairn and Roe's (2003) compiled case studies exemplify how this entails granting material and/or symbolic compensation to the victims, acknowledging responsibility on the part of perpetrators and reaching an unequivocal end to the conflict, without forgetting the experiential dimension of violence and the ensuing retaliation. If this is not achieved, the victims may not be able to put the conflict behind them and are more likely to continue creating trouble.

This is an important point to be considered. The memory of the initial incident of injustice is apparently never free of references to retaliation (Sarat 2002b). If those references are not properly seized and integrated into the production of collective or 'official' memory, retaliatory sentiments may take on a life of their own (Hamber and Wilson 2003). Relinquishing their claim to violent retaliation in exchange for compensation then becomes an unacceptable price to the injured. Compensation can thus not buy out memory; rather, it has to be in direct relation to the requited wrong.

Towards Future Directions in Transdisciplinary Research

The introductory text and this concluding chapter together provide a necessarily biased and limited perspective on the study of retaliation. Nevertheless, it allows us to identify common denominators inherent in all these different approaches, as well as some overlaps and disciplinary differences. Let me start with summarizing the latter first. While the social sciences emphasize the reactive potential of retaliation, which finds expression in making a strategic choice between violence and compensation-oriented action, criminologists and legal scholars focus more on retaliation as the illicit recourse to reactive, even excessive, violence. Moreover, while legal scholars and social scientists agree upon the pre-emptive, conflict suppressing potential of the threat of retaliation, different terms are preferred: anthropologists often speak of avoidance, while criminologists refer to deterrence.

In addition, a strict distinction between the spheres of formal and informal regulation is of decisive importance in legal reasoning. In contrast, social scientists, especially anthropologists, emphasize the inevitable interaction and even the dialectical relationship between these spheres, and assert that they should only be separated for analytical reasons. They are particularly interested in the grey areas between the two realms, which can be seen as an interface of interaction. Thus, they look at the ways in which the so-called informal and the so-called formal depend on and inform each other, and are inextricably intertwined.

Another important disciplinary bifurcation is the exploration of retaliation in terms of either the individual or the collective. Retaliation can be explored as a fundamental and universal characteristic of human nature that finds expression in notions of getting even in interpersonal relations. Alternatively, it may be studied predominantly as a solidarity-enhancing principle of social formations that regulates social relationships far beyond the scope of individual rights and obligations. One aim of the Introduction and its companion conclusion has been to suggest that much can be gained when both perspectives are regarded as mutually constitutive. The focus on the individual human being in some disciplines produces insights that help the other disciplines analyse and theorize social models of retaliation and their reliance on a society's understanding of social cohesion and the construction of social solidarity. The individual thus operates in networks of solidarity that may be based on kinship, territoriality, religious affiliation or adherence to some other formation based on shared markers of identity.

The transdisciplinary exchange on retaliation has led to the identification of thematic fields of common interest that provide new empirical insights and conceptual fine-tuning. Moreover, there is agreement on a basic understanding of retaliation. The chapters in this volume touch upon the interaction between retaliation, violence, the state's monopoly on legitimate punishment, the repertoire of international sanctions, sociopolitical frameworks, individual dispositions, religious interpretations, historical developments, economic processes, deviant behaviour, social transgression and much more. In contrast to other prevailing models of retaliation, all of the contributions here operate with the basic assumption that concepts of retaliation inform individual as well as collective action. They may express more than one truth and follow more than one single logic. As an empirical social fact beyond individual disposition, retaliation is associated with all possible types of social and political organization, is an inherent component (whether implicitly or explicitly) of any given plural legal configuration and is embedded in complex institutional arrangements. Retaliation may co-occur with sanction-based models of conflict regulation, and it can exist independently of or dependent upon central political and juridical authorities.

This transdisciplinary exercise also allows us to identify potential future vectors of research on retaliation: how do the affective dimension of individual retaliatory behaviour and the dynamics of collective retaliation interact with and inform one another? How can we analytically separate out the manifold manifestations of retaliation as, for example, a societal idea? As an expression of responsibility for and challenge to notions of ordering? Such questions are becoming ever more urgent as processes of social diversification pick up speed. It is our sincere hope that, at the very least, the perspectives gathered here have been able to shed light on the myriad ways in which retaliation can be expressed, how it becomes inscribed in the very sites of encounters between people of different origins, how it informs their relatively successful (peaceful and cooperative) or unsuccessful (antagonistic) forms of cohabitation, and how it can and will continue to imbue imbalances of all sorts in human interaction.

Notes

1. Needless to say, it would have been an endless and indeed impossible task to try to cover in one volume all possible circumstances or conditions under which retaliation occurs or plays a role.
2. This timeframe, which most often corresponds to the rules of hospitality, is, for instance, called in Arabic the 'boiling of the blood' (*fort ad-damm*) and amounts in the majority of empirical cases to three days (see Turner 2005). The issue of the time-bound legitimacy of retaliatory claims comes up again in connection with victims' remembering in cases of crimes against humanity (see, e.g., Alonso 2006).
3. See, *inter alia*, Foucault (1995 [1977]); Ignatieff (1983); Rouland (1994); Whitman (1995); Miller (2006); Albrecht (2008); Härter (2008).
4. Retaliation or retribution figures as but one of a number of goals that sanctioning is, in theory, supposed to be able to achieve. Others include deterrence, prevention, incapacitation, societal protection, rehabilitation, restoration, education and denunciation (see, e.g., Tonry 2011).
5. See Wang (2012) for the context of transitional justice.
6. See, e.g., Clouthier and Clouthier (2005); see also the books advertised at http://www.undercoverpress.com/revenge.html, retrieved 1 September 2016.
7. For examples of covert retaliation in the workplace, see Tripp and Bies (2009).
8. On the rights of victims and retaliation as a victim's right, see Sarat (2002a).
9. On the variety of methods and models subsumed under the term 'restorative justice', see Roche (2004); Sullivan and Tifft (2006).
10. For artistic representations of 'revenge versus legality', see Maynard, Kearney and Guimond (2010).
11. For many societies, state justice and (individual) punishment for homicide may exist alongside or intertwined with local regulations. Retaliatory claims remain unaffected by state regulation and necessitate additional informal arrangements (see, e.g., Korsholm Nielsen (2006) for the case of Egypt).
12. For examples, see Verdier (1980–84). On the relationship between reciprocity, violence and religion, see Girard (1979).
13. A less spiritual version is the often described suicide of a person who feels to be in too weak a position even to get involved in a conflict. Suicide and blaming the other party for it is meant to mobilize one's own group to seek retaliation (see, e.g., Malinowski 1926).
14. A similar logic may also be used as justification in multicultural settings, as cases of the 'cultural defence' reported in the literature show (see Foblets and Dundes Renteln 2009; for the case of reconciliation councils, see Hamber and Wilson 2003).
15. See, e.g., recent interpretations of natural disasters such as earthquakes and hurricanes as divine reactions to promiscuous women in Iran (http://www.guardian.co.uk/world/2010/apr/19/women-blame-earthquakes-iran-cleric, retrieved 1 September 2016) and in the United States as a message from God to get the attention of politicians (Belonsky 2011).
16. On the central role of retaliation in the combination of Islamic, traditional and state law in Iran, see Shams Nateri (2006); Osanloo (2012).
17. For details, see http://www.bbc.co.uk/news/world-middle-east-14356886, retrieved 1 September 2016.

18. See the debate on Steven Pinker's controversial 2011 book *The Better Angels of Our Nature: Why Violence Has Declined* (e.g., Lawler 2012).
19. Tuori (2015) claims that this theory continues to exist. Authors like Diamond (2008) seem to confirm this assumption. Without going into the specifics of Diamond's article, it is worth mentioning that it has triggered a vivid and controversial debate because of its comparative view on satisfyingly executed violent retaliation in 'primitive societies' in contrast to the unsatisfying waiving of the right to violent response within emerging 'civilized' modern state systems.
20. For details and references to the literature on the segmentary lineage system, see Turner (2008).
21. See Cooney (2001: 5606) on the association of *feuding* with *stateless societies*, and Dresch (1988: 53) on typical *stateless societies* that have come about as a result of nation-building processes.
22. In other evolutionary approaches, kinship organization is combined with political leadership and modes of production, culminating in the state putting an end to feuding. However, such approaches are purely speculative, based on assuming parallels between contemporaneous social formations and certain stages of evolution (see Boehm 2011).
23. Literature on Mediterranean honour societies has become a genre in its own right in anthropology. For an overview, see Gilmore (1987); Peristiany and Pitt Rivers (1992). On honour and retaliation, see Turner (2005, 2008). For a slightly modified view, see Miller (2006).
24. On intervention by (armed) UN troops in postconflict situations and their contribution to the aspects of conflict regulation discussed here, see Pouligny (2006).
25. It can, however, work the other way round. In the case of Sierra Leone, for example, Shaw (2010b) argues that the Special Court and the Truth and Reconciliation Commission (TRC) are locally regarded as instruments of a retaliatory logic that is opposed to local practices of forgiveness as a means of avoiding the recurrence of violence. In the same vein, Anders (2012) asserts that the tribunals assume that people in Sierra Leone want to retaliate when in fact they want to move on.
26. See, e.g., the respective chapters in Shaw (2010a); see also Chris Coulter's (2006) account of the postwar situation of female combatants in Sierra Leone.
27. See, e.g., Demaria and Wright (2006) on the analysis of types of representation of conflict contexts in postconflict societies. The shaping power of the retaliation principle in postwar situations is discussed by Garb (1995) on the example of Abkhazia and Georgia after the war in 1992–93. The Abkhaz population, referring to mutual unsettled claims of retaliation, threatened Georgian refugees who wanted to return to Abkhazia and thereby rendered their return virtually impossible. See Wang (2012) for an attempt to make – via punishment – a categorical distinction between retribution and revenge for processes of transitional justice.
28. See Minow (2003) on revenge and forgiveness in international jurisdiction.
29. Köchler (2003) argues that a system of global justice can only be ensured by completely independent jurisdiction above and beyond all existing power structures, otherwise it would deteriorate into a system of global revenge guided by political objectives.
30. For a critical analysis of this relation, see Cairn and Roe (2003); Alonso (2006).

References

Aase, T. (ed.). 2002. *Tournaments of Power: Honour and Revenge in the Contemporary World.* Aldershot: Ashgate.

Aladjem, T.K. 2008. *The Culture of Vengeance and the Fate of American Justice.* New York: Cambridge University Press.

Albrecht, H.-J. 2008. 'Strafrecht und Strafe: Belastung oder Entlastung?', in G. Schlee and B. Turner (eds), *Vergeltung. Eine interdisziplinäre Betrachtung der Rechtfertigung und Regulation von Gewalt.* Frankfurt: Campus, pp. 127–48.

Alonso, J. 2006. 'The Passion for Revenge: Semiotics of Time and Memory', in C. Demaria and C. Wright (eds), *Post-Conflict Cultures: Rituals of Representation.* London: Zoilus Press, pp. 311–17.

Anders, G. 2012. 'Juridification, Transitional Justice and Reaching out to the Public in Sierra Leone', in J. Eckert, Z.Ö. Biner, B. Donahoe and C. Strümpell (eds), *Law against the State: Ethnographic Forays into Law's Transformation.* Cambridge: Cambridge University Press, pp. 94–117.

Belonsky, A. 2011. 'Michele Bachman Thinks Hurricane Irene Was Message from God'. Retrieved 1 September 2016 from http://www.deathandtaxesmag.com/135959/michele-bachmann-thinks-hurricane-irene-was-message-from-god.

Black-Michaud, J. 1975. *Cohesive Force: Feud in the Mediterranean and the Middle East.* Oxford: Blackwell.

Boehm, C. 2011. 'Retaliatory Violence in Human Prehistory', *British Journal of Criminology* 51(3): 518–34.

Cairn, E., and M.D. Roe (eds). 2003. *The Role of Memory in Ethnic Conflict.* New York: Palgrave Macmillan.

Carmichael, K. 2003. *Sin and Forgiveness. New Responses in a Changing World.* Aldershot: Ashgate.

Clouthier, G., and A. Clouthier. 2005. *A Woman's Guide to Revenge: Funny, True Stories about Getting Even.* New York: SelectBooks.

Cooney, M. 2001. 'Feud and Internal War: Legal Aspects'. *International Encyclopedia of Social & Behavioral Sciences* 8: 5605–8.

Coulter, C. 2006. 'Being a Bush Wife: Women's Lives through War and Peace in Northern Sierra Leone', Ph.D. dissertation. Uppsala: University of Uppsala.

Darley, J.M. 2009. 'Morality in the Law: The Psychological Foundations of Citizens' Desire to Punish Transgressions', *Annual Review of Law and Social Sciences* 5: 1–23.

Demaria, C., and C. Wright (eds). 2006. *Post-Conflict Cultures: Rituals of Representation.* London: Zoilus Press.

Diamond, J. 2008. 'Vengeance is Ours: What Can Tribal Societies Tell Us about Our Need to Get Even?', *The New Yorker. Annals of Anthropology* 21(4): 74–82.

Dresch, P. 1988. 'Segmentation: Its Roots in Arabia and its Flowering Elsewhere', *Cultural Anthropology* 13(2): 50–67.

Figueredo, A.J., I.R. Tal, P. McNeil and A. Guillén. 2004. 'Farmers, Herders, and Fishers: The Ecology of Revenge', *Evolution & Social Behavior* 25(5): 336–53.

Foblets, M.-C., and A. Dundes Renteln (eds). 2009. *Multicultural Jurisprudence: Comparative Perspectives on the Cultural Defense.* Oxford: Hart Publishing.

Foucault, M. 1995 [1977]. *Discipline and Punish: The Birth of the Prison.* New York: Vintage Books.

Garb, P. 1995. 'The Return of Refugees Viewed through the Prism of Blood Revenge', *Anthropology of East Europe Review* 13(2): 41–44.

Garot, R. 2009. 'Reconsidering Retaliation: Structural Inhibitions, Emotive Dissonance, and the Acceptance of Ambivalence among Inner-City Young Men', *Ethnography* 10(1): 63–90.

Gilmore, D.G. (ed.). 1987. *Honor and Shame and the Unity of the Mediterranean*. Washington DC: American Anthropological Association.

Girard, R. 1979. *Violence and the Sacred*. Baltimore, MD: Johns Hopkins University Press.

Glanville, L.2011. 'On the Meaning of "Responsibility" in the "Responsibility to Protect"', *Griffith Law Review* 20(2): 482–504.

Gollwitzer, M. 2005. *Ist 'gerächt' gleich 'gerecht'?* Berlin: Wissenschaftlicher Verlag Berlin.

Hamber, B., and R.A. Wilson. 2003. 'Symbolic Closure through Memory, Reparation and Revenge in Post-Conflict Societies', in E. Cairn and M.D. Roe (eds), *The Role of Memory in Ethnic Conflict*. New York: Palgrave Macmillan, pp. 144–68.

Härter, K. 2008. 'Strafen mit und neben der Zentralgewalt: Pluralität und Verstaatlichung des Strafens in der frühen Neuzeit', in G. Schlee and B. Turner (eds), *Vergeltung. Eine interdisziplinäre Betrachtung der Rechtfertigung und Regulation von Gewalt*. Frankfurt: Campus, pp. 105–26.

International Commission on Intervention and State Sovereignty. 2001. *The Responsibility to Protect: Report of the International Commission on Intervention and State Sovereignty*. Ottawa: International Development Research Centre.

Ignatieff, M. 1983. 'State, Civil Society and Total Institution: A Critique of Recent Social Histories of Punishment', in D. Sugarman (ed.), *Legality, Ideology and the State*. London: Academic Press, pp. 183–212.

Jacobs, B.A., and R. Wright. 2006. *Street Justice: Retaliation in the Criminal Underworld*. Cambridge: Cambridge University Press.

Kelsen, H. 1982 [1940]. *Vergeltung und Kausalität*. Vienna: Böhlau.

Koch, K. (ed.). 1972. *Um das Prinzip der Vergeltung in Religion und Recht des Alten Testaments*. Darmstadt: Wissenschaftliche Buchgesellschaft.

Köchler, H. 2003. *Global Justice or Global Revenge? International Criminal Justice at the Crossroads*. New York: Springer.

Korsholm Nielsen, H.C. 2006. 'State and Customary Law in Upper Egypt', *Islamic Law and Society Review* 13(1): 123–51.

Lawler, A. 2012. 'The Battle over Violence', *Science* 336(6083): 829–30.

Luhmann, N. 1985. *A Sociological Theory of Law*. London: Routledge & Kegan Paul.

Malinowski, B. 1926. *Crime and Custom in Savage Society*. London: Kegan Paul.

Maynard, K., J. Kearney and J. Guimond. 2010. *Revenge versus Legality: Wild Justice from Balzac to Clint Eastwood and Abu Ghraib*. Oxford: Birkbeck Law Press.

Miller, W.I. 2006. *Eye for an Eye*. Cambridge: Cambridge University Press.

Minow, M. 2003. *Between Vengeance and Forgiveness: Facing History after Genocide and Mass Violence*. Boston: Beacon Press.

Murphy, J.G. 2003. *Getting Even – Forgiveness and its Limits*. Oxford: Oxford University Press.

Osanloo, A. 2012. 'When Blood Has Spilled: Gender, Honor, and Compensation in Iranian Criminal Sanctioning', *Political and Legal Anthropology Review* 35(2): 308–26.

Otterbein, K.F. 1997. *Feuding and Warfare*. Amsterdam: Gordon and Breach.

Palmer, N., P. Clark and D. Granville (eds). 2012. *Critical Perspectives in Transitional Justice*. Cambridge: Intersentia.

Paul, R.A. 2005. 'Reconciliation and the Craving for Revenge in Psychotherapy', in A.B. Brown and K.M. Poremski (eds), *Roads to Reconciliation: Conflict and Dialogue in the Twenty-First Century*. Armonk, NY: M.E. Sharpe, pp. 107–19.

Peristiany, J.G., and J. Pitt-Rivers (eds). 1992. *Honor and Grace in Anthropology*. Cambridge: Cambridge University Press.

Peters, E.L. 1967. 'Some Structural Aspects of the Feud among the Camel-Herding Bedouin of Cyrenaica', *Africa* 37(3): 261–82.

Pouligny, B. 2006. *Peace Operations Seen from Below*. London: Hurst.

Roche, D. (ed.). 2004. *Restorative Justice*. Aldershot: Ashgate.

Rouland, N. 1994. *Legal Anthropology*. London: Athlone Press.

Sarat, A. 2002a. 'Vengeance, Victims and the Identities of Law', in M. Mundy (ed.), *Law and Anthropology*. Aldershot: Ashgate, pp. 347–73.

———. 2002b. 'When Memory Speaks: Remembrance and Revenge in Unforgiven', in M. Minow (ed.), *Breaking the Cycles of Hatred: Memory, Law and Repair*. Princeton: Princeton University Press, pp. 236–59.

Schacht, J. 1986. 'Ḳiṣāṣ'. *Encyclopaedia of Islam* V: 177–80.

Scheff, T.J. 1994. *Bloody Revenge, Emotions, Nationalism, and War*. Boulder, CO: Westview Press.

Schneider, J. 1971. 'Of Vigilance and Virgins: Honor, Shame and Access to Resources in Mediterranean Societies', *Ethnology* 10(1): 1–24.

Shams Nateri, M.E. 2006. 'Formal and Informal Means of Conflict Resolution in Murder Cases in Iran', in H.-J. Albrecht, J.-M. Simon, H. Rezaei, H.-C. Rohne and E. Kiza (eds), *Conflicts and Conflict Resolution in Middle Eastern Societies: Between Tradition and Modernity*. Berlin: Duncker & Humblot, pp. 401–10.

Shaw, R. (ed.). 2010a. *Localizing Transitional Justice: Interventions and Priorities after Mass Violence*. Stanford: Stanford University Press.

———. 2010b. 'The Production of "Forgiveness": God, Justice, and State Failure in Post-war Sierra Leone', in K. Clarke and M. Goodale (eds), *Mirrors of Justice: Law and Power in the Post-Cold War Era*. Cambridge: Cambridge University Press, pp. 208–26.

Sullivan, D., and L. Tifft (eds). 2006. *Handbook of Restorative Justice: A Global Perspective*. New York: Routledge.

Tonry, M. 2011. *Why Punish? How Much? A Reader on Punishment*. New York: Oxford University Press.

Tripp, T.M., and R.J. Bies. 2009. *Getting Even: The Truth about Workplace Revenge and How to Stop it*. San Francisco: Jossey-Bass.

Tuori, K. 2015. *Lawyers and Savages: Ancient History and Legal Realism in the Making of Legal Anthropology*. Abingdon: Routledge.

Turner, B. 2005. *Asyl und Konflikt: von der Antike bis heute*. Berlin: Reimer.

———. 2008. 'Recht auf Vergeltung? Soziale Konfigurationen und die prägende Macht der Gewaltoption', in G. Schlee and B. Turner (eds), *Vergeltung. Eine interdisziplinäre Betrachtung der Rechtfertigung und Regulation von Gewalt*. Frankfurt: Campus, pp. 69–103.

Turner, B., and G. Schlee. 2008. 'Wirkungskontexte des Vergeltungsprinzips in der Konfliktregulierung', in G. Schlee and B. Turner (eds), *Vergeltung. Eine interdisziplinäre Betrachtung der Rechtfertigung und Regulation von Gewalt*. Frankfurt: Campus, pp. 7–47.

Verdier, Raymond et al. (eds). 1980–84. *La Vengeance*, 4 vols. Paris: Éditions Cujas.

Wang, S.P. 2012. 'Transitional Justice as Retribution: Revisiting Its Kantian Roots', in N. Palmer, P. Clark and D. Granville (eds), *Critical Perspectives in Transitional Justice*. Cambridge: Intersentia, pp. 31–50.

Whitman, J.Q. 1995. 'At the Origins of Law and the State: Supervision of Violence, Mutilation of Bodies, or Setting of Prices?', *Chicago Kent Law Review* 71(1): 41–84.

Wilson, R.A. 2001. *The Politics of Truth and Reconciliation in South Africa: Legitimizing the Post-Apartheid State*. Cambridge: Cambridge University Press.

———. 2002a. 'Reconciliation and Revenge in Post-Apartheid South Africa', in M. Mundy (ed.), *Law and Anthropology*. Aldershot: Ashgate, pp. 375–98.

———. 2002b. 'Human Rights and Culture in Post-Apartheid South Africa', in R.G. Fox and B. King (eds), *Anthropology beyond Culture*. Oxford: Berg, pp. 209–34.

Yoshimura, S. 2007. 'Goals and Emotional Outcomes of Revenge Activities in Interpersonal Relationships', *Journal of Social and Personal Relationships* 24(1): 87–98.

Index

S

Integration and Conflict Studies

Published in Association with the Max Planck Institute for Social Anthropology, Halle/Saale

The objective of the Max Planck Institute for Social Anthropology is to advance anthropological fieldwork and enhance theory building. 'Integration' and 'conflict', the central themes of this series, are major concerns of the contemporary social sciences and of significant interest to the general public. They have also been among the main research areas of the institute since its foundation. Bringing together international experts, *Integration and Conflict Studies* includes both monographs and edited volumes, and offers a forum for studies that contribute to a better understanding of processes of identification and intergroup relations.

Volume 1
How Enemies are Made: Towards a Theory of Ethnic and Religious Conflicts
Günther Schlee

Volume 2
Changing Identifications and Alliances in North-East Africa
Vol.I: Ethiopia and Kenya
Edited by Günther Schlee and Elizabeth E. Watson

Volume 3
Changing Identifications and Alliances in North-East Africa
Vol.II: Sudan, Uganda and the Ethiopia-Sudan Borderlands
Edited by Günther Schlee and Elizabeth E. Watson

Volume 4
Playing Different Games: The Paradox of Anywaa and Nuer Identification Strategies in the Gambella Region, Ethiopia
Dereje Feyissa

Volume 5
Who Owns the Stock? Collective and Multiple Property Rights in Animals
Edited by Anatoly M. Khazanov and Günther Schlee

Volume 6
Irish/ness is All around Us: Language Revivalism and the Culture of Ethnic Identity in Northern Ireland
Olaf Zenker

Volume 7
Variations on Uzbek Identity: Strategic Choices, Cognitive Schemas and Political Constraints in Identification Processes
Peter Finke

Volume 8
Domesticating Youth: Youth Bulges and their Socio-Political Implications in Tajikistan
Sophie Roche

Volume 9
Creole Identity in Postcolonial Indonesia
Jacqueline Knörr

Volume 10
Friendship, Descent and Alliance in Africa: Anthropological Perspectives
Edited by Martine Guichard, Tilo Grätz and Youssouf Diallo

Volume 11
Masks and Staffs: Identity Politics in the Cameroon Grassfields
Michaela Pelican

www.ingramcontent.com/pod-product-compliance
Lightning Source LLC
Chambersburg PA
CBHW070908030426
42336CB00014BA/2339

* 9 7 8 1 7 8 9 2 0 0 7 7 5 *